Ben Jonson Revised

Twayne's English Authors Series

Arthur F. Kinney, Editor

University of Massachusetts, Amherst

TEAS 557

ENGRAVED PORTRAIT OF BEN JONSON

Ben Jonson Revised

Claude J. Summers and
Ted-Larry Pebworth

The University of Michigan–Dearborn

Twayne Publishers
New York

Twayne's English Author Series No. 557

Ben Jonson Revised
Claude J. Summers and Ted-Larry Pebworth

Twayne Publishers
1633 Broadway
New York, NY 10019

Library of Congress Cataloging-in-Publication Data

Summers, Claude J.
    Ben Jonson revised / Claude J. Summers and Ted-Larry Pebworth.
        p.   cm. — (Twayne's English authors series ; TEAS 557)
    Rev. ed. of: Ben Jonson. 1979.
    Includes bibliographical references and index.
    ISBN 0-8057-7062-3 (alk. paper)
    1. Jonson, Ben, 1573?–1637 — Criticism and interpretation.
I. Pebworth, Ted-Larry.   II. Summers, Claude J.   Ben Jonson.
III. Title.   IV. Series.
PR2638.S69   1999
822'.3—dc21   99-40559
                                                            CIP

This paper meets the requirements of ANSI/NISO Z3948-1992 (Permanence of Paper).

10 9 8 7 6 5 4 3 2 1

Printed in the United States of America

For
John Edward and Willene Schaefer Hardy

May windes as soft as breath of kissing friends,
Attend thee hence; and there, may all thy ends,
As the beginnings here, prove purely sweet,
And perfect in a circle always meet.

Contents

Editor's Note

Few writers have matched Ben Jonson's noble conception of the significance and utility of a civilizing literature. In this beautifully written account of his life and work, Claude J. Summers and Ted-Larry Pebworth have revised their earlier study of Jonson to incorporate recent scholarship and to add invaluable sections on the masques and the prose. Arguing that Ben Jonson proposed a commonwealth of literature that always combines the private and the public and that his work in part and in whole deals with the poetics of human possibility, they confront a number of recent scholars who have cited his inconsistencies, awkwardnesses, or even (in the later work) "dotages" to show that Jonson never swerved from his original intention. Not merely the neoclassical poet of the Renaissance whose art counters nature through his urbanity, simplicity, and decorum, Jonson is, they argue forcefully, a writer whose works are also playful, witty, earthy, and raucous. The poems, moreover, like the plays, are developmental and often self-correcting, asking the reader and the playgoer to engage with them as they unfold to suggest larger inherent patterns of thought and experience. Aided by the explosion in Jonson criticism over the past 20 years, this study again and again provides deepened readings of Jonson's most cherished achievements to show how he remains, indisputably, one of the major authors not only of the Renaissance but also of the whole of English literature.

Arthur F. Kinney

Preface

The goals of this thorough revision of our 1979 TEAS volume remain much the same as those of the original book. It attempts to satisfy the need for a one-volume critical survey of Ben Jonson's achievement, to reveal the diversity of his art, and to emphasize the social vision that unifies such disparate modes as the masque and the comical satire. A prolific writer who attempted most of the major seventeenth-century poetic and dramatic genres, Jonson is best known for *Volpone, The Alchemist,* and a handful of nearly perfect lyrics, but he is also the author of other superb comedies, two tragedies, a host of masques, and a large canon of excellent poetry. We have tried to respect the integrity of individual works while relating them all to Jonson's poetics of human possibilities.

While we discuss Jonson's works according to their genres, we also attempt to offer an integrative approach. The two largest chapters in the book focus on Jonson's comedies and on his nondramatic poetry. Jonson contributed five comedies to the permanent repertory of English drama. These five, *Every Man in His Humour, Volpone, Epicoene, The Alchemist,* and *Bartholomew Fair,* receive careful attention and close study. In addition, the comical satires and the late plays are also discussed. Jonson's seriousness of purpose, masterful craftsmanship, and boisterous comic spirit render his comedies significant works of literature. The study of the nondramatic poetry examines Jonson's three collections, *Epigrams, The Forest,* and *The Underwood,* and to a much lesser extent, his uncollected verse. Although his poems have been undervalued in comparison with his greatest comedies, they are remarkably rich and varied. The chapter offers close readings of many individual poems and stresses Jonson's mastery as a social poet whose poetic commonwealth includes space for private as well as public emotions. The gracefulness of his lyrics, the dignity of his odes and epistles, the variety of his epigrams, and the surprising accomplishment of his love poetry merit Jonson recognition as a great nondramatic poet.

Briefer chapters consider Jonson's tragedies, masques, and prose works. The two tragedies, *Sejanus* and *Catiline,* both failed on the Jacobean stage, and they are not likely ever to win popular favor. Nevertheless, they have enduring value as imaginative reenactments of ancient history and as gripping reminders of the consequences of social decay. The chapter on the tragedies emphasizes their historical settings and didactic purpose. The masque did not survive the Stuart courts that produced it, but Jonson invested the glittering spectacle with dignity, learning, and ethical force, and his masques repay careful study. The chapter on the masques defines the ritualized mode and its courtly function, sketches Jonson's career as the greatest masque writer of his age, and analyzes three representative Jonsonian masques. The chapter on the prose, entirely new to the revised edition, considers Jonson's *The English Grammar* and *Discoveries. The English Grammar* is valuable for its empirical approach to grammatical questions and for its celebration of the vernacular. *Discoveries,* a miscellaneous collection of works in epitome, in embryo, or in progress, is not a finished or polished work, but it is fascinating when seen as a reader's and writer's notebook.

The first chapter sketches Jonson's life and era, emphasizing the shape of his career and the artistic stance that he assumed. The final chapter briefly outlines his reputation, from his acclaim in the seventeenth century, through his precipitous decline in the eighteenth and nineteenth centuries, to his current recognition as one of the great writers in English literature. The book concludes with a selective bibliography. Space limitations have necessitated restricting that annotated list to the most important book-length studies of recent years. Readers are urged to consult the notes and references to each chapter for important articles on individual works. In addition, readers should be aware of the numerous modern editions of Jonson's poems and plays that are excluded from the bibliography.

The past two decades have been an extraordinary period for Jonsonian scholarship and criticism, as for our understanding of early modern literature in general. Major biographical and critical books and essays have reassessed Jonson's life and works from a variety of perspectives and approaches. In revising our 1979 book, we have attempted to digest and incorporate the most recent biographical and critical discoveries and have vastly increased the level of documentation. In the process we have reconsidered many of our original preconceptions and conclusions. The result is a book that is considerably larger than the 1979 version, one that focuses on current critical concerns and approaches, and one that we hope faithfully reflects a broad consensus of Jonsonian scholarship. We have tried not to be eccentric in our responses, but we are also aware of Oscar Wilde's dictum that criticism is the sincerest form of biography, and we know that our study inevitably presents a Jonson that has been filtered through our own critical faculties and sensibilities.

In the preface to the original edition, we gratefully acknowledged grants from the University of Michigan's Horace H. Rackham School of Graduate Studies and the University of Michigan–Dearborn Campus Grants Committee, which provided financial assistance in our research. The Huntington Library, San Marino, California, offered a pleasant and congenial atmosphere in which to work; our typist, Sue Falconer, proved unfailingly cheerful. We are happy to reaffirm the original acknowledgments, as well as the original dedication to John Edward and Willene Shaefer Hardy, who remain dear friends after all these years.

A Note on the Texts

Quotations from Jonson are from *Ben Jonson,* edited by C. H. Herford, Percy and Evelyn Simpson, 11 volumes (Oxford, 1925–52). The comedies are cited by act, scene, and line numbers; the tragedies, by act and line numbers; the masques, by line numbers; the poetry, by collection, poem number, and line numbers; and the prose, by line numbers. Titles of the plays, masques, and collections of poetry have been modernized; the use of *i, j, u,* and *v* has been regularized; troublesome contractions have been expanded; and lengthy quotations in italics have been silently reversed. Quotations from classical authors, unless otherwise noted, are from the Loeb Classical Library. The following abbreviations are used in citations:

Alch.	*The Alchemist*
Conv.	*Conversations with William Drummond of Hawthornden*
Disc.	*Timber, or Discoveries*
E.	*Epigrams*
E. M. I.	*Every Man in His Humour*
E. M. O.	*Every Man out of His Humour*
F.	*The Forest*
H. & S.	C. H. Herford, Percy Simpson, and Evelyn Simpson, eds., *Ben Jonson,* 11 vols. (Oxford: Clarendon Press, 1925–52)
Hym.	*Hymenaei*
Ind.	Induction
L. T.	*Love's Triumph through Callipolis*
M. Bl.	*Masque of Blackness*
M. L.	*The Magnetic Lady*
M. Q.	*Masque of Queens*
PMLA	*Publications of the Modern Language Association*
Poet.	*Poetaster*
Pro.	Prologue

Chronology

1601–1602   Paid by Henslowe to revise *The Spanish Tragedy.*

1602–1607   Leaves his wife; lives with Esmé Stuart, Lord Aubigny.

1603   Queen Elizabeth dies; James I succeeds her. Begins era of Jonson's "entertainments" and court masques. His son Benjamin dies. *Sejanus* acted by the King's Men and hissed off the stage. Forms "The Mermaid Club."

1605   Voluntarily joins George Chapman, his collaborator on *Eastward Ho!*, in jail for mockery of the Scots.

1606   *Volpone* performed by the King's Men. Jonson and his wife charged for failure to take Anglican communion.

1609   *Epicoene* produced by the Children of Her Majesty's Revels.

1610   *The Alchemist* acted by the King's Men; Jonson returns to the Church of England.

1611   *Catiline* produced by the King's Men.

1612–1613   Travels in France as tutor to the son of Sir Walter Ralegh.

1614   *Bartholomew Fair* performed by the Lady Elizabeth's Men.

1616   Publishes a folio edition of *Works*, including nine plays, *Epigrams, The Forest,* and several masques and entertainments. *The Devil Is an Ass* acted by the King's Men. Granted a royal pension.

1616–1625   Presides over meetings of the "Tribe of Ben" at London taverns.

1618–1619   Makes a walking tour of Scotland; visits Drummond of Hawthornden.

1619   Awarded an honorary M.A. by Oxford University.

1623   Jonson's house and library destroyed by fire. Contributes a commemorative tribute to the first folio collection of Shakespeare's plays.

1625   King James dies; Charles I succeeds him. Jonson's prestige at court declines.

1626   *The Staple of News* performed by the King's Men.

1628   Partially paralyzed by a stroke. Appointed chronologer of the City of London.

Chapter One

The Man and His Age

Among the most important figures in English literature, Ben Jonson resists neat classification. Capable of delicate lyricism as well as savage mockery, he is remembered as both the genial host of the Apollo Club and the stern moralist of the comical satires. A learned neoclassicist, he was also a master of coarse jests and earthy humor, and although noted for his excessive girth and capacity for drink, he was his era's preeminent poet of moderation. The author of some of the most popular plays on the Renaissance stage, he was as well the greatest masque writer of his age, endowing with intellectual substance the extravagant court spectacles of King James I. A convicted felon who became the earlier seventeenth century's foremost man of letters, he articulated a code of civilized values for an era he believed in imminent danger of social and political decay. In his work, he alternately portrayed the men and women of his time as gross and vulgar beasts and as reincarnations of ancient grace. But what animated all of Jonson's work, from the satiric epigrams to the royalist encomia and the love lyrics, was an abiding vision of human possibilities. This idealism informed even the scorn he heaped upon the vices and follies that he found rampant in his society, and it explains how he was able to reconcile in his work the contradictory impulses of satire and celebration, rage and commendation that his age aroused in him.

The Age

Ben Jonson was born 14 years into the long reign of Queen Elizabeth I, who ruled England from 1558 to 1603. The Elizabethan Age was an exciting time, a period of national self-awareness, global exploration, and intellectual ferment.[1] The queen, her nobility, and even wealthy commoners founded scores of new schools and colleges and refounded many older ones with handsome new endowments. The writing, publication, and dissemination of books flourished. While they read widely in the works of continental authors, both modern and ancient, the English became increasingly aware of the importance of their own native litera-

ture. Sophisticated men like Sir Philip Sidney even began to theorize
about contemporaneous literature and to write critically about it, and
discussions of poetry were no longer confined to the universities but
spread into the taverns of London.

Unlike his peripatetic medieval predecessors, Elizabeth's grandfather,
Henry VII, firmly settled the bureaucracy of England in one place, the
royal city of Westminster. Although he and subsequent monarchs occasionally held parliaments in such places as Oxford and frequently took
themselves and their courts into the countryside, spending time in the
numerous royal palaces scattered throughout the kingdom or accepting
the hospitality of their nobles at great country houses, the political and
commercial business of the realm remained centered in Westminster and
its giant neighbor, London. By far the largest city in England, London
was a crowded metropolis of narrow, crooked streets; of magnificent resi-
dential, public, and commercial buildings; and of squalid tenements. It
was a city of buying and selling, of opulence and poverty, of hard work
and boisterous leisure. Already sprawling beyond its medieval walls, it
stretched toward Westminster to the southwest, into the open fields of
the north and northeast, and south to the villages across London Bridge.
By the end of Elizabeth's reign, the city and its suburbs had a total population of well over two hundred thousand inhabitants.

When Jonson was two years old, an important building went up in
Shoreditch, a northern suburb of London. There James Burbage constructed a public playhouse called simply The Theatre. It was the first
permanent home for a professional company of actors in England, and
with its construction and occupancy, English commercial drama began
in earnest.[2] Over the next several years, large and small playhouses pro-
liferated, tenanted both by troupes of adult performers and by companies of child actors. Drawing an eager audience from almost all segments of society, drama flourished for nearly seventy years. On many
occasions during the period, the lord mayors and aldermen of London
tried to suppress the public performance of plays. Considering actors to
be little better than vagabonds and thieves and plays to be lewd and
seductive incitements to immorality and civic irresponsibility, they especially deplored the fact that playgoing took the citizens away from their
proper task, hard work. But theatrical entrepreneurs wisely constructed
most of their playhouses outside the city precincts—initially in the
northern suburbs and later south of the Thames on the Bankside—
where the London administrators had no authority. In addition, the acting companies sought and obtained the patronage and consequent pro-

tection of powerful people such as Lord Chamberlain Hunsdon, Lord High Admiral Howard, and the earl of Essex. Fortunately, too, for the actors and managers, Queen Elizabeth and her successors, James I and Charles I, enjoyed plays, even as they also recognized the potential danger that plays posed by virtue of their power to arouse the populace or to comment on political questions. Although these monarchs exercised censorship through their various Masters of the Revels and often subjected playwrights and actors to punishment for specific infractions (as Jonson himself was to experience on more than one occasion), they allowed the theaters to flourish, even to the point of supporting the establishment of private playhouses within London itself. Commercial acting companies gave frequent command performances at court, and some of them came to enjoy official royal patronage. The only agent that regularly halted the production of plays prior to 1642 was bubonic plague—something that could resist even the power of royal patrons. From 1592 until the year Jonson died, 1637, virulent outbreaks of the Black Death frequently closed the theaters during the summer months.

The plague was only one of many problems that England faced during Jonson's lifetime. Between the 1570s and the 1630s, serious religious, political, economic, and social issues progressively divided the nation's people until, five years after the poet's death, civil war erupted. Queen Elizabeth inherited most of her problems of state and managed to deal with them remarkably well, encouraging her own cult of personality as the Virgin Queen. Her Scottish cousin James, who ruled England from 1603 to 1625, was somewhat less adept, and his son Charles was so inept a politician that his reign and his life were ended on an executioner's scaffold in 1649.

Elizabeth's father, Henry VIII, severed the Church of England from the Church of Rome in 1533. The regents who controlled the minority reign of her younger brother Edward VI (1547–1553) made the English church unequivocally Protestant. Her elder sister Mary, who ruled from 1553 to 1558, returned the country to the Roman fold, by force when persuasion failed. But Elizabeth, who had been reared a Protestant, was by nature a pragmatist. As soon as she ascended the throne, she and her advisors set about to establish a state church that would be acceptable to all but the most determined Roman Catholics. This doctrinal compromise, figured forth in the 39 Articles of Religion (1563), was frankly anti-Roman; but on questions that divided continental Protestants— election, predestination, and the nature and extent of grace—it was purposely vague. Throughout her long reign, Elizabeth refused to be drawn into public controversy concerning her church. As long as her subjects practiced its outward forms, she and her government did not peer closely into their private beliefs. She would probably have ignored the discreet practice of Roman Catholicism had not two popes threatened her throne and her very life. In 1570, Pius V excommunicated her and released English Roman Catholics from all obligations to obey her; and in 1580 Gregory XII went further, endorsing her assassination as a meritorious act: "there is no doubt that whosoever sends her out of the world with the pious intention of doing God service, not only does not sin but gains merit."[3] Reacting to such extreme measures, Elizabeth's government severely repressed Roman Catholicism. In 1605, King James and an entire parliament narrowly escaped annihilation at the hands of Roman Catholic zealots in the infamous Gunpowder Plot, and the repression continued for a while. But in the early 1620s, James made overtures of friendship toward Spain, the most militantly Roman Catholic power in Europe; and in 1625, the year he ascended the throne, Charles married a French princess and thereafter allowed her and members of the court to practice the Roman rite unchecked.

Although few may have realized its full potential at the time, extreme Protestantism proved a far greater threat to the English Crown and to national peace than Roman Catholicism. During the persecutions under Queen Mary, many Protestants fled to safety in the reformed areas of the Continent. When they returned to England after Elizabeth's accession, many of them came back as Puritans. English Puritans were never a unified, cohesive group. The various lines of development within their number reflected differing forms of continental Protestantism, and their sects had numerous, often overlapping designations: Precisionists, Anabaptists, Brownists, Presbyterians, and Separatists, to name only a few. All had as a goal the "purifying" of the Christian religion, stripping away the accretions of Rome to discover and recover the true primitive church beneath. Their religious convictions should be distinguished from their political activities, however. Some remained members of the Church of England and worked for change from within; indeed, for a time Calvinist doctrine dominated establishment theology. The more extreme among them separated themselves from the state church, and some eventually separated themselves from England itself, emigrating first to Holland and later to North America. Elizabeth tolerated Puritanism so long as it was not destructive of the commonweal. James, reared in Scotland by dour Presbyterian regents, despised politically active Puritans, whose resolve to have "no Bishops" he feared would lead inevitably to the corollary "no King"; he harried Separatists out of the realm. Charles, acquiescing to the impolitic goals of his standardizing and ritualizing archbishop of Canterbury, William Laud, inflamed many Puritans—even formerly moderate ones—to frenzied political action, and both Laud and the king died at their hands.

During Jonson's lifetime, Puritans played an increasingly important role in English religious and political life. As a political force, they became especially strong in London and among the commercial and professional classes generally. Most English Puritans lived sober, upright lives and were loyal, valuable, hardworking citizens. They educated themselves, studied the Scriptures, and earnestly sought to imitate Christ's example in their own lives. Others, however, were ignorant, narrow-minded bigots who sought to impose their own rigid beliefs on others, who miserably and hypocritically failed to live up to their professed ideals of rectitude, and who determined to destroy the order and beauty that they themselves could not appreciate. Thoughtful, concerned Englishmen, including Ben Jonson, feared and attacked this second kind of Puritan.

The three monarchs under whom Jonson lived were increasingly troubled by growing parliamentary self-assertiveness. Parliaments became less and less tame servants of the Crown as well-educated, legalistic, and eloquent men began to stand for public office. By tradition, Parliament held the right of taxation; and as the revenue from Crown lands declined, the House of Commons began to demand royal concessions in return for the levying of taxes. Elizabeth managed to hold most of her parliaments in check, often by the mere force of her personality. In addition, despite her love of luxury and show, she lived rather frugally, thus making appeals for extra funds an infrequent necessity. And when she engaged in a war, she made certain that it was a popular one, against Spain, so that public sentiment would incline Parliament to vote taxes with few strings attached. James succeeded in staying out of costly wars, even declining to fight what would undoubtedly have been a popular one in support of his Protestant son-in-law, the Elector Palatine, who was driven from his lands by Roman Catholic powers. But James lived lavishly, and he was in constant need of money. As his reign wore on, he had increasingly difficult relations with his parliaments. His claim that he was entitled by divine right to unquestioned obedience served only to exacerbate his problems, and he bequeathed to his son a governmental crisis. Early in his reign, Charles called parliaments only to dissolve them quickly when they made virtually nonnegotiable demands.

For 11 years (1629–1640), he ruled without a parliament, plunging ever more deeply into debt. The parliament he was finally forced to call late in 1640, with disgruntled Puritans in the majority, eventually declared war on the Crown.

Jonson's age witnessed a drastic and dislocative shift from a medieval economy to capitalism. While ownership of land still carried social status and newly rich merchants and speculators rushed to acquire country estates, wealth and the power consequent to it came to rest in ready money. Furthermore, the influx into the European economy of precious metals from the Americas—particularly silver—cheapened money itself, and prices of goods and services rose steadily, surging at especially alarming rates during the frequent years of crop failure. The whole basis of land tenancy changed, fostering a litigious spirit the breadth, depth, and passion of which are unique in English history. Landowners enclosed once commonly held lands, and many of them turned from the growing of food crops to the grazing of sheep, displacing large numbers of people who had once made at least a subsistence living from the land. The dissolution of religious houses in the reign of Henry VIII and the decay of manorial cohesiveness and responsibility throughout the next several reigns destroyed the old ways in which the poor had been relieved and threatened the web of traditional relationships between landowners and tenants. Many of the old families who stayed on the land—such as the Sidneys, whom Jonson praises in "To Penshurst" (F. 2)—had increasingly less money available to take care of the tenants and neighbors to whom they felt obligated by long tradition. Many of the squires who managed to remain wealthy, by charging exorbitant rents or by involvement in trade, began to live most of the year in London and to spend their money there, leaving the people in and around their estates to fend for themselves. And the newly rich who bought land and built great country houses felt no obligation at all toward their rural neighbors. Elizabeth's government recognized a social responsibility and tried to meet it, sponsoring a succession of comparatively enlightened Poor Laws. But the problems of inflation and unemployment persisted, and most of the progress made against these two evils was quickly offset by a rapid rise in the country's population. This economic upheaval helps explain the often fantastic schemes of exploration, trade, and exploitation of land and people that mark the Elizabethan, Jacobean, and Caroline periods.

One of the most abusive and frequently decried forms of exploitation was the monopoly system. Under it, the Crown granted an individual or a group of people the exclusive right to provide a product or a service to the nation. In some ways monopolies were beneficial. They often provided employment for displaced agricultural workers; they channeled large amounts of money into useful, even necessary enterprises that could never have been accomplished without vast outlays of capital, such as the development of coal mining and transport to offset the swift disappearance of timber fuel; and they provided the English with desirable items that they could not have acquired so easily otherwise—wines, spices, and furs, for example. But monopolists were allowed to set the prices on the goods and services they provided, and the greed of many added significantly to the country's inflationary spiral.

Even with their many economic problems, however, the English on most levels of society generally lived better than most of their continental neighbors, and those who could acquire the money to do so usually lived exceedingly well. They were not misers. What they got, they immediately spent, and not a few borrowed heavily against nebulous expectations to buy present luxuries. They lived in fine houses and apartments, collected expensive possessions, pursued with enthusiasm the latest fads, ate and drank magnificently and immoderately, and wore fortunes on their backs. In 1574, according to Jonson's schoolmaster William Camden, a "very great excesse of Apparell spred it selfe all over *England,* and the habite of our Countrey through a peculiar Vice incident to our apish Nation, grew into such contempt, that men by newfashioned Garments, and apparell too gawdy, discovered a certaine deformitie and insolencie of minde, whilest they jetted up and downe in theyr Silkes, glittering with gold and silver eyther imbroydered or laced. . . . And withall crept in ryot in banquetting, and braverie in building. For now began more Noblemens and private mens houses, to bee raised here and there in *England,* built with neatnesse, largenesse, and beautifull shew, then ever in any other age, and surely to the great ornament of the Kingdome, but decay of the glory of Hospitalitie."[4] In the next several decades, this extravagance did not abate but intensified.

At the head of this glittering society, and sharing both its virtues and its vices, stood the court: the royal presence and the advisors to and chief administrators of the monarchy. Comprising over the years both aristocrats of ancient lineage and new men who were accorded place through personal wealth or merit, the courts of Elizabeth and James governed surprisingly well considering the problems they faced. But there were frequent abuses, some of them leading to scandal. Offices were bought and sold, and their incumbents frequently took advantage of their hardwon positions to demand bribes and embezzle the funds that they administered. Anyone doing business with the Crown, and often with the judiciary, needed money or powerful friends or both if his or her suit was to fare well. Having direct and frequent access to the monarch, royal favorites were particularly cultivated and were both flattered and resented. Elizabeth and James each had a series of handsome young favorites whose chief recommendations seem to have been beauty and charm. Elizabeth was usually astute enough to enjoy her favorites without allowing them undue influence in the government of the realm, though the latter years of her reign were marked by power struggles between her favorites; one of them—the dashing earl of Essex—eventually led a rebellion against her rule and paid for his rashness with his life. James permitted his favorites to grow rich and allowed them some power in domestic matters but gave them little voice in international affairs. Charles inherited, along with the crown, his father's last and most charming favorite, the handsome George Villiers, duke of Buckingham. The young king allowed his headstrong friend to lead the nation into a disastrous foreign policy, and in the duke's defense, Charles antagonized an already obstreperous parliament. After Buckingham's assassination in 1628, the king did not replace him with a similar kind of favorite, but the advisors to whom he did look were inept politicians. Though sincere and often selfless, they were not sensitive to the delicacy of their monarch's increasingly tenuous hold on the government, and they led him into foolish and ultimately fatal mistakes.

The sometimes sordid reality of the royal court was frequently at odds with the celebration accorded that body by poets. Elizabeth, though a huntress and perhaps a perpetual virgin, was no goddess of the moon; James, though learned, was no Solomon; and Charles, though a patron of the arts, was no Apollo. These monarchs and their courts did not in actuality preside over a reincarnation of the Golden Age, and astute English subjects never really believed that they did. But the royal person and court represented the nation's potential for greatness and goodness, its very soul; and poets such as Ben Jonson told the rulers and courtiers of England what they should be, chided them when they fell short, and gloried with them in their successes.

The Man

Jonson was probably born on June 11, 1572.[5] Of Scottish ancestry, he was the son of a Church of England minister who had apparently suffered under the Marian persecution of Protestants and who died one month before the poet's birth. His widowed mother soon married a bricklayer, and the family settled in what was then the village of Charing, midway between London and Westminster. Although Jonson never knew his father, he seems clearly to have identified with his father's status as an educated gentleman and to have resented the loss of social position occasioned by his mother's marriage to a craftsman. He was, however, fortunate in his early education. He began his studies in a school attached to St. Martin-in-the-Fields but soon entered the venerable and prestigious Westminster School, located within the precincts of the abbey.

At Westminster, he came under the influence of William Camden (1551–1623), who was to become one of the age's greatest classicists, antiquarians, and teachers. Best known for his *Britannia* (1586), a historical compendium that achieved wide popularity both in its original Latin and in the English translation by Philemon Holland (1610), Camden was also a conscientious schoolmaster. He earned the adulation of serious students such as the young Ben Jonson, who in a famous poem later credited him with "All that I am in arts, all that I know" (*E.* 14, line 2). The young master taught the boys in his charge to keep commonplace books, encouraged them to compose poetry by first drafting a prose version, and instilled in them a profound love of the classics. Jonson's posthumously published reader's and writer's notebook, *Timber, or Discoveries;* his characteristic method of poetic composition; and his vaunted classicism probably all stemmed from Camden's influence. Certainly Jonson's love of scholarship, a central aspect of his art as well as his life, sprang from his early immersion in languages and learning at Westminster, where he studied poets such as Martial, Catullus, and Horace, who were to have a lasting influence on his own work. And there he was probably first introduced to dramatic productions and to classical drama, including the works of Terence and Plautus.

Jonson was forced by financial straits to end his formal education early, perhaps even before completing the Westminster curriculum. He never ceased to pursue knowledge, however. Study remained a lifelong passion, as the learned authorial notes to his masques and tragedies and the markings in the surviving books of his personal library attest. Indeed, he became one of the best-educated men of his age, proudly asserting in 1619 that "he was better Versed & knew more in Greek and Latin, than all the Poets in England" (*Conv.,* lines 622–23). Still, it must have been a disappointment to Jonson that he was unable to attend either Oxford or Cambridge. In 1607 he expressed gratitude that *Volpone* was favorably regarded at "The Two Famous Universities," and he dedicated the published play to them. With understandable satisfaction, he later boasted to William Drummond of Hawthornden that he had been awarded honorary degrees by both institutions (*Conv.,* line 252).

Instead of attending a university during his late adolescence and young adulthood, Jonson served first as an apprentice to his bricklayer stepfather, then as a soldier, and later as an actor and playwright. In 1598, he obtained the freedom of the Company of Tilers and Bricklayers, thus becoming a journeyman of the craft. Because an apprenticeship normally required seven years, he must have begun working for his stepfather no later than 1591 and probably earlier inasmuch as it is unlikely that he spent seven continuous years as an apprentice. Bricklaying was an ancient and honorable craft, but its practice denoted less than gentle birth and culture; and despite the fact that Jonson came to number nobility and even royalty among his friends and patrons, his antagonists never let him forget that he had been trained as a craftsman. In the second part of *The Returne from Parnassus,* a university play written perhaps as early as 1601, one character described him as "The wittiest fellow of a Bricklayer in England" and another as "so slow an Inventor, that he were better betake himselfe to his old trade of Bricklaying, a bould whorson, as confident now in making of a booke, as he was in times past in laying of a brick."[6] As late as 1632, after Jonson had for 16 years been virtually poet laureate of England, Alexander Gill the Younger remarked of him, in reference to *The Magnetic Lady:*

> A Brickehill's fitter for thee then A stage;
> Thou better knowes a groundsell how to Laye
> Then lay the plott or groundeworke of A playe,
> And better canst derecte to Capp a Chimney
> Then to Converse with Clio, or Polihimny.[7]

Jonson's rise from humble origins may explain his repeated insistence that he was more impressed by virtue and achievement than by title or birth.

In 1594, Jonson married Anne Lewis, who lived in the London parish of St. Magnus the Martyr. The marriage seems not to have been a very happy one. Almost nothing is known of Anne Jonson aside from the poet's 1619 description of her as "a shrew yet honest" (*Conv.,* line 254). The couple probably had several children, though none survived childhood; two of them, a son named Benjamin and a daughter named Mary, were mourned by their father in tender epitaphs.[8] Significantly, Jonson never addressed his wife in any literary production. The couple was separated at least from 1602 through 1607, when Jonson accepted the hospitality first of Sir Robert Townshend and then of the king's cousin Esmé Stuart, Lord Aubigny. The poet's marital difficulties may have been exacerbated by his rise in social status after the accession of King James in 1603, when he came more and more often into intimate contact with members of the nobility who were to become his patrons and friends.

At some point during his late teens or early twenties, Jonson served as a volunteer foot soldier in the Low Countries where, as he told Drummond, "he had in the face of both the Campes Killed ane Enimie & taken opima spolia from him" (*Conv.*, lines 244–46). And by 1597, before officially completing his apprenticeship as a bricklayer, Jonson began yet another apprenticeship, this one to the theater. Early in that year, he acted in a touring company of players, and later in the year, he completed a play begun by Thomas Nashe, *The Isle of Dogs.* It was a singularly inauspicious beginning for a career of playwriting: Queen Elizabeth's Privy Council found the play objectionable, stopped its production, destroyed the script, and imprisoned Jonson and at least two of the actors for sedition. Because the play does not survive, we do not know specifically what dangerous matter it contained; but Jonson must have been able to convince the authorities that he had no seditious intention in his portion of the writing, for within two weeks he and the actors obtained release from Marshalsea Prison. Undaunted by the close call, Jonson assiduously pursued his new career as playwright. During the next two years, he collaborated on at least three plays for the Admiral's Men, all of which are now lost: *Hot Anger Soon Cold,* with Henry Chettle and Henry Porter (1598); *The Page of Plymouth,* with Thomas Dekker (1599); and *Robert the Second, King of Scots* (also called *The Scot's Tragedy*), with Chettle, Dekker, and others (1599).[9] Of more importance, he wrote at least three plays wholly his own: *The Case Is Altered* (1598) for the Children of the Chapel Royal and both *Every Man in His Humour* (1598) and *Every Man out of His Humour* (1599) for the Lord Chamberlain's Men, the most prestigious acting ensemble in London, the company to which Shakespeare belonged. By the end of 1599, Jonson was an established playwright. Indeed, he had achieved sufficient fame (or at least notoriety) within the world of the Elizabethan theater as to be a prominent participant in the so-called War of the Theaters, a battle of satirical wit that extended from 1599 to 1601 and focused unflatter-

ingly on the personalities and artistic theories of Jonson and his antagonists, fellow playwrights John Marston and Thomas Dekker.

By the end of 1599, Jonson was also a convicted felon and a Roman
Catholic convert. On September 22, 1598, Jonson had been provoked
to fight a duel with the young actor Gabriel Spencer and "Killed his
adversarie, which had hurt him in the arme & whose sword was 10
Inches Longer than his" (*Conv.,* lines 247–48). Indicted for manslaugh-
ter, he was held in Newgate Prison and escaped execution only by pleading the ancient right of clergy. He was entitled to such a plea by virtue
of the fact that he could read. But his goods were confiscated, and he
was branded on the thumb.

While in Newgate, he was visited and converted by a Roman
Catholic priest, probably a member of a Jesuit missionary squad who
was himself imprisoned there. It was a dangerous time in which to convert to Roman Catholicism, and Jonson's action provides another
instance of his innate bravery or, as some would allege, his perversity or
foolishness. Jonson always equated valor with Christian fortitude, an
unflinching determination to do what is right even in the face of certain
danger. He also had a strong sense of history and a love of antiquity, to
which Roman Catholicism could justifiably appeal. These, rather than
theological niceties, were probably at the heart of his conversion. His
conversion might also have been at least in part motivated by an unconscious resentment of his father; in rejecting his father's staunch Protestantism, Jonson may have been reacting to his father's abandonment of
him by dying before his birth. He and his wife remained faithful to the
Roman Church for some 12 years. Like most Roman Catholics of the
day, however, Jonson strongly proclaimed his patriotism and loyalty,
vociferously disavowing the activities of extremists such as those
involved in the Gunpowder Plot, whose actions cast the shadow of suspicion on all adherents to the old faith. He and his wife apparently
refused communion in their parish church and in 1606 were cited for
recusancy in a document that accuses Jonson of being "by fame a
seducer of youthe to ye popishe Religion" (H. & S., 1: 220–22). He
denied the charge of seduction but was ordered to consult an approved
priest of the Church of England to resolve his questions of conscience.
When he finally reconverted to the established church in 1610, he may
have been motivated by the antipathy toward Roman Catholics at the
English court following the assassination of King Henri IV of France by
a Roman Catholic extremist. King James's fear that he might also be
assassinated led to a proclamation banning Roman Catholics from his

court. Of his return to the Church of England, Jonson reported to
Drummond that "at his first communion in token of true Reconciliation, he drank out all the full cup of wyne" (*Conv.*, lines 315–16).
Although religion is not the most important subject of his work, Jonson
was widely read in theology and seems to have embraced a kind of Eras-
mian humanism. A deeply felt religious vision informs much of his
poetry, offering consolation in times of grief and faith in times of trouble.
Christian stoicism particularly fortified the poet's repeated depictions of
isolated virtue in a gilded age.

The plays that Jonson wrote for the Lord Chamberlain's Men in 1598
and 1599 mark the beginning of his mature production, work that he
himself deemed worthy of preservation. But even though he had begun
to make a significant mark for himself with plays of his own devising, in
the early years of the seventeenth century Jonson could not afford to
forego play doctoring and collaboration when they were offered to him.
Particularly irksome must have been the revisions he undertook for a
new production of Thomas Kyd's *The Spanish Tragedy,* a popular and
bloody melodrama that he had more than once criticized as a prime
example of a bad play. He may have taken more delight in his 1605 collaboration with John Marston and George Chapman on a rollicking
comedy incorporating the ancient motif of the prodigal son, *Eastward
Ho!* Unfortunately, King James was not amused by the play's mockery
of the Scots and its gibes against the selling of knighthoods. Marston
managed to flee, but Chapman and Jonson were jailed and threatened
with mutilation. The exact way in which the two secured their release is
unknown, but it was probably through the intervention of influential
friends and patrons, including the powerful Robert Cecil, Lord Salisbury,
and William Herbert, earl of Pembroke, to whom Jonson appealed for
help.

Eastward Ho! must have become a cause célèbre, for it was published
immediately and went through three editions in one year. Although
Jonson's name was given on the title page, along with Marston's and
Chapman's, he likely took no part in the publication, and he omitted
the play from his collected *Works.* Indeed, he did not himself preserve
any of his collaborations. The stage version of *Sejanus,* produced in 1603,
was a collaborative effort, probably with Chapman, a leading tragedian;
when Jonson published the play two years later, however, he noted in a
preface that he had rewritten the portions originally composed by "a
second Pen" and that the published play was wholly his own work.
Using documentary evidence from the period, G. E. Bentley has shown

that dramatic collaboration usually followed much the same pattern. After one author had written a scenario approved by the acting company, the playwrights involved were assigned to compose specific acts and scenes individually.[10] This is probably the way in which *Eastward Ho!* was written. Either Marston or Jonson plotted the comedy. Marston apparently wrote the first act; individual scenes in the middle acts were assigned to each of the three collaborators; and Jonson, who had a reputation as a master of the denouement, probably composed most of the final act.

Jonson's negative attitude toward his collaborative works may reflect both his ambivalent attitude toward the stage itself and his self-conscious artistry. He frequently expressed contempt toward the taste and aesthetic standards of playgoers, and he desired to be thought of as a poet rather than a mere playwright. As Bentley has noted, Jonson was only now and then a professional playwright (Bentley 1971, 30–32). Unlike Shakespeare and, at various times, Dekker, Thomas Heywood, John Fletcher, Philip Massinger, James Shirley, William Rowley, and Richard Brome, he was not attached to an acting company as resident writer; and after his theatrical apprenticeship, he did not earn his entire living from the theater. In fact, after 1603, when King James ascended the throne, most of Jonson's income derived from his authorship of entertainments and masques written at the behest of noble and royal employers and from the patronage of the king and members of the aristocracy. Masque writing not only proved far more profitable than playwriting for Jonson but also provided the poet a kind of prestige that a commercial playwright could not expect. Indeed, for the 10 years from 1616 to 1626, he avoided writing for the popular stage altogether. Jonson's particular relationship to the theater had both advantages and disadvantages. He never became rich from it, as did Shakespeare, nor did he derive even a steady income from it, as did the resident playwrights who were not shareholders in their companies. On the other hand, he was free to sell his scripts to the company that offered the most money or the most sympathetic production, and he was able to exercise an unusual degree of artistic independence from both the acting companies and the audiences. Moreover, he was less restricted in the publication of his plays than were the attached playwrights.

For Jonson, publication was extraordinarily important. It countered the ephemerality of theatrical production and allowed the careful shaping of an artistic canon. His first published book was the quarto of *Every Man out of His Humour,* issued in 1600. With it, he began a practice that was unusual for playwrights of his time, the careful publication of plays under authorial supervision. A quarto of *Every Man in His Humour* was issued the following year; and all but one of the plays that he wrote over the next 10 years, among them his most popular stage successes, such as *Volpone* and *The Alchemist,* were published, under his supervision, shortly after theatrical presentation. Jonas A. Barish explains Jonson's passionate concern with the publication of his plays as a measure of his distrust of the stage: "Jonson belongs in a Christian-Platonic-Stoic tradition that finds value embodied in what is immutable and unchanging, and tends to dismiss as unreal whatever is past and passing and still to come. What endures, for him, has substance, what changes reveals itself thereby as illusory."[11] Publication stills in a permanent artifact works that less self-conscious artists might have considered fully alive only in the flux of the stage. Moreover, Jonson's careful presentation of his dramatic works had the effect of claiming for them a seriousness that was only rarely accorded to plays.

Jonson considered himself foremost a poet and his plays and masques species of poetry. He wrote nondramatic poetry throughout his life, and during the reign of King James he was frequently commissioned to write masques and entertainments. James I and his consort, Anne of Denmark, were fond of lavish spectacle, and Jonson invested the masque with new dignity and ethical force. His career as masque writer provided him with money and recognition, and it may have helped mold his conception of himself as a public poet. Certainly access to court provided him the opportunity to study at close hand the ruling class whom he undertook to counsel in his poetry. Generally, Jonson's work advises how best to achieve a good society, inspiring through praise and shaming through ridicule. In his nondramatic poetry, he addressed familiarly some of the most powerful men and women of his age, usually tactfully but sometimes boldly offering counsel. His conviction of the true utility of poetry, as well as his own sense of separateness in rarefied social circles, helped him maintain an essential integrity and protected him from any temptations toward sycophancy even as he became immersed in and dependent on the elaborate patronage system of the day. He became friends with—or at least a client of—such aristocrats as Lucy, countess of Bedford; Sir Robert Sidney; Lady Mary Wroth; and William Herbert, earl of Pembroke, the latter a particularly generous patron. He also cultivated friendships with such members of the intellectual aristocracy as John Selden, Sir Robert Cotton, Sir Francis Bacon, John Donne, and Sir Walter Ralegh, whose high-spirited son Jonson

accompanied as tutor on a journey to France in 1612. Jonson's position
as social poet was solidified by the publication in 1616 of his folio *Works,*
a book that provocatively integrated the two aspects of his career as poet
and playwright.

The 1616 folio is one of the most important books published in seventeenth-century England. A massive, beautifully produced, physically
imposing volume, it established Jonson as an important poet whose literary domain encompassed modes as diverse as the masque and the
comical satire. Perhaps even more significantly, it gave new dignity to
the playwright's craft. The deliberate inclusion of plays originally composed for the popular theater in a folio entitled *The Works of Benjamin
Jonson* boldly asserted the right of plays to be considered serious literature as well as popular culture. Previously, plays had been printed
almost invariably in cheap, often inaccurate quartos. Some measure of
the low esteem in which published plays were held can be gauged from
the fact that when the insatiable book collector Sir Thomas Bodley
made plans for establishing his magnificent library at Oxford, he specifically excluded the acquisition of plays (Bentley 1971, 51–53). Jonson's
own quarto publications were produced in texts distinctly superior to
those of his fellow dramatists. But the act of collecting his plays, including them with his poems and masques, constituted a daring claim for
their permanent value. Jonson was roundly ridiculed for his presumption. One epigrammatist asked, "Pray tell me *Ben,* where doth the mystery lurke, / What others call a play you call a worke."[12] Despite the
chiding of his contemporaries, however, Jonson's confidence was vindicated. The 1616 *Works* set a precedent that undoubtedly inspired the
greatest folio publication of them all, the 1623 collection of Shakespeare's plays, for which Jonson composed his famous tribute, "To the
memory of my beloved, The Author *Mr. William Shakespeare:* And what
he hath left us" (U. V. 26).

Jonson scrupulously controlled the contents of the *Works.* He
included nine plays (*Every Man in His Humour, Every Man out of His
Humour, Cynthia's Revels, Poetaster, Sejanus, Volpone, Epicoene, The Alchemist,*
and *Catiline*) along with two collections of poetry (*Epigrams* and *The Forest*) and several masques and entertainments. The prefatory matter features commendatory verse by John Selden, George Chapman, John
Donne, Francis Beaumont, and others. As W. David Kay remarks, the
publication of the folio and the careful choice of its contents represent
Jonson's attempt "to interpret himself to his age as a writer whose individual works formed a unified corpus animated by his conception of the

poet's function."[13] Although it does not account for the curious absence of *Bartholomew Fair* (1614), this self-conscious making of a canon explains Jonson's decision not to include early works or collaborations in the folio. Jonson's deliberate "canonizing" in the folio obscures his artistic development and imposes greater coherence on his career than it actually had. The care that Jonson lavished on the volume is apparent from his revision and expansion of *Cynthia's Revels* and the minute polishing of *Volpone* and other plays that had already been published in quarto. The inclusion of the masques, often accompanied by descriptions of their productions, especially reveals his desire to "borrow a life of posteritie" for his work (*M. Bl.,* line 5).

The publication of the 1616 folio established Jonson as the leading man of letters in London. King James awarded him a pension, and he became the unofficial poet laureate of England. He gathered about him a host of younger poets and wits, including such individual talents as James Howell, Robert Herrick, and Thomas Carew, who styled themselves "Sons of Ben." Jonson was a notably gregarious man. As early as 1603, he had formed the "Mermaid Club" at the tavern of that name, which was noted for its excellent wine. Like the coffeehouse clubs of the eighteenth century, the Mermaid Club was a group of convivial writers and lovers of literature who met regularly to talk of their common trust in good verses. In 1616, and for many years afterward, the "Tribe of Ben" met at various London establishments, especially at the Apollo Room of the Devil Tavern, to discuss life and literature in feasts of wine and wit. Jonson composed an amusing set of rules or "laws for the beaux esprits," the "Leges Convivales," which were engraved in marble over the fireplace in the Apollo Room, and in a comic poem that was painted on a panel in the tavern, he declared "Truth itself doth flow in wine."

The position Jonson assumed as father figure and teacher was one peculiarly appropriate to him. This status and the new honors he received recognized his attempts to dignify the art of playwriting and to reassert the social function of poetry. Jonson regarded himself as a lawgiver to the stage, and he attempted to make comedy a more serious mode of literature than it had been. As satirist, he was intent on exposing hypocrisy and puncturing pretension. As social poet, he attempted to enunciate a vision of a harmonious society based on enduring ideals. The public recognition he enjoyed after 1616 not only rewarded his past efforts but also placed him in a position to continue as a self-nominated arbiter of civilized values.

Not surprisingly in light of his employment at court and his dependence on noble patrons, Jonson was politically conservative and an ardent royalist. But the poet's conservatism was more than an opportunistic stance. Most profoundly, his political convictions stemmed from his classically rooted conception of his function as a public poet, of his responsibility to lead forth the "many good, and great names" of his time so that they might serve as exemplars of good conduct for his own and future ages. He was always conscious of his role as advisor to the ruling class and of his special obligation to remind those in power of their opportunities and responsibilities. He honored those nobles who were "so addicted to the service of the *Prince,* and Common-wealth, as they looke not for spoyle" (*Disc.,* lines 1127–29), but he also struggled to maintain his independence. He almost never fawned, and he frequently satirized courtiers and indicted the shallowness and misplaced values of the nobility, particularly deriding those who were lazy or who "remove themselves upon craft, and designe . . . with a premeditated thought to their owne, rather then their *Princes* profit" (*Disc.,* lines 1134–36). In an age of political strife and religious dissension, he saw the monarch as a unifying force. *"After God,"* he remarked, "nothing is to be lov'd of man like the Prince" (*Disc.,* line 986). For Jonson, the rise of capitalism and of Puritanism signaled a real danger to the ideal of a united commonwealth. He associated capitalism and Puritanism with financial exploitation, vulgar ostentation, hypocrisy, and intolerance. Puritans were the most persistent targets of Jonson's satire throughout his career. Significantly, he never attacked their religious beliefs; instead, he focused on their political disruptiveness and hypocrisy, characterizing them as divisive and ignorant charlatans who would ruthlessly impose their beliefs on others.

In 1618, Jonson set off on a walking tour to Scotland. The journey attracted much attention among the literary circles of both London and Scotland. To Jonson's delight, Sir Francis Bacon wittily remarked that he "loved not to sie poesy goe on other feet than poetical dactils & spondaes" (*Conv.,* lines 333–34). Less delightfully from Jonson's point of view, John Taylor the Water Poet promptly embarked on an imitative journey. Throughout his trip, Jonson was warmly greeted. The Edinburgh town council staged a dinner in his honor, and various dignitaries entertained him lavishly. Among the literary figures whom Jonson visited in Scotland was William Drummond of Hawthornden (1585–1649), a wealthy squire who kept notes on the famous poet's visit.

Actually, the so-called *Conversations with Drummond* is not so much a record of conversations as a listing of comments made by Jonson, frequently without contexts, and a portrait of him by Drummond. Much of what Drummond reports is literary gossip that Jonson probably did not realize would be recorded for posterity. According to Drummond, Jonson remarked "that Done for not keeping of accent deserved hanging" (*Conv.,* lines 48–49); "That Shaksperr wanted Arte" (line 50); that Sir Philip Sidney "was no pleasant man in countenance, his face being spoiled with Pimples & of high blood & Long" (lines 230–31); and that Jonson himself once "beate Marston and took his pistoll from him" (line 160). Jonson also related to Drummond such revealing personal details as that "he heth consumed a whole night in lying looking to his great toe, about which he hath seen tartars & turks Romans and Carthaginions feight in his imagination" (lines 322–24); that "of all stiles he loved most to be named honest, and hath of that ane hundreth letters so naming him" (lines 631–32); and that "In his merry humor, he was wont to name himself the Poet" (line 636).

Conversations with Drummond is an important document, a source of valuable and curious information, but it ought not to be regarded as an authoritative source for Jonson's considered opinion on any particular subject. Jonson's true estimate of Shakespeare, for instance, was actually far more complex, and far more favorable, than Drummond's account indicates. In *Discoveries,* Jonson condemned "the *running Judgements* upon *Poetry,* and *Poets*" as a preposterous exercise (line 588), one that he almost certainly would not have engaged in had he known his comments to his Scottish host were being recorded. Drummond was apparently a naive, sober, isolated, and sheltered young man, and Jonson probably delighted in shocking him with quick judgments and candid observations. As guest, he may have felt an obligation to perform for his host, to regale him with outrageous anecdotes and bits of gossip. The impression he left with Drummond, however, was that of a blustery and opinionated martinet, too proud and too passionate to please the sensitive Scotsman. "He is a great lover and praiser of himself, a contemner and Scorner of others, given rather to losse a friend, than a Jest, jealous of every word and action of those about him (especiallie after drink) which is one of the Elements in which he liveth," Drummond concluded of his guest (*Conv.,* lines 680–84).

Drummond's assessment of Jonson's personality may be a fair-minded account of the young man's impression of his famous visitor.[14] Nevertheless, it is only a partial account. Jonson's was a proud and self-assertive nature, and there was indeed a coarseness in his manner. Throughout his life, he made enemies and engaged in many quarrels, including particularly those with his sometime collaborators John

Marston and Inigo Jones, the latter of whom described him as "the best of Poetts, but the worst of men."[15] He was always quick to take offense at real or imagined slights, and he frequently found himself in trouble with authorities because of his brashness. His intense competitiveness no doubt contributed to his frequently troubled relationships with other writers, and his irrepressible impulse toward satire probably alienated potential supporters at court. Yet Jonson always had more friends than enemies, and he inspired the personal devotion of many of his poetic "sons." The most gifted of them, Robert Herrick, canonized him as "Saint Ben."[16] Jonson passionately pursued friendships, and in this pursuit he revealed much generosity and a great deal of self-awareness, sometimes disarmingly acknowledging his own character flaws. Physically imposing but not attractive, in middle age he was a mountain-bellied, rocky-faced, gray-haired man. He prided himself on his achievements, yet he could playfully mock his appearance. He valued his honesty and independence, yet he articulated a genuinely felt code of courtesy. He was capable of tenderness as well as bluntness. Jonson's personality was not a simple one, and he imposed its many facets on his poetry, where he is alternately enraged satirist and amused observer, bitter enemy and loving friend, proud poet and courteous host, grieving father and vulnerable lover.

In his later life, Jonson functioned as a kind of literary eminence, the most famous man of letters in England. The honorary degree he received from Oxford in 1619 recognized his scholarship as well as his artistry. He may also have been awarded a deputy professorship of rhetoric by Gresham College; and his name headed the list of candidates to be nominated for a proposed academy of letters. King James offered to confer a knighthood on him, which he refused. He was nominated to the office of Master of Revels, a position he never actually achieved because it was to come to him by reversion, on the deaths of two other appointees. Jonson used his literary prominence well, writing commendatory poems for other authors and apparently urging his friends John Heminges and Henry Condell to collect Shakespeare's plays in the folio of 1623, to which he contributed his own triumphant celebration of his fellow playwright and friend.

But Jonson's years of glory did not extend to the end of his life. A number of misfortunes marred the final years of a career that had been far more successful than the young Jonson could have dreamed it would be. In 1623, a fire destroyed his library, consuming his books and several unpublished manuscripts. At court, as his antagonist Inigo Jones gained ascendancy, Jonson was viewed with decreasing favor. With the accession of King Charles in 1625, he was called upon less frequently to write masques and entertainments. His return to the stage with *The Staple of News* in 1626, after a 10-year absence, was relatively unsuccessful, and that play's unenthusiastic reception was followed in 1629 by the most thorough disaster of Jonson's theatrical career, *The New Inn.* In 1628, the fat, aging poet was paralyzed by a stroke and confined to bed for a long period. In his last years, he was often impoverished. Although King Charles honored his request for an increase in the pension that King James had originally awarded him in 1616, the payments were frequently late.

Thus, Jonson's last years were marred by poverty, illness, and a decline of prestige at court. Nevertheless, he maintained an honored position even under these difficult conditions. Jonson was visited both by the young wits of the town and by such wise old friends as the earl of Pembroke; John Selden; Brian Duppa, later bishop of Chichester; and George Morley, later bishop of Winchester. Although his final plays were neither popular nor critical successes, they represent continued experimentation with theatrical form. When he died, he left an unfinished manuscript of a pastoral drama, *The Sad Shepherd,* perhaps his most lyrical dramatic composition. He continued writing nondramatic poetry in his last years, too, and his final poems show no great diminution of poetic power. Perhaps most remarkably, they avoid despair and sentimentality, embracing instead quiet dignity and gentle humor.

Jonson died in August of 1637. When he was buried in Westminster Abbey the following day, his funeral cortege included "all or the greatest part of the nobilitie and gentrie then in the town."[17] His death was mourned with an outpouring of elegies and tributes, but perhaps the most memorable epitaph is the simple phrase that was carved into the blue marble stone marking his grave, "O rare Ben Jonson."

The Artistic Stance

Few writers have had a more noble conception of literature than Ben Jonson. He considered poetry among the highest and most useful of human expressions, and for him poetry included comic and tragic drama as well as masques and lyrics. Paraphrasing Cicero, he described poetry as an art that "nourisheth, and instructeth our Youth; delights our Age; adornes our prosperity; comforts our Adversity; entertaines us at home; keepes us company abroad, travailes with us; watches; divides the times of our earnest, and sports; shares in our Country recesses, and recreations; insomuch as the wisest and best learned have thought her the absolute Mistresse of manners, and neerest of kin to Vertue" (*Disc.,* lines 2389–96). The principal end of poetry, he declared, is "to informe men, in the best reason of living" (*Vol.,* Dedication, lines 108–109). Precisely because he thought literature so important, he took it seriously. By instinct a reformer, Jonson endeavored throughout his career to impose form and order on the rich but unruly literary traditions to which he was heir.

The literary milieus in which Jonson matured were various and disparate. The late sixteenth century was an age of humanism, of the rediscovery of classical texts and literary theory. It was also a moment ripe for satire, for both the "Toothless Satyres" based on Horace and the "Byting Satyres" imitative of Juvenal.[18] Coming of age artistically in the 1590s, Jonson was profoundly influenced by the humanistic desire to incorporate classical values into his own life and era and by a satirical impulse to cleanse a society widely perceived as corrupt. These two predilections shaped his attitudes toward the literary traditions, both dramatic and nondramatic, that he inherited. On the one hand, the Elizabethan popular theater, while vital and exuberant, seemed too discursive and too reliant on noisy bombast and improbable action to satisfy Jonson. On the other hand, the lyric poetry of the day appeared too decorative, too artificial, and too monotonous to please him. What Jonson attempted in his plays was to fuse classical precepts of structure and decorum with native English vigor and contemporary subject matter. In his nondramatic poetry, he sought to develop an individualized speaking voice and to revitalize classical forms such as the epigram and the epistle.

Unlike many of his contemporaries, Jonson often commented on the nature and aims of his art, self-consciously presenting himself as a "laureate poet" and distinguishing himself from the less ambitious amateur poets of the day. In the dedicatory epistles, prologues, and epilogues to his plays and especially in his reader's and writer's notebook, *Timber, or Discoveries,* he announced his artistic principles.[19] For him, literature was fundamentally didactic. Echoing the ancients, he proclaimed "the impossibility of any mans being the good Poet, without first being a good man" (*Vol.,* Dedication, lines 22–23). He declared that his aim "In all his *poemes,* stil, hath been this measure, / To mix profit, with your pleasure" (*Vol.,* Pro., lines 7–8) and that "this pen / Did never aime to grieve, but better men" (*Alch.,* Pro., lines 11–12). Even masques, he contended, "ought always to carry a mixture of profit, with them, no

lesse then delight" (*L. T.,* lines 6–7). In *Discoveries,* he observed that
poetry "offers to mankinde a certaine rule, and Patterne of living well,
and happily" (lines 2386–87). It is, he continued, "a dulcet, and gentle
Philosophy, which leades on, and guides us by the hand to Action" (lines
2398–99). Of the poet, he said, "Wee doe not require in him meere *Elocution;* or an excellent faculty in verse; but the exact knowledge of all
vertues, and their Contraries; with ability to render the one lov'd, the
other hated, by his proper embattaling them" (lines 1038–41). The
satiric intent of the comedies also clearly mirrors Jonson's essential
didacticism. In these plays he imitated human follies, and occasionally
crimes, in order to cure them by exposure to the wholesome remedies of
laughter. He hoped that foolish people would recognize themselves in
the comedies, realize the absurdity of their follies and vices, and determine to rid themselves of them. Significantly, however, while Jonson
was always didactic in his work, he was very seldom self-righteously or
oppressively moralistic.

Central to Jonson's artistic stance was a respect for discipline and
scholarship. In *Discoveries,* he announced "three Necessaries" for a person
to write well: "reade the best Authors, observe the best Speakers: and
much exercise of his owne style" (lines 1697–99). He also enumerated
five requirements for the poet: natural wit, exercise, imitation, study,
and art. By natural wit, Jonson meant genius or poetical rapture, an
ability "by nature, and instinct, to powre out the Treasure of his minde"
(lines 2412–13). True poets, Jonson believed, were inspired by "a divine
Instinct" (line 2420), and without this natural genius, study and learning are profitless. He quoted Petronius to the effect that only a king or a
poet is not born every year (lines 2433–34). But as he remarked in his
famous celebration of Shakespeare, "a good *Poet's* made, as well as
borne" (U. V. 26, line 64), and the other four requirements he listed are
means of imposing discipline on natural genius. By "exercise," he meant
the capacity for arduous revision. By "imitation," he did not mean the
Aristotelian idea of mimetic representation but more simply the ability
"to convert the substance, or Riches of an other *Poet,* to his owne use"
(*Disc.,* lines 2468–69). In addition, the poet must also possess a critical
faculty, "an exactnesse of Studie, and multiplicity of reading" (lines
2483–84). And, finally, the poet must achieve art, the sum of the discipline necessary to regulate spontaneous genius: "it is Art only can lead
[the poet] to perfection" (line 2495). The qualities Jonson most valued
in the poet—discipline, study, and control—may seem pedestrian to the
romantic imagination, yet they crystallize his rebellion against the

excesses of Elizabethan literature and serve as an index to his own scrupulous artistry.

In the dedication of *Volpone* to the two universities, Jonson audaciously promised to "raise the despis'd head of *poetrie* againe, and stripping her out of those rotten and base rags, wherwith the Times have adulterated her form, restore her to her primitive habit, feature, and majesty, and render her worthy to be imbraced, and kist, of all the great and master-*spirits* of our world" (lines 129–34). Jonson proposed to reform "th'ill customes of the age" (*E. M. I.,* Pro., line 4). He determined to refine comedy by observing "The lawes of time, place, persons . . . / From no needfull rule he swerveth" (*Vol.,* Pro., lines 31–32). He particularly objected to his fellow playwrights' violations of the unities of time, place, and action as well as their frequent mixtures of comic and tragic characters and action. He complained that even Sir Philip Sidney, presumably in his epic romance *The Arcadia,* "did not keep a Decorum in making every one speak as well as himself" (*Conv.,* lines 18–19). In contrast, Jonson confined himself in his comedies to "deedes, and language, such as men doe use: / And persons, such as *Comoedie* would chuse" (*E. M. I.,* Pro., lines 21–22). In his nondramatic poetry, he embraced a plain, though resonant style, reflecting his preference for "Pure and neat Language . . . yet plaine and customary" (*Disc.,* lines 1870–71). He would, he wrote, "rather have a plaine downe-right wisdome, then a foolish and affected eloquence" (*Disc.,* lines 343–45).

Jonson must be regarded as one of the most thoroughgoing neoclassical writers in English literature. Throughout his career, he imitated and adapted classical poets and playwrights and naturalized classical genres and forms. His neoclassicism may be seen in the observance of the classical unities, the verisimilitude and decorum of the comedies, the dignity of the tragedies, and the plain style of the nondramatic poetry. The superb plotting of the mature comedies and the sophisticated tone of the poetry also reflect classical literary influence. More profoundly, Jonson's classical bent made him emphasize the integrity of the whole in producing a work of art and made him conscious of the relationship of the parts to the whole. His discussion of unity of action in *Discoveries,* echoing Daniel Heinsius's 1611 redaction of Aristotle, pointedly stressed the necessity for a prior conception of the whole: "The Fable is call'd the *Imitation* of one intire, and perfect Action; whose parts are so joyned, and knitt together, as nothing in the structure can be chang'd, or taken away, without impairing, or troubling the whole; of which there is a proportionable magnitude in the members" (lines 2681–86).

Most significantly of all, Jonson's acute consciousness of the social role of poetry and the didactic nature of literature was itself a function of his classicism.

Yet Jonson was as independent in his classicism as in every other aspect of his life. In *Discoveries,* he wrote that *"Nothing* can conduce more to letters, then to examine the writings of the *Ancients,"* but he also advised "not to rest in their sole Authority, or take all upon trust from them" (lines 129–31). In addition, he declared that "I am not of that opinion to conclude a *Poets* liberty within the narrowe limits of lawes, which either the *Grammarians,* or *Philosophers* prescribe" (lines 2555–57). He remarked that "Nothing is more ridiculous, then to make an Author a *Dictator,* as the schooles have done *Aristotle"* (lines 2095–97), and he regarded the ancients as "Guides, not Commanders" (lines 138–39). In his classical tragedy, *Sejanus,* he violated the unity of time and omitted "a proper *Chorus,"* explaining that it was unnecessary and impossible "in these our Times, and to such Auditors, as commonly Things are presented, to observe the ould state, and splendour of *Drammatick Poemes,* with preservation of any popular delight" (To the Readers, lines 8, 12–15). Indeed, for all Jonson's appreciation of classical literature and critical theory, he was also very much steeped in native English drama and poetry. English poets and playwrights such as Geoffrey Chaucer, Sir Philip Sidney, Christopher Marlowe, Edmund Spenser, George Chapman, William Shakespeare, and John Donne influenced him as much as his hallowed classical writers, Homer, Horace, Vergil, Martial, Catullus, Cicero, and Plautus. Moreover, as W. David Kay has recently emphasized, Jonson was most often motivated by a spirit of "emulous rivalry" with his contemporary writers: "when we look closely at his literary milieu we discover that he was often reacting very particularly to works by his competitors or seeking to surpass them in some way" (Kay 1995, viii). His works reflect a fusion of classical and English traditions. More accurately, they mirror an English sensibility broadened and refined by thorough immersion in classical scholarship.

Jonson's conscious and scrupulous artistry yielded works that are shapely and controlled, weighty and didactic. But his works are also playful and witty, earthy and raucous. They provide ample evidence of that divine instinct that marked a true poet according to his own definition. His work incorporates those classical virtues of "clarity, unity, symmetry, and proportion," as Douglas Bush enumerates them,[20] but it also embodies the spontaneity, vigor, and excitement of the age he sought to portray. As well as a neoclassical theorist, Jonson was a master of realism. "The true Artificer," he declared, "will not run away from nature, as hee were afraid of her; or depart from life, and the likenesse of Truth" (*Disc.,* lines 772–74). As likenesses of truth, Jonson's various works transcend the rigid barriers suggested by such terms as *classical* or *contemporary.* They express the lives of men and women in "fit measure, numbers, and harmony" (*Disc.,* lines 2349–50).

Chapter Two
The Comedies

Ben Jonson is among the premier writers of comic drama in the English language. Energetic and vital, gritty and satiric, Jonson's comedies are the product of a self-conscious artist who took seriously the Horatian maxim that poetry should entertain and instruct. Best known today as the author of *Every Man in His Humour, Volpone, Epicoene, The Alchemist,* and *Bartholomew Fair,* Jonson actually wrote many comedies during the course of a career that spanned 40 years. The 14 complete comedies that survive are extraordinarily varied, for throughout those four decades Jonson restlessly experimented with approach, point of view, characterization, language, and plotting. But each of them bears the identifying stamps of his artistry: moral seriousness, robust humor, careful structure, and comic energy.

The master of urban comedy, Jonson is primarily a social poet. He believed that the purpose of art was the betterment of society. More specifically, he believed that the aim of comedy was the exposure of those vices and follies that weaken society and disrupt the web of human relationships necessary to a commonwealth. Consequently, his comedies generally have a strong satirical bent, and all are infused with didacticism. Most often, they attack "the ragged follies of the time" (*E. M. O.,* Ind., line 17) in an attempt to shame through ridicule. False values, foolishness, greed, pretentiousness, hypocrisy, and especially self-deception are Jonson's chief targets, both because they are prevalent individual failings and because they typify the failures of his own era. Writing at a time when inflation inspired greed, when social climbing was rampant, when religious unrest threatened domestic tranquility, and when the old manifestations of noblesse oblige seemed dormant, Jonson heaped scorn on his society by exposing the sordid reality that gave urgency to the ideal commonwealth he sought to construct in his nondramatic poetry.[1]

But Jonson is not the rigid moralist he is sometimes thought to be. He never forgets that comedy has a primary responsibility to amuse, and other than in prologues, epilogues, and other extradramatic framing devices, he seldom preaches. In the Prologue to *Volpone,* he declares that his purpose "In all his *poemes,* still, hath been this measure, / To mixe profit, with your pleasure" (lines 7–8), a formulation that emphasizes delight as well as instruction. His conviction that a major function of comedy must be moral edification is supported by both classical example and Renaissance theory. But these two sources also warn that the most effective way to teach through art is to clothe the lesson in a fable so delightful that the audience relaxes its all-too-human defenses against instruction, and Jonson embodies his moral themes in robust entertainment. Moreover, Jonson's didacticism is tempered by his awareness of the complexity of moral choice and by a characteristic ambiguity. He frequently points out the dangers of passing easy judgment on others, and he creates ambiguous situations in which folly and even evil are seductively enjoyable. For instance, the evil of Volpone's enticement of Celia, the false values that underlie Sir Epicure Mammon's dreams, and the baseness of Subtle's trickery are never in doubt, yet the reader is manipulated into admiring—emotionally if not intellectually—all three men and even, at least momentarily, wishing them well. This ambiguity is implicit in the enjoyment with which the plays sport with their galleries of fools and rogues. Although Jonson's comedies use the stage as an intellectual forum to impart a didactic vision, they do so through humor that is often broad and low, and their lessons recognize the reality of flawed human perception and admit the necessity of adaptability and compromise. Sophisticated and worldly, the comedies collectively mirror a moral vision that is serious without being grim. Moreover, for all his didacticism, Jonson himself sometimes seems ambivalent in his own judgments, often investing his comedies with an energy that may be subversive of the very values they ostensibly uphold.

Jonson's moral seriousness is matched by his artistic seriousness. When he began writing for the stage in the mid-1590s, few were willing to admit that popular drama could be considered literature. Plays were published almost invariably in cheap, hastily produced, often inaccurate quartos that were read once or twice and then either thrown away or sold to wastepaper dealers. In 1616, when Jonson included seven of his comedies and two of his tragedies in a folio publication of his *Works,* conferring on them the status then reserved for a writer's serious production, he was chided by his friends and ridiculed by his enemies for his presumption.[2] But Jonson had a noble conception of drama. To him, plays, whether written in verse or prose, were or should be poems, and he considered poetry one of the highest and most useful of human expressions. Preeminently a humanist, Jonson attempted to make popular comedy a more serious mode by adapting classical ideals of comedy to his contemporary material.

The neoclassicism of Jonson's comedies consists largely in their observance of the classical unities of time, place, and action and in their sense of decorum: their reliance on "deedes, and language, such as men doe use: / And persons, such as *Comoedie* would chuse" (*E. M. I.*, Pro., lines 21–22). From classical comedy, Jonson appropriated disciplined structure, concentrated action, and serious purpose, and he imposed them on the rich vitality of the middle- and lower-class London material he knew so well. The result is a comedy that is carefully shaped but earthy, artfully designed but unlabored, enriched by ancient tradition yet contemporary and topical. Although the comedies are informed with the self-conscious artistry of a determined neoclassicist, they have very little of the scholarly affectation sometimes attributed to this lawgiver of the stage. Jonson insisted that the ancient writers he admired were "Guides, not Commanders" (*Disc.*, lines 138–39), and he was never a slave to theory. As he remarked, "rules are ever of lesse force, and valew, then experiments" (*Disc.*, lines 1757–58).

The conscious artistry of Jonson's comedy can best be appreciated by comparing it to the carelessly conceived and artlessly executed comedy of many of his contemporaries. Almost exclusively concerned with the problems encountered and eventually overcome in romantic pairings, most of these comedies were far removed from the everyday lives of their audiences. Characters and situations were frequently brought up only to be dropped without resolution or explanation. Comic materials were mixed with pathetic and even tragic elements. Plots were improbable, relying heavily on coincidence and accident. Settings were exotic in place and time. Locales often changed drastically from scene to scene, and two-hour plays often galloped through 10 or 20 years of action. Dukes and cobblers mingled freely and even joined in unlikely fraternity, and the dialogue of both was sentimental and artificially poetic.

By contrast, Jonson's comedies possess internal unity and coherence. Characters and situations are carefully integrated into the fabric of the whole play. Pathetic and tragic materials are excluded. Although the plots are far from simple, they are composed of believable action that gives the impression of spontaneity. Characters are restricted to the middle and lower classes, and whether in verse or prose, they speak in the words and rhythms appropriate to them. The passage of time is held within the bounds of credibility; usually no more than 12 hours elapse during a play. And locales are restricted to places within easy walking distance of each other. Moreover, Jonson moved comedy to his own milieu and that of his audience, the city, and he made its setting contemporaneous. The formal limitations he imposed on his comedies actually led to a broadening of scope and theme. Featuring few women characters and almost none in leading roles, Jonson largely eschewed romantic comedy's preoccupation with love and marriage, concentrating instead on intrigues involving money and status. While marriage is frequently used as a plot device in the comedies, it is nearly always treated unsentimentally, as more practical than romantic. Rather than focusing on amorous adventures or any other single aspect of life, Jonson sought to paint an "Image of the times" (*E. M. I.,* Pro., line 23), realistically detailing (though comically exaggerating) the men and manners of his age. Peopled with representatives of nearly all segments of the broad middle class, the plays are fully grounded in the contemporary reality of London.

Jonsonian comedy does not begin with a plot that is then fleshed out with characters but rather with characters whose natures are the source of the action. Each of his plays brings together people who have individual eccentricities, or "humours"—follies, and occasionally vices, that compel them to act in ways counterproductive to themselves and to society. These people may be ruled by single passions, such as greed or anger or self-righteousness; or they may have pretensions to abilities or positions that they do not actually possess, such as wit, learning, fashion, or social prestige. Their passions and their distorted views of themselves lead them into ridiculous action and interaction and make them easy prey for manipulators of all kinds. The gulling of them or the sporting with them to make them display their follies to the world constitutes the action of Jonson's plays. Many of his comedies also contain individuals of genuine cleverness and integrity who, as representatives of the best aspects of society, serve both as normative figures and as moral pointers. All of Jonson's comedies from *Every Man in His Humour* onward are humor comedies; some, notable among them *Epicoene,* are also comedies of manners, balancing criticism of an imperfect society against the implied faith that the wit and sophistication of its intelligent members are sufficient to discover and root out shortcomings. Jonson's characters tend not to be unambiguously sympathetic, and the result is unsentimental, tough-minded comedy.

Although most of Jonson's characters begin as types, they are seldom merely caricatures. Almost all are given individualizing traits or aspects that contribute to their credibility as actual, albeit exaggerated, human beings. Most of them have prototypes or sources in classical comedy, in native English drama, and in nondramatic literature of all periods, but they are given fresh life by the playwright's own acute observations of the world about him. He consistently gives clues to his characters' natures by the names he assigns them.[3] Some, such as Clement, Bonario, Morose, Truewit, and Purecraft, are transparent; others are recondite but no less revealing. Fabian Fitzdottrel, in *The Devil Is an Ass,* for example, translates as "licentious son of silliness"; Dauphine Eugenie, in *Epicoene,* as "well-born heir." Many of Jonson's major characters have extraordinary presence: Volpone, Subtle, Sir Epicure Mammon, and Zeal-of-the-Land Busy, to name only a few. A real mark of his ability as a comic writer, however, is his capacity for making even minor characters surprisingly memorable: Bobadill, Sir Politic and Lady Wouldbe, the Ladies Collegiate, Dapper, and Ursula the pig woman are unexpectedly affecting. Moreover, Jonson is always careful to distinguish between characters and to individualize them even when they appear superficially similar, as do Volpone and Mosca, for instance, and even when they function collectively, as do Truewit, Clerimont, and Dauphine. Jonson's characters generally have a one-dimensional single-mindedness, yet they are fully, realistically, and recognizably human even in their comic exaggerations. Although they lack the psychological complexity and depth of Shakespeare's characters, they are nevertheless fascinating in their eccentricities and obsessions.[4]

Perhaps the most obvious excellence in Jonsonian comedy is the superb execution of the plots. The kinds of plots Jonson uses vary widely, from the apparent structural sprawl of *Every Man in His Humour* and *Bartholomew Fair* to the tightly wound construction of *The Alchemist.* But all his plots are animated by characters with believable motives, and all events are realistically accounted for, even in plays that employ a deus ex machina. He generally uses a five-act form in which the first two acts introduce the characters and set up the conflicts, the third act provides a complication, and the fourth act ends in a false conclusion, only to have a new twist introduced in the final act, which effects the real conclusion. Often the action is accelerated, with event piled on event, episode interlocked with episode, and duplicity linked with duplicity, until finally a perceptive character steps forward to sort out the confusion and dispense the comic justice. The enormous number of incidents and the unpredictable action of Jonson's plays contribute immensely to their exuberant vitality.

Another source of the excitement of Jonsonian comedy is the brilliant manipulation of language.[5] Although he eschewed the artificial wordplay of romantic comedy, he nevertheless fills his comedies with the cant and jargon of contemporary London, from the alchemical technicalities of Subtle to the biblical cadences of Zeal-of-the-Land Busy. He perfectly matches speech to character, and the large number of characters in the comedies provides him the opportunity for a broad range of style. There is Marlovian richness and seductive power in the exalted celebrations of luxury that pour from the mouths of Volpone and Sir Epicure Mammon. There is the crystal purity of lyric song in Clerimont's "Still to be neat." There is the polite but witty banter of Truewit and Clerimont. There is the testy railing of Humphrey Wasp and the beleaguered dignity of Celia. But most of all, there is the energetic billingsgate of rogues and cheaters, whose vigorous vituperation becomes intoxicating. The plays are filled with catalogues of exotic unguents, cosmetics, chemical elements and processes, news items, and misquoted canon law, all designed to tempt the unwary and the foolish. And when the low characters strip down to reveal their true selves, they sling epithets of stable, street, and privy with exuberant abandon. Jonson is a master of colloquial idiom and speech rhythm, and the characteristic speech of each figure is a kind of signature as revealing as his or her actions. The sheer vitality of Jonson's language energizes his comedies, and the range of his style contributes to the comprehensiveness of that "Image of the times" he sought to portray.

The Early Comedies (1596–1601)

The first phase of Jonson's career may be conveniently terminated in 1601, when he took temporary leave of "the *Comick* MUSE" to "trie / If *Tragoedie* have a more kind aspect" (*Poet.,* To the Reader, lines 222, 223–24), a sabbatical from comedy that was to last three years. The plays of this early period include *Every Man in His Humour* (1598), *Every Man out of His Humour* (1599), *Cynthia's Revels* (1600), and *Poetaster* (1601), which Jonson collected in his *Works* (1616), as well as an unknown number of apprentice efforts of which only one survives, *The Case Is Altered.* The variety of these comedies is instructive, for Jonson's early career may be described as a struggle to find his most comfortable and effective voice. The early plays include an experiment in an uncharacteristic and uncongenial mode—romantic comedy—as well as types that were to become particularly identified with Jonson—the "humour" play and the "comicall satyre." Near the beginning of his career, Jonson moves toward the compression of time, place, and action; toward the development of realistic dialogue; and toward the themes and the artistic stance that were to be uniquely his. This movement culminates in an early success, *Every Man in His Humour,* only to be followed by an excursion into satire. Significantly, by the expiration of his three-year hiatus from writing comedy, Jonson came to realize where his true genius lay. He masterfully revised *Every Man in His Humour* and produced even greater successors in the comedic triumphs of his middle years.

The earliest surviving example of Jonson's apprentice work, *The Case Is Altered,* was likely written in 1597. It is probably the last of his compositions before *Every Man in His Humour.* It exists only in a revised state, but the revisions, which consist largely of an interpolated attack on a contemporary figure, the pageant poet Anthony Munday, were probably made only a few years after the original version. *The Case Is Altered* is a romantic comedy, a genre Jonson was later to attack for its absurdities of plotting, characterization, and diction. Its two plot lines, drawn from different Plautine comedies, double the instances of long-lost children ultimately restored to their families and multiply the love interests and eventual pairing of couples. The play follows the pattern of romantic comedy in freely mixing noble and base characters, even to the point of having noblemen and clownish servants vie for the hand of the same young lady. But despite its genre, there are actually relatively few love scenes, and Jonson imposes on the play some of the formal strictures characteristic of his later work. Although the plot of *The Case Is Altered* is far more diffuse than the later comic triumphs, Jonson compresses the passage of time as much as possible, allowing only a few weeks to transpire between the first and last acts; he restricts place to a few locales in close proximity; and he attempts (not altogether successfully) to tie the plot lines together and to integrate the concerns of the low characters with those of the nobility. Moreover, *The Case Is Altered* contains incidental speeches and episodes, most notably the exaggerated mourning of Count Ferneze for his wife (1.6 and 1.9), that anticipate the humor characterization and comedy of manners of *Every Man in His Humour.*[6]

Jonson's first undisputed success, *Every Man in His Humour,* premiered in 1598 at The Curtain, the second oldest of the Elizabethan playhouses. Produced by the Lord Chamberlain's Men, its original cast included Will Kempe, the most famous comic actor of his generation; Richard Burbage, a player of both comic and tragic genius; William Shakespeare, the company's leading playwright-actor; and John Heminges and Henry Condell, the pair who in 1623 (probably with the

aid and encouragement of Jonson) collected and published Shakespeare's plays. In its original version, issued in quarto in 1601, *Every
Man in His Humour* is set in Italy, and most of its characters have Italian
names, although both setting and characters are recognizably English.
Some years after its original production, perhaps for presentation at
court in early February of 1605, perhaps as late as 1612, Jonson
rewrote the play, abandoning the Italian locale and names in favor of a
London setting and descriptive English names. He also tightened the
play, most notably by abbreviating the speeches in praise of poetry that
slow the original fifth act.[7] In its revised form, Jonson placed *Every Man
in His Humour* first among the plays in the 1616 *Works,* indicating
thereby his own judgment of the play's importance as the earliest of his
comedies worthy of preservation. A comedy of manners molded from
both classical and native English traditions, the play is self-consciously
conceived as a revolutionary attempt to create a new genre of satiric
city-comedy.[8]

   Although original in its details, Jonson's first major play owes much
of its shape to Latin comedy, particularly to Plautus. In a frenetic series
of episodes, two witty gallants and a wily, frequently disguised servant
manipulate their foolish relatives and companions to supreme heights of
folly, all for the sport of it. When the numerous threads of the action are
thoroughly complicated, a fun-loving old magistrate sets everything
right, and the play ends with an invitation to a banquet celebrating the
marriage of one of the gallants to a wholly appropriate young woman. A
deliberate synthesis (and sometimes parody) of diverse elements, both
dramatic and nondramatic, the play self-consciously adheres to classical
ideals of structure and decorum, but its characters, situations, and language are informed and enriched by native English dramatic traditions;
by the rogue literature, satirical poetry, and humor psychology of the
Elizabethan period; and by Jonson's own robust enjoyment of city life in
all its manifestations. The work's originality lies both in its unique synthesis of diverse material and in its flouting of generic expectations and
conventions.

   In the Prologue to the revised version of the play, Jonson expounds
on his adherence to classical structure and decorum by contrasting the
virtues of his comedy with "th'ill customes" of other playwrights (line
4). Unlike his contemporaries, including Shakespeare, he will not allow,
in a two-hour play, "a child, now swadled, to proceede / Man, and then
shoote up, in one beard, and weede, / Past threescore yeeres" (lines
7–9). After the scene is set, he will allow no chorus suddenly to waft his

audience "ore the seas" (line 15). And he will not mix comedic and tragic personages, actions, or language, but will confine himself to

> deedes, and language, such as men doe use:
> And persons, such as *Comoedie* would chuse,
> When she would shew an Image of the times.
> (lines 21–23)

Jonson thus distinguishes his work from that of his contemporaries and describes *Every Man in His Humour* as a decorous comedy that illuminates contemporary life and manners while observing the unities of time, place, and action.

In *Every Man in His Humour,* the classical strictures that Jonson voluntarily adopts never intrude as artificially enforced rules; rather, they serve to strengthen design and to reenforce theme. The settings of *Every Man in His Humour* are the streets, warehouses, and residences of a single city and a house in the countryside a short walking distance away; and when characters move from one locale to another, they do so at a natural pace. Furthermore, when Jonson uses letters and messengers, those old standbys of Greek and Roman drama, he does so in functional ways that do not violate probability. They are not used to relate events that, because of the confinement to a single locale, cannot take place within the audience's view. They serve instead to bring characters together and to complicate the plot. Similarly, although few plays call attention to the exact hours of the day as insistently as *Every Man in His Humour,* the unity of time is as unforced as the unity of place. All of the action transpires between the early morning and the early evening of a single day. Those 12 or so hours are crowded with events, but the crowding does not strain credibility. Indeed, the frequent references to the passage of time and the tumbling together of events have thematic points, reflecting the crowded and hurried nature of urban life. The many decisions that have to be made must be made quickly, without the luxury of prolonged consideration. To survive in the city, and certainly to flourish, one needs a wit both quick and penetrating.

While *Every Man in His Humour* is crowded with events, it is unified in action. The one action is the making of "sport with humane follies" (Pro., line 24), and all the events in the play contribute to that end. Each event is designed to show either the folly of the fools, the perception of the wits who manipulate them, or both simultaneously. And just as the action of the play is of one piece, although crowded with details, so is the theme single but multifaceted. Fools lack self-knowledge and, as a consequence, do not perceive the true nature of the world and fail to participate positively in human society. Wits, on the other hand, know themselves and thereby the world about them. Such knowledge makes them able both to perceive and to uphold desirable social values. The conclusion of the Prologue states this theme, although it avoids overt moralizing. If loved and perpetuated, rather than despised and banished, human follies can become crimes. Jonson's term for these failings, "popular errors" (line 26), not only indicates that they are widely accepted and practiced but also suggests that they are faults harmful to society as a whole. This implication is strengthened in the final line of the Prologue, where Jonson expresses the hope that his comedy will cause the audience to purge itself of its affection for "monsters" and to appreciate "men," well-balanced human beings in a harmonious society. The playwright is, however, somewhat disingenuous here, for the obvious delight that the play takes in the antics of fools actually reveals a more ambiguous attitude than the Prologue allows. Nevertheless, the moral intention of the play is manifest, if expressed in robust entertainment.

Although the action of *Every Man in His Humour* is of one piece, it is woven of many strands. Preeminent is the sport made with the pretentiousness of the three fools, Bobadill, Matthew, and Stephen. Another strand has older men (Knowell and Downright) foolishly attempting to protect their young relatives (Edward and Wellbred) from corruption by loose society. Closely related to this concern is the jealousy plot, centered on Kitely and his wife. Also included, although minimized in importance, is the courtship motif, with Bridget as the prize and Matthew and Edward as the juxtaposed foolish and sensible suitors. Finally, although it is more prominent in the earlier version than in the revision, there is a concern with distinguishing true and false poetry, again pitting Edward against Matthew as well as against his father. All of these plot lines may be combined into two large considerations, one focusing on gentility and the other centering on human relationships, both familial and sexual. The true gentility of Wellbred and Edward contrasts with the futile aspirations of Bobadill, Matthew, and Stephen, who think that to be gentlemen they have only to fight, swear, and parrot verse. The concern with relationships subsumes blood ties, notably represented by Downright's anxiety over his brother Wellbred and old Knowell's fear about his son Edward, and conjugal relationships, including the jealousy of Kitely and the courtship of Bridget. These two parts of the main plot

are masterfully parodied in a subplot centered on the low characters Cob
and Tib. Cob mirrors the pretentiousness of the would-be gentlemen of
the main plot in his admiration of outrageous oaths and in his concern
with his own distinguished lineage, tracing his family back to King Her-
ring, while at the same time he professes disgust with the gentlemanly
affectation of tobacco. The water bearer also reinforces the jealousy of
Kitely in his own suspicions of Tib, while Tib duplicates Dame Kitely's
essential blamelessness in her own innocent but raucous behavior.

A comedy deliberately composed within the strictures of the unities
runs the risk of appearing mechanical and contrived in its plotting. In
Every Man in His Humour, Jonson avoids that pitfall. Once the various
parts of the plot are set in motion, specific incidents give the impression
of flowing naturally from unpremeditated occasions. For instance,
Edward decides to "furnish our feast with one gull more" only because
the foolish Stephen happens to be at the Knowell house when Wellbred's letter arrives (1.3.70–71). Similarly, Wellbred apparently has no
thought of matchmaking when he invites Edward to London for a day
of sport. Only after he perceives that Edward has fallen in love with
Bridget does he determine to aid their union (4.5). Stephen's altercation
with Downright comes about entirely through a happy convergence of
circumstances. The character who most often improvises is the witty
servant Brainworm. Without premeditation, he takes advantage of the
situation at hand to gull Stephen into buying a cheap sword at a dear
price (2.4). He uses Formal's offer of a drink to disguise himself as "the
Justices man" (4.8.50). And he grabs occasion by the forelock in the
quarrel between Bobadill and Downright, selling the blustering soldier
and Matthew a warrant against the angry squire (4.9). Throughout, the
plot of *Every Man in His Humour,* while unified and tightly controlled,
gives the impression of spontaneity as actions seem to arise naturally
from unexpected situations.

As is clear from the Prologue, Jonson is concerned with decorum in
the selection of characters, voluntarily restricting himself to "persons,
such as *Comoedie* would chuse" (line 22). His model of decorum is Greek
New Comedy, as transmitted to the Renaissance through the comedies
of republican Rome. Inspired by Athenian democratic ideals, this comedy is peopled with characters from the middle and lower classes only.
To the squires and burghers of these classical prototypes, Jonson adds a
third group of middle-class citizens prominent in Elizabethan England,
the merchants, and for the slaves of Roman comedy, he substitutes free
servants and menial laborers. Although restricted by considerations of

decorum (and the practical limitations of acting companies), the range and number of characters in the play are nevertheless large enough to "shew an Image of the times" (Pro., line 23), particularly because Jonson places them in realistic settings that accentuate social relationships. Most of the characters may also be described as "humourous," or eccentric in one way or another. Cash's definition of humor as "a gentleman-like monster, bred, in the speciall gallantrie of our time, by affectation; and fed by folly" (3.4.20–22) explains Jonson's title for a comedy of manners intent on exposing pretension and folly.

The sources for the specific characters are many and varied, and Jonson often mixes traits from two or more sources in a single character or subtly modifies a stock figure to give it fresh life. Bobadill, for instance, is ultimately the *miles gloriosus,* the braggart soldier of Roman comedy, but with a significant difference. Unlike his classical ancestors, he is poor. He has no mistress or parasite in his retinue. His only companion is the equally poor and pretentious Matthew. The result of this modification is that while Bobadill is a ridiculous liar and coward, he is also curiously affecting. His desire that Matthew "possesse no gentlemen of our acquaintance, with notice of my lodging" (1.5.33–34) reveals his affected gentility; he wants no one to know that he is reduced to renting a room from a water bearer. But it also indicates how poorly society treats its soldiers when there are no wars in which they are needed. Moreover, although Bobadill is a coward, he faces his poverty with a kind of bravery as well as bravado, making do with radishes, salt, wine, and tobacco "to close the orifice of the stomach" (1.5.167).

In another instance, Jonson adds to a characterization a self-awareness not usually found in its prototype. The old husband of a young and pretty wife, Kitely is dominated by jealousy and is basically a humor character. But Jonson makes him aware of the irrationality of his behavior. In a long speech (2.3.57–74), Kitely warns himself that jealousy works "upon the phantasie," that it "soone corrupts the judgement," and that it "Sends like contagion to the memorie." He tries to "shake the feaver off," and as a consequence he becomes a more interesting figure than the stock jealous husband of Roman and Elizabethan comedy. Finally, for comic effect and thematic point, Jonson sometimes places characters in positions where they seem, at least for a time, to be types that they actually are not. Old Knowell, for instance, is not the *senex amans,* the lecherous old lover of Latin comedy, although his appearance at Cob's door makes Kitely think that he is, and the old man suffers much verbal abuse as a result (4.10). Similarly, Wellbred and Edward appear to be the dissolute gallants of earlier comedy, prodigal young men who need to be rescued from bad company, but in fact they are not dissolute. They revel in the antics of what could be corrupting companions, but both are in reality wise enough not to be tainted by their associates.

The low characters of *Every Man in His Humour* are carefully drawn, and even the least important of them are used to good effect. Cash, with whom Kitely would "trust my life" (2.1.23), is quite easily persuaded to desert his master's cause for his mistress's (4.8). The stuffy Formal is a perfect foil to his fun-loving master, Clement, and his formality is comically compromised by his affection for drink and shattered entirely when he is reduced to appearing before his employer in Brainworm's rusty armor. Cob and Tib, the quarrelsome but fundamentally devoted peasant couple of medieval drama, provide a farcical element in the play and underscore some of its more serious concerns. And finally, Brainworm, whose complex ancestry includes the wily slave of Roman comedy, the vice character of medieval and early Renaissance drama, and the coney catcher of Elizabethan pamphlet literature, is a kind of comic overreacher, anticipating such later creations as Mosca in *Volpone* and Face in *The Alchemist*. Successful beyond expectation in his early manipulations, he becomes so enamored of his wit that he takes a dangerous risk that leads to his comic fall.

The duped characters in the play may be divided into two groups: those who are permanently foolish and those who are foolish for a time only. The three gulls, Bobadill, Matthew, and Stephen, are all pretenders to what they are not, and they are all so insensitive to their own realities that they are incapable of becoming rational creatures. Bobadill is a pretender to gentility and to martial prowess. Although he may actually have fought in a battle or two, he is ridiculous in the role of officer and tactician. He is a fencer out of books and a coward. Matthew, a fishmonger's son, is a pretender to gentility and to poetry, but the verse he claims as his own is invariably stolen and mutilated in the process. He pretends to melancholy because it "breeds your perfect fine wit" (3.1.90), but he has none of the useful introspection that accompanies that humor, and in no way is his wit improved by it. Stephen, a dense young man of "rustical cut" (3.1.18), is the country bumpkin come to town to learn the latest fashions of gentlemanly deportment. He is so out of touch with polite society that he is just now taking up the sport of hawking, already passé. Like Matthew, he affects the melancholy humor, and from Bobadill he is eager to learn to swear and to take tobacco. All three are such fools that they are easily manipulated. As Justice Clement perceives, they are unable to abandon their folly and must be exiled from convivial society—Bobadill and Matthew to fast in the courtyard, Stephen to eat with the menials in the kitchen.

Old Knowell, Kitely, and Dame Kitely are fools for a time only and then only partially so. Dame Kitely is fundamentally sensible. She recognizes and is untouched by the folly of the gulls. Wellbred is able to persuade her that Kitely is a lecher (4.8), however, and for a time she is outraged without true cause. Old Knowell, although somewhat too self-satisfied and pompous, is a loving father of good motives. He knows that Edward is a dutiful young man, but he is concerned that his son, having studied only poetry, knows so little of the real world that he may be led astray. The father's failure to appreciate the true utility of poetry and his lack of faith in his son are failures of perception. And like Knowell, Kitely acts foolishly against his own better judgment. At the end of the play, Justice Clement asks the three "to put of[f] all discontent. . . . you, master KNO'WELL, your cares; master KITELY, and his wife, their jealousie" (5.5.70–72). There is reason to hope that the exposure of their foolishness has cured them of it.

Downright is a special case among the manipulated characters. A no-nonsense country squire, he is a humor character; but his humor, anger, is potentially more dangerous to society than the affectations of simpletons, the misplaced anxiety of a parent, or the jealousy of a husband. Wellbred and Edward recognize the difference. They comment on Downright's anger, and they bait it, but they cannot find the same kind of amusement in it that they find in the irrational behavior of the other dupes. Although a misanthrope may despise the follies and vices of mankind, his all-engrossing anger is not an answer to them, and his rantings disturb the comic spirit. Downright cannot distinguish between relatively harmless folly and more harmful vice, and in treating the two alike, he makes a serious error in judgment. Justice Clement tells him to leave off his anger, but his destructive humor is so fundamentally a part of his personality that it is unlikely he can alter it.

The positive aspect of the play's moral thrust is embodied in Wellbred, Edward Knowell, Justice Clement, and to a lesser extent, Bridget. All four recognize folly when they see it, and although they make sport of it, their own actions and essential natures remain untouched. Bridget obviously enjoys the outrageous wooing of the false poet, Matthew, but she comes to love and to marry the true poet, Edward. Ironically, he does not court her with verse. The play's focal characters, Wellbred and

Edward Knowell, are more thoroughly developed than Bridget. Well-bred is a spirited but sane young man. As his name indicates, he is a true gentleman. He is the prime mover of the action, which begins as a lark to expose the follies of two gulls, progresses through some unexpected fun with Kitely's jealousy, and ends with the romantic and sensible match of Edward and Bridget. Edward is a studious young man but one who can enjoy a jest. He respects his father but thinks him too sober and too protective. He has the exuberance of youth and the good sense to fall in love with a wholly suitable young woman.[9]

Justice Clement is the play's deus ex machina, but he is "a god with a sense of humour."[10] As his name indicates, he tempers justice with mercy, although, as in the cases of both Cob (3.7) and Brainworm (5.3), he finds amusement in making a culprit squirm. As the embodiment of justice, Clement resolves all the plot complications and metes out appropriate rewards and punishments. (It may be indicative of Jonson's own growth of maturity that the punishments meted out in the revision of the play are considerably more lenient than they were in the original version.) In the comic spirit of the play, Clement's role of judge is primarily one of seeing through foolish pretension and irrational conduct. He banishes Bobadill, Matthew, and Stephen from the festivities; he cautions Old Knowell, the Kitelys, and Downright; and he creates the appropriate conditions for the happy reconciliation of master and servant, husband and wife, and father and son. Tellingly, he pardons Brainworm "for the wit o' the offence" (5.3.113–14).

Every Man in His Humour is a considerable achievement. In it Jonson synthesizes classical and native traditions of drama into a new kind of comedy, concretely illustrating the adaptability of ancient practice to his contemporary stage; he adds unexpected dimensions to stock figures; and he captures the excitement of Elizabethan city life. Perhaps most important of all, however, the play's exuberant comic spirit and its serious social intent perfectly complement each other. The attitude the work expresses toward human follies is serious but urbane and sophisticated. It recognizes the dangers of social pretension and of failures of perception, but it delights in the city's sport. This balance of moral seriousness and comic joyousness distinguishes *Every Man in His Humour* from the harsh works that immediately followed it.

One difference between *Every Man in His Humour* and the three subsequent plays is revealed by Jonson's designation of *Every Man out of His Humour, Cynthia's Revels,* and *Poetaster* as comical satires rather than comedies. Unlike the earlier comedy, these plays are not good-natured correctives that delight as well as instruct. Rather, they instruct by means of overt and biting attacks on faults and individuals seriously harmful to society. While they are frequently amusing, these plays present a less appealing vision than that "Image of the times" incorporated in *Every Man in His Humour*. Moreover, they lack the mastery of organic form and characterization that enriches the earlier play. Indeed, the comical satires may represent an attempt to dramatize the verse satires of the period; plot and characterization are thus subordinated to the presentation of didactic episodes and abstractions that contribute to a generalized thesis. While they do not much engage the emotions or capture the imagination, the comical satires are interesting, even revolutionary experiments and reveal Jonson's conception of the poet's role as censor or moral arbiter of the age.[11]

Every Man out of His Humour premiered late in 1599. Like its immediate predecessor, it was first acted by the Lord Chamberlain's Men but in the newly completed Globe Theater. During the Christmas season, it was also presented at court. Although its title might imply that it is either a sequel or a companion piece to *Every Man in His Humour,* it is neither, although both plays expose and reform humors. In contrast to the earlier comedy's intent to "shew an Image of the times," *Every Man out of His Humour* is designed to show "the times deformitie / Anatomiz'd in every nerve, and sinnew" (Ind., lines 120–21). In it, Jonson sets forth a gallery of grotesques: a self-commending, vainglorious knight; an affected courtier; an empty-headed lady of the court; a greedy farmer who would let the masses starve while his barns are full; and two aspiring courtiers, one a country fool, the other a law student in love with fine clothes. Even the two characters who expose the deformities of the others are themselves representatives of undesirable passions. One is an envious malcontent; the other, a profane jester. The only sensible character is Cordatus, but his role is to comment on the play as an ideal spectator rather than to participate in it. The framing device of which he is a part heightens the sense that the diverse characters and episodes are intended as object lessons and not as illusions of real human beings engaged in actual human behavior. The result is that the play fails to evoke empathy. Whereas Jonson's best comedies appeal simultaneously to the mind and to the emotions, *Every Man out of His Humour* speaks only to the intellect. While the work may be seen as daringly innovative in its repudiation of the traditions of English popular theater, sacrificing, for example, a linear plot for an "eddying circular structure designed entirely for the display of eccentricity,"[12] it is more interesting conceptually than successful theatrically.

The second and third of Jonson's trio of satirical comedies, *Cynthia's Revels* and *Poetaster,* were written for the Children of Queen Elizabeth's Chapel. Both premiered at Blackfriars Theater, which attracted a more select audience than did the Globe, the former late in 1600, the latter early in the next year. *Cynthia's Revels* is an attack on false courtiers; *Poetaster,* on false poets. Even more so than *Every Man out of His Humour,* these plays sacrifice structure to portraiture, and both are collections of good and bad exempla only occasionally animated by drama.

In *Cynthia's Revels, or the Fountain of Self-Love,* Jonson deserts the milieu he knew best and could best represent on stage, the world of the middle and lower orders of London society, to present a confusing mixture of mythological, allegorical, and humor characters centered in the court of the virgin huntress-queen of Gargaphie, a "fustian countrie" (Ind., line 43). In a progression of loosely connected scenes, characters whose names translate into such abstractions as voluptuousness, impudence, prodigality, money, and self-love exhibit their respective humors and, rather superfluously, drink from the Narcissan fountain. With the encouragement and support of a lovely woman whose name means "sobriety," Crites, a discerning critic-poet ("A creature of a most perfect and divine temper. One, in whom the humours and elements are peaceably met" [2.3.123–25]), exposes the follies of the "light, and emptie ideots" (1.5.26) at court and, in a pair of masques presented before Queen Cynthia (an allegorized Queen Elizabeth), delineates the characteristics desirable in courtiers: natural affection, pleasant conversation, wit, simplicity, elegance, courage, and good nature.

Cynthia's Revels may best be understood as an attempt by Jonson to fulfill his perceived role of advisor to the ruling classes, a role he would assume in fact only after the death of Queen Elizabeth. With its static plot, overt moralizing, predictable didacticism, and tedious allegorizing, the play is not exciting theater. Yet it deserves interest as a serious experiment to create an idealistic, intellectual form of comedy capable of excoriating pretentiousness and moral failure in the highest levels of society.[13] The play was frankly designed as a revolutionary departure from the "beaten path" of popular drama and directed toward "learned eares" (Pro., lines 10, 11). It contains some of Jonson's loveliest lyrics, such as Echo's Song (1.2.65–75) and the Hymn to Cynthia (5.6.1–18), and the masques within the play adumbrate Jonson's later role as court poet. Characteristically, it expresses great ambivalence toward the court: Even as it anatomizes the foolishness and failures of the court, it betrays Jonson's own ambition for a place there, implying that the secret to its reform is the presence of a figure like Crites, who seems to be a self-

portrait of the author. The satiric cleansing of the court by a collaboration between the monarch and a Jonsonian moralist is a fantasy quite
revealing of Jonson's own fondest hopes. If the play is an unsuccessful
amalgam of scarcely compatible modes—comedy, satire, allegory, lyric
poetry, and masque—it usefully anticipates Jonson's later achievements
as the greatest masque writer of his age and an accomplished lyric poet.

Although *Every Man out of His Humour* and *Cynthia's Revels* may both
contain incidental skirmishes in the so-called War of the Theaters, *Poetaster, or His Arraignment* is unquestionably a major attack in the conflict.
Several theories have been offered as to the exact nature of the altera-
tion: that it was a personal quarrel between Jonson and his antagonists
John Marston and Thomas Dekker, that it expressed the rivalry between
the public adult acting companies and the private children's companies,
that it centered in the conflicting artistic principles of Shakespeare and
Jonson, and that it was merely a ploy to increase box-office revenue for
all parties concerned. In any case, the war broke out in 1599, but
whether the *poetamachia* was initiated by Marston or Jonson is not altogether clear. Until recently it had been thought that Marston began the
conflict by modeling the character of the pedant Chrisoganus in his play
Histriomastix on Jonson, who then retaliated by aping Marston in the
inflated diction of the fop Clove in *Every Man out of His Humour* (3.4).
But James Bednarz, in centering the war in the growing split between
elite and popular culture in the period, has recently argued that *Histriomastix* is actually a response to *Every Man out of His Humour*.[14] Regardless of who struck the first blow, the rivalry between Jonson and
Marston (and their differing conceptions of poetry and theater) is at the
heart of the war. In 1600, Marston and fellow playwright Dekker recognized themselves in the characters of Hedon and Anaides in *Cynthia's
Revels*. To revenge these unflattering portraits, they began a collaborative play entitled *Satiro-mastix, or the Untrussing of the Humourous Poet*.
But before that work could be staged, Jonson recaptured the offensive
by a devastating satire of his opponents in *Poetaster*.

Poetaster is, however, far more than an attack on Marston and Dekker,
who are actually represented in the rather small roles of Crispinus and
Demetrius. Written in the unusually short time of 15 weeks, the play is
set in imperial Rome, where Augustus Caesar as a matter of course looks
to poets for advice. The subject of the play is poetry itself, more particularly the relationship of poetry and society.[15] In the initial plot revolving
around Ovid and Julia, Jonson raises questions about the effect of the
poet's private life on his public role. In the major plot, activated by the

satirist Horace, with whom the playwright clearly identifies, Jonson examines the public obligations of the poet. Horace explains that his satirical bent is motivated by his love of virtue and hatred of vice. He will "spare mens persons, and but taxe their crimes" (3.5.134). The ideal poet is Vergil, and his poetry is of indisputable utility, as Tibullus explains:

> That, which he hath writ,
> Is with such judgement, labour'd, and distill'd
> Through all the needfull uses of our lives,
> That could a man remember but his lines,
> He should not touch at any serious point,
> But he might breathe his spirit out of him.
>
> (5.1.118–23)

With Vergil as judge and Caesar as supporting authority, Horace arraigns greater and lesser enemies of poetry. Among the lesser malefactors is the "play-dresser" Demetrius, easily recognizable as Dekker; among the more serious culprits is Crispinus, representing Marston, who in the play's climactic scene is given an emetic and forced to vomit up bombastic words and phrases.

Poetaster is the most successful of Jonson's comical satires. It does seem to have been written too hurriedly; its plots are not well integrated, and the incidental action is not always focused clearly. But the play is genuinely amusing. It contains some of Jonson's most interesting characters, particularly the complex Ovid and the wonderfully boorish Captain Tucca. As in the best of Jonson's comedies, the satiric force of the play does not preclude delight in sporting with folly. In fact, the play seems to endorse a tolerant and urbane Horatian approach to satire, rejecting harsh Juvenalian satire as surely as it rejects indulgent Ovidian sensuality.[16] And although it may have originated in a personal quarrel, *Poetaster* transcends its origins to express a lasting vision of the poet's active function in a receptive society. The play has particular interest as "the first and still one of the most powerful statements of an Augustan literary programme in English" and as a drama deeply engaged with contemporaneous political concerns (Cain, 1). Containing a number of allusions to the Essex rebellion of 1600 and throughout implying a contrast between Elizabethan England and Augustan Rome, *Poetaster* is a political as well as poetic satire.

The first period of Jonson's career is marked by experimentation and innovation. In *Every Man in His Humour* he successfully imposes classical ideals of form and decorum on contemporary material. The result is realistic comedy that breathes an air of city life. The excursion into comical satires did not yield great plays, but Jonson's restless experimentation indicates an attempt to revitalize the popular stage as a forum for intellectual issues. And if the War of the Theaters no longer interests us—however bitter Jonson's quarrel with Marston, the two were sufficiently reconciled by 1604 to join George Chapman in collaboration on *Eastward Ho!*—it provided an opportunity for Jonson to assert in *Poetaster* the profound seriousness of poetry and its usefulness to society, a lifelong theme. After *Poetaster,* Jonson abandoned the comic muse for a time to attempt tragedy. When he returned to comedy with a play of his own devising, he produced *Volpone,* a work that combines the organic form and control of *Every Man in His Humour* with the seriousness of the comical satires.

Volpone (1606)

Jonson's second major comedy, *Volpone, or The Fox,* was first presented by the King's Men (formerly the Lord Chamberlain's Men) at the Globe Theater, probably early in 1606. Within a year, the play was produced at both Oxford and Cambridge, and when it was published, Jonson dedicated it "To the Most Noble and Most Equall Sisters the Two Famous Universities." Jonson wrote *Volpone* in only five weeks (Pro., line 16), for him an extraordinarily rapid rate of composition, but he was justifiably pleased with the result. When he prepared the play for inclusion in his *Works,* he altered the text only slightly. Although in some respects unlike anything else he was to write, *Volpone* is masterful both in conception and in realization. Its characters and its actions are sources of unflagging interest, and the language of the play is rich and evocative.

The situation from which the action springs in *Volpone* was no doubt suggested to Jonson by a medieval beast fable in which a fox feigns imminent death in order to catch and eat carrion birds.[17] Using details from the legacy-hunting literature of classical Rome, including Petronius's *Satyricon,* and from an important Renaissance satire, Erasmus's *The Praise of Folly,* Jonson transforms the fable's appetite for food into an appetite for riches and adds a host of complications. With the assistance of his parasite, a Venetian magnifico named Volpone ("the fox") pretends to be terminally ill in order to extract expensive gifts from three wealthy old men, named appropriately Voltore ("the vulture"), Corvino ("the crow"), and Corbaccio ("the raven"), leading each to believe that he will be made sole heir if his gifts find favor with the dying man. Volpone is a luxurious, quick-witted man who becomes enamored of his own ability to scheme. His voluptuous nature manifests itself in his lust for Celia, the virtuous young wife of one of his gulls, and his determination to bed her, culminating in attempted rape, causes the play's first catastrophe. Volpone averts public exposure but deludes himself into believing that he was saved entirely by his own quick wit. His already high opinion of his cleverness soars, and he elaborates on his scheme so much that he unwittingly provides an opportunity for the parasite Mosca ("the fly") to seize his fortune. The rivalry of master and servant leads to a second and complete catastrophe.

The subjects of *Volpone* are vices, not follies: greed so great that it disrupts both the familial and the broader social order, luxuriousness so excessive and unchecked by conscience that it countenances rape, and perversions so fundamental that human beings descend to the level of beasts.[18] Carried to the extent that they are, these human failings, themselves outgrowths of a self-love that overpowers all other considerations, cannot be considered merely humors, and thus the major plot of *Volpone* cannot be considered a comedy of manners. It does not contain a single normative figure.[19] On one side are the vicious characters, Volpone, Mosca, and the three gulls; on the other side are Bonario and Celia, their innocent victims, who are so naive that they lack even that moderate amount of calculating wit necessary for self-preservation in a far-from-perfect world. In the middle stand the Avocatori, who should be the wise guardians of society but who are actually foolish old men easily led astray. If the play had only this one plot and if it were not presented with such comic zest, it might be bleak indeed. But Jonson not only presents the main plot with inventiveness and energy but also deftly weaves into its fabric a subplot that is a comedy of manners in miniature, using it both to ameliorate the tension of the major plot, which frequently threatens to become a tragedy, and to show the ultimate danger of what appears to be relatively harmless folly.

Scattered throughout *Volpone* are scenes that feature an expatriate English couple, Sir Politic and Lady Wouldbe, and a young gentleman traveler named Peregrine. Both Sir Pol and his wife are pretenders to that which they do not have, the husband to worldly wisdom and an intimate knowledge of state secrets, his wife to beauty, intelligence, and fashion. The manipulation of Lady Wouldbe by Volpone and Mosca clearly demonstrates the ease with which folly can be used by vice. In Venice primarily to learn the cosmetic and fashion secrets of the city's famous courtesans, she is readily made partner to the unjust persecution of Celia and added to the company of greedy legacy hunters. Sir Pol's function is more subtly connected to the play's chief action. His most egregious folly is alleging the existence of political plots where none really exist. This proclivity pointedly complements the inability of the Avocatori to detect the actual conspiracies of Volpone and Mosca. Sir Pol also serves as a telling foil to Volpone himself, his naïveté and sociability contrasting with the cynicism and antisocial proclivities of the magnifico. Peregrine, in the manner of the gentlemen wits of other Jonsonian comedies, at first finds amusement in Sir Politic's pretensions. But when he thinks that he himself has become a victim of the English couple's foolishness (4.2 and 3), he exposes the old knight's absurdities in an appropriately humiliating way, although in doing so, he may also ironically expose himself as someone very like Sir Pol in that he is responding to an imaginary threat rather than a real one.[20]

The range of characters in *Volpone* is great, from simply developed figures of minor interest to completely realized individuals of memorable presence and power. The four Avocatori are defined only by their collective judicial blindness, self-satisfaction, and obsequiousness to wealth and social position. The three gulls are somewhat more fully drawn. All are characterized by a greed so great that they are willing to sacrifice for material gain those things they should most love. Voltore, an eloquent lawyer, should of all men respect truth, but his tongue is "mercenary" and "His soule moves in his fee" (4.5.95,96). Corbaccio should cherish his dutiful son, but he is willing to disinherit the young man for the promise of great wealth. Corvino, insanely jealous and defensive of his reputation, should appreciate the virtue of his wife, whom he treats as a possession. But after locking her away from the world to avoid even the appearance of impropriety, he then willingly prostitutes her in the hope of increasing his wealth. The manipulation of the gulls abounds in irony. None of them believe that they actually endanger the values they profess, but their subordination of everything to the hope of gold reveals their true natures. In contrast to the gulls, Celia and Bonario are defined by an innocence so complete that they are unequipped to deal with the real world.[21] As their names indicate, Celia is "heavenly" and Bonario is a "good man." When faced with rape, Celia naively believes that she can win over her attacker by appealing to his conscience, honor, and pity. And even after learning of his father's plan to disinherit him, Bonario remains dutifully obedient. Their only defense to counter the perjuries sworn against them in their trial are the touching but naive and ineffectual witnesses of "Our consciences. / And heaven, that never failes the innocent" (4.6.16–17).

Peregrine is characterized in much the same fashion as the witty gallants of Jonson's other comedies.[22] Basically blameless, he is clever enough to recognize folly. While he enjoys the city's sport, he can, when necessary, manipulate a foolish character into an embarrassing exposure of his inadequacy. The two humor characters he confronts are quite thoroughly drawn, and both became enduring types in comedies of manners. Sir Politic Wouldbe is full of assumed dignity, self-importance, and even bluster when he is away from his wife but is a slave to her shrewish tongue when she is present. Some of his speeches, such as the "advice to travelers" passage that begins act 4, are among the most sophisticated bits of comic writing in the play. But Lady Wouldbe is the masterpiece of humor characterization in *Volpone*. Full of recipes for medicines and cosmetic unguents, furnished with the names of authors and titles—but not the contents—of books, and completely oblivious to her own ridiculousness and to the havoc she wreaks on her mother tongue, she chatters her way through the play, to the frustration of its characters and to the delight of its audience. As an autonomous (and therefore threatening) woman, she serves as a foil to Celia, who is valued and commodified not only because of her beauty but also because of her dependence. Lady Wouldbe may be used negatively to point up a moral lesson, but she is a brilliant creation; and her numerous daughters and granddaughters enliven the comedy of manners throughout the Restoration and beyond.

Most of Jonson's comedies are focused widely. They present the actions of people in groups, and the audience follows the fates of several characters simultaneously. In *Volpone*, however, attention is almost unrelentingly directed toward the title character and his parasite. Both are superb improvisers of comic action who delight in intrigue and conspiracy, and both ultimately overreach themselves, but Jonson carefully distinguishes between them. The keys to Mosca's character are his self-love, his contempt for others, and his conviction that his wit entitles him to a status higher than that of a mere servant. He recognizes the monstrosity of his deeds. As he tells Bonario, even here using the truth for his own deceitful purposes,

> I have done
> Base offices, in rending friends asunder,
> Dividing families, betraying counsells,
> Whispering false lyes, or mining men with praises,
> Train'd their credulitie with perjuries,
> Corrupted chastitie. . . .
>
> (3.2.25–30)

But he scorns the social fabric he endangers. Acutely aware of being, in
the words of the judge who sentences him, "a fellow of no birth, or
bloud" (5.12.112), he is alienated from a body politic that restricts his
ambition and fails to recognize him as "a most precious thing, dropt
from above, / Not bred'mong'st clods, and clot-poules, here on earth"
(3.1.8–9). He takes pleasure in undermining the society from which he
feels excluded and, as he observes of his own evolution, begins "to grow
in love / With my deare selfe" (3.1.1–2). The gulls of the play merit his
disdain, but his contempt for fools gradually broadens to include
Volpone himself. Mosca comes to believe that he is more clever than his
master and that his own wit, rather than the magnifico's, is responsible
for cozening the dupes. In this context of social resentment, Volpone's
praise begins to smell of condescension. Mosca chafes at the subservient
role, and when the opportunity arises, he seizes the wealth and social
position he believes are due him.

The relationship between Volpone and Mosca is complex and defined
by their roles as master and servant. Mosca attempts to reverse these
roles, but Volpone's pride in his own status precludes allowing himself
to be tricked by a parasite. Moreover, the fox's sense of his own uniqueness makes it impossible for him to acquiesce in a compromise settle-
ment with his subordinate. If the magnifico must accept defeat, his ruin
will be at the hands of his social peers. "My substance shall not glew
you, / Nor screw you, into a family" (5.12.87–88), he declares to
Mosca, even though his exposure of the parasite necessarily causes his
own severe punishment. By making Mosca resentful of his social position and using this alienation to help motivate his actions, Jonson deepens his portrait and, without mitigating his confessed evil, makes him
more complex and affecting than he might otherwise be. Jonson also
complicates and deepens the relationship between Mosca and Volpone
by infusing it with a subtle homoeroticism that is occasionally made
explicit, as when Volpone describes his parasite as "my pride / My joy,
my tickling, my delight!" (3.7.68–69).[23]

Unlike Mosca, Volpone does not acknowledge the evil he does or causes others to do. Indeed, he congratulates himself that he earns his money by wit rather than by such "destructive" occupations as trading, farming, mining, manufacturing, shipping, or banking:

> I use no trade, no venter;
> I wound no earth with plow-shares; fat no beasts
> To feede the shambles; have no mills for yron,
> Oyle, corne, or men, to grinde 'hem into poulder;
> I blow no subtill glasse; expose no ships
> To threatnings of the furrow-faced sea;
> I turne no moneys, in the publike banke;
> Nor usure private.
>
> (1.1.33–40)

He complacently accepts Mosca's praise of his generosity and "sweet nature" (1.1.48), and he apparently misses the irony in his servant's commendation of him for abhorring the ruthlessness of capitalists, although in fact his schemes lead exactly to the abuses catalogued by Mosca (1.1.40–51).

Completely egocentric, Volpone is a narcissist and a sadist[24] as well as a jaded voluptuary who delights in feasting the senses. He keeps as household entertainers his putative children, the dwarf Nano, the eunuch Castrone, and the hermaphrodite Androgyno, their physical abnormalities mirroring his spiritual unnaturalness. Even the satisfaction he derives from his clever scheming is sensual. "The pleasure of all woman-kind's not like it" (5.2.11), he exclaims. But for all his intelligence, Volpone is not as unique as he thinks he is. In fact, he shares the lack of self-knowledge of his dupes, as becomes apparent in his overreaching in act 5. Moreover, he partakes of their failure of perception, as when he neglects to notice that "loving Mosca" (1.2.122) is not loving at all. He fails to recognize that Mosca has his own designs and that even his exposure to Celia may have been more in the service of his parasite's interests than his own. What Mosca says of the gulls in act 5, that they are so stuffed with their own hopes that they resist any evidence that would contradict them, is true of the magnifico as well.

Volpone's lack of conscience makes him a monster, but he is nevertheless enormously appealing, at least for a time. Despite the perversion of values implicit in his worship of gold, he certainly evokes far more admira-

tion than Corbaccio, Corvino, and Voltore; they share his debased values
but not his appealing wit or his excellent acting in this intensely theatrical
work. Indeed, Volpone's playing the role of an invalid actually serves to
emphasize his vitality. When he preys on individuals as monstrous as he,
his attractiveness insulates him from moral censure. Not only is his cleverness far greater than that of his dupes, but his vision is also larger than
theirs and contains elements of nobility, however corrupted they may have
become. Even when the excess of his luxuriousness grows to outweigh its
apparent attractiveness, when he attempts to destroy—in the persons of
Celia and Bonario—both heavenly and earthly goodness, his agile wit
continues to command respect. The attempted seduction of Celia betrays
the grotesquerie of Volpone, and the futility of his desire for her links him
with the gulls, who are equally frustrated, yet the episode also provides an
opportunity for him to display his comic energy. His false values represent
the dark side of human nature, but in him that side shines with a brilliant,
tempting luster. And despite (or because of) his profoundly serious moral
failings, Volpone remains a fascinating character, complex and compelling
and always entertaining.

A measure of Jonson's genius in *Volpone* is that the play's dark vision
of spiritual malaise is presented delightfully. Still, the play's fun does not
obscure its serious social and religious insights. Focusing on an animat-
ing materialism so complete that it becomes religious, the play studies
the worship of riches that translates men into beasts. The inversion of
Volpone's values is clear from his blasphemous opening hymn to gold,
"the worlds soule, and mine" (1.1.3):

> O, thou sonne of SOL,
> (But brighter then thy father) let me kisse,
> With adoration, thee, and every relique
> Of sacred treasure, in this blessed roome.
>   (1.1.10–13)

All the characters of the main plot, except the symbolic innocents, join
to greater or lesser degrees in the worship of the false god gold. This
worship of riches impoverishes them spiritually. Their materialism yields
subhuman behavior and the ironic physicality of the sensualist who
knows, even as he tries to suppress the knowledge and even as he catalogues the exotic pleasures wealth can buy, that gold cannot purchase
health, youth, or eternal life.

The limits of materialism are stretched in Volpone's gorgeous speeches designed to seduce Celia, whom he may desire primarily for the challenge her inaccessibility poses to his ingenuity. Although the magnifico dismisses Corvino as one who "would have sold his part of paradise / For ready money" (3.7.143–44), his own soaring imagination does little more than attempt to buy her. Even the carpe diem appeal of the famous song, "Come, my Celia, let us prove," is itself a recognition of limitations: "Time will not be ours, for ever" (3.7.168). His appeals escalate from predictable offers of "a rope of pearle" and "A diamant" (3.7.191, 195) to temptations of exotic food ("The heads of parrats, tongues of nightingales, / The braines of peacoks, and of estriches" [3.7.202–203]) to visions of luxuries that delight the entire body:

> Thy bathes shall be the juyce of july-flowres,
> Spirit of roses, and of violets,
> The milke of unicornes, and panthers breath
> Gather'd in bagges, and mixt with *cretan* wines.
>   (3.7.213–16)

When these prove no temptation, he lures her with the almost total involvement of sensation implied in the erotic novelty of fantastic role-playing, a temptation that may inadvertently reveal his own desire to escape the limitations of the self :

>   my dwarfe shall dance,
> My eunuch sing, my foole make up the antique.
> Whil'st, we, in changed shapes, act OVIDS tales,
> Thou, like EUROPA now, and I like JOVE,
> Then I like MARS, and thou like ERYCINE,
> So, of the rest, till we have quite run through
> And weary'd all the fables of the gods.
>   (3.7.219–25)

Volpone continues, offering more "moderne formes" than those of the ancients, but his imagination is exhausted, and the thematic and metaphorical point has been made. Volpone's materialistic universe, for all its Faustian appeal, is severely bounded by its earth-centeredness, a diminishment emphasized by the earlier reference to paradise and by

Celia's symbolic name and function. Moreover, the allusion to Ovid's *Metamorphoses,* in which human beings are not ennobled but transformed into plants or animals, inadvertently acknowledges the bestial proclivities of materialism. Tellingly, when the lady resists his persuasion, Volpone resorts to the brute physicality of rape.

The frequent allusions to physical illness in the play reflect the spiritual sickness of Venice, but they also indicate the limitations of materialism.[25] The complexity of Volpone's attitude toward illness and old age, a mixture of contempt and dread, is especially revealing. Shamming disease for profit, Volpone pretends to be ill throughout much of the play. But being a true voluptuary, he scorns the reality he imitates, especially the infirmities that affect the enjoyment of physical pleasures. He unfeelingly catalogues the "feares attending on old age," describing the elderly in contemptuous terms (1.4.145–50). In the mountebank scene (2.2), where the consummate actor brilliantly performs a noted charlatan—a part naturally congenial to his talents—he callously hawks a "precious oyle" that offers false hopes of remedy and eternal youth. Beneath the voluptuary's easy derision of the aged and the ill, however, is a barely submerged dread. Fittingly, while feigning disease to trick the Avocatori, he is struck by the initial symptoms of a real malady. As he recounts to Mosca, with momentary foreboding:

> 'Fore god, my left legge 'gan to have the crampe;
> And I apprehended, straight, some power had strooke me
> With a dead palsey.
>
> (5.1.5–7)

He tries to deny this intimation of mortality ("well, I must be merry, / And shake it off"), but his merriment does not last long. When his doom is sealed, the sentence passed on Volpone is grimly ironic and altogether appropriate:

> thy substance all be straight confiscate
> To the hospitall, of the *Incurabili:*
> And, since the most was gotten by imposture,
> By faining lame, gout, palsey, and such diseases,
> Thou art to lie in prison, crampt with irons,
> Till thou bee'st sicke, and lame indeed.
>
> (5.12.119–24)

The fate that Volpone had most mocked and feared becomes his own. Not only is he stripped of the wealth and freedom that made voluptuousness possible, but the conditions of his imprisonment will also rob him of sensation itself. The punishment is the greater because his materialism has never allowed him to transcend the physical.

The materialism of the gold worshipers limits their human potential and causes them to express the bestiality within, to become less than fully human. Appropriately for a play based on a beast fable, the names of most of the characters suggest their animal natures—fox, fleshfly, vulture, raven, crow, and the diminutive "Pol" for parrot. But these names are only the comedy's most overt identification of human beings with animals. Bestiality abounds in the play, from the epithets applied to nearly all the characters to the actions that reek of carrion. Only Mosca and Volpone admiringly identify themselves with animals, however—Mosca with the "subtill snake" (3.1.6) and Volpone with the fox (e.g., 1.2.94–96). Their frankness makes them more attractive than the other, equally animalistic characters who never admit their resemblance to beasts. Yet the honesty does not alter their bestiality, particularly because the snake and the fox are traditionally potent emblems of evil and cunning. The materialistic limitations and spiritual poverty of animalism are strikingly revealed in Volpone's reaction to the judgment pronounced against him, the single sentence, "This is call'd mortifying of a FOXE" (5.12.125). This simple phrase—the last words he speaks in the play proper—neatly concentrates a number of important insights and focuses the play's irony. In the early seventeenth century, *mortifying* did not mean "causing extreme embarrassment," its common modern meaning, but "causing to die." Moreover, two specialized meanings are implied as well. As a religious term, it refers to a denial of the physical appetites, and as a kitchen term, it denotes the hanging up of dead animals to allow the first stages of putrefaction to tenderize their flesh before being cooked and eaten. Thus, in the one word Volpone acknowledges his fate in three areas. His fears regarding old age and death will be horribly realized, his voluptuousness will be thoroughly checked, and his identification with an animal will be made unpleasantly total.

Significantly, the conclusions of both plots are effected in terms of the pervasive animal metaphor. The subplot ends with a farcical scene in which Peregrine, whose name means "falcon" as well as "traveler," brings down Sir Politic Wouldbe, the parrot of fictional intrigues. He illustrates the foolish knight's descent from the human sphere to the animal by frightening him into a giant tortoise shell (5.4). Although Sir

Politic's hilarious punishment is the exposure of his foolishness, a fate less harsh than that apportioned to the vicious characters, it is effected in terms that echo and parody the tortures of the main plot. The main plot ends with an ironically self-congratulatory moral delivered by one of the foolish Avocatori and stated in terms of the slaughterhouse:

> Let all, that see these vices thus rewarded,
> Take heart, and love to study 'hem. Mischiefes feed
> Like beasts, till they be fat, and then they bleed.
>   (5.12.149–51)

But the play's vision of our animalistic instincts and its depiction of justice and goodness as impotent have been too complete to allow the Avocatori's smug sententiousness to be reassuring.

Indeed, *Volpone* is not a reassuring comedy. The discovery of truth is not effected through societal safeguards—or even by a witty, basically good individual as in other Jonsonian comedies—but solely through the confession of the play's chief criminal, who decides he prefers vengeance to safety. The play may illustrate the self-defeating futility of vice and the ability of true innocence to resist the temptations of materialism; moreover, conforming as it does to the "triumph of truth" tradition of the period, the play's plot may express the comforting Renaissance idea that the truth will eventually be brought to light.[26] Yet the fact remains that Celia and Bonario are so symbolic as to be scarcely imitable and the earthly institutions of justice so inept and dishonest as to offer little solace. The play is peopled exclusively by knaves and fools, and the discourse of morality is systematically robbed of any meaning by being co-opted into the service of knavery.[27] That the vision of *Volpone* is a negative one requires no apology, however. The brilliant depiction of materialistic corruption is its own justification, documenting the betrayal of human nature itself by people in the service of the false god gold. Jonson defended the harsh ending by remarking, in the letter dedicating *Volpone* to Oxford and Cambridge, that "the office of a *comick-Poet*" is, among other things, "to imitate justice, and instruct to life" (lines 121–22). As instruction and imitation, *Volpone* achieves the combination of moral seriousness and delight its author always sought.

Volpone is a major achievement, a totally successful experiment in mixing profit with laughter. The aims Jonson confesses in his Prologue are daringly realized. A play providing serious moral insight, it is nevertheless a "quick *comoedie*"; with its lessons conveyed in "salt" rather than in "gall," it is a work of great "pleasure" (lines 8, 29, 33, 34). Although "refined, / As best Criticks have designed" in its adherence to "The lawes of time, place, persons" (lines 29–30, 31), it nonetheless seems both spontaneous and plausible. Moreover, its two plots, though different in kind, are perfect complements to each other. The comedy of manners in the subplot periodically relieves the tension built by the main plot as vice temporarily yields the stage to foolishness. The language of the play, while always highly evocative, is satisfyingly varied, ranging from coarse bestial invective to soaring voluptuous fantasy, but always suited to character and situation. And finally, the major characters of *Volpone* are so well conceived and developed that they transcend the limits of time, place, and custom. By all the tests applied to imaginative literature, *Volpone* is a masterpiece.

Epicoene (1609)

The subplot of *Volpone* touches briefly on the subject of gender roles. Lady Wouldbe dominates her husband, and in one scene she mistakes Peregrine for a loose woman in disguise, describing him as "A female devill, in a male out-side" (4.2.56). In his next comedy, a work very different from *Volpone,* Jonson explores the issue more fully. *Epicoene, or The Silent Woman* was first presented in late 1609 or early 1610 by the Children of Her Majesty's Revels at Whitefriars Theater. Its plot combines situations from Ovid and Juvenal, Plautus's *Casina,* the sixth declamation of Libanius, Shakespeare's *Twelfth Night,* Aretino's *Il Marescalco,* and other sources, but with much elaboration and transformation. The action is so carefully and naturally developed according to classical precepts that John Dryden described it as "the greatest and most noble of any pure unmixed comedy in any language."[28]

In *Epicoene* Jonson returns to the exuberant manners comedy of *Every Man in His Humour,* a mode he abandoned for the comical satires and used only in the underplot of *Volpone.* The action takes place on a single day in a London neighborhood and centers on the efforts of young Dauphine Eugenie (abetted by his friends and fellow gallants Truewit and Clerimont) to secure his rightful share of his eccentric uncle's estate. Morose, the uncle, is addicted to silence and wrongly believes that his nephew has harassed him with unnecessary noise. The old man determines to find a mute woman, marry her, beget an heir, and deprive Dauphine of his inheritance. Working in secret, Dauphine creates a "silent woman," Epicoene, and arranges for Morose to discover her. Although the scheme is almost upset by the well-intentioned but misplaced efforts of Truewit, the old man proposes to her. As soon as Morose marries Epicoene, however, she turns into an incessantly chattering shrew. When the miserable husband offers his fortune to his nephew if he will rid him of such a hateful wife, the young man reveals the bride to be a boy in disguise and the marriage, therefore, invalid.

Although its plot hinges on the disposition of money, *Epicoene* is primarily concerned with sex roles and sexual stereotyping. Hence, it is not surprising that it is highly controversial. There simply is no critical consensus about some basic issues concerning interpretation of the play. Is it a light comedy or a grim satire? Is Morose a victim tortured by his sadistic nephew, or is he a misanthropic sociopath? Do the young gallants represent Jonsonian values, or are they themselves satirized? Does Jonson flatter his courtly audience, or does he criticize it? Are the minor characters merely foolish, or are they rather embodiments of social decay and perversion? Is the play misogynistic, or is it protofeminist? Is it homophobic or homoerotic? *Epicoene* has been described as both "a grimly serious play which exposes moral disease" (Knoll, 115) and as a high spirited, even affectionate comedy. Critics who conceive of Jonson as invariably satirical tend to see *Epicoene* as a harsher work than do critics who find Jonson more various and flexible, capable of lightness and tolerance as well as of censure. The play evinces ambiguities of tone, as is perhaps inevitable in a work that is indebted to both Ovid and Juvenal,[29] but it is not the humorless satire that some critics describe.

Unlike *Every Man in His Humour,* which it resembles in many respects, *Epicoene* does not present an "Image of the times." Although designed for a wide audience, as both its Prologue and its mixture of low comedy and learned wit indicate, it focuses narrowly on a group of Londoners on the periphery of the court.[30] This element of upper-middle-class society is in flux, especially in the area of sexual expression, and the very absence of unchallenged conventions provides the source of much of the play's laughter. As guides through the competition of aims and ideals expressed by the diverse characters, Jonson places at the comedy's center a trio of young gallants, Dauphine, Clerimont, and Truewit. These handsome youths expose the follies of the other characters and establish the play's criteria of sophistication and wit by which everyone else is measured. The comedy has a satiric edge. It ridicules violations of decorum by its bizarre cast. But the play delights in many of the frivolities it criticizes, and its comic vision is good-naturedly tolerant.

Dauphine, Clerimont, and Truewit are among the most attractive characters in Jonsonian comedy.[31] Although it may be true that the gallants, as Diana Benet and others have pointed out, themselves partake of their society's deceptions and falsifications, they are nevertheless sharply differentiated from the fools.[32] Intelligent, well-educated, and sensible, they delight in living well and in observing the world about them. All three are exuberant young men who enjoy the city's sport, but they are capable of seriousness as well. They are sophisticated in their casual acceptance of the varieties of sexual expression and in the high value they place on wit. As Dryden remarked, Jonson "has here described the conversation of gentlemen in the person of True-wit, and his friends, with more gaiety, air and freedom, than in the rest of his comedies" (Dryden, 1:86). The confident tone of comic banter with which the young men rally each other is clear in Truewit's early description of Clerimont as a "man that can melt away his time, and never [feele] it! what, betweene his mistris abroad, and his engle at home, high fare, soft lodging, fine clothes, and his fiddle" (1.1.23–26). This passage indicates the gallants' easy familiarity and urbane values, particularly in regard to sexual matters.[33]

The three wits function collectively in the play, but they are highly individualized. Clerimont, for instance, is retiring and writes beautiful poetry. Truewit, on the other hand, is gregarious, even impulsive. He visits the court, attends sporting events, and enjoys amorous adventures. Dauphine seems younger and less experienced than the other two, and he suffers from lack of money. But he has the wit necessary to improve his finances and an eagerness to learn from his friends. Indeed, the willingness and ability of all three to learn from the world and from each other are particularly important in the unsettled society of *Epicoene,* where conventional roles are questioned at every turn. The gallants encourage, support, and teach each other. Their education often takes the form of witty argument and spirited disagreement, as in the famous discussion of cosmetics that neatly crystallizes conflicting notions of art's relationship to nature. Clerimont comes to accept Truewit's approval of artifice, and Dauphine requests Truewit's instruction in wooing the Ladies Collegiate. But the experienced Truewit also learns from his friends, and at the end of the play he awards the garland of wit to Dauphine and Clerimont. The youths' openness to new ideas and to revision of old ones is a function of their urbanity.

If the gallants may themselves be flawed to the extent that they embrace some of the faults of their society, the other characters in *Epi-*

coene are far more seriously blemished. Morose, for example, is deeply disturbed. His humor manifests itself in his unreasonable determination to make the world around him silent. But his full passion is broader in scope, as he reveals in his first speech: "all discourses, but mine owne, afflict mee, they seeme harsh, impertinent, and irksome" (2.1.4–5). His real desire is to be the complete and unquestioned master of his household. In fact, he wants to be obeyed far beyond his own domain. For his nephew's suspected disobedience, he vows to "thrust him out of my bloud like a stranger" (2.5.100–101). He tries to silence all noises of the street and the neighborhood, and when Cutbeard brings Epicoene for an interview with Morose, the old man requires the barber to answer questions in the same silent, ridiculous, but broadly comic manner demanded of the servant Mute. Furthermore, his passion for total obedience is tellingly betrayed in his initial examination of Epicoene, whose poverty pleases him, for it will make her "more loving, and obedient" (2.5.93). Morose attempts to trick the prospective bride into revealing an inclination for fine company and expensive clothes as well as for talking. He determines to marry her only after her meek answers convince him that she will be completely submissive to him in all matters, including, but by no means limited to, silence.

The nature of Morose's humor and the seriousness of its consequences have often been misunderstood. Its statement in terms of physical ailment has afforded it sympathy, and it has been seen merely as a comic extension of the right of paterfamilias.[34] But Morose's passion, if realized, would result in an unconscionable dictatorship that could threaten the social fabric. Even the specific manifestation of total silence except for one lone, sullen voice is a symbolic denial of human communication. Many of the world's noises are as silly and annoying as the chatter of Daw and LaFoole and "The spitting, the coughing, the laughter, the [s]neesing, the farting" of the marriage banquet (4.1.8–9), but an indiscriminate denial of all sound would also silence poets, teachers, musicians, and other conveyors of compassion, wisdom, delight, and inspiration.

The fate that Dauphine engineers for the old bridegroom fittingly punishes the excessiveness of his desire for dominance. Although some critics believe that Morose is treated cruelly by his nephew, it is worth remembering, as Alexander Leggatt observes, that the torment of Morose is for one day only.[35] Significantly, Dauphine does not take unfair advantage of the misanthrope's discomfort. He refuses to be "unreasonable" when Morose offers him the entire estate (5.4.176); he accepts only one-third of his uncle's income and the assurance that he will be named heir. Morose's real punishment is not the recognition of his legitimate obligations to his nephew, however, but his public admission of impotence. The announcement, "I am no man, ladies" (5.4.44), is a surrender not only of dominance but also of the symbol of maleness that conventionally justifies it.

That Morose's punishment is effected in sexual terms is particularly significant in a play entitled *Epicoene*. The word means "androgynous," or having the characteristics of both sexes. Appropriately, the comedy abounds in sexual innuendo of all kinds.[36] The world of the play is a world in sexual flux, a society in which conventional sexual distinctions are reversed, blurred, or comically exaggerated. The bizarre cast of minor characters exemplifies this society's unsettled sexual attitudes. These characters are, in varying degrees, foolish, but the questions of sexual identity they raise and the assumptions they challenge are very real. Although the play has been seen as misogynistic and homophobic,[37] it actually treats issues of sexuality more deftly than such charges would suggest. Indeed, it embodies an urbane vision of sexual accommodation that implicitly criticizes stereotyped wisdom about the relationships of the sexes.

Two of the play's most amusing minor characters are the pretentious fools, Sir John Daw and Sir Amorous LaFoole. Daw affects wit and poetry but understands neither. Like Lady Wouldbe in *Volpone,* he passes weighty judgment on books he has not read. He even goes further than his fellow bird to insist that *Syntagma Juris civilis, Corpus Juris civilis,* and other titles are actually the names of authors. The *"Corpusses"* he claims to have known personally: "they were very corpulent authors" (2.3.88–89). The poetry he recites includes a trite, self-contradictory tribute to his "mistress" Epicoene, which, as the true poet Clerimont comments, "chimes, and cries tinke i' the close" (2.3.42). His companion, Sir Amorous, is an equally empty-headed fop with social pretensions. He is absurdly proud of his family and its coat of arms, not recognizing that the latter is the traditional motley of fools: *"Yellow,* or *Or,* checker'd *Azure,* and *Gules,* and some three or four colours more, which is a very noted coate, and has, some-times, beene solemnely worne by divers nobilitie of our house" (1.4.42–45). Similarly, his knowledge of polite society is so superficial that he misunderstands its etiquette, as Clerimont explains: "Hee is one of the *Braveries,* though he be none o' the *Wits.* He will salute a Judge upon the bench, and a Bishop in the pulpit, a Lawyer when hee is pleading at the barre, and a Lady when shee is dauncing in a masque, and put her out" (1.3.29–33). He renders courtesy counterproductive.

Both Daw and LaFoole are pretenders to manliness as well. They wear swords, constantly seek the company of women, and boast of their sexual prowess. But they are actually cowards, and neither knows how to court ladies successfully. Daw attempts to seduce Epicoene by praising her modesty, and LaFoole uses banquets and sweetmeats "for a bait" (1.3.41). Understandably, neither is successful. Women use them for amusement, not love. Their problem with women rests in their own effeminacy. Clerimont describes LaFoole as "a precious mannikin!" (1.3.25), and the phrase fits Daw as well. Especially important in a comedy that plays upon the stereotype of women's loquaciousness, both chatter pointlessly. Truewit ironically defines Daw as "The onely talking sir i' th' towne!" (1.2.66), and Clerimont scornfully exclaims of LaFoole, "Did you ever heare such a wind-fucker, as this?" (1.4.79). The fools' constant noise often consists of gossiping and boasting of their (imagined) sexual exploits, slandering the women of their acquaintance in the process. This breach of decorum contradicts all the courtesies of polite society that they profess, and it violates the code of discretion upon which social arrangements are based.

Daw and LaFoole, like Morose, are punished in progressive stages. The gallants first trick the two knights into a farcical public demonstration of their cowardice and then manipulate them by means of their cowardice and egotism into swearing before the assembled company that they have enjoyed Epicoene's sexual favors. Mavis's outcry against them, "Now out upon 'hem, informers!" (5.4.125), although uttered by one of the play's foolish characters, is fully warranted. Subsequently, the revelation of Epicoene's true sex also reveals Daw and LaFoole as ridiculous liars. Their indiscretion is their worst fault, and it is far more serious than their cowardice. Truewit dismisses them as "cuckowes. . . . You are they, that when no merit or fortune can make you hope to enjoy [ladies'] bodies, will yet lie with their reputations, and make their fame suffer. Away you common moths of these, and all ladies honors" (5.4.236–40). Their punishment is fitting: banishment from the society whose code of decorum they have violated.

Morose's exaggerated desire for dominance has a comic foil next door in the household of Otter. Truewit may have the Otters in mind when, in his attempt to dissuade Morose from marriage, he warns that if the bride is rich, "you marry her dowry, not her; shee'll raigne in your house, as imperious as a widow" (2.2.70–72). Mistress Otter's pride in her family—she is of "the LA-FOOLES of *London*" (1.4.35)—is as ridiculous as her social climbing, but she has the money, if not the wit, to support her pretensions. In both title and status, she far outranks her husband. He may have been a captain at sea, but on land he is an impoverished nobody, and "She commands all at home" (1.4.29). Captain Otter, the *"animal amphibium"* (1.4.26), is even more fatuous than his wife. In Truewit's estimation, he is "An excellent animal, equall with your DAW, or LA-FOOLE, if not transcendent" (2.4.52–53). While he affectedly spouts tags of Latin, and does so marvelously in his impersonation of a learned divine, his wit is so shallow that when he adopts a humor, he states it in terms of his three drinking cups: "these things I am knowne to the courtiers by. It is reported to them for my humor, and they receive it so, and doe expect it. TOM OTTERS bull, beare, and horse is knowne all over *England,* in *rerum natura*" (3.1.11–15).

The Otters' marriage reflects a deliberate reversal of traditional gender roles. Truewit describes the relationship succinctly, with a mixture of ridicule and titillation: "hee is his wifes Subject, he calls her Princesse, and at such times as these, followes her up and downe the house like a page, with his hat off, partly for heate, partly for reverence" (2.4.54–57). If the Captain's position is undignified, at least it is of his own choosing. As he explains it, he fell in love with his wife's "sixe thousand pound" (4.2.78) and signed a marriage agreement acknowledging her right to be "Princess" and rule the household. Their marriage has sometimes been described in moralistic terms as a reversal of the "natural order."[38] But such a description assumes that the natural order allows the husband dictatorial power, and the play uses the Otters to question that common assumption. The comic shock afforded by their marriage is only partly attributable to its reversal of conventional roles. The greater jolt arises from the recognition that the relationship parodies—and thus exposes to ridicule—the domination men ordinarily exert over women. When Mistress Otter asks, "Who gives you your maintenance, I pray you? who allowes you your horse-meat, and mans-meat? your three sutes of apparell a yeere? your foure paire of stockings, one silke, three worsted? your cleane linnen, your bands, and cuffes when I can get you to weare 'hem?" (3.1.38–43), she unwittingly mocks the attitudes husbands often display toward wives. Mistress Otter's domination of her husband is no more—and no less—unnatural than the more common domination of women by men. In fact, her treatment of Captain Otter is considerably more humane than Morose's initial plans for the obedient, silent Epicoene he thinks he is marrying. Interestingly, the Otters provide their own punishment for each other in the play. Their foolishness should not obscure the seriousness of the issues they parody.

The characters who most directly challenge conventional sex roles are the Ladies Collegiate: Madame Haughty, Madame Centaure, and Mistress Mavis. Early in the play, Truewit describes them as "an order betweene courtiers, and country-madames, that live from their husbands; and give entertainement to all the *Wits,* and *Braveries* o' the time, as they call 'hem: crie downe, or up, what they like, or dislike in a braine, or a fashion, with most masculine, or rather hermaphroditicall authoritie" (1.1.75–80). Like men, they address each other by their surnames, and Haughty proudly announces that "CENTAURE has immortaliz'd her selfe, with taming of her wilde male" (4.3.27–28). As promiscuous as men, they entertain a "pluralitie of servants, and doe 'hem all graces" (4.3.31). Moreover, they control the rituals of courtship, as their active wooing of Dauphine demonstrates. This wonderfully comic scene reverses the conventional roles of sexual pursuit. Centaure and Mavis are frankly sensual in their praise of Dauphine's physical charms, and each invites him to a private rendezvous. Haughty, on the other hand, parodies the Petrarchan lover's idealism, masking her sensual appetite in the praise of higher things: "I assure you, sir DAUPHINE, it is the price and estimation of your vertue onely, that hath embarqu'd me to this adventure, and I could not but make out to tell you so; nor can I repent me of the act, since it is alwayes an argument of some vertue in our selves, that we love and affect it so in others" (5.2.1–6). Although Haughty protests that "It is not the outward, but the inward man that I affect" (5.2.17–18), her ends are the same as those of Mavis and Centaure. The comic reversal of sex roles in this scene brilliantly parodies the conventional courtship ritual. Indeed, the targets of Jonson's satire here are the absurdities and hypocrisies of courtship conventions, not the "unnaturalness" of women pursuing men.

The independent Ladies Collegiate are undeniably the subject of ridicule, but they are not merely ridiculous. They are foolish enough to be manipulated by anyone who is even moderately clever; as Truewit explains, "all their actions are governed by crude opinion, without reason or cause; they know not why they doe any thing: but as they are inform'd, beleeve, judge, praise, condemne, love, hate, and in aemulation one of another, doe all these things alike" (4.6.64–69). They are silly enough to think that Daw and LaFoole are actually wits and to be impressed with the brave shows of wealth and status. Yet their rebellion against the restrictions placed on their sex is not without just cause.

While presented in a comic context, their protest raises serious issues that cannot be jokingly dismissed as "hermaphroditicall" or sneeringly denounced as unnatural (Partridge 1958, 162–65; Knoll, 111–13). In a society that freely allows promiscuity to men, for instance, their revolt against the double standard is reasonable. "Why should women denie their favours to men?" Haughty asks, "Are they the poorer, or the worse?" (4.3.32–33). Similarly, her justification of birth preventives is valid: "How should we maintayne our youth and beautie, else? Many births of a woman make her old, as many crops make the earth barren" (4.3.59–61). The ladies' practice of birth control is not evidence of the "sterility" of their lives, as one critic asserts (Partridge 1958, 165). Haughty's protest is not against childbearing itself but against the numerous pregnancies expected of a woman, the cost of which in early modern England was often disability or early death.

The comic ambiguity of Jonson's presentation of the Ladies Collegiate is perfectly illustrated in their carpe diem arguments justifying promiscuity:

> HAU. Besides, ladies should be mindfull of the approach of age, and let no time want his due use. The best of our daies passe first.
>
> MAV. We are rivers, that cannot be call'd backe, madame: shee that now excludes her lovers, may live to lie a forsaken beldame, in a frozen bed.
>
> CEN. 'Tis true, MAVIS; and who will wait on us to coach then? or write, or tell us the newes then? Make anagrammes of our names, and invite us to the cock-pit, and kisse our hands all the play-time, and draw their weapons for our honors? (4.3.40–50)

The shallowness of their values is obvious in their addiction to fashionable amusements and in their trivialization of a very serious issue. Still, there is melancholy truth in their perception that women face grim futures in the sexual arena as they age. That this reflects a double standard is obvious from Morose's easy arrangement of marriage to the youthful Epicoene. Moreover, the passage strikes to the heart of the play's exposure of the inequities of early modern England's sex-gender system. To defend their promiscuity, the ladies use arguments traditionally employed by men to convince coy mistresses to grant sexual favors. This reversal of roles parodies the conventional male arguments by revealing the inequity on which they are based. The further irony is that the ladies' active pursuit of men must be expressed in passive terms: The females must appear to be the recipients of male courtship.

In his instruction of Dauphine in the art of seduction, Truewit observes that women "would sollicite us, but that they are afraid. Howsoever, they wish in their hearts we should sollicite them" (4.1.77–78). The fear of which he speaks underlines the danger in the courtship ritual and, more particularly, the risk women face in a brave new world of sexual etiquette. Their boldness may damage their reputations or may frighten men into retreat. The sophistication of their social circle can protect their honor, but only if its code of discretion is observed—hence Clerimont's admonition to Dauphine, "you must not tell" (5.2.51), and the necessary ejection of Daw and LaFoole, who are too witless to understand the need for decorum. The risk of frightening away suitors may be ameliorated only if men are urbane enough to realize that the ladies' boldness is not emasculating. Dauphine is unthreatened by the Ladies Collegiate, and he is eager to learn how to win their favors. With the aid of his friends, he succeeds in his quest. Although the Ladies Collegiate are comic characters whose follies are exposed, their collective name implies not only that they are able to educate Dauphine in the art of love but also that they—unlike the other ridiculous characters—may themselves be educable.

Epicoene is a play of suggestion rather than of definitive statement. Jonson is fully aware of the profound mystery that surrounds human sexuality, and he does not presume to offer revolutionary formulas for society. But he does suggest that certain assumptions concerning the roles considered proper to the sexes are unreasonably confining, and in his exposure of the absurdities of the courtship ritual, he points toward a freedom for both sexes to express their desires. The final comment on the play's title character implies the possibility of sexual accommodation. As Epicoene stands revealed as a boy on the edge of puberty, Truewit commends him to the Ladies Collegiate in these words: "let it not trouble you that you have discover'd any mysteries to this young gentleman. He is (a'most) of yeeres, & will make a good visitant within this twelve-month. In the meane time, we'll all undertake for his secrecie, that can speake so well of his silence" (5.4.246–51). The word "mysteries" is resonant and suggestive. It refers to the code of discretion necessary to the society of the play, and in the name of all three gallants, Truewit pledges that Epicoene will observe that code. The deeper impli-

cation of "mysteries," here as in the reference to "The mysteries of manners, armes, and arts" (line 98) in "To Penshurst" (*F.* 2), is intimate
knowledge of the essence of things. Epicoene has been in a uniquely
instructive position. His experience far transcends the assumption of a
wig and female clothing. For a time he has been treated by women as
one of themselves, sharing intimacies they would normally never reveal
to men. The experience bodes well for both Epicoene and the ladies in
his future. What he has learned from his experience will help make him
a good lover when he is a man. The sexual accommodation Jonson envisions in the play is one to be achieved through education.

Although the depiction of women in *Epicoene* clearly draws upon a
long history of misogynistic representations and stereotypes, Jonson's
intent is not so much to further an antifeminist agenda as it is to provoke a reexamination of gender and sex roles and to interrogate the sex-
gender system of his day.[39] Moreover, his exploitation of the conventions
of the transvestite Renaissance stage in order to feature a male actor who
portrays an apparently female character only finally to reveal the character as male may indicate his awareness that masculinity and femininity
are social constructions rather than immutable natural characteristics.
In this regard, it is noteworthy that the cross-dressing at the center of
the plot furthers a strong homoerotic theme in the play, since Epicoene
is an object of desire for both men and women. Although Jonson is frequently accused of misogyny and homophobia, Richmond Barbour may
well be right to assert that in sexual matters, "Jonson is deeply divided,
by turns authoritative and subversive."[40]

Epicoene is among Jonson's most interesting works. Its plot, always
controlled and completely integrated with theme, balances calculated
plan with spontaneous action and reaction. The decision to withhold the
full details of Dauphine's scheme from the other gallants was inspired.
Enormously influential on the Restoration masters of the form, *Epicoene*
is a model comedy of manners. It perfectly achieves the delicate balance
demanded by the genre: equally criticizing the flaws of an imperfect,
polite society and affirming its sophistication as sufficient remedy for
those shortcomings. It places a high value on wit yet humanely punishes
only that witlessness that is dangerous to the social fabric. It explores
serious issues but with an urbanely light touch. It luxuriates in variety of
character and language yet unobtrusively observes decorum. Most of all,
while it does not underrate the need for privacy and solitude, it joyously
celebrates men and women as social beings.

The Alchemist (1610)

Jonson's most famous comedy, *The Alchemist*, was written for the King's
Men, who premiered it at the Globe (or possibly the Blackfriars, which
is located in the district where the play is set) near the middle of 1610
and included it in the repertory of their autumn tour. In it, the playwright turns from the restricted social milieus of *Volpone* and *Epicoene* to a
canvas even broader than that of *Every Man in His Humour* to paint a
detailed "Image of the times" with the deft strokes of a master at the
height of his powers. Although its cast of characters includes representatives of all but the lowest and highest social strata, *The Alchemist* is the
most concentrated of Jonson's comedies. All its events take place in one
house and in the lane adjacent, the time it covers is at most seven hours,
and all its parts add up to a single action. Yet the play is unforced, exciting, and provocative, suggesting the complexity of an entire city.
Unmistakably a London comedy, it teems with her varied citizenry and
visitors; it speaks with her particular range of accents; it breathes with
her odoriferous air; and it bustles with her chief preoccupation, the
acquisition of money and status. Or, in the words of the Prologue:

> Our *Scene* is *London*, 'cause we would make knowne,
> No countries mirth is better then our owne.
> No clime breeds better matter, for your whore,
> Bawd, squire, impostor, many persons more,
> Whose manners, now call'd humors, feed the stage.
>   (lines 5–9)

Furthermore, the play has a special sense of immediacy. Set in an
autumn day of the year of its initial production, its events are presented
in the context of the time's chief horror, the plague, and its subject is the
"vices" bred in the "clime" and "age" of London, 1610 (Pro., lines 7, 13,
14), in particular the lust for power and the propensity for self-delusion.

Using materials from such disparate sources as Plautus's *Mostellaria*,
Erasmus's *De Alcumista*, alchemical and religious treatises, rogue pam-
phlets, and the written and oral reports of contemporaneous quackery of
all kinds, Jonson constructed a comedy of enormous vitality and freshness. To escape the plague's contagion, the prosperous London citizen
Lovewit spends the summer months in his country hopfields. In his
absence, Jeremy, the butler left in charge of his Blackfriars townhouse,

forms an alliance with Subtle, a starving cheater, and his prostitute companion Dol Common. They set up a laboratory in the deserted house and fleece a variety of gulls with ruses that promise wealth and success through alchemy, astrology, and demonology, used alone or in various combinations. On the climactic day of the scheme, their alliance shows the strain of mutual suspicion and distrust, but the three rally together sufficiently to attend to the host of London citizens and visitors who flock to them almost begging to be cozened: a law clerk, a shopkeeper, a Separatist elder and his parson, a city knight, his skeptical gamester companion who later returns disguised as a Spanish grandee, and a young country squire and his rich widowed sister. To succeed in their schemes, the three tricksters contrive to keep the gulls separated from one another, and as the latter crowd in for return visits, the cozeners rise to extremes of improvisation. When the action reaches a frantic pace, Lovewit returns unexpectedly, and the whole fabric of deceit crumbles. Subtle and Dol are forced to flee penniless, but by giving the ill-gotten wealth to his fun-loving master and arranging for him to marry the rich young widow, Jeremy saves himself.

Although its masterful plot is a series of replications of a single action, cozenage, *The Alchemist* is varied and complex. Set during a time of "the sickness hot" (Pro., line 1), the drama depicts a diseased society peopled by a wide variety of egocentrics and sensualists who are preyed upon by swindlers and cheats.[41] Incident succeeds incident at breakneck speed until the final act, when the return of Lovewit restores order and imposes an ending. As the title suggests, the play focuses on transformation. The aspirations of the individual gulls differ, but each comes to the house used by Subtle, Face, and Dol hoping to escape the realities of a narrow and unfulfilled self. Ironically, they only become more completely what they already are.[42] Even the three cozeners who offer the hope of metamorphosis effect for themselves only superficial and temporary transformations. Their identities are as false as the hopes they hold out to their gulls, and when faced with reality, they are as vulnerable as the most stupid of the victims. The play is vitalized by tensions—the tension between reality and desire in both the gulls and the tricksters and the tension between the attractiveness of many of the desired transformations and the ugliness of the values that animate them. As an exposé of human fallibility, of the human capacity for deception and especially self-deception, and of false values and the cynical veneers of altruism and piety that mask greed and corruption, *The Alchemist* is a deadly serious play. Yet it wears its didacticism lightly, and the delight it takes in its rogues and fools reflects the characteristic ambiguity at the heart of the Jonsonian comic spirit. *The Alchemist* clearly reveals the flawed reality of the human condition, but its "wholsome remedies are sweet" (Pro., line 15): the fair correctives of robust laughter.[43]

Most of the play's exposure of vice and folly is improvised by Subtle, Face, and Dol. The three tricksters are among Jonson's most triumphant inventions. Intelligent, resourceful, and accomplished in the arts of seduction, they are united in a tenuous alliance that threatens to fall apart at various points in the play. They manipulate the gulls with consummate skill, illustrating their insight into the nature of folly and greed. They even help the fools to articulate repressed desires and unacknowledged aspirations, prompting the dupes to expand their dreams (even as they also reveal their egocentricity and childishness in the process). The rogues are brilliant in assessing the different needs and weaknesses of their clients. But they forget their own realities as petty cheats and swindlers, and their attempts to transmute themselves are as doomed as Mammon's and Wholesome's hopes of the philosopher's stone. The rivalry of Face and Subtle, who are engaged in a competitive game of one-upmanship, is exacerbated by the trio's early success and by the opportunity for the main chance that Dame Pliant represents.[44] The alliance is only barely held in check by the ministrations of Dol and by the rogues' mutual dependence on each other. The appearance of Lovewit merely hastens the inevitable collapse of the collaborators' uneasy truce. Because they are so adept at their confidence games and because their gulls are so ripe for cheating, Subtle, Face, and Dol command the audience's sympathetic interest. Like the three gallants in *Epicoene,* they function collectively to expose the folly of others yet are highly individualized.

As befits the range of connotations in his name, Subtle is a complex figure. He is intelligent and knowledgeable. He knows the theory, the history, and the processes of alchemy, and he uses its terminology accurately.[45] He is acquainted with scholastic reasoning; he knows the vocabularies of palmistry, astrology, and demonology; and he is proficient even in the etiquette of quarreling.[46] He also knows something of the theology and practices of the separatist Anabaptists, and he is a quick and able casuist. He skillfully plays the role of *homo frugi,* a "pious, holy, and religious man / One free from mortall sinne, a very virgin" (2.2.98–99). But he uses his intelligence and knowledge merely to transform himself into appearances that temporarily disguise his reality. Ironically, however, the successes of his schemes in the Blackfriars house lead him to believe that he has actually become what he pretends to be, a man whose knowledge entitles him to dominion and respect. He boasts that it was his power that transformed the shabbily dressed menial Jeremy into the resplendently uniformed Captain Face. He demands of the erstwhile butler:

> Thou vermine, have I tane thee, out of dung,
>
> . . . .
>
> Rais'd thee from broomes, and dust, and watring pots?
> *Sublim'd* thee, and *exalted* thee, and *fix'd* thee
> I' the *third region,* call'd our *state of grace?*
>
> (1.1.64, 67–69)

The process described is alchemical, and it is clear that Subtle believes himself a real alchemist, of men if not of metals, a transformer of base matter into a higher state. But the terms he uses are also theological, and the language reverberates with ironic blasphemy. In the questions that climax the tirade, "have I this for thanke? Doe you rebell?" (1.1.78), Subtle assumes the persona of God rebuking an unworthy creature whom he has favored with his ultimate blessing of grace. Indeed, in his role as the alchemist, he consistently forces his dupes into postures of submission and worship. But in reality he is a petty cheat, one so unsuccessful that he was starving and homeless when Face first noticed him. The discrepancy between desire and reality renders his pretensions pathetic.

While the specific manifestations of his role vary as occasion demands, Subtle always presents himself as extraordinarily knowledgeable, and his name remains constant. His male confederate, on the other hand, assumes different kinds of roles and is a man of many names: Jeremy, Face, Lungs, Ulenspiegel. Although used only rarely, Ulenspiegel is a key both to his dramatic genealogy and to his function as a person of multiple identities. Ulenspiegel is the merry prankster of German legend, a low character who uses his wit to trick his social betters. Thus the Face of *The Alchemist* betrays kinship to the vice of medieval drama. He is less learned than Subtle, but he has a keen knowledge of human nature. He quickly perceives each fool's hidden desire, and he exploits his insight to lure the prospective victim into cozenage. He is the chief possessor of the deceiving wit necessary to the triumvirate. In exercising his wit, he assumes the outward show, the face, of a number of roles. To those awed by the paraphernalia of science, he is Lungs, the conscientious laboratory assistant. To those impressed by swagger and worldliness, he is Captain Face, successful gambler and gallant about town. But, like Subtle, he confuses his appearance with his reality. Convinced by his own ego that the success of the collaborative venture is due much more to his cunning wit than to Subtle's knowledgeability, he demands priority in the trio. He angrily reminds Subtle that when all his "conjuring, cosning, and your dosen of trades" could not relieve his penniless condition, "I ga'you count'nance," "Built you a fornace, drew you customers, / Advanc'd all your black arts" (1.1.40, 43, 45–46). Subtle may be the master of knowledge, but as Face emphatically points out, "You must have stuffe, brought home to you, to worke on" (1.3.104). Face's early success deludes him into the belief that he really is a master of men, yet the reality he can never escape is that of the subservient housekeeper Jeremy.

Dol Common is less complex than her two male associates, but she has comparable wit and intelligence. She functions largely as peacemaker between the quarreling Subtle and Face. She reminds them of the terms of their collaboration, stressing the "equalitie" of their roles and the agreement that no one should have "prioritie" (1.1.134, 136). Dol flatters the two men with titles that play to their conceptions of themselves. She addresses Subtle as "Soveraigne" and Face as "Generall" while referring to herself with the less exalted but equally telling term "your *republique*" (1.1.5, 110), a title that may pun on the Latin words *res publica,* "public thing," indicating both her profession and the claims her confederates make on her in and out of bed. But Subtle exalts her with the epithet "Royall DOL" (1.1.174), and as the comedy progresses, she plays in turn a noble lady and the Queen of Faery. She functions in a variety of roles, adapting herself to the needs of the various swindles and of the dupes, acting, for instance, as a surrogate mother for the immature Dapper and as a courtly lady for the smitten Mammon. Like her collaborators, she too confuses her role-playing and her reality, as is evident when Subtle tries to coach her in the part she is to play with Mammon. When he reminds her that as "my lord WHATS'HUM'S sister, you must now / Beare your selfe *statelich*" (2.4.6–7), she exclaims:

> I'll not forget my race, I warrant you.
> I'll keepe my distance, laugh, and talke aloud;
> Have all the tricks of a proud scirvy ladie.
>   (2.4.8–10)

She clearly relishes the disguise and hopes to be transformed into a genuine lady. But her reality as a slatternly whore mocks the transmutation she desires.

The individual threads of plot in *The Alchemist* are essentially variations of the same action, and all develop the same broad theme, but Jonson avoids any sense of mere repetition. The gulls are strikingly differentiated from one another. Spread widely across the social and occupational ranges of the middle class, they vary in levels of intelligence and sophistication. Thus, they demand different stratagems from the tricksters. Some are in the process of being cozened by slow degrees over a period of weeks, whereas others visit the Blackfriars house for the first time, so the various schemes are shown in different stages of maturity. What the gulls share in common is their capacity for self-deception, a capacity concomitant with their overwhelming desire to escape their own small and repugnant realities. This desire to escape the self is sometimes expressed through indulgence in millenarian dreams, most notably in the cases of Sir Epicure Mammon and the Puritans, but as Gerard Cox has argued, in this "anti-apocalyptic comedy" Jonson "satirizes not only the wish-fulfillment of the gulls, not only the hypocrisy of the false pretenders, but the inanity of escaping the present by envisioning a better future state."[47] Each of the dupes attempts to find fulfillment in increasingly expansive fantasies of desire and power that, as Wayne A. Rebhorn observes, are expressed in terms of infantile and regressive visions, fully in keeping with the scatological language that pervades the play.[48] The fools are, in effect, their own victims as well as the dupes of Subtle, Face, and Dol. By making them responsible for their own cozening, Jonson preserves the play's comic spirit and maintains sympathy for the mischievous triumvirate, who are themselves trapped in unpalatable realities that can only be temporarily escaped through role-playing.

The least sophisticated of the fools are Dapper and Drugger, both recruited by the dashing Captain Face, who offers to intercede for them with the necromancer Subtle. Dapper, a young law clerk who "Consorts with the small poets of the time," who can write "sixe faire hands," and who "can court / His mistris, out of OVID" (1.2.52, 54, 57–58), desires transmutation into a successful gambler. Abel Drugger, a slow-witted young man just entering the livery of the Grocers Company and setting up his own tobacco shop, wants to know "by art," "by *necromancie*," how to arrange his premises and what sign to erect over the door in order to become a successful businessman (1.3.10, 11). Exploiting Dapper's romantic sensibility and childlike faith, Subtle claims to recognize him as a favorite nephew of the Queen of Faery and promises that if he will endure "a world of ceremonies" (1.2.144), his aunt will grant him a personal audience and present him a "Fly" that will guarantee him luck at gambling. Dapper spends most of the play in a stinking privy, gagged with stale gingerbread, waiting for the queen to appear, until finally the gingerbread dissolves in his mouth and he can stand the stench no longer and cries out plaintively, "For gods sake, when wil her *Grace* be at leisure?" (5.2.65). Subtle satisfies Drugger's unimaginative simplicity with extemporaneous readings in astrology and palmistry, with authoritatively stated directions for ordering the tobacco shop, and with a "mystick" rebus on his name (2.6.15). The rogues also encourage the young tradesman's scarcely acknowledged desire for an advantageous marriage to the rich young widow who lives next door, despite the fact that he knows "shee'll never marry / Under a knight" (2.6.50–51). Though manipulated by the schemers, Dapper and Drugger are more truly victims of their own gullibility and greed.

The snappish Kastril and his sister Dame Pliant are unwittingly added to the list of gulls by Drugger. The brother is a rich country squire who has "come up / To learne to quarrell, and to live by his wits" like the "angrie Boyes" of London (2.6.60–61, 3.4.22). The worldly-wise but scholarly Subtle impresses him with "the *Grammar,* and *Logick,* / And *Rhetorick* of quarrelling" (4.2.64–65). In some respects, Kastril is reminiscent of Stephen in *Every Man in His Humour,* but he has an ugly cast to his character. He bullies his sister, and he wants to learn city vices so that he can be an ungenerous tyrant to his country tenants and neighbors alike. He, too, is a victim of his own stupid ambitions. Fortunately, he is as incapable of being transformed into his unlovely vision as all the other characters, and at the end of the play he remains the ridiculous, easily manipulable fool he is at the beginning. In addition to seeking to learn how to quarrel, Kastril has also come to town to seek a match for his rich, beautiful, and unrelentingly stupid sister, one that will "advance the house of the Kastrils" (4.4.88). A widow of 19, Dame Pliant is especially interested in learning the current fashions, and she longs "to know her fortune" (2.6.39). The Subtle of palmistry and crystal balls forecasts that she will shortly meet "a souldier, or a man of art" who will soon have "some great honour" (4.2.48–49), thus setting in motion the competition for the rich widow's hand that will animate much of the plot. She will hear the prediction as confirmation of her most romantic fantasies of marriage to a dashing aristocrat, but the honor Subtle has in mind for her is her own prostitution and marriage to a cheat. Though she is blatantly commodified and effectively silenced by the men—she speaks fewer than 10 lines in the entire play—her vacuity victimizes her as much as the schemers do, and appropriately she becomes the somewhat dubious prize Face offers to his master.

Considerably superior to these four simple creatures in cunning and imagination are Tribulation Wholesome and Sir Epicure Mammon. They are clever men, and while they are as selfish as their more foolish fellows, they use causes greater than themselves to mask the reality of their true desires. They can be cozened only by a Subtle who is a serious and learned alchemist. The tricksters have been working on these two gulls for several weeks, gradually bleeding them for the largest swindle of all, the promise of the philosopher's stone itself. As an emblem of Renaissance aspiration, the philosopher's stone symbolizes our hope to control our own reality, including the reality of nature. In *The Alchemist,* however, Jonson insists that self-knowledge is the sine qua non of any attempt to cope successfully with the reality of an imperfect world. Thus, the gullibility of Sir Epicure Mammon and Tribulation Wholesome is a function of their self-delusion and their indulgence in millenarian pipe dreams. Although Tribulation Wholesome and Sir Epicure Mammon may at first glance seem polar opposites, each is in fact a complex if distorted mirror image of the other. In their messianic ambitions to reform the world and usher in a golden age, the Puritan and the Epicurean share a similar pride and self-delusion.

Pastor of a congregation of exiled English Anabaptists in Amsterdam, Tribulation Wholesome is a hypocrite who conceals his lust for power beneath the cloak of a holy cause. He defends the Separatists' scandalous exploitation of others as effective "Wayes, that the *godly Brethren* have invented, / For propagation of the *glorious cause*" (3.2.98–99). The specific end he seeks is "the restoring of the *silenc'd Saints*" to the pulpits of England (3.1.38). But his real desire is to be transformed into a man of power. As a source of gold, the philosopher's stone, Subtle assures him, can be used for "hiring forces" to fight the enemies of their church (3.2.22). As a medicine and restorative, it can be doled out to the infirm and aged among persons of influence to "make you a faction, / And party in the realm" (3.2.25–26). With great satisfaction, Wholesome contemplates an England in which he and his brethren may be "temporall lords, our selves" as well as spiritual leaders (3.2.52). By specifically identifying Tribulation Wholesome as a member of one of the most rabid of Separatist sects and attributing to him political ambitions, Jonson is able to exploit popular associations of radical Puritans with anarchy and sedition and to satirize their millenarian dreams of worldly rule.[49]

Because the Separatists have complained of the time involved in the production of the philosopher's stone, Subtle offers a more immediate temptation. If the "holy purse" is low and "the *Saints* / Doe need a present summe," the alchemist proposes counterfeiting "as good *Dutch* dollers, / As any are in *Holland*" (3.2.140, 141–42, 144–45). When Tribulation worries that coining might be considered unlawful by the brethren, Subtle bests him at his own hypocritical game by speciously distinguishing between coining and casting, assuring him that the process would be casting. Wholesome, though obliged to "make a question of it, to the *Brethren*" (3.2.157), is clearly tempted, and Ananias's later report to Face comes as no surprise:

> the Holy *Synode*
> Have beene in prayer, and meditation, for it.
> And 'tis reveal'd no lesse, to them, then me,
> That casting of money is most lawfull.
> (4.7.75–78)

The distance between Tribulation's image of himself as a holy Christian and his reality as a hypocritical crook is a measure of his self-delusion.

Unlike Tribulation Wholesome, Sir Epicure Mammon has wealth and a respected social position; furthermore, if Surly can be believed, the knight was at one time considered wise. Mammon is the most intelligent of the gulls and by far the most imaginative. His is the most audacious dream of all: to use the philosopher's stone to rectify all the shortcomings of nature. In effect, he will use it to transform himself into a god who will "turne the age, to gold" (1.4.29). He will eliminate all disease, even the plague; restore youth and vigor to the aged; and enrich the poor. But most of all (and in consonance with the meaning of his name, which highlights his sensuality and greed), he will indulge himself in a life of unparalleled luxury. He will have "a list of wives, and concubines, / Equall with SALOMON," and he will make his back as tough as Hercules' "to encounter fiftie a night" in his seraglio (2.2.35–36, 39). He will eat only the most exotic foods, dress only in the finest raiment, enjoy the most exquisite pornography—in short, do all the things that Volpone would do but with the added power to escape the Venetian's limitations by maintaining eternal youth and health, "And so enjoy a perpetuitie / Of life, and lust" (4.1.165–66). Subtle realizes that Mammon's fantasy and lust are so great and so unfettered by either rationality or decorum as to be self-delusive. The cozener brilliantly feeds the knight's selfish dreams not by direct encouragement but by frequent reminders that the stone cannot provide what Mammon really wants. Such cautions not only strengthen Mammon's faith in Subtle as an "honest wretch, / A notable, superstitious, good soule" (2.2.101–102) but also confirm the knight's assumption that he knows better than the unworldly alchemist, that he really can have all he desires. Mammon's combination of selfishness and heroic magnanimity makes him far more affecting than any other character in the play. Indeed, he is one of Jonson's greatest creations. The defeat of his Faustian vision does in fact make the commonwealth poorer, yet his egocentrism blinds him to the reality of his own absurdity.

The secondary cheating of Sir Epicure that the tricksters initiate—the introduction of Dol Common as a noble lady driven mad by biblical studies—not only cozens Mammon of additional money but also strikingly demonstrates and exploits his self-delusion. Refusing to identify the lady, supposedly because reports of her madness would greatly embarrass her illustrious family, Face and Subtle present her to Sir Epicure, who immediately professes to see "the *Austriack* princes" in her eyes, lips, and chin; "The house of *Valois*" in her nose; and "the *Medici* / Of *Florence*" in her forehead (4.1.56, 58, 59–60). Mammon determines to make the common prostitute his consort in a perpetual life of luxury, as though she were ennobled by his desire to see nobility in her. Like all the other gulls, Mammon cozens himself.

Wholesome is frequently accompanied by his elder Ananias; Mammon, by his friend Pertinax Surly. Although Ananias and Surly are less important than the men they attend, both are used to significant effect in the play. Ananias is a zealous but ignorant Separatist, and Surly is a cheating gambler and pimp. Both are hypocrites, and both feel smugly superior to Subtle and Face. Although their motives differ, both are skeptical of the philosopher's stone, and each tries to dissuade his companion from its pursuit. Ironically, the objections they raise spur their friends onward. They are ineffective spokesmen for truth because they know themselves insufficiently, and they confuse the roles they assume with the realities in which they are imprisoned. Ananias is not gifted with the divine revelation he claims, and Surly is not the honest reformer he pretends to be.

Surly boasts that he will not "willingly be gull'd" (2.1.78). When he enters the Blackfriars house, hears Subtle's learned disquisitions, sees Dol Common, and is handed a message from "Captain Face," he recognizes his own kind. He perceives in Subtle's speeches the cant of the cozener and sees in alchemy "a pretty kind of game, / Somewhat like tricks o'the cards, to cheat a man, / With charming" (2.3.180–82). He accurately labels the three inhabitants of the house "confederate knaves, and bawdes, and whores" (2.3.248). But Surly's "foolish vice of honestie" (5.5.84) is itself only a scam designed to gain Dame Pliant for himself and thereby alter his own status from that of a cardshark to a gentleman as well as to dupe his fellow schemers. Significantly, however, when Surly reveals the truth, only Dame Pliant will believe him, and—as her name suggests—she believes anything that anyone tells her. Face convinces the other gulls present that Surly is an enemy, and because they prefer to believe their illusions rather than to accept their realities, they force the would-be reformer from the house. Surly's ill-fated attempt to expose the cheaters illustrates the ineffectuality of direct instruction of fools.

Moreover, and most ironically, Surly's disguise as an honest man actually contributes to his gulling. He quite deliberately refuses to take advantage of Dame Pliant when he has the opportunity, telling her that "Your fortunes may make me a man, / As mine ha' preserved you a woman" (4.6.13–14). But as Lovewit tells him, his uncharacteristically chaste courting of Dame Pliant was not welcomed by her:

> shee do's blame yo'extremely, and sayes
> You swore, and told her, you had tane the paines,
> To dye your beard, and umbre o'er your face,
> Borrowed a sute, and ruffle, all for her love;
> And then did nothing.
>
> (5.5.50–54).

Rather than appreciating Surly's restraint and regard for her honor, the young widow interpreted his scrupulosity as "an over-sight, / And want of putting forward" (5.5.54–55).[50] Honesty—in either of its two Renaissance meanings, truthfulness and chastity—is not a virtue much appreciated in the world of *The Alchemist*.

The only other character who will not be tricked is Lovewit, the master of the house whose return (perhaps but not certainly at the summons of Face) brings about the play's catastrophe. When Face, necessarily reverting to his role as Jeremy the butler, tries his self-vaunted cleverness on Lovewit in an attempt to salvage as much of the situation as possible, the man who is his social superior seems to emerge as his intellectual master as well. Because the neighbors contradict each other in their tales of comings and goings over the past several weeks, Lovewit is prepared to credit Face's claim that they are mistaken. But the master will not believe that Dapper's plaintive cries from the privy are "Illusions, some spirit o'the aire" (5.3.66), and he sternly demands of his servant, "No more o' your tricks, good JEREMIE, / The truth, the shortest way" (5.3.73–74). But Lovewit's urbanity and commitment to the truth may not actually protect him from the machinations of Jeremy and, especially, from his own capacity for self-deception. That is, he may himself be duped at the end of the play.

Like the audience itself, the master loves a "teeming wit" (5.1.16) and forgives Face, but in doing so, he may himself (like the audience) be gulled by the butler, who offers him the very lures that had motivated the dupes: the prospect of sex, the restoration of youth, and the promise of wealth:

> I'll helpe you to a widdow,
> In recompence, that you shall gi' me thankes for,
> Will make you seven yeeres yonger, and a rich one.
> (5.3.84–86)

But while the alliance with Dame Pliant may enlarge his fortune, Lovewit's marriage to the 19-year-old widow is not likely to be happy. For all his boasting about his sexual prowess, the elderly gentleman is not likely to be able to satisfy his lusty bride, and the promise of sexual rejuvenation and youth is not likely to be fulfilled. As Richard Dutton comments, "the traditional fate of the old man with the young wife is cuckoldry, and this is surely what lies in store for Lovewit" (Dutton 1983, 122). Moreover, despite Lovewit's appearance of assurance and control as the play ends, there are indications that the wily servant is actually in charge. "I will be ruled by thee in any thing, Jeremie" (5.5.143), Lovewit remarks. It may well be that the butler has actually triumphed over the master, who is as self-deluded as the other dupes. If so, the play ends with Face having achieved his greatest coup.

Still, Lovewit functions as a deus ex machina to restore order to the confused world of the play. He has been seen as both an ironic character, "A Falsewit rather than a Truewit,"[51] and as the embodiment of the play's urbane attitude toward foolishness and vice in a society rife with both.[52] Duped or not, Lovewit dispenses a form of justice that is consonant with the play's ambiguous comic spirit. The tricksters who improvise the action have hardly preyed on innocents as did Volpone and Mosca, and they do not deserve the harsh sentences passed on the earlier villains. Subtle and Dol Common thus escape external punishment for their misdeeds, but in making their hasty getaway "over the wall, o' the backside" (5.4.133), they suffer confinement to their own unacceptable realities. The man who would be a powerful sovereign and the woman who would be a great lady become once more the cheat and whore they have always been. Jeremy's wit advances him in his master's tolerant eyes, and he may indeed succeed in gulling Lovewit, but the price is his acknowledgment of a reality far below the delusions of importance he had entertained as Captain Face. The gulls must also accept the realities their ambitions attempted to deny. Lovewit offers to return the confiscated goods if Mammon "can bring certificate, that you were gull'd of 'hem" (5.5.68). The knight's response, "I'll rather loose 'hem" (5.5.71), indicates the fools' continuing reluctance to recognize themselves as they actually are. Because true reform must begin with self-knowledge, the play's comic justice can not initiate reform. It does, however, enforce order: Tribulation Wholesome, who would be a temporal lord, is awed into nervous patience by the threat of cudgeling; and the would-be pampered lord of a golden globe resolves to "goe mount a turnep-cart, and preach / The end o'the world, within these two months" (5.5.81–82). Sir Epicure's vow to preach the end of the world is not only a touching and altogether characteristic extravagance but also indicates that he "is in fact transformed from a temporal or optimistic alchemical millennialist . . . to a raving apocalyptic, or pessimistic, millennialist" (Schuler, 197).

Despite the appropriateness of the comic justice dispensed by Lovewit, however, the play's ending is shadowed by serious concerns that lurk just beneath the surface. In the first place, Lovewit remains a dubious figure who cannot easily be seen as the voice of true justice. Insofar as he profits from the greed and foolishness of others, he is little better than the cheats and swindlers whose work he completes, and insofar as he is gulled by Face, who conspicuously escapes punishment, he is a fool to be ranked with the other, more grotesque gulls. The ambiguity of the play's ending may be observed as well in its mirroring of the beginning. As Robert Schuler asks, "what else is the Face-Lovewit-Dame Pliant arrangement but another 'venture tripartite' (the 'old man' Lovewit re placing the aging Subtle, and a pliant widow replacing the common whore) based on trickery and blackmail?"[53] The circularity of such a dramatic structure suggests the continuation of foolishness and vice in human nature and in society. Moreover, the epilogue raises troubling questions of audience complicity in such a state of affairs, as Face throws himself on the mercy of the audience:

> And though I am cleane
> Got off, from Subtle, Surly, Mammon, Dol,
> Hot Ananias, Dapper, Drugger, all
> With whom I traded; yet I put my selfe
> On you that are my countrey: and this pelfe,
> Which I have got, if you doe quit me, rests
> To feast you often, and invite new guests.
> (5.5.159–65)

While mere observers may simply applaud Face's success, the audience that Jonson most sought, that of "Judging Spectators" or "understanders" (to use his terms from the Prologue and the epistle prefaced to the play, "To the Reader"), will have a more complicated response, perceiving that our very enjoyment of rogues and fools may itself implicate us in the play's satire.

The Alchemist is one of the greatest comedies in the language. Masterfully crafted with a plot that Samuel Taylor Coleridge considered one of the three best in literature and with a sure grasp of time and place, the play transcends calendar and geography to speak to enduring questions of human nature itself.[54] Our capacity for self-delusion is an enormously important subject, one with serious consequences on both the individual and the social levels. The satire of *The Alchemist* thus indicts not merely the fools and rogues but also the audience as well, at least insofar as it also engages in self-deception and encourages the egocentricity that infects society like a sickness. Jonson never forgets the serious purpose of his depiction of human foolishness and vice, but his "faire correctives" (Pro., line 18) permit genuine laughter as well as scorn. Perhaps Jonson's greatest single achievement in the theater, the play is neither a simple gallery of idiocy nor a bitterly satiric diatribe but an incredibly vital comedy that depicts human weakness. Combining a robust enjoyment of eccentric characters and colorful language, accelerated action and moral insight, *The Alchemist* is a work of mature genius.

Bartholomew Fair (1614) and *The Devil Is an Ass* (1616)

After writing *The Alchemist,* Jonson took a second leave of absence from the comic stage, this sabbatical lasting four years. He returned to comedy in 1614 with the production of *Batholomew Fair* and followed that play two years later with *The Devil Is an Ass. Batholomew Fair* is among Jonson's comic triumphs, and *The Devil Is an Ass* is an interesting example of topical Jacobean city comedy that in some ways breaks new ground. The plays lack the obvious unity of *Volpone, Epicoene,* and *The Alchemist,* recalling more vividly the structural sprawl of *Every Man in His Humour* and the frank theatricality of the comical satires. In these plays, however, Jonson's theatricality is in the service of comic realism, and he avoids the overt moralizing and static commentary of *Every Man out of His Humour* and *Cynthia's Revels.* Like *Every Man in His Humour* and *The Alchemist,* the new plays are firmly rooted in London.

Bartholomew Fair was premiered by the Lady Elizabeth's Men in their new theater, The Hope, on Halloween 1614, and was presented at court the following day. A play of great and exciting extremes, extraordinarily crowded, noisy, and episodic, it provides a panoramic view of London low life. It hosts a large gallery of bawdy characters given to broad humor and rowdy action, and its setting at a great civic festival allows the inclusion of these robust outlaws without a breach of decorum. Moreover, the play is unusual in Jonson's canon for the prominence and complexity of its women characters, ranging from the virtuous and intelligent Grace Wellborn to earthy and dishonest but vital low characters such as Ursula the pig woman or Joan Trash the vendor of stale gingerbread.[55] *Bartholomew Fair* exposes folly and vice as serious as that presented in *The Alchemist* or even *Volpone,* yet its perspective is significantly different. The play presents life in all its squalor and vulgarity, its foul smells and natural functions, but reserves its censure for those who would pretend to be aloof from the common humanity represented by the denizens of the fair. If *The Alchemist* illustrates our capacity for self-deception, *Bartholomew Fair* repeats the lesson in a new guise. It insists upon a commonality that unites human beings: The prerequisite for self-knowledge is acceptance of the fact that human nature is so flawed as to make judgment tentative at best. Although this recognition of human limitations may seem grim and pessimistic in the abstract, the comedy realizes its theme through playful action that celebrates the human capacity for laughter.

Although specific incidents in the play may have been suggested to
Jonson in the course of his reading, the plot of *Bartholomew Fair* is of his
own devising, and it owes its complex fascination to his firsthand knowledge of London's underworld. As Anne Barton has observed: "Struc-
turally, *Bartholomew Fair* sustains the most delicate balance between order
and chaos, between form and a seemingly undisciplined flow which sets
out to imitate the random, haphazard nature of life itself, while maintaining an artistic control so tight that no episode, no character, however
minor, can be removed without causing damage to the whole. The sheer
abundance characteristic of much popular Elizabethan and early
Jacobean comedy is combined here with an extraordinary discipline"
(Barton, 197). The plot consists of a large number of events loosely connected by personal relationships among its characters. Two family groups
go out from London to nearby Smithfield to attend the St.
Bartholomew's Day Fair. Through most of the day they meet and inter-
act with the crowd of low characters who provide the fair's food, drink,
trinkets, and assorted amusements. For a time the members of each family separate from their fellows and have various adventures, some of
which center on the marriage arrangements of the wealthy widow Dame
Purecraft and the young ward Grace Wellborn. In the late afternoon, all
come together at a puppet play.[56] Toward nightfall, after some regroup-
ing of personal alliances, they retire to supper at the home of a London
Justice of the Peace, whose own investigations into the "enormities" of
the fair have been hilariously ineffectual. The characters who set themselves up as censurers of others must acknowledge their own limitations,
but the play ends with a feast from which no one is excluded.

Bartholomew Fair opens with an induction that self-consciously calls
attention to the comedy's artifice. The Stage-Keeper complains that
what is to be presented "is like to be a very conceited scurvy [play], in
plaine English. When't comes to the *Fayre*, once: you were e'en as good
goe to *Virginia*, for any thing there is of *Smith-field*" (Ind., lines 9–11).
He is driven away by the Book-Holder and the Scrivener, who present
"Articles of Agreement" between the spectators and the author. In
return for the audience's commitment to "remaine in the places, their
money or friends have put them in, with patience," Jonson promises "a
new sufficient Play . . . merry, and as full of noise, as sport: made to
delight all, and to offend none. Provided they have either, the wit, or the
honesty to thinke well of themselves" (Ind., lines 77–79, 81–84). The
promise of a decorous, inoffensive comedy is disingenuous, but it enlists
the audience's engagement as understanding judges. While the framing

device distances the spectators from the events presented on stage, in some sense insulating them from the festivity at Smithfield, it also invites the observers to test the play's artifice against their own realities and, by extension, to match their own judgments against those of the play's characters. Moreover, the provision that the spectators have "either, the wit, or the honesty to thinke well of themselves" sets the terms of the comedy's examination of human folly. As L. A. Beaurline comments, "If they are conscious of their worth and think well of their potential good, they can relish whatever fare is put before them, without offense."[57] More pointedly, the provision enunciates a nexus between self-knowledge and good judgment. Wit and honesty are necessary to self-knowledge, and self-knowledge is essential to good judgment and ought to preclude facile judgment of others.

Bartholomew Fair is in some respects similar to Shakespeare's festive comedies;[58] and as the first act of *As You Like It,* for instance, establishes the "envious court" (2.1.4) that contrasts with the "liberty" of the Forest of Arden (1.3.138), so the middle-class setting of the opening act of *Bartholomew Fair* functions as a foil to the holiday world of Smithfield where inhibitions are relaxed. For most of the middle-class characters, the carnivalesque world of the fair beckons as an escape from everyday restrictions to freedom and even license. That the delights of Smithfield are sordid and ordinarily forbidden only increases its attractiveness as a temporary respite from the pressures of polite society. But Jonson's presentation of the fair is complex. It provides a rich setting in which fools can be gulled of their money and pretensions by a whole host of unsavory hucksters, yet it is by no means romanticized. As Jonathan Haynes remarks, "The way the Fair is presented is calculated to put us on our guard, to suggest that if we cannot . . . master its noise and confusion, its tricks and deceptions, we had better stay aloof. . . ."[59] Moreover, for a Jacobean audience, aware of Smithfield's historical association with religious persecution and iconoclasm, the fair's setting may have seemed somewhat ominous or at least ironic.[60]

What unifies the play is its consistent concern with judgment and, relatedly, with the motif of disorder, or "enormity."[61] The issue of judgment is faced squarely in the opening act, set in Littlewit's London house, where most of the middle-class characters who presume to judge the denizens of the fair are introduced. Some of the characters go to the fair in order to enjoy an escape from the workaday world, but others go to Smithfield to pass judgment on still others. These characters attempt to deny their need for the holiday spirit and seek "enormities," as in the case of Justice Overdo, or they disguise their pleasure-seeking as an opportunity to "be religious in midst of the prophane" (1.6.73), as in the case of Zeal-of-the-Land Busy. The irony of the play, however, is that while the enormities and the profanity of the fair are indeed exposed, the greater satire is directed against the middle-class characters, particularly against those who would peremptorily or self-righteously judge others. As Brian Gibbons remarks, "The main satiric force is directed towards Puritanical attitudes to art and life: the didactic purpose of Jonson is to demonstrate that here, in 1614, these attitudes are more of a threat to the Commonwealth than even the crassest stupidity, fashion-following, or pretentiousness. . . ."[62]

Most of the play's middle-class characters are variations of types already familiar in the Jonson canon. John Littlewit, a proctor of an ecclesiastical court, is a would-be wit and poet. His wife, Win-the-Fight Littlewit, is—despite her imposing Puritan name—an empty-headed, pretty little woman easily impressed with the outward show of things. Dame Purecraft, her mother, is a widow of apparently sober Puritan rectitude; and her suitor of the moment, Zeal-of-the-Land Busy, is a former baker of Banbury, now a purifying prophet and self-appointed arbiter of morals in the Littlewit household. Also attached to the Littlewit group, if only tenuously, is Ned Winwife, a gentleman of real wit whose courtship of Dame Purecraft has been eclipsed by the arrival of Busy. Accompanying Winwife is his clever friend Tom Quarlous, a gambler given to drink and foolery.

The other group of visitors to the fair is the entourage of Bartholomew Cokes, a rich but exceedingly foolish young country squire. This eager and resolute ninny is accompanied by Humphrey Wasp, a self-important, testy old servant who tries, unsuccessfully, to control the idiocies of his young master. An unwilling member of the group is Grace Wellborn, Cokes's scornful young fiancée, the ward of Justice Adam Overdo. Serving as Grace's chaperone is Dame Overdo, the Justice's wife and Bartholomew Cokes's sister. A social climber of proud dignity, she constantly reminds everyone of her own importance. Also present at the fair, but arriving separately and disguised, is Justice Overdo himself. And haunting the festival is Trouble-All, a man driven mad by having been wrongly discharged by Overdo from his position as a minor official of the court of Pie-Powders, who now insists on having Overdo's written warrant for any action he takes.

The fair itself is crowded with still a third group—low characters, some there to provide its wares and services, others to prey on its customers by the more direct means of thievery. These are among the most colorful people Jonson ever invented. Their very names—Joan Trash, Lantern Leatherhead, Ezekiel Edgeworth, Jordan Knockhum, Nightingale, Punk Alice, Captain Whit, Mooncalf, and Ursula the pig woman—indicate their earthiness. Much of the play's vitality stems from its depiction of the moral and physical depravity of these prostitutes, pimps, and petty criminals, and they provide the comedy with its pungent air of humanity at its basest and most basic levels. These characters share good-natured contempt for the pretensions of their social betters, an honesty with themselves regarding their own shortcomings, an accurate perception of the world about them, a facility for trickery, and a jovial spirit of camaraderie with their fellow rogues. They display far more loyalty toward each other than do their respectable visitors and gulls. Collectively, they test the characters and wits of their middle-class customers.

The more foolish customers are easy prey for the rogues. Assured by her imperceptive and irresponsible husband that the men he leaves her with, the horsetrader and whoremaster Jordan Knockhum and the pimp Captain Whit, are "honest Gentlemen . . . they'll use you very civilly" (4.5.8–10), Win Littlewit succumbs to the offer of fine clothes and the promise that she will be worshiped as a lady and thereby unwittingly becomes part of Whit's merchandise. The proud Dame Overdo, having overindulged in drink and neglected her chaperonage of Grace, confesses drunkenly that she admires "Men of warre, and the Sonnes of the sword" (4.4.228), and she too is added to the Captain's stable. These two women who begin the play as proud matrons are exposed in the course of the play as no better than the prostitutes who work the fair. The prominence of prostitution in the play serves to emphasize how easily human beings can be commodified and how the fair caters to appetites for human flesh no less than for pig flesh and makes little distinction between the two. Although Littlewit does not knowingly prostitute his wife, his tendency to objectify her and show her off to others (most notably to Winwife in the opening scene) is not much different from the more open form of trade practiced by Whit and Knockhum; indeed, it may be that he has been so generous with his wife's charms as to have been cuckolded by Winwife, who may be the father of her expected child.[63] The proctor's foolishness is indicated by his name as well as his failures of perception. Tempted by the occasion of the fair to display his poetic skill, Littlewit arranges for Leatherhead's puppet theater to present a play he has written. The drama, in halting poulter's measure, combines the myths of Hero and Leander and Damon and Pythias and absurdly trivializes them. In puppetmaster Lantern Leatherhead's explanation, Littlewit has reduced the classical stories "to a more familiar straine for our people" (5.3.111–17).

The many temptations of the fair prove over and over again Bat Cokes's fundamental foolishness, as he delightedly goes from one attraction to another, merrily living up to the meaning of his surname: "nitwit." He buys the entire stock of Lantern Leatherhead's toys to serve as his wedding masque and the lot of Joan Trash's gingerbread men to furnish his nuptial banquet and then leaves his purchases behind, trusting the dishonest vendors to deliver them at a later date. He persists in disregarding the advice of Wasp and keeps company with men who twice rob him of his purse and eventually steal his hat and cloak as well. He is thoroughly impressed by the absurd puppet play and becomes so engrossed with the puppets that he treats them like real people. The most naive character in the play, he cannot distinguish between surface and substance in either objects or people. Cokes's irrepressible good humor makes him endearing, but it does not disguise his egocentrism and foolishness. Nevertheless, for all his losses at the fair—including his fiancée—Cokes may at least gain some freedom from the domination of Wasp, who at the end of the play resigns his authority.[64]

The foolishness of these four characters may have serious consequences for themselves, but it is of little danger to society as a whole. Four other characters are in positions where their foolishness can affect the lives of others, however, and the fair provokes the public discovery of their more serious folly. Humphrey Wasp not only has charge of Bat Cokes but defiantly also assumes leadership of the whole group that accompanies the young man to the fair. Although basically honest and intelligent, Wasp is constantly angry, and his expression of testiness toward everyone he presumes to correct—his favorite phrase is "turd i' your teeth" (1.4.53)—makes his admonitions offensive and thereby ineffectual. Even Mrs. Overdo recognizes that Wasp needs to "also governe your passions" (1.5.23). His indiscriminate indignation blinds him to worth where it does exist and prevents an accurate assessment of the situations in which he finds himself. His loss of Cokes's marriage license, the immediate cause of his ultimate humiliation, is only the most tangible reflection of the serious flaws in Wasp's perception.

Dame Purecraft, matron and ruler of the Littlewits as well as an officer in her Puritan congregation, reveals in response to the temptations offered by the fair not only the shallowness of her faith and a boundless

sexual hunger but also the serious crimes she has committed while hypocritically clothing herself in precisionist self-righteousness. The fair
offers Purecraft, in the person of Quarlous disguised as Trouble-All, the
madman of gentle birth that a fortune-teller has prophesied she should
marry. To get him, she must overcome his prejudice against Puritan
hypocrisy, and the "truth" she tells him about herself is a chilling confession of venality: "These seven yeeres, I have beene a wilfull holy widdow,
onely to draw feasts, and gifts from my intangled suitors: I am also by
office, an assisting *sister* of the *Deacons,* and a devourer, in stead of a dis-
tributer of the alms" (5.2.53–56). Fortunately for her, the man to
whom she proposes is just as fond of money as she is, and he responds
favorably to her invitation to "enjoy all my deceits together" (5.2.72),
although it may be questionable whether he will be able to satisfy her
sexual desires.

Zeal-of-the-Land Busy, who for the three days of his visit has
assumed moral leadership in the Littlewit household, is drawn to the fair
by his gluttony. But once there, he is tempted to use his divinely
inspired zeal for the correction of the whole community of the ungodly
at the Smithfield celebration: "I was mov'd in spirit, to bee here, this
day, in this *Faire,* this wicked, and foule *Faire;* and fitter may it be called
a foule, then a *Faire:* To protest against the abuses of it, the foule abuses
of it, in regard of the afflicted Saints, that are troubled, very much troubled, exceedingly troubled, with the opening of the merchandize of
Babylon againe, & the peeping of *Popery* upon the stals, here, here, in the
high places" (3.6.86–93). As intolerant as he is hypocritical, Busy's
attempt to overturn the tents of Baal—or, more precisely, the stall of
Jane Trash, which is seen by the would-be iconoclast as "a shop of
reliques" and a "basket of Popery" (3.6.96, 73)—causes him to be confined in the stocks for disturbing the peace, and his railing at the presentation of the play results in exposing the ignorance that underlies his
fanaticism. Although he calls upon his zeal to "fill me, fill me, that is,
make me full" (5.5.45–46), he is bested in a theological argument by a
puppet manipulated by a low character. A swindler as well as a religious
extremist, Busy is the target of the play's most scathing satire. He is the
source of much laughter, but the Puritanical attitudes that he espouses
and the hypocrisy he embodies remain at least potential threats to the
peace and safety of the commonwealth.[65]

The occasion of the fair tempts Justice Overdo to don "the habit of a
foole" to discover firsthand the "enormities" perpetrated there (2.1.9,
45). Like the elder Knowell in *Every Man in His Humour,* he is well inten-

tioned and basically good. His reasoning is sound: Judges too often "heare with other mens eares; wee see with other mens eyes; a foolish Constable, or a sleepy Watchman, is all our information" (2.1.29–31). His cause is admirable: "in Justice name, and the Kings; and for the Commonwealth" (2.1.48–49). But he exaggerates his importance and the seriousness of the "enormities" he seeks to expose. Most significantly, however, his perception, like that of so many others in this play, is sadly deficient. For example, he seems not to realize that in forcing the engagement of his wealthy ward to his foolish nephew, he is himself guilty of a true enormity. Moreover, so intoxicated is he by his own rhetoric that he fails to notice the discrepancy between the external reality he actually sees and what he describes. Indeed, he consistently misinterprets what he observes, a serious failing in anyone but disastrous in a judge. Thinking Ezekiel Edgworth "has a good Clerks looke with him" (2.4.33), Overdo mistakes the cutpurse for a "proper young man" who needs to be rescued from his "debaucht company" (3.5.2, 3) and protected from a dangerous tendency toward poetry. He is not so much duped by others as deluded by his own inability to see and judge accurately. As his surname indicates, he overdoes and overdramatizes everything. Even his well-intentioned attempt to make amends with Trouble-All provides an example of this overdoing as well as of his inability to see clearly: He gives a signed, blank warrant to Quarlous (disguised as Trouble-All), who uses it for his own purposes. Lacking any sense of proportion, Overdo inadvertently surrenders his authority even as he exercises it.

In the course of the play, Overdo is beaten, placed in the stocks, almost cuckolded, and thoroughly humiliated. His attempt to pass judgment at day's end begins in bombast: "looke upon mee, O *London*! and see mee, O *Smithfield*; The *example of Justice*, and *Mirror of Magistrates*: the true top of formality, and scourge of enormity. Harken unto my *labours*, and but observe my *discoveries*" (5.6.33–37). Yet all his judgments are mistaken, and the play ends with his exposure. Although Justice Overdo is foolish, he may have the capacity to learn from his experience, and his late realization that he needs to be more gentle when he returns to his official role as judge is a direct result of his firsthand contact with common humanity at the fair.

The characters in *Bartholomew Fair* who come nearest to a normative balance of wit and self-knowledge are Ned Winwife, Tom Quarlous, and Grace Wellborn. Tellingly, these three characters are the least involved in the fair itself. They are neither as enthusiastic about the fair as simple-

tons such as Cokes and Littlewit nor as condemnatory as enormity-seek-
ers like Busy and Overdo. At once intelligent and wary of the fair, they
avoid being gulled by the hucksters and in fact use the fair for their own
benefit. As a direct result of their participation in the fair, these three
characters reach acceptable if somewhat problematic marriage settlements. In *Bartholomew Fair,* marriage is not presented as an elevated or
inspiring institution; still, these settlements profit the men financially
and rescue Grace from the ignominy of marrying Bartholomew Cokes.

It is, however, difficult to see these figures as heroic characters. Like
the witty gallants of other Jonsonian comedies, Winwife and Quarlous
are perceptive and intelligent, and they enjoy sporting with fools. But as
their names suggest, one is preoccupied with winning a rich wife, and
the other is inclined to quarreling. Furthermore, when the fair offers
each the possibility of wedding the young and wealthy Grace, their first
instinct is not to aid each other but to settle the question by swordplay.
Their choice of Palamon and Argalus as their code names in the marriage lottery only underscores their failure to live up to the ideals of
romance and friendship suggested by the literary allusions. The fragility
of their friendship when they become rivals contrasts with the stronger
bonds of friendship displayed among the low characters. And when
chance awards Grace to Winwife, Quarlous takes advantage of Justice
Overdo's signature to make Grace his ward and forces Winwife to pay
for the privilege of marrying her. Moreover, even though Quarlous has
often scorned old wives and hypocritical Puritans, he all too easily yields
to the proposal of Dame Purecraft, with her "sixe thousand pound . . .
and a good trade too" (5.2.76–77). But this unsavory marriage may
itself signify Quarlous's recognition of human imperfections, including
his own. Thus, as the character most grounded in reality and the one
most alert to the hypocrisies and poses of the other characters, it is fitting that Quarlous should untangle the plot complications at the end of
the play and propose that Overdo invite everyone home to supper:
"There you and I will compare our *discoveries;* and drowne the memory
of all enormity in your bigg'st bowle at home" (5.6.99–100).

Grace Wellborn is "discrete, and as sober as shee is handsome"
(1.5.55–56). One of Jonson's most successful female portraits, she is
trapped in an untenable situation as the ward of Justice Overdo, who
intends to marry her to his nephew, Bartholomew Cokes. Justifiably
scornful of the foolish young man her guardian expects her to marry, she
scorns the fair as well: "there's none goes thither of any quality or fashion" (1.5.131–32). Undoubtedly, her reluctance to attend the fair has

less to do with fashion than with her embarrassment at being accompanied by her idiot of a fiancé. Ironically, however, the fair offers her the
opportunity to escape Cokes by marrying either Winwife or Quarlous,
both "reasonable creatures" with "understanding, and discourse"
(4.3.35–36), and she seizes the occasion. After protesting that she cannot make "a choyse [between the two], without knowing you more"
(4.3.32), she devises a plan to have the next passerby pick her husband,
an impetuous and irrational action. That the man who makes the actual
decision is the mad Trouble-All underscores the irrationality of the marriage lottery and may validate her opinion that "*Destiny* has a high hand
in businesse of this nature" (4.3.51–52) even as it may also suggest that
for most women in Jacobean society marriage is, at best, a gamble. She
may be wrong to think that she can make Quarlous and Winwife work
cooperatively together "friendly, and joyntly, each to the other's fortune"
(4.3.64–65), but her trust that "if fate send me an understanding husband, I have no feare at all, but mine owne manners shall make him a
good one" (4.3.36–38) may be justified. While her marriage to Winwife is unsentimental and unromantic, it is nevertheless a perfectly suitable and eminently practical match. Grace's successful coping with her
difficult predicament highlights not only the exploitation of women and
the abuse of marriage customs in a patriarchal society but also her own
active virtue and intelligence.[66]

Although *Bartholomew Fair* contains some of Jonson's most serious
examinations of folly and vice, especially the human propensity to
descend to the level of beasts, its didacticism is conveyed in some of his
most robustly comic characters and situations. Ursula, the fat and foul-
mouthed purveyor of roast pig who sweats so profusely that she waters
the ground "like a great Garden-pot" (2.2.52), may in her frank gluttony and open dishonesty serve as a foil to Busy, but she is a magnificent
creature in her own right. In Justice Overdo's somewhat skewed observation, she is "the very *wombe,* and *bedde* of enormitie!" (2.2.106). For all
her colorful invective against others, she is goodhearted—in her own
words, she is merely "a plaine plumpe soft wench o' the Suburbs . . .
juicy and wholesome" (2.5.84–85). As Knockhum remarks of her,
"there's no malice in these fat folkes" (2.3.22). Busy, though an arch
hypocrite, has a memorable comic presence, as he assumes various roles
for which he is absurdly unqualified: prophet, martyr, saint, spiritual
advisor, and biblical exegete. The casuistry by which he justifies his eating of pig flesh and the ridiculousness of the way in which his lack of wit
is exposed—by a puppet talking him into a corner and then raising its

skirt to show that it has no sex—are howlingly funny. Wasp may be thoroughly disagreeable, but his cleverness in escaping the stocks earns him the respect of delighted laughter. Although in the strictest sense undeserved, the whipping Punk Alice administers to the proud Dame Overdo when she mistakes the drunken matron for a "privy rich" whore who steals trade from "poore common whores" (4.5.70, 69) is comically appropriate to Dame Overdo's folly. Trouble-All, potentially the grimmest reminder of the serious consequences of justice without mercy and whose plight convinces Overdo that "compassion may become a Justice" (4.1.82–83), is comic in his exaggerated obsession.

Even the puppet play, which embodies all the faults Jonson saw in Jacobean drama and reflects the debasement of love and friendship that is apparent as well in the play as a whole, is not without positive charm. When Hero, transformed by Littlewit into a Bankside trollop, first sees Leander, a dyer of Puddle Wharf, she notes his "naked legge, and goodly calfe" and casts on him an affecting "Sheepes eye, and a halfe" (5.4.124, 125). Indeed, in squelching Busy's Puritanical objections to theater by echoing St. Paul's reminder, "There is neither male nor female: for ye are all as one in Christ Jesus" (Gal. 3:28), the puppets articulate the play's central insight about the commonality of humankind. They also, in Debora K. Shuger's words, help define "the almost tragic gulf between men's ideals—their awesome sense of their own significance and vast potentiality—and their pitiful reality."[67]

With such good humor throughout, there is no compulsion to enforce strict justice at the end of the play. All of its characters are in some way compromised, and Overdo's final words, a quotation from Horace, perfectly suit the mood in which all have been tested: *"Ad correctionem, non ad destructionem; Ad aedificandum, non ad diruendum"* [For correction, not for destruction; for building up, not for tearing down] (5.6.112–13).[68] Wasp's comment, "He that will correct another, must want fault in himselfe" (5.4.99–100), crystallizes the play's attitude toward those who would too easily judge others. The most serious offenders, those who have held themselves apart from common humanity, have all been shamed in the course of the play. Certainly Justice Overdo has gained a new awareness of his limitations and, consequently, of his possibilities. His justice will be more compassionate and more constructive in the future.

The epilogue that Jonson wrote for the production at court makes the monarch the ultimate arbiter of whether the playwright has used his liberty well. Addressing King James directly, Jonson remarks, you

Can best allow it from your eare, and view.

You know the scope of Writers, and what store

of leave is given them, if they take not more,

And turne it into license: you can tell

if we have us'd that leave you gave us, well.

(lines 1–6)

Inasmuch as the play in effect defends royal authority by exposing the limitations and hypocrisies of those who would challenge or usurp it, especially the Puritans but also London officials like Overdo, the tribute to the king is altogether appropriate.[69] By focusing here on questions of liberty and perception, Jonson emphasizes the preeminence of the theme of measured judgment in the work. Although the play may enjoy the rogues and rascals it presents, it neither endorses license nor rages against the "enormities" that it exposes. In its recognition and acceptance of the fact that all human beings, irrespective of class or sect, are united by frailties and failings, the play seeks accommodation. Its values are those of accurate perception, due proportion, religious tolerance and moderation, and careful judgment.

Bartholomew Fair is one of Jonson's most fascinating plays. Alternately "indignant and compassionate, farcical and serious,"[70] it embraces a tolerant view of human nature while never suppressing unpleasant aspects of human experience. Devastatingly anti-Puritan, the play nevertheless refuses to banish even Zeal-of-the-Land Busy from the feast that includes rich and poor, witty and witless, justice and cutpurse, ladies and whores alike. As a celebration of humanity in all its diversity, and as an affirmation of the holiday spirit, it teaches all to "remember you are but *Adam,* Flesh, and blood! you have your frailty" (5.6.96–97). Zestful and exuberant, earthy and vital, *Bartholomew Fair* is one of the most energetic plays in English literature.

Although far less complex and crowded than *Bartholomew Fair, The Devil Is an Ass* shares the earlier comedy's theatricality. First presented by the King's Men at Blackfriars Theater late in 1616, *The Devil Is an Ass* is framed by infernal scenes that are unique in the Jonsonian canon. A realistic, topical city comedy on the subject handled so brilliantly in *The Alchemist,* cozenage, the play uses its framing device to set its comic depiction of human foolishness within a witty allegorical context. It satirizes some of Jonson's favorite targets: people who are ruled by fashion, affected travelers, social climbers, empty-headed playgoers who visit the theater only to be seen, and Puritans. The human characteristics of pretentiousness and gullibility are exposed with particular reference to a serious economic and social abuse of the day, the granting of monopolies.[71] *The Devil Is an Ass* breaks with its immediate predecessors in important ways, however, and signals a new departure for Jonson. Unlike even those few of his comedies that contain fully realized women, it has in the person of Mistress Frances Fitzdottrel an actual heroine, and it is the first of his comedies since *The Case Is Altered* to explore romantic love seriously. Moreover, as Anne Barton remarks, "*The Devil Is an Ass* celebrates trust in human relationships, and the ability of at least some people to change and grow."[72]

A minor devil, Pug, wheedles permission from a reluctant Satan to work evil on earth for a single day. Set down in London in the young and handsome body of a just-executed cutpurse, Pug attaches himself as serving man to a foolish, pretentious, and gullible squire from Norfolk, Fabian Fitzdottrel. Through the events of the day, especially his attendance at a "school" where women are taught to be fashionable, Pug makes two related discoveries, the first of which is that humans are more sophisticated in evil than devils are. "You talke of a *University!*" he exclaims, "why, *Hell* is / A Grammar-schoole to this!" (4.4.170–71). The corollary discovery is that hell has a lesser array of torments than does London society. Having disgraced his calling by letting "men know their strength, / And that they'are able to out-doe a *divel*" (5.6.57–58), Pug is carried back to hell on the broad shoulders of old-fashioned Iniquity.

The play contains three familiar Jonsonian types among its human characters: a greedy cozener, foolish gulls who deserve to be cozened, and witty gallants who see through the tricksters as well as the gulls and who manipulate both groups, initially "for the mirth" inherent in the game (3.4.26) and eventually to effect justice. The cozener is Meercraft, a "projector" of monopolistic schemes. He is clever and quick-witted, but as his name implies, he can be bested by someone who relies on a higher, more humane intelligence. Unlike Jonson's other cozening plays, however, *The Devil Is an Ass* focuses not on the trickster but on the victim; and although several people are gulled in the play, Fitzdottrel is always the center of attention. Meercraft proposes many projects to make the squire rich, the distillation of wine from raisins and the manufacture of fine gloves from dog skins, for example; but the scheme that most excites Fitzdottrel is the draining of fenlands to make them arable, a project that will not only enrich him but will also be of such value to the kingdom that he can expect a dukedom for his efforts.[73]

The gallant Wittipol, assisted by his friend Manly, engineers two of the best schemes in the play. Knowing Fitzdottrel's passion for fine clothes, Wittipol trades a rich cloak for the foolish squire's permission to speak to Mistress Fitzdottrel, whereupon he proceeds to woo the young woman in the presence of her husband, who—according to the terms of the agreement—must remain silent or forfeit the cloak (1.6). Later, in a scene replete with characteristic Jonsonian catalogues and high-sounding doubletalk, Wittipol, disguised as a young English widow lately come from Spain, holds a "school" for fashionable ladies at Lady Tailbush's house, instructing them in exotic manners and elaborate cosmetic concoctions (4.3–4). The ultimate and serious action of the gallants, however, is to trick Fitzdottrel into giving his power of attorney to his sensible young wife before he can waste his entire fortune on the toys of fashion and on Meercraft's impossible schemes.

The Devil Is an Ass contains the most passionate and fully realized courtship in all of Jonson's dramatic canon. In professing his love for Mistress Fitzdottrel, Wittipol uses most of the devices available to seventeenth-century lovers. Courting her in the presence of her foolish husband, he invokes the arguments of suitability and of carpe diem (1.6.122–32). In a later scene, alone with the young woman, Wittipol runs his hands over her body and describes her charms in the conventions of the sonneteer's *blazon* while at the same time arguing the "naturalness" of their love (2.6.71–87). One of the most sympathetically drawn women in Jonsonian comedy, Mistress Fitzdottrel is sensible, beautiful, intelligent, and much aggrieved in being yoked to an extraordinarily foolish husband. Wittipol is a handsome, sound young man of wit who truly loves her. He would make a far more appropriate mate for her than the witless man to whom she is wed. She is undoubtedly tempted by Wittipol's advances, and the expectation is raised that somehow, by the end of the play, the two lovers will be united. But Mistress Fitzdottrel is irrevocably married, and Jonson resists the easy solution of romantic comedy in favor of realism. In the last scene, Manly assures Fitzdottrel that his wife has remained "chaste, and vertuous" (5.8.151). Wittipol, an "honest" man (5.8.152), respects the woman he loves; although he would prefer things to be otherwise, he contents himself with being her platonic admirer: "Lady, I can love *goodnes* in you, more / Then I did *Beauty*" (4.6.37–38).

The Devil Is an Ass is not a profoundly moving comedy. It fails to strike below the surface of cleverness and comic incident. Fitzdottrel's dream to become Duke of Drown'd-Land and to cut a gallant swath through London society is superficial. It does not touch the deep, secret longings in the human psyche that Volpone's and Mammon's voluptuous fantasies excite. Similarly, the cozener Meercraft, while extraordinarily clever, is basically simple. Motivated entirely by greed, he possesses none of the self-delusive complexity that makes Subtle such an interesting character. Moreover, the form that his cozenage takes, the projection of monopolistic schemes, lacks the imaginative appeal of alchemy, with its mystical promise of perfecting all creation. But *The Devil Is an Ass* is nonetheless a sophisticated, witty comedy. Its topicality may render it inaccessible for many readers, but the play dwells enough on the universal follies of mankind to merit a respectable place in the history of Jacobean comedy. Although it cannot be ranked among Jonson's greatest plays, *The Devil Is an Ass* is exhilarating and inventive.

The Late Comedies (1626–1633)

Jonson's third leave of absence from comedy lasted almost ten years. When he returned to the genre, he produced a festive and topical city comedy, *The Staple of News* (1626); a much misunderstood romantic comedy, *The New Inn* (1629); a farewell humor comedy, *The Magnetic Lady* (1632); and a nostalgic rustic comedy, *A Tale of a Tub* (1633). Until recently, the critical attitude toward all four has largely been dismissive: *The New Inn, The Magnetic Lady,* and sometimes *The Staple of News* have often been referred to as Jonson's "dotages," and *A Tale of a Tub* has been viewed as an early apprentice work resurrected and tricked out for a Caroline production by the addition of a character and scenes ridiculing Inigo Jones. The three so-called dotages do not in fact betray any decline in Jonson's inventiveness, as that term implies, and neither does *A Tale of a Tub* reflect an unsure playwright at the beginning of his career. Indeed, all four comedies break new ground and show that, while aging and infirm in body, Jonson maintained to the end a mind and an imagination that was open to new ideas and new ways of expressing them. Although none of these four final plays measure up to the comic masterpieces written during his prime, all are deserving of unbiased consideration.

The Staple of News was first presented by the King's Men at Blackfriars Theater shortly before the beginning of Lent in 1626, with a court performance following, probably on Shrove Tuesday. Like *Bartholomew Fair,* it is a festive comedy.[74] Its holiday tone is set by Gossip Mirth, "the daughter of *Christmas,* and spirit of *Shrovetide*" (Ind., lines 11–12), and her three companions—Gossips Tattle, Expectation, and Censure—who interrupt the prologue, demand seats on the stage, and proceed throughout the play to "interpret" everything they see. The play itself, though it does not contain supernatural materials, shares with *The Devil Is an Ass* an allegorical significance. Its central plot is a variation of the ancient motif of the prodigal son, and its theme is the equally venerable ideal of the "golden meane" (5.6.64). Also like *The Devil Is an Ass, The Staple of News* comically dramatizes the abuses possible in a current London phenomenon, in this case the fledgling journalism of the early period of the Thirty Years' War. The Staple of the play's title is an office where news is not only collected but also manufactured out of rumor and even out of thin air and then categorized, packaged, and sold to an eager and gullible public at prices based on bulk.

The play's focal character, Penniboy Junior, has recently been told by an old vagabond—whom he subsequently adopts into his retinue as Penniboy Canter—that his father has died, leaving him heir to a fortune. The young man spends the day that he comes of age in prodigal misuse of that wealth. He buys elaborate new clothes at exorbitant prices; he purchases a position on the Staple for his barber, a man who, by profession, is a natural peddler of "news"; and he courts, at considerable expense, the city's most eligible and sought-after young heiress, Lady Aurelia Clara Pecunia Do-All. This "princess" of Cornish tin and copper, grandly referred to as "Infanta of the Mines," is, with allegorical aptness, the closely guarded ward of young Penniboy's miserly uncle, Richer Penniboy. When Penniboy Canter has seen enough to be thoroughly disgusted with Penniboy Junior's behavior, he reveals himself to be the young man's father and explains his disguise and the report of his own death as a test of his son's ability to manage money. The young man is left in disgrace, but when his father is threatened with ruin at the hands of the dishonest lawyer Picklock, Penniboy Junior summons the wit to thwart the attempted fleecing and thereby redeems himself in his father's eyes and wins the hand of Pecunia.

The subjects of money and news come together at the exact center of the play. In an effort to impress Pecunia, Penniboy Junior takes her to the Staple of News, whereupon the master of the establishment, Cymbal, tries to steal her away from the young prodigal, correctly perceiving that her patronage of his place of business will draw customers. When he calls her the "*State,* and wonder, / Of these our times" and bids her to "dazle the vulgar eyes, / And strike the people blind with admiration" (3.2.238–40), Penniboy Canter, who embodies the play's "humane scheme of values,"[75] exclaims:

> Why, that's the end of wealth! thrust riches outward,
> And remaine beggers within: contemplate nothing
> But the vile sordid things of time, place, money,
> And let the noble, and the precious goe,
> Vertue and honesty; hang 'hem; poore thinne membranes
> Of honour; who respects them? O, the *Fates!*
> How hath all just, true reputation fall'n,
> Since money, this base money 'gan to have any!
>
> (3.2.241–48)

The play does not suggest that money should be despised, only that it should be kept in proper perspective and used wisely. The Staple fails because it caters to the worship of money. Richer Penniboy goes mad when his desire to enslave money is thwarted. Penniboy Junior, who almost loses Pecunia when he prostitutes her to the Staple, succeeds in his courtship of her only when he finally realizes that he should "use her like a friend, not like a slave, / Or like an *Idoll*" (5.6.22–23).

Because much of its comedy is based on the ridiculousness of the "news" offered by the Staple, this play is even less accessible to the modern reader than *The Devil Is an Ass.* It presupposes fairly detailed knowledge of the background and the events of the early part of the Thirty Years' War, the complex religious situation in Europe, the state of science and technology in 1626, the era's exploration and exploitation of the non-European world, and even something of the infancy of the English "newspaper." In addition, many of the characters in *The Staple of News* are so flatly representative of abstractions and occupations that they fail to engage more than superficial interest as individuals. Finally, the plot lacks the kind of unity that one expects in a Jonsonian comedy. The Staple itself, which is ostensibly the play's chief concern and which offers the greatest opportunity for comedy, is postponed until the third act, after which it virtually disappears. What in fact dominates the play is the prodigal son plot, which had been seen so often on the stage that in the intermean that follows act 1, Jonson in effect admits its lack of originality and suspense by having Gossip Expectation predict, fairly accurately, the play's outcome: "here's nothing but a young *Prodigall,* come of age, who makes much of the *Barber,* buyes him a place in a *new Office,* . . . and his man o' Law to follow him, with the Begger, to boote, and they two helpe him to a wife" (lines 5 –9). Although these two plots are loosely unified in the theme of a foolish prodigality of language and money and although they overlap in the third act, they are not effectively interwoven throughout the play, as in the best of Jonson's comedies, and neither are they equally present and fused in the play's denouement. In enough passages to make the play rewarding, however, the topical is tied recognizably to the universal, and the comic overrides the particular. And while many of the characters are flat, the dialogue is sparkling and varied, ranging from sophisticated barb to crude scatology. Moreover, the play is perfectly suited to the occasion of its Shrove Tuesday production. Through festive comedy, *The Staple of News* sets the house of flesh in order, an appropriate prelude to the otherworldly contemplations of Ash Wednesday and the Lenten season that it inaugurates.

Jonson's next comedy, *The New Inn. Or, The Light Heart,* received its first and, for almost three hundred years, its only performance by the King's Men at Blackfriars Theater early in 1629. In materials appended to the first printing of the play (1631), Jonson blamed its poor reception on bad acting and on the insensitivity and boorishness of the spectators. But even given a good performance, the play demands extraordinary sophistication from its audience to see behind its facade. In some ways, *The New Inn* is the most daring experiment that the constantly experimental Jonson ever attempted. It is a comedy about decorum and role-playing, and indeed, the whole play may be seen as a dramatization of many of Jonson's theories concerning drama.[76] Its points are made by such indirect means that they can easily be missed, however. The prologue and epilogue give little hint as to how the play is to be viewed, and there are no audience pointers such as Jonson provides in the inductions and intermeans of several other comedies. What is presented in *The New Inn* is a presumably straightforward play that is extremely indecorous and excessively flawed by the compounded absurdities of the worst examples of romantic comedy. But the play's breaches of decorum serve to comment, by indirection, on appropriate conduct in several interrelated spheres of human affairs: love and courtship, social position, and responsibility toward others. Moreover, the plot of *The New Inn,* also by indirection, makes three points. On the simplest level, it criticizes by exaggeration the romantic comedy that it imitates. On another level, it graphically illustrates the illusory nature of much that human beings experience and think they understand. And on still another level, it demonstrates the truth that can emerge through theatrical feigning. *The New Inn* concerns discovery of the self in the maze of conscious and unconscious role-playing.

A frivolous but virtuous young noblewoman, Lady Frances Frampul, accompanied by her waiting maid Prudence and a brace of young gallants, Lords Latimer and Beaufort, determines to sport for a day in a country inn near London, The Light Heart. Unknown to her, that particular hostelry, presided over by a determinedly jovial host, Goodstock, is the refuge of Lovel, a middle-aged gentleman who loves her but who has promised a dying friend, old Lord Beaufort, that he will look after the welfare of that nobleman's son, now coincidentally Lady Frampul's chief suitor. To fool young Latimer and Beaufort, Prudence suggests that the innkeeper's adopted son, a pretty lad sold to him by a drunken old woman now employed as a nurse and char at the inn, be dressed as a girl and introduced to the company as a relative of Lady Frampul's. As the main entertainment of the day, Lady Frances, assisted by the host, decides to tease the melancholy Lovel by having him pay suit to her in a formal court of love presided over by Prudence. With long set speeches on the nature of love and honor, paraphrased from popular neoplatonic literature, Lovel rather improbably sobers the flippant young lady and wins her love. In the meantime, Latimer falls in love with Prudence; and Beaufort succumbs to the charms of the host's disguised son and, much to the delight of the company, marries "her" in a hastily arranged ceremony in the stables. Intermingled with these events, the servants and other low characters banter, drink, and quarrel below stairs. Finally, in an unmasking scene going beyond that of the most outrageous of romantic comedies, the innkeeper announces that he is the long-lost Lord Frampul, the drunken charwoman proclaims herself the equally long-lost Lady Frampul, and Goodstock's adopted son is revealed to be his real younger daughter Laetitia. Lady Frances, who for many years has thought herself an orphan, thus suddenly has her entire family restored to her, and the play ends in the happy pairing of Lovel and Frances, Latimer and Prudence, Beaufort and Laetitia, and the reunited Lord and Lady Frampul.

In *The New Inn*, characters and situations are both not what they seem and more than what they seem. The inn itself is a theater, recalling the genesis of the Elizabethan playhouse, and the host its appreciative audience:

> I imagine all the world's a Play;
> The state, and mens affaires, all passages
> Of life, to spring new *scenes,* come in, goe out,
> And shift, and vanish; and if I have got
> A seat, to sit at ease here, i' mine Inne,
> To see the *Comedy;* and laugh, and chuck
> At the variety, and throng of humors,
> And dispositions, that come justling in,
> And out still.
>
> > (1.3.128–36)

The host is also a character, Goodstock; and most of the characters in the play, like actors, have assumed identities not their own or else attempt to do so. Some, with indecorous presumption, try to rise above their abilities and worth. The servant Fly assumes the dignities of "Deacon," "Doctor," "Captaine," "Lieutenant," and "Professor" (2.4.33–34, 5.1.2). The tailor's wife, Pinnacia Stuff, dons the clothes that her husband makes for great ladies, assuming a dignity she does not have for purposes of erotic stimulation.[77] Some of the characters assume roles to evade responsibilities. Lord Frampul, having spent years in the company of "Pipers, Fidlers, Rushers, Puppet-masters, / Juglers, and Gipseys" (5.5.96–97), presides over an inn rather than over his family. Even more grotesquely, his wife has deserted one of her daughters, reared the other as a boy, and lives in the inn as the drunken widow of a Welsh herald.

In some cases, however, the assumption of a false identity points toward a character's true self. The innkeeper's adopted son, dressed as a girl and presented as a kinswoman of Lady Frances, is actually that noblewoman's sister. The host, who recognizes virtues beneath Lovel's melancholy inertia and assists in forcing the lovesick man to woo Frances, is the lady's father; and even though he has for a long time evaded his responsibilities toward his daughter, he is brought to an indirect performance of his fatherly function. Lovel is made to assume openly the role of suitor to Frances, realizing, although unwillingly, his secret wish.

The character in whom all the elements of the play come together is Prudence, the chambermaid. She recognizes the importance of decorum, she questions the validity of appearances, and she carefully distinguishes between role-playing and real life. When Frances forces her to be queen of the court of love, Pru protests, calling attention to the unsuitability of such a role: "To be translated thus, 'bove all the bound / Of fitnesse, or *decorum*" (2.1.54–55). But her conduct in that assumed role proves that in wit and good sense she is suited to a high station, and without presuming to think herself worthy of it, she wins the love of Lord Latimer. Judged by the Host to be the "best deserving / Of all that are i' the house, or i' my Heart" (5.5.130–31) and by Latimer to be "all-sufficient in her vertue and manners" (5.5.144), Prudence is raised above her allotted place in society. She is a unique creation in the Jonsonian comic canon, an indirect though eloquent plea that human beings be judged on their merits and behavior rather than on the accidents of birth.

The New Inn is an intriguing play, one whose riches are still being explored with sympathetic understanding, although opinion is divided on whether it is a romantic comedy or a parody of one and on whether it harkens back to Shakespearean romance or reflects the new emphasis on neoplatonism fostered by Charles's French queen, Henrietta Maria.[78] But the play may be more satisfying in the study than on the stage. Most of its subtleties reveal themselves only through diligent probing and quiet reflection. The prolonged antics of its low characters and the lengthy disquisitions of Lovel, while making important statements, are tedious, and both hobble the dramatic flow. In fact, until the staccato bursting forth of hitherto unsuspected—as well as improbable—plot lines in the fifth act, there is very little action at all, and the improbabilities of the play have a force that virtually overpowers the serious intent. But the lessons of *The New Inn* are both valid and humane, and the play deserves the attention it is now receiving.

The Magnetic Lady: or, Humours Reconciled was presented by the King's Men at Blackfriars Theater in the autumn of 1632. Apparently it had three public performances, all unsuccessful, and it may have been presented at court. Although *A Tale of a Tub* dates from 1633 and in the last years of his life Jonson may have worked on *The Sad Shepherd,* a pastoral romance left unfinished, both the subtitle and the tone of the induction and choral intermeans suggest that *The Magnetic Lady* was intended as a valediction to the stage, rounding off 34 years of mature production. As the Boy of the House explains:

> The *Author,* beginning his studies of this kind, with *every man in his Humour;* and after, *every man out of his Humour:* and since, continuing in all his *Playes,* especially those of the *Comick* thred, whereof the New-Inne was the last, some recent humours still, or manners of men, that went along with the times, finding himselfe now neare the close, or shutting

up of his Circle, hath phant'sied to himselfe, in *Idaea,* this *Magnetick Mistres.* A Lady, a brave bountifull House-keeper, and a vertuous Widow: who having a young Neice, ripe for a man and marriageable, hee makes that his Center attractive, to draw thither a diversity of Guests, all persons of different humours to make up his *Perimeter.* And this hee hath call'd *Humors reconcil'd.* (Ind., lines 99–111)

The play places its humor characters, most of them pretentious and greedy, in a situation appropriate to romantic comedy. It introduces characters not seen before in Jonsonian plays, and it modifies significantly some familiar types.

A group of people gathers in the house of Lady Loadstone, most of them attracted, as the Boy notes, by the presence of the lady's wealthy young niece, Placentia Steel, an orphan who has reached the marriageable age of 14. During an altercation at dinner, the young girl goes into labor and gives birth. Although there are desperate attempts to hide what has happened, the girl's miserly uncle who has charge of her fortune, Sir Moth Interest, discovers the truth and delightedly takes his niece's immorality as an excuse to keep her property. Compass, the focal character of the play, discovers that Placentia's nurse, Mistress Polish, substituted her own daughter, Pleasance, for the heiress when the two were infants, whereupon he marries the false Pleasance, whom he has loved for some time; reveals her true identity to the company; and demands her dowry. The false Placentia is given to Lady Loadstone's steward Needle, the father of her illegitimate child, and Lady Loadstone offers herself to Compass's adopted brother, Captain Ironside, who accepts her hand and her fortune.

The Magnetic Lady presents, with modifications, some familiar humor characters, including a miser, Sir Moth Interest; a foppish and cowardly courtier, Sir Diaphanous Silkworm; and an unscrupulous lawyer, Mr. Practice. Among the play's characters, however, are some types new to Jonson, among them a hedonistic Anglican priest, Parson Palate; a greedy and subornable physician, Doctor Rut; and a devious politician, Mr. Bias. One of the liveliest characters in the play, also new, is Mistress Polish, the loquacious, scheming, and wholly unrepentant "she-Parasite" who advances her child at another's expense. But one of the most interesting aspects of the play is what Jonson does with the witty gallants. Compass, who sports with folly and manipulates fools, and Captain Ironside, who exposes Silkworm's cowardice, are not young. Like Lovewit in *The Alchemist,* they are experienced men of maturity and achievement, and the whole comedy has an aura of worldly wisdom that tempers exuberance.

The allegorical intent of *The Magnetic Lady* seems imperfectly realized. Lady Loadstone is shadowy almost to the point of passing unnoticed, and her niece attracts the company to the house, not the lady. In addition, while Jonson's personal device—a broken compass, its circle left incomplete—is no doubt the source of the major character's name, the Compass of the play is at times the needle drawn to a magnet, a very different instrument altogether, and the relationship between his two functions remains unclear. Moreover, Compass and Ironside expose the follies of many of the play's fools, but exposure is not synonymous with reconciliation, and neither the Boy's remark in the induction nor Lady Loadstone's comment near the end of the play—"Well, wee are all now reconcil'd to truth" (5.10.126)—is wholly satisfying as an explanation of the comedy's subtitle. But the plot of *The Magnetic Lady* is carefully constructed, its induction and intermeans provide a systematic and useful statement of Jonson's comedic intent and practice, and many passages in the play are witty and pointed. This last of Jonson's humor comedies may lack the spark of his greatest achievements in the genre, but it should not be dismissed out of hand as a dotage.[79]

While *The Magnetic Lady*, like Shakespeare's *Tempest*, was obviously designed by its author as a valedictory play, it was in fact not Jonson's final composition for the stage. That distinction belongs to *A Tale of a Tub*, which was licensed for Queen Henrietta's Men on May 7, 1633, and probably performed by them at The Cockpit not long afterward. The only recorded performance took place before the royal court on January 14, 1634. Because the play is so unlike Jonson's other mature works, many critics have argued that it is a very early play—written about 1596 or 1597 but not thought worthy to be included in the 1616 *Works*—that the enfeebled and impoverished Jonson of the early 1630s resurrected and revised for a new production, chiefly by adding a satirical portrait of Inigo Jones. This view of the play's origin and subsequent textual history was reflected, argued, and virtually canonized in the Herford and Simpson edition. It was questioned as early as 1924, however, by W. W. Greg; challenged outright in 1978 by L. A. Beaurline; and refuted point by point in 1984 by Anne Barton, who asserted that "this charming and unjustly neglected play makes sense only when read—in its entirety—as a Caroline work."[80] Whether it incorporated earlier materials or was a wholly new play in 1633, the received text of *A Tale of a Tub*, as published in the 1640–41 folio, is a unified work that deserves consideration as Jonson's final production for the popular stage.

Like *The New Inn* of four years earlier, *A Tale of a Tub* is a romantic comedy concerned with marriage, although on a decidedly less refined level. Also like its recent predecessor, Jonson's final comedy is set in the countryside, in this case the even more determinedly rustic hamlets and fields of the hundred of Edmonton, at that time a rural area to the north of London since swallowed up by the city. Unlike any of Jonson's comedies with English settings, however, the action of *A Tale of a Tub* is not contemporaneous with the time of its production but instead is set almost a hundred years in the past, during the reign of Mary Tudor (1553–58), and the play reflects the Caroline nostalgia for a Merry England now perceived as lost. In addition, *A Tale of a Tub* might well be called a festive comedy. Set on St. Valentine's Day, its plot is driven by the ancient rural custom of selecting a mate on that holiday, and it concludes with a parodic masque celebrating two weddings.[81]

The extraordinarily convoluted plot revolves around the marriage of Mistress Awdrey Turfe, daughter of Toby Turfe, the High Constable of Kentish Town. As Canon Hugh, Vicar of Pancrace, explains to Squire Tub of Totten-Court, who made his fortune mining saltpeter, the previous night Awdrey "did draw . . . for her *Valentine*" John Clay, a tilemaker of Kilborne; and her sentimental parents, who were paired under similar circumstances 30 years before, "will have her married" to Clay "To day by any means" (1.1.46–50). During the course of the day, four men seek in various ways to thwart that marriage, because each wants Awdrey for himself. In addition to Squire Tub, who had earlier been promised Awdrey by her father, these include Justice Preamble of Maribone; Ball Puppy, the High Constable's man; and Pol-Marten, usher to Squire Tub's mother. To remove him from the scene, Clay is falsely accused of a crime but escapes and goes into hiding. While he and Awdrey are separated, she secretly marries Pol-Marten, "A Groome . . . never dreamt of" (5.4.18). In addition, Puppy woos and wins Dido Wispe, Lady Tub's woman; he tells Canon Hugh, "If you dare knit another paire of strangers, / *Dido of Carthage,* and her Countrey-man, / Stout *Hannibal* stands to't" (5.5.3–5). All the characters are then reconciled, save the jilted John Clay, who "will not eate his meat, but cryes at th'boord, / He shall be hang'd" (5.8.6–7). The two couples are feted by a masque designed by In-and-In Medley of Islington, a cooper. Through comically strained symbolism that Medley has to explain at every turn, it recapitulates the events of the play.

It is the character of In-and-In Medley, of course, that is intended to satirize Inigo Jones. For some time, Jonson and Jones had disagreed over which was the more important element of a masque, the verbal or the visual. Their disagreement flared into a bitter feud in 1631, when Jonson put his own name first on the title page of their collaborative masque *Love's Triumph through Callipolis,* angering Jones, who retaliated by persuading their royal patron to end Jonson's employment as poet of the annual Christmastide masques. In addition to writing at least three poems excoriating Jones for this action (U. V. 34, 35, and 36), Jonson made his attack public in *A Tale of a Tub.* As devastating as it is in the received text of the play, the satiric portrait of Jones in the version submitted to Sir Henry Herbert, Master of the Revels, for licensing may have been worse. In it, the Jones character bore the name Vitruvius Hoop, alluding to Jones's devotion to ancient architecture. Herbert "allowed" the play only with the proviso that "Vitru Hoop's parte [be] wholly strucke out, and the motion of the tubb, by commande from my lorde chamberline; exceptions being taken against it by Inigo Jones, surveyor of the kings workes, as a personal injury unto him" (H. & S., 3:3). In the text of the play that survives, Hoop's name has been changed to Medley, but the attack on Jones is still prominent. Appearances by Medley occur throughout the play, and the tub remains as the focus of the wedding masque that concludes it. Medley's pomposity, self-assurance, and sense of his own worth are everywhere. In justifying the device of the masque—the tub—to the patron who commissioned it, Squire Tub, Medley, alluding to Jones's position as royal surveyor, asserts that he has

> Survey'd the place Sir, and design'd the ground,
> Or stand-still of the worke: And this it is.
> First, I have fixed in the earth, a *Tub;*
> And an old *Tub,* like a Salt-Peeter Tub,
> Preluding by your Fathers name Sir *Peeter,*
> And the antiquity of your house, and family,
> Originall from Salt-Peeter.
>
> (5.7.2–8)

To which Squire Tub exclaims, "Good yfaith, / You ha' shewn reading, and antiquity here, Sir" (5.7.9–10). The wittiest part of the satire, however, is that the only scenic actions during the masque are five "motions" of the tub, and Medley is forced to prove Jonson correct in his quarrel with Jones by having to explain, in words, what each motion signifies. Jonson's attempt to humiliate Jones apparently failed, however, for Herbert records that the play was "not likte" when performed at court.

Jonson's last four comedies are not great, but they are far from negligible. *The Staple of News* is energetic, robust, and witty. *The New Inn* deserves respect for what it attempts. *The Magnetic Lady,* while it may not rank with the best of Jonson's humor comedies, nevertheless betrays no real decline in his inventive powers and serves as a fitting farewell to the stage. All three of these plays are urbane and humane, concerned with drama as a meaningful art form and with educating their audiences to a full appreciation of what they experience in the theater. Finally, *A Tale of a Tub* proves that though old, ill, and bitterly disappointed, Jonson could still scrap with the best of them and was still capable of boisterous humor, both affectionate and barbed. The career that these four comedies complete, while often interrupted and not uniformly successful, never wavered in vision or in aim, and the circle that they close has a just and true shape.

Ben Jonson must be ranked in the very forefront of English comic dramatists. He contributed five plays to the permanent repertory of English comedy, and his other experiments in the "*Comick* thred" (*M. L.,* Ind., line 102) repay interest as well. More than any other of his contemporaries, he took seriously the writing of comedy and gave to his craft a sense of dignity. He imposed discipline and structure on the disorderly comedy of his age while preserving its boisterous vitality. He ridiculed the vices and follies of his era, portraying the men and manners of seventeenth-century England in images of grossness, vulgarity, and disease. But he never abandoned an abiding vision of human possibilities and a sophisticated stance that accepted the flaws of human nature even as he derided them. Indeed, the impetus for his scorn was always a social ideal that the reality of his gilded age mocked. Perhaps his greatest achievement was to articulate a comic spirit that could be simultaneously didactic and delightful, serious and earthy, scornful and genial, satiric and celebratory.

Chapter Three
The Tragedies

Ben Jonson's two surviving tragedies were conspicuous failures on the Jacobean stage, and although he was defiantly proud of them, they are not likely ever to win general approval.[1] Their failures as popular drama may be attributable to the bleakness of their themes and to their relative lack of attention to individual psychology and motivation. They are bitter indictments of social disease, and they deliberately avoid exploring individual predicaments. Because they fail to engage much interest in their characters as human beings and because they provide little hope of heroic action, they seem oppressively didactic. Nevertheless, Jonson's tragedies constitute an important aspect of his career as a social poet, and they merit our attention. Jacobean intellectuals hailed *Catiline* as the one of the supreme dramatic achievements of their age, and *Sejanus* is a notable accomplishment.

The relative failure of Jonson's tragedies has sometimes been explained as the result of their alleged neoclassicism. In fact, however, the plays are rooted far more securely in English dramatic tradition than in either classical theory or practice.[2] Indeed, they adhere to the classical unities far less strictly than do most of Jonson's comedies. Their action is clearly influenced by the Machiavellian intrigue of the Elizabethan revenge tragedy, their characterizations owe much to the medieval morality tradition, and their occasional mixture of the farcical and the tragic recalls Christopher Marlowe and William Shakespeare more vividly than it does classical models. The didactic spirit and pessimistic vision of the plays owe far more to the influence of George Chapman than to Aristotle. Jonson, however, considered the plays thoroughly classical. In the address "To the Readers" prefaced to the 1605 quarto of *Sejanus,* Jonson admitted his departure from some conventions and rules governing classical tragedies (specifically, his failure to observe the unity of time and his lack of a chorus), but he insisted that the play nevertheless conforms to the best neoclassical standards: "in truth of Argument, dignity of Persons, gravity and height of Elocution, fulnesse and frequencie of Sentence, I have discharg'd the other offices of a *Tragick* writer" (lines 18–22). Although one may question whether the characters of *Sejanus* and *Catiline* are very dignified, the dramas nevertheless embody a tragic gravity that might be described as classical, and they incorporate superb classical scholarship.

Sejanus and *Catiline* are history plays, yet Jonson's purpose is not simply to dramatize historical events. Not only does he alter historical facts for dramatic purposes and interpret for thematic point some events of the past that were unverifiable, as, for example, his indictment of Julius Caesar for complicity in the conspiracy of Catiline; but also and more significantly, he imposes on the past his own moral viewpoint. The thoroughness of Jonson's humanistic scholarship in these plays convinces the reader of their "truth of Argument," their faithfulness as representation of actual events, yet the tragedies do not really present accurate and disinterested history. As Philip J. Ayres points out, "to the materials of history he has so carefully sifted and assembled Jonson brings not the subtly discriminating mind of an historian but . . . [the] critical, simplifying eye of the moralist."[3] Jonson did not recreate the past for its own sake or merely as an academic exercise. For all his obsession with the minute details of historical facts, Jonson seems to have intuited the contemporary notion of history as a social construct created by historians rather than a reality that can be faithfully resurrected; hence, his historiography may be both less constrained and more skeptical than his elaborate apparatus of scholarly notes and annotations suggest. For him, as for most Renaissance historians, history was primarily important as a source of lessons valuable to the present. In his tragedies, Jonson depicts ancient Rome in order to cast light on the England of his own and future days. The lessons he derives from the corrupt imperial Rome of *Sejanus* and the beleaguered republican Rome of *Catiline* are lessons of social irresponsibility. The plays recreate the past to warn the present of the dangers of social decay. Their moral urgency stems directly from their faith in the continuing relevance of history as interpreted from the perspective of the present. Moreover, the plays probably have specific topical meaning as well as more general application. The plays' classical settings provide an excellent means of evading the Jacobean prohibition against direct comment on political matters, especially for an audience trained in discovering analogies between ancient and contemporary predicaments.[4] Indeed, Jonson was suspected of having infused his work with seditious matter when he was brought before King James's Privy Council to answer unspecified charges of treason soon after *Sejanus* was acted in 1603.

As recreations of ancient Rome, Jonson's tragedies are brilliant successes. Yet they suffer dramatically, for the inevitability of their action robs their characters of spontaneity. Jonson's bleak view of the periods of Roman history that he depicts allows very little opportunity for heroic action. His deterministic interpretation of history emphasizes broad social currents rather than individuals. Thus, the would-be Tamburlaine, Sejanus, is finally understood as merely a consequence of social decadence, and the success of the courageous Cicero is placed within a historical context that renders his victory hollow. The tragedies generally present flatly drawn characters, types rather than individuals, embodiments of vice or virtue rather than believable human beings. Jonson was certainly capable of creating memorably realistic serious characters, as his portrait of Tiberius—a masterpiece of dramatic subtlety—illustrates. But he deliberately chose not to write tragedies that pivot on individual action or inaction. This choice, which doomed the plays on the popular stage, may have been fatally mistaken. But it was a choice consistent with the role Jonson adopted for himself as public poet, as counselor to his age. His tragedies are profoundly political. They are concerned not with the dilemmas of particular politicians but with the intimate connection between the health of a society and the quality of its political life. The plays achieve tragic intensity by the fierceness of their indignation and tragic scope by the breadth of their concern.

The tragedies' gravity results largely from their didactic purpose, but it is intensified by their weighty diction. The language and tone of Jonson's tragedies are not, it is true, entirely of a single piece: In *Catiline,* the conspirators speak quite distinctly, and the comic scene between Fulvia and Sempronia features colloquial dialogue; in *Sejanus,* Tiberius's characteristically evasive manner of communication both perfectly mirrors his Machiavellian personality and delineates his speech from that of anyone else in the play. But the speeches in both tragedies tend to be tediously long, and too often the characters speak at the same oratorical pitch. Although it is too unvaried to be dramatically satisfying, the diction of the tragic characters is poetically pleasing: a grave, deliberative, and carefully balanced language. Often there is a disparity between the bombastic content of a speech and the solid blank verse in which it is delivered. For instance, when Sejanus exultantly recapitulates his evil and dares his destiny shortly before his fall, there is a marvelous tension between the horrors he rehearses and the dignified language he uses:

> Fortune, I see thy worst: Let doubtfull states,
> And things uncertaine hang upon thy will:

. . . .
I, that did helpe
To fell the loftie Cedar of the world,
GERMANICUS; that, at one stroke, cut downe
DRUSUS, that upright Elme; wither'd his vine;
Laid SILIUS, and SABINUS, two strong Okes,
Flat on the earth; besides, those other shrubs,
CORDUS, and SOSIA, CLAUDIA PULCHRA,
FURNIUS, and GALLUS, which I have grub'd up;
And since, have set my axe so strong, and deepe
Into the roote of speading AGGRIPPINE;
Lopt off, and scatter'd her proud branches, NERO,
DRUSUS, and CAIUS too, although re-planted;
If you will, destinies, that, after all,
I faint, now, ere I touch my period;
You are but cruell. . . .

                                              (*Sej.*, 5.236–37, 241–55)

The poetry here, as throughout the tragedies, helps rescue the play from the melodrama implicit in the events recounted. The clarity, balance, and solidity of the expression counter the excesses that the plays depict and so give the tragedies an air of classical dignity.[5]

Sejanus (1603)

Sejanus His Fall was premiered by the King's Men in 1603 or possibly 1604, perhaps at court, with Burbage, Shakespeare, Heminges, and Condell in the cast. The acted version included scenes written by a collaborator, probably Chapman;[6] but when the play was issued in quarto in 1605, Jonson substituted passages of his own for those written by the "second Pen" ("To the Readers," line 45). *Sejanus* aims for and largely achieves those qualities its author declared essential in tragedy: "truth of Argument, dignity of Persons, gravity and height of Elocution, fulnesse and frequencies of Sentence" ("To the Readers," lines 19–20). Its picture of a corrupt age, with values so distorted that an emperor and his favorite cynically practice evil while an indecisive and fawning senate acquiesces, is chillingly grim. Yet the play offers only superficial motives for the actions of its vicious characters, depicts their natures unrelieved by any elements of nobility, and makes no positive suggestions as to desirable conduct in so debased an era.

In constructing *Sejanus,* Jonson relied most heavily on Tacitus's *Annals,* but he also incorporated materials from Dion Cassius's *Roman History,* Suetonius's anecdotal "Life of Tiberius," Seneca's "On Tranquility," and Juvenal's tenth satire. For all the elaborate citations of sources in the published version of *Sejanus,* however, the play is more coherent and original than such indebtedness might suggest. As Wilson F. Engel III has written, "*Sejanus* transcends its historical sources by means of its compression and arrangement of incidents according to familiar literary patterns; its sharp, clear characterization; its reiteration of fearful, vivid images; and its elaborate uses of irony. The Roman world of *Sejanus* is achieved through the transformation of history by art."[7] While Jonson insists on the truth of his argument and the integrity of his story, he is a poet, not a historian, and he does not merely translate his sources—he creates from them an original synthesis.

The play is set in Rome and covers events that took place over approximately eight years, but the action is carefully modulated, from the slow beginning to the fast pace of its conclusion. In this play talk has precedence over action, with most of the sensational events occurring offstage; the author's refusal to dramatize some of the most crucial plot elements helps impart to the tragedy a curiously static quality and a certain *gravitas,* despite its notably lurid scenario involving murder, mayhem, and public and private depravity of all kinds. Sejanus, a Roman of obscure background, manipulates himself into the favor of the emperor Tiberius. By being both an encourager of the ruler's licentious nature and a tool through which Tiberius can, without soiling his own hands, carry out vicious acts against those who threaten him or oppose his desires, Sejanus rises to a position that "wanted nothing, but the name, to make him a copartner of the Empire" ("The Argument," lines 5–6). He seduces Livia, the wife of Tiberius's son Drusus, and with her aid poisons the prince. That hindrance removed, he feeds Tiberius's fears that the virtuous widow and popular children of the noble Germanicus are a threat to the imperial throne. Tiberius gives his favorite permission to destroy them and their followers, but Sejanus, thinking the emperor a manipulable fool, betrays the extent of his personal ambition by asking for permission to marry Livia. A sly man who only pretends to indecision and dotage, Tiberius determines to check his favorite. In secret, the emperor solicits another ambitious man, Macro, to spy on Sejanus. At the suggestion of the unsuspecting favorite, Tiberius retires to a life of luxury and lust on Capri. But from his retreat, the emperor sends letters to important Romans that alternate between praise and condemnation of Sejanus and create confusion among the sycophants. When the time is right, Tiberius calls an extraordinary session of the senate, ostensibly to honor Sejanus, but the imperial letter that is read to the senators after much vacillation ultimately blames the powerful favorite for excesses and hints that he may be guilty of treason. Macro, who has gained control of the Praetorian guard, arrives to accuse Sejanus in person and is acclaimed savior of Rome by the foolish senators. The senate, without according him a trial, sentences Sejanus to death; the mob that witnesses his execution tears his body to shreds; and Macro delivers the dead traitor's innocent young children to rape and strangulation.

While it is unclear exactly what Jonson's accusers before the Privy Council objected to in *Sejanus,* it is not difficult to see how the play could have been interpreted as subversive, or at least as a presumptuous commentary on contemporary politics, which may have seemed all the more audacious when presented at court. Jonson may have intended an analogue between the reigns of Tiberius and the recently deceased Elizabeth, in which case the Sejanus figure would be the earl of Essex, who had been executed only two years before the play's production. Conversely, the playwright may have intended for the audience to recognize similarities between Sejanus and Robert Cecil, the earl of Salisbury, the rival of Essex. Or the play may have been conceived as a more generalized warning to the newly crowned King James of the danger of favorites and of authoritarian rule. Jonson may have been more daring still and intended his play to reflect on the recent and notorious miscarriage of justice that was Sir Walter Ralegh's show trial on trumped-up charges of treason in late 1603. What Silius says of Tiberian justice in the play could have been said by Ralegh himself of his prosecutors: "This boast of law . . . is but a forme, / A net of Vulcanes filing, a meere ingine, / To take that life by a pretext of justice, / Which you pursue in malice" (3.244–47). Jonson himself, of course, denied any topical allusions and attacked those who claimed to find such meaning in the play, expressing disdain for "those common Torturers, that bring all wit to the Rack: whose Noses are ever like Swine spoyling, and rooting up the *Muses* Gardens, and their whole Bodies, like Moles, as blindly working under Earth to cast any, the least, hilles upon *Vertue*" ("To the Readers," lines 29–33). But this denial, alluding significantly to instruments of authoritarian control and oppression, is no doubt disingenuous. It is consistent with the playwright's tactic throughout his career of disavowing any intent to libel others or to engage in topical controversies while, instead, blaming the charges frequently leveled against his work on the misconstructions of his enemies, but it is not convincing and may not even mean to be so. As Annabel Patterson has pointed out, in the seventeenth century readers were accustomed to discerning in such disclaimers an invitation to pursue the very kinds of interpretations being warned against.[8]

When the play was published in 1605, it came decked out with an impressive array of scholarly footnotes that highlighted its dependence on classical sources, particularly Tacitus. The scholarship functioned as a defense, shifting responsibility for the depiction of state terror from Jonson to Tacitus and other historians; at the same time, however, the invocation of Tacitus in particular signaled to politically savvy readers Jonson's identification with a historian embraced by opponents of authoritarian rule.[9] Particularly interesting in light of Jonson's questioning by the Privy Council is his depiction of the historian Cremutius Cordus, a champion of "old liberty" who is accused of being "a man factious, and dangerous / A sower of sedition in the state, / A turbulent and discontented spirit" (3.380–82). Among his alleged crimes is that of drawing parallels between his own and former ages. He is ordered held for trial and his books burned. If Jonson added this portrait to the play in his revision for publication, it is a defiant gesture that calls even more attention to the parallels between Jacobean England and Tiberian Rome: in both eras historians and writers are subject to abuse and censorship as corrupt regimes "thinke they can, with present power, extinguish / The memorie of all succeeding times!" (3.473–74). Jonson no doubt is warning his own rulers when he has Sabinus say of the Tiberian censorship: "Nor doe they ought, that use this crueltie / Of interdiction, and this rage of burning; / But purchase to themselves rebuke, and shame, / And to the writers an eternall name" (3.477–80).

The play revolves around two characters, Sejanus and Tiberius; as the drama progresses, emphasis gradually moves from the former to the latter. Despite his importance as the title character, however, Sejanus is sketchily drawn. A "villain-hero" rather than a tragic hero, Sejanus lacks any real stature. He is, as William Blissett observes, a "lethal bureaucrat" and "civil servant"; even in his villainy, he remains petty, a creature of the emperor rather than a person in his own right and certainly not a great man.[10] Jonson fails to explore his interior in any depth, and as a result he seems, in the words of Anne Barton, a character with whom "it is impossible to sympathize, or even take seriously. He is a bogeyman, as hollow as his own statue in the theatre of Pompey, unreal, and despite the carnage he wreaks, always verging on the absurd" (97). A proud and ambitious man who has risen from very low origins as a serving boy and male prostitute to the very pinnacle of command, the favorite apparently seeks power only to commit "A race of wicked acts" that will be a wonder to the world (2.151).

Like many of the overreachers in Jonson's comedies, Sejanus is also a poor judge of character, blinded as he is by his own self-delusion. The face that Tiberius presents to him, one of indecisive servility, causes him to despise the emperor and to underestimate him. As honor piles upon honor until Sejanus is worshiped as a god in the temples of Rome alongside Tiberius, the favorite's pride outdistances his wit even further, and he rashly comes to believe that he has completely mastered fortune. Believing himself destined to fulfill a plan decreed for him by Fortuna, the blind goddess to whom he sacrifices but who finally averts her face from him, Sejanus uses his power ever more recklessly both to fulfill his unslakeable ambition and to avenge real or imagined slights. At the peak of his success, he discovers that "Rear'd to this height, / All my desires seeme modest, poore and sleight, / That did before sound impudent" (5.9–11) and wonders whether even becoming Caesar would satisfy him. "Must we rest there?" (5.14), he asks, as he contemplates what he thinks will be his greatest triumph but turns out to be his catastrophe, his fall from a great height. As is the case with many of Jonson's comic characters, however, Sejanus is actually manipulated and brought low not by the *de casibus* turn of fortune's wheel but by his own self-delusion and by the wit of a greater Machiavellian than himself.[11]

The true master of fortune—at least for the moment—is Tiberius. The emperor is personally corrupt and, like Sejanus, evinces no concern at all for the commonwealth. But he has the wit and the deviousness to survive. He is both cautious and cunning. He is deeply enigmatic and a genius of equivocation. In private sessions with his advisor, he pretends to be indecisive and oblivious to political reality, but he, rather than Sejanus, actually manipulates the events of the play. Tiberius carefully transfers the odium of unjustly persecuting his greatest rivals—the family of Germanicus and their supporters—onto his favorite. On public occasions, he allows Sejanus to reveal himself as a vicious zealot while he strives to seem magnanimous and merciful. He pretends to respect the ideals of liberty and due process that characterized republican Rome even as he systematically subverts them. He recognizes that Sejanus's own ambition soars as high as the throne itself, and he carefully plots the downfall of the favorite even as he uses him. Tiberius also knows how to manipulate the senate for his own purposes. Realizing that its members fear his spies and want only to be left to their lives of ease, he confuses them with contradictory letters until they are ready to accede to anything. As Anthony Miller (1983) observes, "Tiberius's oracular utterances are heeded by the subservient senators with the puzzlement and fear due to a god; and the control he exerts from afar over the senate is a parody of God's working through second causes to determine history" (190).

A consummate actor (according to Arruntius, he acts "his *tragedies* with a *comick* face" [4.379]), Tiberius is also a kind of dramatist figure: He both causes things to happen and assumes readily a variety of false faces to hide the monstrous deeds for which he is responsible. A thoroughgoing Machiavellian, Tiberius is totally unprincipled, but in the relentlessly secular and utterly debauched world of imperial Rome he prevails by dint of his own cunning statecraft, his command of "arte" and "practice," as Lepidus refers to his toying with Sejanus (4.447, 466). His artfulness is seen most ingeniously in the long prose letter he sends to the senate in act 5 to topple his erstwhile favorite. The letter is, as William W. E. Slights describes it, "a tissue of equivocations, ambiguities, and deferrals" (38). Most remarkably, Tiberius so confidently calculates the effect of his self-consuming prose that he does not even bother to leave his lustful retreat on Capri, characteristically preferring to work offstage. It is altogether fitting that Tiberius, having raised the practice of manipulation to a high art, should triumph in the world of intrigue and terror that he has created. Yet an audience familiar with Roman history would know that the emperor's victory is pyrrhic. The very creature he raises to dispose of Sejanus, Macro, will—appropriately enough—eventually betray him as well.

The foils to these selfish schemers are the aristocratic partisans of the Germanicus family, notable among them Silius, Cordus, Sabinus, Arruntius, and the matriarch Agrippina. All upright citizens, they bemoan the age they live in, complaining that the commonwealth has been degraded and enslaved by "one mans lusts" (1.63), that the senate has abdicated its responsibility to the people, and that civic morality is a thing of the past, an "old vertue" that died with Germanicus (1.119). Their disgust is well founded, yet their inability to counter the evil around them is itself both a source and symptom of the disease that corrupts their society. They congratulate themselves that they are morally superior to Tiberius and Sejanus, but they retreat into detached self-examination and accomplish nothing constructive. Spectators rather than actors, they merely indulge their nostalgia for an idealized past when "mightie spirits" lived and condemn their present age as decadent: "we are base, / Poore, and degenerate from the exalted streine / Of our great fathers" (1.97, 88–90). Arruntius's public complaints against the emperor and his favorite are so ineffectual that Sejanus recommends that he be permitted freedom of speech in order to lull other malcontents into a false sense of security. Even Silius's dramatic suicide in the senate is equally futile, a mere gesture that removes him from an unpleasant situation and furthers Sejanus's ends.

The passivity of the Germanicans is ironically underlined by the terms in which they praise their republican heroes, Cato, Brutus, and Cassius, as great men of action. Germanicus himself is remembered as a leader who joined audacious action and sober judgment:

> a man most like to vertue'; In all
> And every action, neerer to the gods,
> Then men, in nature; of a body' as faire
> As was his mind; and no lesse reverend
> In face, then fame.
>
> (1.124–28)

In contrast, the Germanicans of the play only talk, perform meaningless gestures, or practice a passive fortitude in suffering that proves politically disastrous. As the spy Latiarus remarks provocatively but more truthfully than he may realize, "It must be active valour must redeeme / Our losse, or none" (4.157–58). The Germanicans are further diminished by the fact that Germanicus's eldest sons, including the cruel future emperor Caligula, are easily manipulated by Tiberius and set against each other. That the Germanicans are aristocrats only exacerbates their failure of responsibility. The conditions of which they so frequently and justly complain are at least partially the result of their own abdication of leadership, their refusal to oppose actively the evil that they recognize around them. Marvin L. Vawter comments pointedly, "As always in Jonson's plays, the health and strength of a society is, or should be, most clearly reflected in its nobility. When the nobility ceases to be actively virtuous, when the 'seedes of the old vertue' no longer bear fruit, the entire garden decays and becomes overgrown with the weeds of evil."[12]

The world of Sejanus is the amoral world of political terror, of spies and whispers, of murder and pillage. One outrage succeeds another. Individuals are murdered with impunity; political dissidents are peremptorily convicted of crimes against the state; laws and due process are honored only in their breach; history is ordered rewritten and books burned; surveillance is constant, and freedom only a memory. Suspicion, hypocrisy, ambition, and brute force pervade all aspects of human life. Jonson depicts this degenerate police state with remarkable clarity, and he offers no consolation that the excesses of Sejanus are merely temporary aberrations. The fall of Sejanus, the play's central event, changes nothing except the cast of characters; one villain is replaced by another. "The wittily, and strangely-cruel MACRO" (5.851) is as frightening a product of imperial Rome's civic disease as Sejanus himself. Utterly ruthless and unprincipled, Macro would scruple at nothing to please his master. He is governed only by his own ambition, his knowledge that in Tiberian Rome, "The way to rise, is to obey, and please" (3.735). His triumph is anything but comforting, although our knowledge that he will eventually betray his master allows us to place in ironic perspective Tiberius's ploy of elevating him to destroy Sejanus. But the sweetness of that irony pales before the sobering knowledge that Tiberius's barbarities will be succeeded by the equally repellent degeneracies of Caligula.

Two related aspects of the sordid world of Sejanus deserve special note: the familial disruptions in the play and the savage dismemberment of the title character's body. A great deal of attention in the play is paid to the relationships by which the characters identify themselves, particularly those who belong to or are allied with powerful families. Dynastic and family terms define political and social relationships among all the characters, perhaps most incessantly among the Germanican faction, as when Agrippina, according to the spies, reminds her allies "Whose niece she was, whose daughter, and whose wife" (2.223) . At the same time, however, the families in the play are all conspicuously dysfunctional, and the villains of the play take a special pleasure in disrupting familial bonds and, indeed, in destroying families altogether. Quite tellingly, when Sejanus rehearses his accomplishments during his rise to power, he does so in terms of having violently toppled entire family trees, particularly the "loftie Cedar of the world, / GERMANCUS" and "DRUSUS, that upright Elme" (5.242–43, 244), to say nothing of lesser trees, limbs, branches, and shrubs. Similarly, when Macro swears his allegiance to Tiberius, he does so by enumerating the family members whom he would gladly destroy should his master demand it:

> Were it to plot against the fame, the life,
> Of one, with whom I twin'd; remove a wife
> From my warme side, as lov'd, as is the ayre;
> Practice away each parent; draw mine heyre
> In compasse, though but one; worke all my kin
> To swift perdition. . . .
>
> . . . .
>   I would undertake
> This, being impos'd me, both with gaine, and ease.
>   (3.726–31, 733–34)

Not even the emperor's own family relationships are valued. Tiberius countenances the murder of his son Drusus by Sejanus, who is assisted by Drusus's unfaithful wife, Livia, the sister of Germanicus. Clearly, family loyalty is a rare commodity in imperial Rome, although individuals are persecuted simply for being members of or allied with particular families. Even more appallingly, Tiberius, Sejanus, and Macro are all specifically identified as destroyers of children. Tiberius maintains a "slaughter-house, at *Caprae;* / Where he doth studie murder, as an arte" and where he tortures and molests boys and girls from "our noblest houses" (4.388–89, 393). Sejanus murders a number of children whom he regards as potential rivals. And in a particularly poignant account, Macro delivers the young daughter of Sejanus to "be deflowr'd, and spoil'd, / By the rude lust of the licentious hang-man, / Then, to be strangled with her harmlesse brother" (5.852–54).

Jonson's emphasis on the destruction of families contributes, of course, to the depiction of imperial Rome as a degenerate society where politics and the apparatus of state terror intrude into even the most private of realms. In destroying the great Roman families, Tiberius and Sejanus subvert the basis of republican civic virtue, and in their valuing of power and ambition over human bonds, they reveal their own savagery and monstrosity. In this light, it is significant that the rift between Tiberius and Sejanus develops when the favorite requests permission to marry Livia and thereby become the emperor's son-in-law and presumptive heir. Hence, John Gordon Sweeney III reads the play as a dramatization of Oedipal conflict, in which the "son" Sejanus attempts to displace the "father" Tiberius. In contrast, David Riggs suggests that the play's concern with destroyed families and murdered children may have a more personal origin in the deaths of the author's own children and the failure of his marriage.[13]

The crisis of generativity that is apparent in the destruction of families may also find expression in the play's confluence of homosexuality and political violence and, particularly, in the dismemberment of the title character. The play establishes homoeroticism as a notable characteristic of both Tiberius and Sejanus. Sejanus is described as having been a prostitute in his youth, and Tiberius is accused of having become "the ward / To his owne vassall, a stale *catamite*" (4.404). As a transgression of traditional sex roles and practices, the homosexuality of the emperor and his favorite may be presented satirically in the play as emblematic of the spiritual disorder and social chaos of imperial Rome, but it may also function more seriously and complexly. Gail Kern Paster, for example, regards Sejanus's status as a "noted *pathick of the time*" (1.216) as parodic of "Rome's ideal of self-denying service, giving one's body to the state."[14] The ferocious brutality visited upon Sejanus may also be related to his sexuality. Not only is he beheaded, but in an extraordinarily feral response, Terrentius reports to Lepidus, "the rude multitude" also tore the former favorite's body limb from limb:

> These mounting at his head, these at his face,
> These digging out his eyes, those with his braine,
> Sprinkling themselves, their houses, and their friends;
> Others are met, have ravish'd thence an arme,
> And deale small pieces of the flesh for favours;
> These with a thigh; this hath cut off his hands;
> And this his feet; these fingers, and these toes;
> That hath his liver, he his heart: there wants
> Nothing but room for wrath, and place for hatred!
>   (5.787, 808–16)

Observing that Sejanus is condemned to the punishment prescribed for a sodomite under English law, Bruce Smith contends that the violence at the end of the play "has as much to do with the desires engaged in the spectators as it does with desires professed by characters in the play."[15] While there may be some poetic justice in the fate experienced by the monstrous Sejanus, the emphasis on the bestial response of the multitude signals once again that Jonson's interest is less in individuals than in the larger society. In any case, the dismemberment of Sejanus's body is carefully prepared for by a pattern of allusions to dismemberment throughout the work, and it is at the very least symbolic of the dismemberment of the body politic that has taken place in imperial Rome.

Sejanus is a bitter satire that achieves tragic scope by the relentless single-mindedness of its vision. The tragedy it depicts is that of an entire society. It has no heroes, and it offers no hope for happy endings. Even the traditional private consolations of "plaine, and passive fortitude" (4.294) ring hollow in *Sejanus,* for they are indicted as failures of leadership. A grim warning to Jonson's own and future ages, the tragedy depicts the moral and political bestiality of individuals like Tiberius, Sejanus, and Macro as reflections of a debased age and as inevitable consequences of social degeneration. Its lack of interest in individual motivation and its severity may limit its popular appeal, yet its determined and sophisticated exposure of corruption gives *Sejanus* continuing interest. As J. W. Lever remarks, "Without stage horrors or sensational effects, Jonson's play depicts with timeless relevance a society in the grip of state terror."[16] By locating the sources of that terror in the degenerate values of the society itself, Jonson translates what might have been the stuff of historical melodrama into an incisive statement of social tragedy.

Catiline (1611)

Catiline His Conspiracy was presented by the King's Men in 1611 and published in quarto the same year. Like its predecessor *Sejanus,* and for many of the same reasons, the play was initially unsuccessful on the stage, although it ultimately gained a measure of popularity during Jonson's lifetime and enjoyed several revivals after the Restoration. Indeed, it eventually became "the most respected play of the [seventeenth] century."[17] Although Jonson severely criticized the original audience for liking the first two acts, the "worst" part of the play ("To the Reader in Ordinarie," line 7), and for disliking Cicero's long oration in the fourth, it is difficult not to sympathize to some extent with the audience's judgment. The first two acts, despite their faults of Senecan melodrama and boudoir farce, contain interesting actions and move at a satisfying pace. Much of the fourth act is static, with almost 300 of its 842 lines devoted to a single speech that is seldom, and then only briefly, interrupted. In some respects more "classical" than *Sejanus*—it employs a chorus, and the action is reduced to a shorter span—*Catiline* is less unified in tone and single-minded in purpose than the earlier tragedy. Nonetheless, it is an interesting reenactment of an episode in Roman history that would have been both very well known to its original audience and quite susceptible to topical application.

Jonson's decision to write a tragedy based on the Catiline conspiracy may well be related to his conversion from Roman Catholicism and his return to the Anglican Church in 1610, following the assassination of King Henri IV of France by a religious fanatic. The murder of King Henri created a crisis of confidence across the channel that led to enhanced suspicion of Roman Catholics in England. King James became increasingly fearful for his own safety, the assassination of Henri no doubt reviving painful memories of the Gunpowder Plot of 1605, in which Catholic conspirators allegedly plotted to blow up both the king and Parliament. Jonson's decision to abandon his religion was probably intended to dissociate himself from extremist elements and to assert his loyalty to king and country. Similarly, *Catiline* itself may also have been intended to express the playwright's patriotism, particularly his belief that "no religion binds men to be traitors" (3.369). The play is haunted by the Gunpowder Plot, to which it alludes a number of times and to which it may be a "parallelograph." If Jonson did intend his tragedy to be seen as an analogue to and commentary on the Gunpowder Plot, then the play may also be regarded as a tribute to Jonson's sometimes patron, Robert Cecil, earl of Salisbury, who was the Cicero of the 1605 affair, the faithful public servant who saved his country from a demonic conspiracy.[18]

The principal sources of *Catiline* are Sallust's *Bellum Catilinae* and Cicero's *In Catilinum,* with materials added from other Ciceronian orations, Dion Cassius's *Roman History,* Plutarch, and the Renaissance jurist-historian Constanzo Felice. As in the case of *Sejanus,* however, Jonson here does not merely dramatize his sources but rather creates an original synthesis from his historical scholarship, mediating the conflicting views of the interpreters of a controversial period of ancient history. Particularly interesting is the way in which he juxtaposes and creates tension between Sallustian and anti-Sallustian historical perspectives as regards the roles of Cicero and Julius Caesar. Jonson reaches a compromise between his opposing sources, creating a Caesar who is almost certainly involved in the conspiracy and therefore quite different from Sallust's view of the historical figure while also depicting Cicero as more flawed than the anti-Sallustian perspective of Felice would have it.[19]

Jonson compresses the events of several months into three days and sets the play in Rome, with two brief scenes in the country near Fesulae. Inspired by the ghost of Sulla, a former dictator who was blamed by Sallust for precipitating the moral degeneracy that ultimately engulfed Rome, the impoverished patrician Catiline determines to overthrow the Roman republic and draws into his conspiracy several malcontents, notable among them the outcast senators Curius and Lentullus and the rash and cruel Cethegus. The first step in Catiline's plan is to be elected to one of the two consulships. Although he is supported by such powerful people as Julius Caesar, Catiline is not chosen: The people elect the nonentity Antonius and the "new man" Cicero, the latter favored by the wise Cato. Catiline furiously determines to subject the city to a bloodbath, beginning with the murder of Cicero; Caesar advises him in his plans, but does not actively join the conspiracy. Fulvia, a dissolute young woman, gets details of the conspiracy from the braggart Curius. Jealous of one of Catiline's partisans, the learned and proud older woman Sempronia, she reveals the plot to Cicero. The new consul protects himself from assassination by surrounding himself with friends and impartial observers, and the next morning he delivers an oration against Catiline in the senate. Catiline threatens revenge on both Cicero and the senate and rushes to join his army at Fesulae. Cato warns Cicero of Caesar's secret support of Catiline, but the consul decides against an open break with the powerful man. Instead, he sets about gathering incriminating evidence against Catiline. When the evidence is presented to them, the senators, against the advice of Caesar, condemn Catiline and his known cohorts to death. After the execution of some of the conspirators, a leader of the Roman army arrives from the field to report Catiline's defeat and death, and Cicero, honored by the senate, gives thanks to the gods for the rescue of Rome.

As he had done with Sejanus, Jonson oversimplifies the character of Catiline and robs him of any potential heroism. A monster guilty of unspeakable atrocities, he lacks any redeeming qualities. His inhumanity is made chillingly manifest in the ugly scene in which he and his followers, later fittingly described by himself as "Th' rash, th' ambitious, needy, desperate, / Foolish, and wretched, ev'n to the dregs of mankind" (3.714–16), seal their conspiracy by drinking wine mixed with the blood of a slave freshly killed for the occasion. Ironically, they drink to "freedom" and "libertie" (1.421, 410). Jonson no doubt intended his title character to be a figure of demonic horror, but the villainy of Catiline and his associates is so overdone that they constantly verge on the comic. The glee that he and his henchmen express when they contemplate murder and mayhem of all kind smacks of melodrama rather than of tragedy. Lacking any psychological subtlety, Jonson's portrait of Catiline is less that of an individual than of an embodiment of the depravity that is destroying the Roman republic. As one critic comments, Jonson "imbues Catiline with a barely credible stock of sins, ranging from incest to parricide, not in order to make him a convincing personality . . . but to suggest that in his own person, he represents the cancer which is eating Rome apart."[20]

The conspirator is given two specific motives for his attempted overthrow of the state. One is the need to achieve power to protect himself from prosecution for his past crimes—incest, murder, rape, parricide, and a previous, unsuccessful conspiracy against the senate. His other motive, and the one on which he most dwells, is a conviction that Rome has used him badly, turning him down when he "stood *Candidate*, / To be commander in the *Pontick* warre" (1.89–90). His defeat in the race for the consulship feeds this grievance and makes him more determined than ever to avenge the slights. But more generally, he is motivated simply by a love of evil and a competitive desire to gain fame by outdoing all previous destroyers. "The cruelty, I meane to act, I wish / Should be call'd mine, and tarry in my name," he declares in soliloquy, adding that "were the power of all the fiend let loose, / With fate to boot, it should be, still, example" (3.745–46, 750–51).

Although something of a cartoon figure of villainy, Catiline is a good manipulator of those less intelligent than himself but is no match for the superior intellect of Cicero. He urges his fellow conspirators to desperate action by asserting strongly what they want to believe, that the "giants of the state" have enslaved them (1.348). And like demagogues in all ages, he cloaks selfishness in a glorious ideal: "We doe redeeme our selves to libertie, / And break the yron yoke, forg'd for our necks" (1.344–45). Moreover, he provides his unappetizing crew of supporters with vivid visions of devastation and revenge as well as a plentiful supply of male and female slaves to minister to their sexual appetites, as graphically illustrated in act 1 when he performs the role of pimp to his page boy, warning him on the pain of death not to show "any least aversion i' your looke / To him that bourds you next" (1.511–12). Catiline carefully masks the disappointment that he feels over his defeat for the consulship, but when provoked, he acts rashly and is easily outmaneuvered by Cicero, who knows just how to bait him. Disregarding Caesar's advice to "Be resolute" (3.491), he does not calmly deny Cicero's charges against him in the senate, which are for the most part unprovable at that point. Instead, he flares out at the impertinence of the upstart Cicero and betrays himself publicly, allowing the state sufficient time to arm itself against his plot.

Although he has been seen as a kind of "good twin" foil to Catiline, with whom he shares some characteristics, Cicero is much more subtly drawn. Whereas the title character is intent on destroying Rome, Cicero is an unselfish patriot, a vigilant guardian of the city, "Whose vertue, counsell, watchfulnesse, and wisedome, / Hath free'd the common-wealth" (5.305–306). And whereas Catiline is a haughty patrician, the representative of a decaying and corrupt nobility, Cicero is a "new man" who has "no urnes; no dustie moniments; / No broken images of ances-tors, / Wanting an eare, or nose; no forged tables of long descents" (3.14–17). Described as "A meere upstart, / That has no pedigree, no house, no coate, / No ensignes of a family" (2.119–21), Cicero possesses only civic virtue, which in a depraved society is regarded as "vice" and "sawcinesse" "where there is no bloud" (2.122, 123). So devoted is he to the safety of Rome that he even gives the rich province of Macedonia, conferred on him by the senate, to his fellow consul Antonius to make the latter "that which he is not borne, / A friend unto the publique" (3.475–76).

Foremost of Cicero's abilities is, of course, his mastery of language. In the Renaissance, the historical figure was regarded as a philosopher and orator whose learning, insight, and skill with words made him a model prose stylist. Hence, Jonson presents him as a great orator who van-quishes a military conspiracy primarily by means of his speeches.[21] The point of the superiority of the pen to the sword in politics is underlined by Jonson's making the orator something of a physical coward while emphasizing the personal bravery of Catiline. Although he is denigrated by his antagonist as a mere "tongue-man" (4.161), Cicero, with his com-mand of rhetoric, makes hash of Catiline in their confrontation before the senate. In addition to his intelligence and mastery of prose, Cicero also has an acute sense of the politically possible. Always conscious that most of Rome's aristocrats scorn him, Cicero moves carefully through the maze of political intrigue. While he shares the ideals and the percep-tion of Cato, he is more realistic and flexible than his plain-spoken ally, the great "conscience of Rome." He knows that his allegations against Catiline will not be persuasive without unimpeachable evidence, and he is savvy enough not only to marshal his evidence but also to bait Cati-line into incriminating himself. At the same time, however, he proceeds more cautiously against more powerful enemies of the state.

Although there is no question that Cicero's vigilance saves the republic and that he deserves credit for heroic action, he is not presented
unambiguously, and his tactics and character are not above criticism.
Proud and altogether too self-satisfied and eager for glory, he displays
the kind of vanity that limited the historical figure's effectiveness. Moreover, he does not scruple very much as to the means he uses to prosecute
Catiline. He gets proof any way that he can, even stooping to meanness
of conduct. He flatters Fulvia and Curius, the one "a base / And common strumpet" (3.450–51), the other a selfish turncoat, both motivated by ambition and rivalry rather than by the patriotic piety Cicero
cleverly attributes to them. He also establishes an elaborate system of
spies and counterspies, and he promises (but does not always deliver)
rewards to informers. In light of Jonson's frequent expressions of hatred
of spies and ridicule of intelligencers, Cicero's resort to such means cannot help but qualify his character.

Most problematic of all is Cicero's treatment of Caesar. Like Cato, the
consul is certain that Caesar is somehow involved with the conspiracy.
Unlike Cato, however, he realizes that Caesar, a much more powerful
and intelligent man than Catiline, has hidden his involvement well and
is virtually impervious to attack, and he refuses to press the point. "If
there were proofe 'gainst CAESAR," he declares, "or who ever, / To
speake him guiltie, I would so declare him" (5.89–90). The allegations
of Vectius and Curius, without strong documentary substantiation, are
not enough to convict Caesar, and Cicero contents himself with watch-
ing him closely, believing it "an unprofitable, dangerous act, / To stirre
too many serpents up at once" (4.528–29). Cicero's refusal to pursue
the allegations against Caesar has been variously interpreted as prudence and as cowardice. He has consequently been seen as both a virtuous statesman and as a man guided by political expediency rather than
principle, as someone whose means are suspect and who lacks the
courage to save the republic by prosecuting its real enemies, Caesar and
Crassus. Both views of Cicero's character seem too extreme. Although
Cicero certainly has flaws, it is difficult to reconcile the criticism of him
for using base means in prosecuting Catiline with the criticism of him
for not pursuing Caesar more vigorously. Still, the play is haunted by the
fact that the real destroyer of the Roman republic is not Catiline but
Caesar, to whom Cicero in effect gives a free pass. It may well be that in
portraying Cicero as a virtuous but flawed human being, Jonson wants
to demonstrate the possibilities of virtuous action in difficult circumstances while also subjecting those actions to judgment from the per-

spective of history. Our knowledge that Caesar and Crassus will in effect destroy the republic is a knowledge that Cicero obviously could not have possessed, yet it shadows our judgment of his character and political astuteness. As Katherine Eisaman Maus observes, "Cicero cannot perceive that his calculated disinclination to confront serious dangers merely postpones them and eventually contributes to the downfall of the system he now triumphantly redeems" (75).

Jonson's portrayal of Caesar is particularly interesting. Caesar was an ambiguous figure to the Renaissance: On the one hand, he was sometimes depicted as among the most heroic figures of the ancient world; on the other hand, he was frequently attacked as an ambitious and unscrupulous politician and the destroyer of the Roman republic. Jonson abandons his primary source, Sallust, and goes beyond a secondary source, Plutarch, to make Caesar unquestionably a partisan of Catiline.[22] He pictures him as an unprincipled man totally committed to Machiavellian intrigue. Caesar makes pious and patriotic comments in the senate, while at the same time he advises Catiline on the overthrow of the republic. The play implies that the more complex and subtler Caesar uses the simpler Catiline as a stalking horse to test the possibility of seizing control of the commonwealth himself.[23] What is tragic in *Catiline* is not what happens within the time frame of the play but what is to occur beyond it. The drama ends with thanksgiving to the gods that Rome has been preserved from Catiline's bloody designs, but Jonson's original audience would have known that Caesar, in little more than a dozen years, will put an end to the effectiveness of the republican institutions of Rome. The victory celebrated at the end of the play is real enough— Catiline has been defeated—yet from the perspective of history as intimated by the presence of Caesar, it may be regarded as illusory.

Like *Sejanus, Catiline* is less a tragedy of character than it is of social decay. As J. S. Lawry contends, Rome is the hero of the play, "the subject and object" of the tragedy.[24] Although set in a less bleak period of history than the earlier play, when Rome is at the height of her powers and her institutions—the consuls and senate—are still capable of effective action, *Catiline* nevertheless suggests that the real enemy of Rome is her own decadence. This argument is made most consistently by the Chorus, which functions less as "a participant than [as] a voice of the author."[25] The Chorus, on its first appearance, poses the crucial question in regard to the Roman republic: "Can nothing great, and at the height / Remaine so long? But it's own weight / Will ruine it?" (1.531–33). The Chorus not only repeatedly stresses the need for leaders like Cicero

who will restore the old virtues to the Roman state but also points out
that Rome's worldly success has in it the seeds of the subsequent
depravity that *Sejanus* depicts:

> Rome, now, is Mistris of the whole
> World, sea, and land, to either pole;
> And even that fortune will destroy
> The power that made it: shee doth joy
> So much in plentie, wealth, and ease,
> As, now, th'excesse is her disease.
>   (1.545–50)

Rome is beginning to fall prey to avarice and riot; her offices and laws
can be bought and sold, and her senators can be bribed: "Such ruine of
her manners *Rome* / Doth suffer now, as shee's become /. . . . Both her
owne spoiler, and owne prey" (1.583–84, 586). It is still possible for a
good man to effect good public ends, and Cicero does, but the price he
must pay is discouraging, and his success is limited. Catiline is
destroyed, but a far more intelligent and subtle threat to the state must
be left untouched because he is "mightie" (4.531). Although the degeneracy it exposes is not as advanced as it is in *Sejanus, Catiline* is equally a
tragedy of social decay.

Just as *Sejanus* seems to be obsessed with the question of family disruptions, so, too, is *Catiline,* although with a difference.[26] Whereas in
Sejanus all the families are dysfunctional and the villains are particularly
intent on murdering children, here things have not progressed to quite
so horrendous a state. It is true that Catiline is identified as a par-
racide—he has apparently also killed a wife, a brother, and a son and is
guilty of incest with his sister and daughter—and there is no limit to the
atrocities that he and his henchmen are capable of committing. But
family bonds are also more positively presented, as, for example, in the
family relations of Cicero. Although from a modest background, "a
burgesse sonne of *Arpinum*" (4.480), Cicero exhibits great loyalty to his
family. He not only refers to his wife affectionately but also relies on his
brother for support and protection. Most significantly, Rome itself is
repeatedly characterized as a maternal figure, "our common mother," a
"thankefull, and a bounteous mother" (3.365, 431). The test of all the
characters in the play is their loyalty to this powerful archetype. It is as
natural or unnatural sons or daughters of Mother Rome that all the

characters are judged. Fittingly, at the end of the play, in recognition of his having saved the beleaguered city, Cicero is honored as "Great parent of thy countrie" (5.610).

Jonson's two tragedies are not great plays, but they merit respect as profoundly serious experiments. It may be that Jonson's satiric cast of mind prevented his depiction of heroic action or that his dramatic genius was comic rather than tragic. His decision to concentrate not on individual tragic dilemmas but on the predicaments of entire societies probably explains the plays' failure to capture the popular imagination, as does his related choice to present his title characters as devoid of any redeeming qualities. But such easy explanations of the relative failures of the tragedies beg the essential question of Jonson's actual achievement in them. As pointed reenactments of ancient eras and as chilling reminders of the consequences of social decay, the plays are of enduring value. *Sejanus,* particularly, is among the finest social tragedies of the age. The two plays are also important as evidence of Jonson's lifelong commitment to public poetry, a vocation he fulfilled less obviously in the comedies and most successfully in the masques and the nondramatic poetry. The failure of his tragedies on the stage puzzled and frustrated Jonson, but in the "apologeticall Dialogue" appended to *Poetaster* ("To the Reader," line 3), which announced his intention to pursue the tragic muse, he expressed his characteristic scorn for the popular audience. He hoped only to "prove the pleasure but of one, / So he judicious be; He shall b'alone / A Theatre unto me" (lines 226–28). Appreciation of Jonson's tragedies will always be confined to a judicious minority. As he prophesied they would, these plays remain "high, and aloofe, / Safe from the wolves black jaw, and the dull asses hoofe" ("To the Reader," lines 238–39).

Chapter Four

The Masques

Ben Jonson probably earned more money and received more advantageous contemporary recognition from his masques and other courtly entertainments than from even his most successful plays. His career as court poet is a long one, beginning at least as early as 1603, when he wrote *The Entertainment at Althorp* to welcome the new royal family to England. It embraces the glittering Christmas-season celebrations he and such collaborators as the architect and scene designer Inigo Jones, the composer Alphonso Ferrabosco, and the choreographer Thomas Giles prepared for the courts of King James, Queen Anne, and Prince Henry, and it concludes with masques and entertainments written for King Charles near the end of Jonson's life. The access to the royal courts that this employment afforded him is particularly important, for it may have helped to foster Jonson's entire conception of himself as a public poet, and it provided him opportunity to study at close hand the ruling class whom he undertook to counsel in his poetry. But the masques, although they are difficult for a modern reader to comprehend and to appreciate fully, are important in and of themselves. They "eyther have bene, or ought to be the mirrors of mans life" (*L. T.*, lines 3 – 4), Jonson declared, metaphorically crystallizing their ability to reflect profound truth about human activity.

The Masques and the Court

Developing from several native and foreign traditions of mummers' pageants, triumphs, and dances, the masque combines music, choreography, spectacle, and poetry into a theatrical presentation that largely excludes the conflict and tension of the popular drama. Lavishly produced and featuring illusionistic stage settings animated by spectacular machinery, the masque celebrates the seventeenth-century court hierarchy, ritualizing social and political realities into an idealistic vision of harmony and order. Essential to its very conception is the royal presence and the court setting. The king is always the center of the masque, seated strategically and addressed directly or indirectly. Professional actors and singers perform the speaking parts, but the masquers are noble ladies and gentlemen whose very presence provides the impetus for the idealized fictions of the usually slight plot. The masque culminates in a dance in which the courtly spectators join the masquers in a self-congratulatory celebration of aristocratic community.[1]

It is easy to dismiss masques as ephemeral and expensive entertainments, occasional, extravagant, and wasteful spectacles characterized by unrealistic and shameful flattery. Indeed, they were often attacked on precisely these grounds in the seventeenth century. But the masques in general, and Jonson's in particular, were more serious than such easy dismissals allow. Jonson considered them important enough to publish his texts, even though he knew that the bare words of a masque might seem hardly more than a scenario that needs to be fleshed out by scenic invention, musical accompaniment, and choreographic art. He believed the poet's vision to be the soul of the masque, capable of existing independently of the immediate circumstances of production. By publishing the texts, often accompanied by detailed descriptions of his collaborators' contributions, he sought to counter the ephemerality of performance, to "borrow a life of posteritie" for them (*M. Bl.*, line 5).

In the introduction of *Hymenaei,* Jonson proclaims the essential seriousness of his intention and justifies publication: "This it is hath made the most royall *Princes,* and greatest *persons* (who are commonly the *personaters* of these *actions*) not onely studious of riches, and magnificence in the outward celebration, or shew; (which rightly becomes them) but curious after the most high, and heartie *inventions,* to furnish the inward parts: (and those grounded upon *antiquitie,* and solide *learnings*) which, though their *voyce* be taught to sound to present occasions, their *sense,* or doth, or should always lay hold on more remov'd *mysteries*" (lines 10–19). The "more remov'd *mysteries*" of the poet's vision enable the masque to survive the occasional nature of production, just as the soul survives the death of the body. Jonson's conception of poetic meaning as more important than the choreographic, musical, and scenic elements led to a bitter and protracted controversy with Inigo Jones.[2]

The enormous expense devoted by the Jacobean and Caroline courts to the production of masques can best be understood as displays of liberality and magnanimity. Renaissance ideals, and Realpolitik theory as well, held that princes should give the appearance of magnificence. These ideals, and this theory, were especially congenial to the Stuart monarchs and their evolving pursuit of the divine right of kingship. The sumptuous show, the outward form of the masque, Jonson remarks, "rightly becomes" princes

and other great persons. In addition, the productions justify their stagger-
ing costs by elevating the court, if only for a moment, beyond the petty
concerns of transient politics; by reminding the king and his courtiers of
the duties and opportunities resulting from their positions; and by providing them a glimpse of individual and civic possibilities.

Modern readers are apt to recoil from praise that appears to be ful-
some, as, for example, the hymn to Pan in *Pan's Anniversary,* where Jonson describes King James as "our All, by him we breath, wee live, / Wee
move, we are" (lines 191–92). But the praise in these works is not only
flattery; it is also a function of the masque's intrinsic didacticism. Jonson
held that masques and entertainments "ought always to carry a mixture
of profit, with them, no lesse then delight" (*L. T.,* lines 6–7). This profit
is often conveyed by means of *laudando praecipere,* a kind of praise Sir
Francis Bacon describes as "a Forme due in Civilitie to Kings, and Great
Persons . . . When by telling Men, what they are, they represent to
them, what they should be."[3] Jonson acknowledges this principle in "An
Epistle to Master *John Selden*" (*U.* 14), where he admits that he has sometimes praised undeserving individuals but adds " 'twas with purpose to
have made them such" (line 22). The praise in the masques, as in the
poems, is fundamentally a kind of counsel. As Stephen Orgel observes,
the masque "is the opposite of satire; it educates by praising, by creating
heroic roles for the leaders of society to fill" (40).

Thus, Jonson's intention is not simply to flatter the king and his
court but to create in his "most high, and heartie *inventions*" an ideal
society, founded on ancient principles and nurtured by a wise, divinely
anointed monarch. Jonson was a notably independent individual who
respected achievement and virtue more than title or position. He knew
that the monarchs and courtiers who participated in his masques were
not in reality gods and superhuman heroes and that seventeenth-century England did not in fact represent the restoration of a Golden Age.
He wrote many satiric epigrams attacking courtiers, and in "To Sir
Robert Wroth" (*F.* 3) he specifically indicts masquing, "the short
braverie of the night" (line 10), for its wasteful expense and vanity.[4] But
the exalted depiction of king and court in the masques is intrinsic to the
ceremonial form. In his masques, Jonson ritualizes experience and transforms the literal and mundane into the symbolic and eternal. If the realities of life at court seem far removed from the ideals of order and harmony, love and virtue that the masques celebrate, the transcendent
vision that could perceive an English Golden Age among rather sordid
circumstances is not on that count ignoble or dishonest. The gap

between the realities of court life and the ideals of the masque may be directly proportional to the need for such ideals. "To the extent that the actuality falls short of the ideal," Jonas Barish remarks, "the masque may be taken as a kind of mimetic magic on a sophisticated level, the attempt to secure social health and tranquility for the realm by miming it in front of its chief figure."[5]

As a form of mimetic magic, the masque is a highly complex ritual. It is essentially nondramatic, for its ceremonial mode allows no room for tension or conflict or character development. It is assertive and dogmatic rather than argumentative or tentative, and its characters are symbolic rather than realistic. Drama is possible only within the *antimasque,* which Jonson developed as a "foyle, or false-*Masque*" (*M. Q.,* line 13) and incorporated as an important structural feature of his masques from *The Masque of Queens* onward. Performed by professional actors, the antimasque is a grotesque world of vice or comic disorder that is subdued or displaced by the courtly masque. The tension between the two is purely artificial, for there is never any question that the harmonious masque will supersede its unruly foil. Nevertheless, the juxtaposition of masque and antimasque is an essential structural development because it makes possible an important basis of contrast and provides needed lightness and variety.

Much of the complexity of the masque form stems from its need simultaneously to represent and to transcend the realities of the court. Jonson's masques frequently reflect political concerns and rivalries. Several of his earliest masques were commissioned by Queen Anne and seek to assert her importance in her husband's patriarchal court; his later Jacobean masques are centered on Prince Henry, whose political agenda was largely opposed to his father's, and on the king's male favorites— notably Robert Carr, earl of Somerset, and George Villiers, duke of Buckingham—whose influence was frequently problematic. The Caroline masques are largely designed to conceal the growing impotence of the court.[6] Occasionally Jonson's masques offer rather daring though indirect advice concerning specific political issues.[7] Moreover, the masquers themselves add topical significance to a production by their very presence. As well as participating as symbolic characters in the "more remov'd *mysteries*" of the poet's invention, the courtiers remain themselves. Indeed, they are selected to be masquers precisely because of who they are and the positions they command in the court hierarchy.

Yet if the topical realities of the court can never be totally obliterated in a masque production, the masque itself is never merely topical. Its whole purpose is to elevate the temporal realities of power and politics by subsuming mundane concerns into allegorical representations of absolute and eternal harmony. This process of elevation is the most interesting challenge confronting the masque writer. Jonson accomplishes it by grounding his poetic fictions upon "*antiquitie,* and solide learnings" (*Hym.,* line 16). He links his fanciful actions to classical and native mythology and to Renaissance philosophical and iconographical traditions.[8] By making his lavish and occasional entertainments the mirrors of enduring ideals, Jonson invests the superficial glitter of the Jacobean and Caroline courts with transcendental meaning and creates a ceremonial and humanistic literature of continuing relevance.

The Early Masques

Jonson probably came to the attention of the court as a result of the entertainments he provided early in the reign of King James: the welcome at Althorp in June 1603, the King's coronation in March 1604, and the royal visit to Sir William Cornwallis's home at Highgate in May 1604. These slight entertainments combine classical and native lore, dignified and weighty counsel, and arcane and learned symbolism. It was Queen Anne, however, and not King James who commissioned Jonson's first masque, and she continued to be his primary patron in the genre for several years.[9] *The Masque of Blackness* was written for performance on Twelfth Night 1605, and Jonson credits the queen for its governing trope: "It was her Majesties will," he writes in the introduction, "to have [the masquers] *Black-mores* at first" (lines 21–22). From this royal direction, Jonson derived a graceful fable adapted from the legend of Phoebus and Phaeton. The queen and 11 of her ladies are presented as "twelve *Nymphs, Negro's;* and the daughters of NIGER" (lines 55–56). In an elaborate setting designed by Inigo Jones, they appear on the shores of Albion (England) "in a great concave shell, like mother of pearle, curiously made to move on [the] waters, and rise with the billow" (lines 58–59). Their father Niger asks the moon goddess Aethiopia to "Beautifie them" (lines 225, 230), causing her to break into a paean to

> BRITANIA (whose new name makes all tongues sing)
> . . . .
> Rul'd by a SUNNE, that to this height doth grace it:

> Whose beames shine day, and night, and are of force
> To blanch an AETHIOPE, and revive a *Cor's*
> His light scientiall is, and (past mere nature)
> Can salve the rude defects of every creature.
> (lines 251, 253 – 57)

At the culmination of the masque, their father Niger is sent back "to the *lake*," while the nymphs "Must here remayne the *Ocean's* guests" (lines 328, 330). Aethiopia then commands them to perform a magic rite: "Thirteene times thrise, on thirteene nights" over the next year they are to "steepe" their

> bodies in that purer brine,
> And wholesome dew, call'd *Ros-marine:*
> Then with that soft, and gentler fome,
> Of which, the *Ocean* yet yeelds some.
> (lines 335, 338 – 42)

At that point, they will achieve "perfection"—that is, they will turn white—and dry their faces "in the beames of yond' bright *Sunne*," the king sitting enthroned as chief spectator (lines 346, 349). This view of blackness as needing perfection is distinctly Eurocentric. Yumna Siddiqi has termed this attitude "protocolonial" and remarks, "In this masque, Africans are depicted as potentially disruptive, but at the same time desirable, meriting 'refinement.' "[10]

The Masque of Blackness contains most of the elements that came to characterize Jonson's masques: erudite mythologizing, poetry and song, elaborate costume design and scenery, music and dancing. Its celebration of King James is both general and topical. He is the sun that animates and enlivens all, but here he is also particularly the king who has recently joined the crowns of Scotland and England into a united Britain.[11] Also fulfilled in the masque is a second, implicit political concern, Queen Anne's desire that she and the ladies of her court be placed in a position of prominence in her husband's court. As the chief masquers, they receive that prominence, but in reality the only true source of power in the masque remains its chief spectator, the king.

The Masque of Blackness was notably successful at court and led to other commissions, including a sequel intended for the next year's festivities, *The Masque of Beauty,* where the nymphs of the earlier masque return with "their beauties varied" (lines 6–7), that is, no longer black. The performance of this companion piece was delayed for two years (until January 1608) because of two politically important weddings that took place during the Christmas festivities of 1606 and 1607, respectively. For the first of these, the marriage of the young earl of Essex to Frances Howard, intended to lessen the rivalry between factions in the court, Jonson wrote the wedding masque *Hymenaei,* which added to the grace of *The Masque of Blackness* more severe learning and more recondite symbolism.[12] Jonson's masque for another marriage promoted by King James, that between the Scottish Lord Haddington and an English heiress, is sometimes given the title *The Hue and Cry after Cupid.* Performed in February 1608, it contains an antic dance of boys. This embryonic form of the antimasque adds a gently comic spirit to the solemnity of the whole. But the Jonsonian masque did not reach full maturity until the performance of *The Masque of Queens* in February 1609.

The Masque of Queens is the earliest truly ensemble production in which the disparate elements of scenic and costume design, stage machinery, music, choreography, and poetry all are functional parts of a unified whole, and it contains the first fully developed antimasque. Jonson accompanies his text with copious annotations and detailed descriptions of the performance. The annotations, requested by King James, give a sense of the form's seriousness and provide evidence of the poet's learning. In describing the performance, Jonson announces that "it was my first, and speciall reguard, to see that the Nobilyty of the Invention should be answerable to the dignity of theyr persons. For which reason, I chose the Argument, to be, *A Celebration of honorable, & true Fame, bred out of Vertue:* observing that rule of the best *Artist,* to suffer no object of delight to passe without his mixture of profit, & example" (lines 3–9). The masque, then, combines Horatian didacticism with careful observation of social decorum. Its earnest moral is simple and easily comprehensible but especially appropriate for the court, which needs to be particularly sensitive to the relationship of fame and virtue, and it is buttressed by enormous literary and iconographical learning.

The Masque of Queens was commissioned by Queen Anne, again to assert the importance of her court, and Jonson attributes the development of the antimasque to her suggestion: "because her Majestie (best knowing, that a principall part of life in these *Spectacles* lay in theyr variety) had commaunded mee to think on some *Daunce,* or shew, that might praecede hers, and have the place of a foyle, or false-*Masque*" (lines 10–13). In response, the poet devised a grotesque company of 12 witches, "sustayning the persons of *Ignorance, Suspicion, Credulity,* &c. the opposites to good *Fame*" (lines 17–19). This antimasque is a "spectacle of strangenesse, producing multiplicity of Gesture, and not unaptly sorting with the current, and whole fall of the Devise" (lines 20–22). The antimasque adds variety to the production, but it also plays an important thematic function, serving as a foil that sets off the main masque.

The production begins with the courtly spectators in their assigned places, awaiting the spectacle prepared by Inigo Jones and the allegorical fiction by Jonson. "First, then, his Majestie being set, and the whole Company in full expectation, that which presented it selfe was an ougly *Hell.* . . . These Witches, with a kind of hollow and infernall musique, came forth from thence" (lines 23–30). Jonson describes the scene and costumes in great detail, justifying the most minute representations by reference to classical and iconographical lore.[13] He gives full credit to his collaborators, but he subordinates all the individual elements of design, stage machinery, costuming, and choreography to the unifying moral vision of the poet's fiction.

In the antimasque, that moral vision is presented by means of antithesis. The 11 hags and their Dame are defined solely in terms of their impossible mission: "And come We, fraught with spight, / To overthrow the glory of this night" (lines 111–12). They are "faythfull Opposites / To *Fame, & Glory*" (lines 132–33). By antithesis, their chaotic evil defines the harmonious virtue to be represented in the main masque and assumed to be present in the courtly audience presided over by King James. The hags hate "to see these fruicts of a soft peace, / And curse the piety gives it such increase" (lines 144–45), thus indirectly but unmistakably alluding to the pacific king. The spells and incantations of the witches culminate in a frenzied but futile moment of parodic revelry, characterized by dissonant sound and boisterous movement: "with a strange and sodayne Musique, they fell into a *magicall Daunce,* full of praeposterous change, and gesticulation" (lines 344–46).

In the midst of the grotesque dance, however, the antimasque is suddenly ended, subdued by the appearance of the real masquers: "on the sodayne, was heard a sound of loud Musique, as if many Instruments had given one blast" (lines 354–56). The hags and their hell vanish; the attempt to forestall the appearance of virtue has failed. The scene alters to reveal "a glorious and magnificent Building, figuring the *House of Fame,* in the upper part of which were discovered the twelve *Masquers* sitting upon a Throne triumphall, erected in forme of a *Pyramide,* and circled with all store of light" (lines 359–63).

It is Inigo Jones's genuis that effects the triumphant transformation scene. His House of Fame is adorned with statues, visually announcing a crucial relationship between poetry and fame. On the lower tier are "the most excellent *Poets,* as *Homer, Virgil, Lucan,* &c. as beeing the substantiall supporters of *Fame"* (lines 684–86); on the upper are *"Achilles, Aeneas, Caesar,* and those great *Heroes,* which those *Poets* had celebrated" (lines 686–88). The design thus functions to further the humanist vision that finds inextricable links between poetry and heroism and between fame and virtue.

Heroique Virtue comes forth to explain the transformation that has taken place: "at FAMES loud Sound, and VERTUES sight / All poore, and envious Witchcraft fly the light" (lines 367–68). He reveals that he is the father of Fame and her strength. He points to his daughter's house and describes it as "Built all of sounding brasse, whose Columnes bee / Men-making *Poets"* (lines 385–86), emphasizing poetry's immortalizing power. He introduces the mythological and quasi-historical queens, culminating with Bel-anna, Queen of the Ocean, who "alone, / Possest all vertues" (lines 416–17) and who was represented by Queen Anne herself. Heroique Virtue addresses King James directly, complimenting him and explaining the benefits of fame based on virtue, as exemplified in the masquers. Fame herself comes forward to the accompaniment of music and directs the procession of queens. The masquers descend from their pyramidal throne and mount chariots that are drawn across the stage by appropriate "Birds, & Beasts" (line 465) and by the vanquished hags of the antimasque.

The performance concludes with lovely, self-consciously formal songs and graceful dances that starkly contrast with the ugly incantations and unnatural contortions of the antimasque. One of the dances in the main masque is *"graphically* dispos'd into *letters,* and honoring the Name of the most sweete, and ingenious *Prince, Charles, Duke of Yorke"* (lines 750–52). Choreographed by Thomas Giles, this dance was so graceful that "if *Mathematicians* had lost *proportion,* they might there have found it" (lines 754–56). The final song specifically denies any necessary connection between the queens' military glory and their fame:

> Force Greatnesse, all the glorious wayes
> You can, it soon decayes;

> But so *good Fame* shall, never:
> Her triumphs, as theyr Causes, are for ever.
> (lines 770–73)[14]

Jonson offers as epilogue a simple list of the masquers, revealingly indicating the intimate relationship between the poet's fiction and the court's reality.

The political import of *The Masque of Queens* is complex.[15] The time of its staging is connected to the religious division within the royal family. It was originally intended for performance during the Christmas celebrations of 1608–1609 but was postponed until February 2, 1609, the Feast of the Purification of the Virgin Mary, a date of considerable significance to the Roman Catholic Queen Anne, and she insisted on including a number of her coreligionists as dancers. This embarrassing defiance of her husband's position as head of the Church of England did not go unremarked. In addition, the text of the masque deals specifically with issues of gender politics. For some time prior to its production, the patriarchal James had attacked in various ways women who asserted independence; no doubt to please the king, Jonson and Jones subtly problematized the masque's ostensible purpose—to proclaim the importance of the queen and her court—in several ways.

The first is the introduction of witches. It is important to note that while Jonson credits the queen for the general concept of the anti-masque, he clearly states that the choice of witches is his idea and not hers (lines 10–22). In addition to alluding in a flattering way to James's condemnation of witches in his *Daemonologie* (published in Edinburgh in 1597 and again in London in 1603) and his continuing fascination with them, the introduction of ultimately powerless witches into the masque might be seen as marginalizing women. But it is the appearance of the female masquers—the queens—that causes the witches to fly, and as Lawrence Normand observes, the masque ultimately fashions "an image of legitimate female power in the queens that challenges as much as supports patriarchy" (120). The second way in which the purpose of the masque is problematized lies in Inigo Jones's design of the House of Fame. Until recently, the inspiration for this device has been traced back to Ovid's *Metamorphoses* by way of Chaucer's *Legend of Good Women*. Recently, however, John Moffitt has argued that the design of the House of Fame in *The Masque of Queens* (a sketch of which survives) owes its details to Antonio di Piero Avelino's description of a "house of virtue and vice" in *Trattato di Architectura,* a fifteenth-century work probably known to Jones, in which virtue is "consistently personified as masculine while vice is personified as feminine."[16] If this identification is correct, then the masque subtly undercuts the virtues represented by Queen Anne and her ladies by placing them in a context associated with vices. Finally, in the transformation scene is an echo of King James's claim that he is both father and mother to his kingdom,[17] a dual role that effectively strips women of even their childbearing function. The masculine figure of Heroique Virtue proclaims himself the "Parent" of Fame (line 380), presumably her only parent as no mother is mentioned, and it is clear from her own speeches as well as his that she exists only to serve him. As a consequence, even though the inhabitants of the House of Fame—Queen Anne and her ladies—are themselves worthy of fame, they are reminded in a passage spoken directly to King James that a chief purpose of their fame is to enlarge his (lines 432–445).

What is striking about *The Masque of Queens* is Jonson's deftness in managing to satisfy the contradictory agendas of both James and Anne, to the apparent satisfaction of both. Of course, one should realize that in the masques that she commissioned, Queen Anne obviously did not intend to displace her husband as monarch but only to assert what she believed to be her own importance in a royal court that increasingly ignored her. In that context, she was not so much protesting the prevalent idea of gender hierarchy as she was demanding the full recognition of her position as queen consort and the respect due to that position. Because she continued for some time to commission masques from Jonson, she was obviously pleased with the honor he accorded her in them. At the same time, the king was also obviously pleased that he remained the primary focus of the praise accorded in these lavish spectacles.

The Later Masques

The Masque of Queens marks a pivotal point in the development of the Jonsonian masque, but it does not mark a final point. In the years following 1609, the masque developed further. It remained preoccupied with broad ethical issues, and it continued to envision almost limitless social possibilities, reminding the courtly audience of responsibilities as well as blessings. In the later masques, Jonson returns again and again to the myth of the Golden Age, evoking classical and mythological glories with affecting nostalgia and fervid optimism in such works as *The Golden Age Restored* (1616) and *Time Vindicated* (1623). He continues to concern himself with the questions that dominate the early works, exploring issues of love and beauty, virtue and reason in masques like *Love Restored* (1612) and *Lovers Made Men* (1617) and informing his explorations with the same kind of erudition and philosophical seriousness that mark *The Masque of Queens*. But in the later years, the masque becomes a more subtle and more complex species of poetry.

Although the famous quarrel between Jonson and Jones reflected their profound disagreement about the relative importance of the verbal and nonverbal elements of the masque, Jones's eventual triumph did not lead, as some have supposed, to an increasing emphasis on spectacle.[18] Indeed, the movement is in the other direction. The settings of Jonson's masques become less spectacular in the years following *The Masque of Queens,* including those designed by Inigo Jones. They come to have less of an independent existence and to function more effectively as media for dramatic and poetic action, merging the stage's illusion with the court's reality. The very absence in the later masques of the kind of detailed descriptions of the performance, the scene designs, and the stage machinery that are so prominent in *The Masque of Queens* indicates the form's developing literary integrity and its capacity to sustain an imaginative existence separate from the circumstances of production. Although not true of *Love's Triumph through Callipolis* and *Chloridia* (both 1631), the later masques generally rely more on poetry to effect their various transformations than on spectacular stage machinery.

In the later works, the antimasque develops into a more supple device. It continues to provide variety and contrast but tends to rely less on simple antithesis. The worlds of antimasque and masque become less rigidly separated, and the antimasque is sometimes subsumed positively into the world of the revels, as in *Oberon* (1611), where the satyrs of the antimasque are converted to the service of Prince Henry.[19] Most significantly, the antimasque comes more often to represent comic disorder rather than abstract vice, as in *Mercury Vindicated* (1615), *The Gypsies Metamorphosed* (1612), and *Neptune's Triumph* (1623). It grows more worldly, and its values become less obviously evil. Indeed, the antimasque and main masque, rather than contrasting absolute representations of vice and virtue, occasionally contrast a lesser good with a higher one.

Poetry and song more completely dominate the main masques of the later works than they do in *The Masque of Queens*. *Lovers Made Men* has some claim to be considered the earliest English opera, because the entire masque was sung in recitative "after the Italian manner" (lines 26–27), and *The Golden Age Restored* is a sequence of lyric poems, its resolution accomplished by the invocation of English poets Geoffrey

Chaucer, John Gower, John Lydgate, and Edmund Spenser. Jonson uses
the songs of the later masques to effect scenes of transformation, as in
Neptune's Triumph, where the presentation of the masquers is accomplished by means of music and song as well as by elaborate machinery.[20]
Apollo and a Grand Chorus sing as the scene is transformed from an
almost bare stage, which had served as the backdrop for the antimasque,
into the island of Delos: "some *Muses,* & the Goddesse *Harmony,* make
the musique, the while the Iland moves forward, *Proteus* sitting below,
and APOLLO sings" (lines 334–39). This integration of song and music
with action marks a considerable advance in fusing the disparate elements of the masque. Similarly, songs rather than prose or spoken
poetry come regularly to persuade the dancers to dance and to interpret
the significance of the dances. In *Pleasure Reconciled to Virtue* (1618), for
example, Daedalus invites the masquers to dance in a lovely song that
both instructs the dancers and explains the thematic relevance of the
dance:

> Come on, come on; and where you goe,
>> so enter-weave the curious knot,
> as ev'n th'observer scarce may know
>> which lines are Pleasures, and which not.
> . . . .
> Then, as all actions of mankind
>> are but a Laborinth, or maze,
>> so let your Daunces be entwin'd,
>> yet not perplex men, unto gaze.
> But measur'd, and so numerous too,
>> as men may read each act you doo.
> And when they see the Graces meet,
>> admire the wisdom of your feet.
>> > > > (lines 253–56, 261–68)

This song, with its emphasis on the hieroglyphic nature of dance, is
more than ornamental: It gracefully explicates the masque's theme of
the reconciliation of pleasure and virtue, and it helpfully interprets the
significance of dance in realizing that theme.

  The songs admirably crystallize the ideas more fully developed in the
blank verse and the nonverbal elements in which they are embedded.

Simple, brief, elegant, and characterized by brilliant stanzaic variations, they reveal numerous aspects of Jonson's talent. A song like "The faery beame uppon you," from *The Gypsies Metamorphosed,* demonstrates his gift of delicate grace; while the Satyr's catch from *Oberon,* "Buz, quoth the blue Flie," illustrates his comic spirit; and the song for Comus in *Pleasure Reconciled to Virtue,* "Roome, roome, make roome for the bouncing belly," indicates his ability to use poetry and music to reveal character. Jonson often creates unusual effects in his songs by alternating solo and choral passages, a technique used brilliantly throughout *Neptune's Triumph.* Most significantly, however, in the later works the songs become an integral part of the masque, used for various purposes but always central to the form itself.

Perhaps the most important development in the later masques is the progressive movement away from moral absolutism, already noted in reference to the antimasques. This development is reflected in the evolution of the characters in the masques: Those of the main masques remain symbolic but less singularly so than in the early works; they become less static and more capable of action. Increasingly, they are faced with decisions and internal conflicts. They function more as exemplars than as abstractions. For instance, in *Pleasure Reconciled to Virtue,* Hercules enters the antimasque world of excess and rejects it in favor of the masque's world of higher pleasures, illustrating the human obligation to make moral choices. Although he may have made his choice long before the masque begins, Hercules functions as an allegorical type of the hero "who can enter the world of misrule, assess it, and lead us from it into the masque."[21]

Pleasure Reconciled to Virtue, first performed on January 6, 1618, is an especially important masque, for it epitomizes the tendency of the later works to reconcile apparent opposites rather than merely to contrast them through antithesis.[22] Pleasure in the masque is finally revealed as only ostensibly opposed to virtue. Comus, the lord of misrule, is exposed as a god of base sensuality and tired excess rather than of true pleasure. The masque transforms the court into the innocently pleasurable garden of Hesperus; tellingly, entrance to the garden is dependent on virtue. The masquers are called forth in a song that stresses the relationship of pleasure and virtue:

> Descend,
> descend,

> though pleasure lead,
>   feare not to follow:
>   they who are bred
>   within the hill
>   of skill,
>   may safely tread
>   what path they will:
>   no ground of good, is hollow.
>   (lines 226–35)

Pleasure, thus, can lead to wisdom, and those wise in the *"hill of knowledge"* (line 204) are able to enjoy pleasure safely and innocently. As a result of a "roial education" (line 223), which combines pleasure and virtue, Prince Charles qualifies as chief "of the bright race of *Hesperus*" (line 205). Presided over by King James as Hesperus, the Hesperidean garden reconciles pleasure and virtue by subordinating the former to the latter and by defending pleasure as an impetus to virtue.

The religiopolitical import of *Pleasure Reconciled to Virtue* is located in its depiction of the Hesperidean garden. Jonson's masque is a comment on the recent defiance of the king by adherents of the two religious extremes in England and Scotland. On the one hand, the Scottish Presbyterians and the English Puritans attacked the king and the Anglican Church for promoting too much pageantry and allowing too much mirth, to the detriment of sober piety, and some refused to observe the rules of hospitality. On the other hand, recusant English Catholics, especially in Lancashire, were frequently so boisterous in their Sabbath dancing and games that they disrupted religious services. By various means, including the proclamation of the *Book of Sports,* a document that defined the proper role and limits of country pastimes within an Anglican framework, James tried to bring both extremes toward a middle ground that allowed for both decorous worship and innocent sport, to reconcile virtue and pleasure. Jonson's *Pleasure Reconciled to Virtue* celebrates the efforts of the king and is, in the words of Leah Marcus, "his tribute to the comely *via media* of the Anglican Church and the king's attempts to preserve it against the extremes of popery and puritanism"[23]

Not surprisingly, *Pleasure Reconciled to Virtue* influenced John Milton's *A Masque Presented at Ludlow Castle* (1634) and in more significant ways than simply providing Milton with the name of his antagonist Comus.[24] Both masques pivot on questions of choice and create highly ritualized worlds that are nevertheless grounded in human experience. *Pleasure Reconciled to Virtue* and *A Masque Presented at Ludlow Castle* both depict the conflict of virtue and license without simplifying the attractions of either. Jonson's later masques are not truly dramatic any more than Milton's magnificent achievement in the genre is dramatic, but Jonson's work develops in that direction to the extent that it comes more and more to admit of human conflict and moral complexity.

The masque, although it did not survive the era that produced it, greatly influenced the development of the illusionistic stage and on that count alone merits sympathetic consideration in the history of English theater. But the masque is a form of literature as well as theater, and Ben Jonson more than anyone else made it so. He was the greatest masque writer of his age. In his hands, the form became a medium for the presentation of a humanist vision that perceives connections between the world of experience and the world of ideals and interprets these connections as faithful mirrors of human potential. He invested the masque with dignity, learning, and ethical force. In his sumptuous shows, he mixed profit with delight and attempted to translate the mundane into the transcendent.

Chapter Five
The Poetry

Today casual readers probably know Ben Jonson best as a comic playwright, but in the seventeenth century his nondramatic work was thought to be his more secure claim to fame. In fact, he was the most honored poet of his age. When King James awarded him a pension in 1616, he became unofficially poet laureate of England. The pension was probably in recognition of Jonson's masques, work that may seem remote today, yet the position of poet laureate is peculiarly appropriate for him. He is preeminently (though not exclusively) a social poet who "can faine a *Common-wealth* . . . can governe it with *Counsels,* strengthen it with *Lawes,* correct it with *Judgements,* informe it with *Religion,* and *Morals*" (*Disc.,* lines 1035–37). The commonwealth metaphor is more than fanciful: it enunciates a nexus between poet and society that is crucial to appreciating Jonson's achievement.

Jonson's role as social poet, and the consequences of that role, help distinguish him from his great contemporary John Donne. Born within a year of each other, the two men helped create a new kind of poetry in the early seventeenth century, and they share as many similarities as they exhibit differences.[1] What they have in common are a proclivity for the "plain style" of strong lines, colloquial language, natural rhythms, and economy of expression; a disdain for the sensuous ornateness and pictorial diffuseness of their Elizabethan predecessors and neo-Spenserian contemporaries; a willingness to explore individual sensibilities; and a dedication to philosophical truth and moral principle. Both created distinct and personal voices. Perhaps most influenced by the example of Sir Philip Sidney, their poetry is an intellectual, tough-minded verse in which the formal properties of rhythm and meter emphasize meaning; the individual poems are organic, each part governed by a prior conception of the final form and growing into a highly structured, precisely crafted, untransposeable whole. For both men, poetry is a means of "expressing the life of man in fit measure, numbers, and harmony" (*Disc.,* lines 2349–50).

One can easily exaggerate the differences between the two, so it is worthwhile to remember that each occasionally wrote the kind of poetry most often associated with the other. They differ chiefly and most clearly in that Donne is more often a private poet than Jonson. Intro-verted and sometimes eccentrically, unclassically individual, Donne is more intent on fashioning realms of private emotion than on creating a poetic commonwealth. Consequently, his poetry is more arcane and more often inaccessible than Jonson's, and he writes more frequently of extremely private subjects, of sex and religion. He characteristically devises elaborate and extended conceits, self-consciously affecting wit and worrying minute points of logic and learning in order to startle his readers into recognition and acquiescence. Jonson, while capable of the imaginative perceptions of Donne, is not as interested in discovering unexpected resemblances between unlike phenomena. Although he is a far better love poet than is generally conceded, love is not his foremost poetic subject, and only once does he approach a religious question with an intensity comparable to Donne's. Even when he is at his most per-sonal—mourning his children, for instance—Jonson is never eccentri-cally private, and he rarely attempts to capture the kind of emotional ecstasy Donne achieves in his verse. Moreover, unlike Donne, who dis-dained print and remained an amateur rather than professional poet, Jonson earned his living from his pen and pioneered in adapting to the period's emerging print culture, utilizing it to create and fix his canon and individual texts as unchanging and unchangeable artifacts. Finally, as C. A. Patrides has observed, whereas Donne remained distant from the classical tradition, Jonson enriched English poetry by accommodat-ing in his poems the spirit of the classical lyric. Moreover, by the practice of *imitatio,* he not only drew from rich classical traditions, but he also self-consciously added to them.[2]

Jonson's role as social poet is a function of his classicism. He boasted to William Drummond of Hawthornden that "he was better Versed & knew more in Greek and Latin, than all the Poets in England" (*Conv.,* lines 622–23). He had a profound admiration for classical literature, but tellingly he regarded ancient authors "as Guides, not Commanders" (*Disc.,* lines 138–39). The classical qualities of Jonson's poetry may be located in a number of specific manifestations. Certainly the urbanity, simplicity, and decorum of his lyrics are the products of a classical sensi-bility, as are their restraint, clarity, and economy of expression. Jonson frequently alludes to and even translates or paraphrases Greek and (more often) Roman authors, and he self-consciously identifies with poets like Martial and Horace. He adopts as his own the classical ideals of balance and stoic self-sufficiency, incorporating for himself and his age an ethical code or moral philosophy derived from, or at least paralleled in, the works of great Roman writers, especially Horace, Cicero, and Seneca. The weighty statement and broad generality of his verse, often employing vividly concrete detail only to illustrate received wisdom, are classical qualities. In addition, Jonson revives classical forms such as the epigram, the epitaph, the ode, and the verse epistle, and he does so with a scholar's knowledge of the origins and conventions of each genre. But the most fundamental reflection of his classicism is the social and public nature of his poetry, his vision of an ordered society in which the poet plays an indispensable role as arbiter of civilized values.[3]

Jonson's poetry is, for the most part, didactic. Although Jonson's entanglement in the elaborate and frequently treacherous patronage system of the day complicated his performance as counselor to the ruling classes, much of his poetry does indeed advise the noble men and women of his acquaintance on how best to achieve a good society. He praises in order to inspire and ridicules in order to shame. Jonson is sometimes the convivial drinking companion singing the pleasures of love and friendship; frequently he is the energetic satirist echoing the Ciceronian lament *O tempora! O mores!* Nearly always, he is the self-nominated maker of a moral vision of the integrated life. In satiric verses, he exposes the vice, disorder, and exploitation he observes around him. But in his poetic commonwealth, he also creates a positive ideal of the harmonious society, one founded on enduring notions about the good life. He sees the great and virtuous men and women of his age as mirrors of old and still vital truths and frequently as anachronistic reincarnations of ancient grace. That this positive ideal and these exemplary individuals are often defined by contrasting them with the negative and the flawed is a measure of Jonson's realism and of the perceived vulnerability of his values in a time of change and peril. The poet's personal emblem was the broken compass; he entertained no illusions about the possibility of perfection in the real world. But he never forsook the ideal as an individual and public goal, and his verse is supremely a poetics of human possibilities. If the possibilities Jonson envisions are in real life achieved only infrequently and in the artifice of verse realized only in fragmentary and nostalgic glimpses of an older and increasingly threatened civilization, the integrity of the vision is none the less for that. The functional aspect of Jonson's classicism is his faith in the continuity of ethical principles and in the living relevance of timeless questions about the nature of the good life.

To say that Jonson is a social poet is not to imply a lack of personal engagement, and to call him didactic is not to deny him subtlety.

Indeed, few poets have ever displayed in their work so complete and so assertive a personality as does Jonson, and still fewer have permitted large preconceptions to inform individual poems so naturally and so easily. Central to his work is the felt presence of Jonson's persona: the plain, blunt man of judgment and discrimination. His poetry is sustained by moral vision and energy, but it is almost never moralistic in any narrow or self-righteous way. Poems that celebrate occasions and persons now long forgotten can still excite interest precisely because of the poet's engagement. Moreover, the large scope and continuing relevance of his ethical concerns help make even the most topical and time rooted of his poems more than simply documents of a culture now lost.

Jonson's appeal may be more clearly intellectual than emotional. He is seldom ecstatic, and rarely does he create poems of private sensation. Nevertheless, there is a great deal of emotion in his verse, although it has been too little appreciated. He expresses anger and joy, grief and gratitude, dejection and exhilaration, passion and love, and he manipulates his poems so that they stir these emotions in his readers as well. He is capable of conveying fine shades of feeling and of orchestrating delicate shifts of tone. From poem to poem, he assumes a variety of dramatic poses, each of them true to one or another facet of his personality and all of them invested with individualized emotion. He is tactful advisor, respectful admirer, proud poet, grieving father, courteous host, affectionate parodist, enraged satirist, amused observer, witty commentator, loving friend, loyal subject, unhandsome lover. Most often his persona is characterized by enormous dignity and fierce independence, and sometimes he exposes himself as affectingly vulnerable. Frequently, Jonson surfaces in his poetry as a man very much aware of the precariousness of his social and professional status within a harshly competitive society.

The variety of voices Jonson adopts, or more accurately, the number of facets of a single personality he reveals, usefully reminds us that he is a great dramatic poet. Each voice is decorously suited to the situation of the individual poem. The dramatic qualities of the poetry help place in perspective Jonson's penchant for weighty statement and broad generality. As Sara van den Berg observes, "Whatever its occasion, literary form, or social assumption, a Jonsonian poem consists of two central actions: the poet describes the person he addresses and dramatizes his own response."[4] The vivid dramatic situations rescue the poems from any potential for dullness or banality. Although the poetry is frequently motivated by a didactic impulse and its concerns are with ethical commonplaces, this didacticism and these concerns are presented in highly particularized situations of masterfully controlled drama. The drama is sometimes suggested rather than stated, as in the lovely lyrics "Drinke to me, onely, with thine eyes" (*F.* 9) and "Oh doe not wanton with those eyes" (*U.* 4). At other times, as in "An Elegie On the Lady Jane Pawlet" (*U.* 83), it is self-consciously exaggerated and theatrical. But whether implied or explicit, Jonson's articulation of dramatic context is at the heart of his illumination of human experience in the poetry.

At first glance, the bulk of Jonson's verse may seem somewhat prosaic in its scarcity of startling imagery, its paucity of metaphor, its dearth of ornamentation, and its apparent lack of ambiguity. As he remarked, "Pure and neat Language I love, yet plaine and customary" (*Disc.,* lines 1870–71). On his schoolmaster's instruction, he composed his poetry by first writing it out in prose and then turning it into verse. Moreover, he gives highest priority in poetry to "matter." The poet, he says, "must first thinke, and excogitate his matter; then choose his words, and examine the weight of either" (*Disc.,* lines 1701–02). Jonson aims for clarity and artful shapeliness. As Drummond remarks, "his inventions are smooth and easie" (*Conv.,* lines 693–94). But the appearance of placidity and conventionality is often simply an appearance, a calm surface that makes possible surprising and resonant reverberations. Jonson's poetry is active, animated by verbs rather than adjectives; it is fresh, vital, symmetrical; it typically reinvigorates tired conventions and exhausted traditions; it is sometimes inventive, playful, and imaginative; and it is nearly always carefully controlled and neatly unified.[5]

Perhaps the most consistent tools Jonson uses to impart expansive meaning unobtrusively are his careful diction and versification. A master of metrics, Jonson typically uses versification to restrain excess and to emphasize thought and modulate feeling.[6] His use of words is always precise, although he is sometimes thought not to be evocative. Actually, he often gains richness of implication by choosing a single word or phrase that echoes with meaning. For instance, near the end of his famous tribute to the Sidney family, "To Penshurst" (*F.* 2), he remarks that the Sidney children, by observing their parents, may learn "The mysteries of manners, armes, and arts" (line 98). The word "mysteries" here gives transcendence to what might appear merely a conventional compliment. Suggesting as it does a whole wealth of meaning, from secret social rites or mastery of a craft to the Christian religion itself, the word infuses powerful implication into the rest of the line and into the work as a whole. Similarly, at the end of this poem, Jonson contrasts the

owners of ostentatious, new country homes with the owner of Penshurst: "their lords have built, but thy lord dwells" (line 102). Deriving
naturally from all that has come before in the poem, this simple but precise opposition of building and dwelling implies a wealth of meaning,
much of it nonparaphrasable but all of it appropriate to the central distinction between the imposing "heaps" (line 101) erected for the sake of
vanity and the organic, living embodiment of civilized values that is
Penshurst. A final example of Jonson's subtle but imaginative diction
may be cited from "A Hymne On the Nativitie of my Saviour" (*U*. 1. 3).
Depicting Christ as *Theantropos,* the Word of God become human, Jonson writes of the nativity, "The Word was now made Flesh indeed" (line
17). There is a marvelous suggestiveness in the word "indeed." It
exclaims Christ as the perfection of humankind, and it also coolly states
a fact: By assuming our nature, God became flesh in deed. By this simple, seriously witty device, Jonson effectively locates Christ's birth as an
active fulfillment of ancient prophecy, a pivotal moment in human history.

Semantic play abounds in Jonson's poetry, enriching the texture of
the seemingly smooth poetic surfaces. But perhaps even more important
than the verbal and linguistic skill of the poet is the tension he generates
through the balancing of various oppositions throughout his work. He
sometimes depicts idealized landscapes only to intrude realistic figures
upon them, allowing experience to impinge on innocence and realism to
temper idealism. In "An Elegie" (*U*. 22), for instance, idealistic assumptions about love are placed in a realistic perspective that adds deep and
surprising poignancy to the poet's celebration of neoplatonic virtue.
Sometimes Jonson will force attention on the artifice of his poetry in
order to emphasize the reality that animates it. Often he juxtaposes one
emotion with another, as in "My Picture left in *Scotland*" (*U*. 9), where
playful wit balances and then intensifies pathos. Sometimes contradictory attitudes are placed in opposition, and the poet refuses to reconcile
them. "On My First Daughter" (*E*. 22), for example, gains great power
by never reconciling its oppositions of soul and body, heaven and earth,
allowing them to coexist as discrete elements in the paradox of human
love. And perhaps equally miraculous is Jonson's ability to mingle seemingly opposed emotions without ever permitting them to develop into
oppositions, as in the "Epitaph on S[alomon] P[avy]" (*E*. 120), where he
is at once witty and sincere, playful and earnest.

Finally, the *textuality* of Jonson's poems—their writerly and readerly
qualities—needs to be emphasized. Jonson's poems are artfully designed

written constructs, consciously adapted for a print rather than a manuscript culture. They may be intended to be read more than to be heard,
and to be reread in order to correct original misreadings. Hence, he
characteristically employs circular structures that encourage the reread-
ing and reevaluating of his poems, as his conclusions compel the reader
to circle back to his beginnings. Like the poems of George Herbert,
which may owe their circular strategies to the example of Jonson, Jonson's poems are frequently self-correcting, as their conclusions reveal
unexpected complexities that require rethinking on the part of the
reader. Much of the pleasure in reading the poems lies in this process of
correction, whereby the reader revises his or her original impressions in
light of the entire poem. At the same time, however, the poems, which
lack much visual imagery, are also meant to be heard and to be read
aloud. Their heavy punctuation and their use of enjambment and
caesura seem calculated to create the illusion of a speaking voice and to
guide the reader in the apprehension of intonation.[7] Despite their
appearance of perfect lucidity, Jonson's poems pose complex interpretive
challenges; they insist on the active participation of the reader in the
creation of meaning.

When one generalizes about Jonson, it is easy to forget the great
variety of his poetry. As social poet, he frequently employs public modes
of expression such as the ode, the verse epistle, and the epigram, revital-
izing these public forms with refreshing intimacy and confident familiarity. But he also incorporates into his poetic commonwealth a space for
the private and the personal, mastering the less philosophical forms such
as the love elegy, the song, and even—though rarely—the sonnet. Jonson's various art can best be illustrated by discussion of the individual
poems, among which are some of the best-crafted works in the English
language.

Epigrams (1616)

Jonson seems to have prepared his *Epigrams* for publication in 1612,
when it was entered in the Stationers' Register. Apparently, however,
the collection was not printed until its inclusion in the 1616 *Works*. Dedicating them to William Herbert, earl of Pembroke, Jonson refers to his
epigrams as "the ripest of my studies," distinguishes them from the
scurrilous lampoons that had come to be synonymous with the term *epigram,* and extends to Herbert "the honor of leading forth so many good,
and great names (as my verses mention on the better part) to their

remembrance with posteritie," even as he also expresses some anxiety as to having "praysed, unfortunately, any one, that doth not deserve; or, if all answere not, in all numbers, the pictures I have made of them" (lines 4, 18–24). This preface indicates both the seriousness with which Jonson regards his collection and the consciousness of his departure from the practice of such contemporary epigrammatists as John Davis of Hereford and John Weever, from whom he dissociates himself in *Epigram* 18.

For Jonson, the epigram is not merely a satiric mode; it is also a medium for the praise of "good, and great names." He does not desire "with lewd, prophane, and beastly phrase, / To catch the worlds loose laughter, or vaine gaze" (*E.* 2, lines 11–12). By conceiving the epigram as a vehicle for praise as well as blame, he realizes that many of his readers may be startled, as he admits in "To My Meere English Censurer" (*E.* 18): "To thee, my way in *Epigrammes* seemes new, / When both it is the old way, and the true" (lines 1–2). As T. K. Whipple has shown, Jonson finds "the old way, and the true" in the classical form of the epigram, particularly as perfected by Martial.[8]

The epigram may best be defined as a brief poem, generally no more than 20 lines long and usually shorter, that points toward a witty, ingenious, or surprising conclusion or turn of thought. The qualities most appropriate to an epigram are conciseness and wit. Jonson especially prizes subtlety, irony, and implication in preference to the obviousness and the direct abuse he found in the work of his contemporaries. The style of his epigrams is colloquial; the tone, familiar and conversational. The poems benefit from being read aloud, and the heavy punctuation seems calculated to help the reader in this regard. Following Martial, Jonson thought of the epigram as a form admitting of a wide variety of subject and feeling. In theory, no theme is too exalted and no feeling too intense to be conveyed in an epigram; in practice, Jonson rarely treats explicitly religious subjects, and the collection contains no love poems. He most often uses the genre to satirize the foibles of his fellows, to celebrate his king, to compliment the worthy, to perform the various rites of friendship, and to commemorate the loss of loved ones. And in his collection, Jonson mingles forms other than the epigram, including the epistolary "Inviting a Friend to Supper" (*E.* 101) and the burlesque epic "On the Famous Voyage" (*E.* 133).

For all the variety of subjects, however, *Epigrams* is not haphazardly put together. Rather, it is a coherently arranged collection in which poems are meaningfully juxtaposed to each other (as when a satiric denunciation of an unnatural father, "On Chuffe, Bancks the Usurer's Kinsman" [*E.* 44] is paired with the moving elegy "On My First Sonne" [*E.* 45]) and sometimes form small clusters or sequences of contrasting or complementary works. The collection gains unity by the coherence of its vision and the mastery of its expression. In this collection, satiric and panegyric, comic and serious poems occur almost randomly, but what emerges from the whole is an individual sensibility, one that both sees the follies of the age and celebrates its ideals. Because these ideals are only rarely realized in "the sloth of this our time" (*E.* 66, line 5), they are all the more to be prized. Jonson is not rigidly moralistic in the *Epigrams.* His common sense and his appreciation of the comic are too pervasive to permit his verse to become oppressively didactic. But he is concerned with moral questions and social issues, and these concerns are never sacrificed to the demands of wit. The persona of these poems is the poet *par excellence:* a good man armed with moral authority, exercising his responsibility to expose and to extol by means of "*Poesy,* a dulcet, and gentle *Philosophy,* which leades on, and guides us by the hand to Action, with a ravishing delight, and incredible Sweetnes" (*Disc.,* lines 2398–2400). By exposing types of vice and foolishness and by extolling particular exemplars of virtue and achievement, Jonson's book aspires to what he saw as the end of all true poetry. It becomes a collection the study of which "(if wee will trust *Aristotle*) offers to mankinde a certaine rule, and Patterne of living well, and happily; disposing us to all Civil offices of Society" (*Disc.,* lines 2386–88).[9]

The seriousness with which Jonson regards his epigrams can best be measured by the large number of poems that comment on his book, as he addresses the book itself, its readers, its critics, and its seller. The very first poem instructs the reader:

> Pray thee, take care, that tak'st my booke in hand,
> To read it well: that is, to understand.
>
> (*E.* 1)

This epigram states a recurrent theme, the need for a fit audience. In its stress on the final word, it illustrates in a minor way Jonson's technique of allowing a single precise, low-keyed but expansive phrase or word to infuse the understated whole with unexpected force. The importance Jonson attaches to readers who "understand," in all senses of that word, can scarcely be overestimated: Not only must the reader be capable, but he or she must also be an active participant in the poetry. Jonson makes a similar point in *Epigram* 17, where he addresses "the Learned Critick" (the poem's title), as opposed to the mere English censurer of the poem that immediately follows. From the learned critic alone comes "a legitimate fame" (line 3). The poet expresses honest ambition for the praise of intelligent and educated readers: "a sprigge of bayes, given by thee, / Shall outlive gyrlands, stolne from the chast tree" (lines 5–6). This brief poem, with its concentrated energy, careful diction, and unified imagery based on various forms of "legitimacy," clarifies Jonson's desire for discerning readers from whom he can demand much and to whom he can look for poetic immortality. He realizes that lasting poetic laurels cannot be stolen; they must be freely given by a learned audience. By submitting his work to understanding critics, he seeks, in the words of one of his epigrams to fellow poet John Donne, "great glorie, and not broad" (*E*. 96, line 12).

Jonson's confessed ambitions for his work are nicely tempered by humor in "To My Booke-seller" (*E*. 3), where his self-regard is leavened by his ability to laugh at himself without sacrificing his dignity. It begins with the poet's acquiescing in the profit motive of his bookseller, although from a position of implied superiority:

> Thou, that mak'st gaine thy end, and wisely well,
>   Call'st a booke good, or bad, as it doth sell,
> Use mine so, too: I give thee leave.
>
> (lines 1–3)

The poet does, however, insist that the bookseller not pander his work by advertising it in undignified ways to unworthy or incapable readers. But in the conclusion, the poem reverses itself to a comic close: "If, without these vile arts, it will not sell, / Send it to *Bucklers-bury*, there 'twill, well" (lines 11–12). Bucklersbury was a commercial street lined with grocery and apothecary shops; there the leaves of the book would be used as wrapping paper, a fate that haunted several classical writers who worried about the popularity of their books. Horace himself declined "to be praised in verses ill-wrought, lest I have to blush at the stupid gift, and then along with my poet, outstretched in a closed chest, be carried into the street where they sell frankincense and perfumes and pepper and everything else that is wrapped in sheets of useless paper" (*Epistles* 2, lines 265–70). By ironically alluding to Horace's observations on the fate of badly written poetry, Jonson draws a significant distinction between Augustan Rome and Jacobean England. In his own age, it is not poor verse but good poetry that is neglected. Jonson's poem satirizes the bookseller's greed, the undiscriminating readers of his time, and the failure of the general public to appreciate the true utility of serious poetry. But the humor and gentle mockery of the ingenious conclusion precludes bitterness. Jonson's tone here, as in many of the epigrams, is that of a good-natured observer of the human condition who is aware of the flaws in his society but is able to be amused as well as occasionally enraged by them.

Not surprisingly, Jonson is most aware of the flaws of his society in the satiric epigrams. In these poems, which dominate the first half of the book but recede in the second, the poet presents a wide panorama of foibles. Affected courtiers and plagiarists receive much of Jonson's attention, but he satirizes almost all elements of his society from pretenders to learning, unscrupulous professionals, and phony intelligence-mongers to vainglorious captains, jaded voluptuaries, and country bumpkins. The subjects of these epigrams are not identified in such a way as to be readily recognizable in the real world. This discretion is both aesthetic and prudential: It reflects Jonson's greater interest in exposing foibles and vices common throughout his society than in attacking particular individuals who possess these characteristics as well as his practical knowledge that such attacks could have serious consequences. Nevertheless, the real genius of these epigrams is that they are unusually vivid. By the careful selection and accumulation of concrete details, the poet makes his gallery of contemporary types seem individualized in spite of their generic names and the wide application of the satire. Projecting himself as a rational and virtuous man, he avoids the bitter invective of the verse satirists of his day in favor of a restrained discourse of cool reasonableness.[10]

What distinguishes the satiric epigrams is their quality of wit and their verbal dexterity. These characteristics often take the form of puns and other kinds of wordplay, irony, and aphoristic ingenuity, and they are often achieved by masterful control of syntax and meter. The ironic wit of "To Alchymists" (E. 6) is achieved through reticence. It rests on our awareness of the alchemical attempt to turn base metals into gold:

> If all you boast of your great art be true;
> Sure, willing povertie lives most in you.

Similarly, "To Pertinax Cob" (E. 69) depends for its wit on our knowledge that one meaning of the Latin *pertinax* is "stiff." This squib on sex-

ual exploitation is not a great poem, but it honestly achieves the epigram's aim of concision, subtlety, and wit:

> COB, thou nor souldier, thiefe, nor fencer art,
> Yet by thy weapon liv'st! Th'hast one good part.

Central to this small poem is Jonson's extraordinary sense of comic tim-
ing, as the exclamatory "Yet by thy weapon liv'st!" yields to the understatement of the punch line. The incongruous name that yokes a Latin
adjective to a vernacular noun focuses attention on the comic juxtaposi-
tions within the poem. Cob's "sword" is not a martial weapon but an
erect penis; his is not an art of war but an art of love. To make this poem
a bitterly satirical and narrowly moralistic attack, as one critic does, is to
miss the comic tone of Jonson's wit.[11]

In several of the finest satiric epigrams, Jonson manipulates refrains
to great comic effect, unifying colorful details and establishing comic
patterns that the turns of the final couplets elaborate or refute. In "On
Lieutenant Shift" (E. 12), for instance, the shifty lieutenant welshes on
his debts "with this charme, god payes" (line 4), repeated throughout
the poem as Shift's invariable excuse in all circumstances. But in the
conclusion, his attempts to defraud his whore lead to his own syphilitic
retribution:

> Not his poore cocatrice but he betrayes
>   Thus: and for his letcherie, scores, god payes.
> But see! th'old baud hath serv'd him in his trim,
>   Lent him a pockie whore. Shee hath paid him.
>   (lines 21–24)

The refrain in "On Giles and Jone" (E. 42) is not a repeated word or
phrase but a recurring sentiment, a kind of discordant *concordia concors*. It
begins with the question, "Who sayes that GILES and JONE at discord
be?" (line 1), and proceeds to demonstrate their complete agreement:
each is equally ill-disposed toward the other.

Several of the epigrams concern courtiers, and these tend to be
among the most satiric of all. Jonson often attacks the hangers-on at
court by depicting them as dehumanized poseurs. The title of "On
Some-thing, That Walkes Some-where" (E. 11) points toward its subject's lack of humanity. The poem itself is beautifully constructed, all of

its parts carefully arranged into a whole of unexpected force and taut power. The poet's contempt is perfectly conveyed in the dehumanizing pronouns applied to the courtier and in the account of his ineffectuality. Although the lord thinks he is an otherworldly creature trapped in a fleshly existence, in actuality he is less than human because he has betrayed the possibilities—and the responsibilities—of his position. Like the English monsieur of *Epigram* 88 and the rapacious court-worm of *Epigram* 15, this lord is a mere mannequin of fashion, too concerned with appearances and too dead to real life to accomplish anything, either good or ill. If the final pronouncement, "Good Lord, walke dead still" (line 8), seems a little flat at first reading, one must notice how it echoes "buried" in line 5 and "grave" in line 2: death in life is its own punishment. In fact, the echoes and parallelism throughout this brief, carefully balanced poem are remarkable, particularly because it remains colloquial and dramatic despite its formality of construction.

The poems that satirize courtiers and other highly placed individuals such as Lord Ignorant (*E.* 10), Sir Cod (*E.* 19, 20, 50), Sir Voluptuous Beast (*E.* 25, 26), and Fine Lady Would-Be (*E.* 62) help preserve the independence of Jonson's persona in the *Epigrams* as a whole. It is a central fact of Jonson's personality and of his integrity as a poet that he is impressed by virtue and achievement rather than by title or position. He told Drummond that "He never esteemed of a man for the name of a Lord" (*Conv.,* line 337), and in *Epigram* 9 he asserts, "I a *Poet* here, no *Herald* am" (line 4). His emphasis on achievement is deeply felt and probably reflects religious conviction. As he says in one of the two overtly religious poems in the volume, "The ports of death are sinnes; of life, good deeds: / Through which, our merit leads us to our meeds" (*E.* 80, lines 1–2). In addition, the emphasis on achievement serves as a counter to the suspicion of sycophancy—and self-doubt—inevitably generated by the patronage system.

Jonson's hierarchy is one of worth and accomplishment. He is not a democrat, but his position is not unlike that of Robert Burton when the latter asks, "What man thinks better of any person for his nobility? . . . we are all born from one ancestor, Adam's sons, conceived all and born in sin, &c. We are by nature all as one, all alike, if you see us naked."[12] Undoubtedly, Jonson's expressions of independence, all the more striking in light of his political conservatism, reflect his awareness of his own rise from humble origins. They may also function as a defensive mechanism that both acknowledges his consciousness of the necessity to flatter the powerful men and women on whom he is dependent and also denies his servility in doing so. He pays tribute to Sir Henry Nevil (*E.* 109) by establishing criteria for poetry that transcend those of birth. And in "To Sir William Jephson" (*E.* 116), he makes clear that merit and title are not synonymous. Praising Jephson's merit, the poet presents him as an anachronistic figure, representative of a time when "bloud not mindes, but mindes did bloud adorne: / And to live great, was better, then great borne" (lines 11–12). Jonson's stress on his own integrity is not mere puffery. It functions in many ways throughout all of his poems, but it is especially important in the complimentary epigrams, where it is invoked to inoculate him against the suspicion of insincerity and to reassure himself of his autonomy.

If Jonson finds the court corrupt and the nobility often contemptible, this is not to say that he rejects the political hierarchy of seventeenth-century England. He praises King James in several poems, and in *Epigram* 4 he addresses James as both king and poet. In *Epigram* 36, Jonson specifically contrasts his own position with that of his classical model Martial, who shamelessly flattered the despotic Emperor Domitian, while James "cannot flatter'd bee" (line 4). In "On the Union" (*E.* 5), he celebrates James's "marriage" of England and Scotland in an elaborate and imaginative conceit that may have been suggested by the king himself:

> When was there contract better driven by *Fate?*
>   Or celebrated with more truth of state?
> The world the temple was, the priest a king,
>   The spoused paire two realmes, the sea the ring.

The first two lines announce a riddle whose solution is indicated in the title and explicated in the final couplet.[13] The poem easily integrates the natural and the artificial, the fated and the contrived. The ocean that surrounds England and Scotland and separates the two from other geopolitical entities becomes a natural wedding ring, symbolizing the inevitability of the union. The artificial linking of the two realms by a shared crown is celebrated as a fated event, preordained by God and contrived by the priestly King James. A graceful compliment, the poem is a serious political comment as well. By equating a political union with a holy sacrament and envisioning King James as an anointed agent of fate, Jonson reveals his conservatism. In *Epigram* 35, a poem that celebrates the king's preservation from attempts on his life, Jonson asks,

"Who would not be thy subject, JAMES, t'obay / A Prince, that rules by'example, more than sway?" (lines 1–2).[14] In these poems, the poet embraces the conventional religious claims of the Stuart monarchy. Jonson's royalism is not an isolated or opportunistic political attitude; it reflects a deep-seated philosophical commitment. This commitment is expressed most clearly in *Discoveries:* "*After God,* nothing is to be lov'd of man like the Prince: He violates nature, that doth it not with his whole heart. For when hee hath put on the care of the publike good, and common safety; I am a wretch, and put of[f] man, if I doe not reverence, and honour him: in whose charge all things *divine* and *humane* are plac'd" (*Disc.,* lines 986–91).

The obligations of being a poet weigh heavily on Jonson in the complimentary poems. As he states in the Dedication, he wants to lead forth the "many good, and great names" of his time, but he also worries that he may indiscriminately praise the undeserving. In "To My Muse" (*E.* 65), he admits to just such an indiscretion but remembers "Who e're is rais'd, / For worth he has not, He is tax'd, not prais'd" (lines 15–16); and later in an *Underwood* poem, he will admit that he has sometimes praised too much, explaining " 'twas with purpose to have made them such" (*U.* 14, line 22). But if there is danger of "smelling parasite" (*E.* 65, line 14), there is equal peril in overlooking the virtuous. Jonson's fine tribute to the famous actor Edward Alleyn, *Epigram* 89, capitalizes on the poet's sense of obligation in this regard. "How can so great example dye in mee, / That, ALLEN, I should pause to publish thee?" (lines 7–8), he asks and neatly closes: " 'Tis just, that who did give / So many *Poets* life, by one should live" (lines 13–14). To fail to celebrate deserving individuals is to injure the poet, the subjects, and the age. By naming illustrious individuals in his poems and thus preserving them for the remembrance of posterity, the poet helps create what Edward Partridge describes in a Wordsworthian phrase as "one great society of the noble living and the noble dead."[15]

Jonson is acutely conscious of the power of poetry and its potential to bestow immortality on both the poet and his subject. Yet he is also aware that the relationship between poet and subject is reciprocal. In *Epigram* 43, he constructs an elaborate compliment by modifying the conventional relationship and asking Robert Cecil, earl of Salisbury, "What need hast thou of me? or of my *Muse?* / Whose actions so themselves doe celebrate" (lines 1–2).[16] He explains that although the poet cannot add to the statesman's fame, yet the reverse may be true. Similarly, in celebrating Lord Monteagle's role in foiling the infamous Gunpowder Plot, Jonson boasts that his own work will "out-last common deeds" but adds that Monteagle's work "much exceeds" the poet's craft (*E.* 60, lines 6, 8). In praising these dissimilar men of action at the expense of his own art, Jonson gracefully compliments them and courteously effaces himself, acknowledging the mutual dependency of poet and patron, doer and recorder of deeds. While the acknowledgment that the poet needs individuals to celebrate entails a certain cost in self-esteem and no doubt betrays the anxieties implicit in the patronage system itself, Jonson translates these anxieties into an opportunity to project an unwonted modesty. His modesty makes his compliments the greater precisely because he did care deeply for his work. If "to write [is] lesser then to doo," writing "is the next deed, and a great one too" (*E.* 95, lines 25–26). Tellingly, Jonson praises Clement Edmonds in *Epigram* 110 for translating Caesar's *Commentaries;* by virtue of the translator's "learned hand, and true *Promethean* art" (line 17), Caesar "can dye no more" (line 22). Jonson most prizes the capacity of poetry to recreate the past and to preserve the present for the future. If he respects men of virtuous action and occasionally assigns them places of honor higher than those given to poets and scholars and if he can never escape his painful knowledge of the poet's marginality in the halls of power, he also never fails to assert the enduring power of art.

Whereas the subjects of the satirical epigrams are given imaginary or generic names, the subjects of the complimentary poems are identified as real people existing in actual situations outside the artifice of the poems. They function as exemplars of ideals seriously threatened in the real world of Jonson's society. Sir Henry Cary's valor upbraids "the sloth of this our time" (*E.* 66, line 5). The life of William Herbert, earl of Pembroke, is such that all who "hope to see / The common-wealth still safe, must studie thee" (*E.* 102, lines 19–20). Of Susan, countess of Montgomery, the poet asks, "Were you advanced, past those times [of former ages], to be / The light, and marke unto posteritie?" (*E.* 104, lines 11–12). Sir Thomas Overbury "mak'st life understood" (*E.* 113, line 3). Even Sir Henry Goodyere's hawk "doth instruct men by her gallant flight" (*E.* 85, line 5). Jonson's exemplary heroes are particular men and women whose lives and deeds are emblems of good conduct that need to be preserved for emulation by others both in his own and in future ages.

The celebration of exemplars is a public ceremony and fills a public need. But the poet's personal engagement can add deep feeling to such celebrations, giving them emotional as well as intellectual force. The best of the commendatory epigrams are at once public and private. Among the most affecting of such poems is "To William Camden" (*E.* 14), where the poet's personal attachment enriches his celebration of his subject's public achievement. An antiquarian and historian, Camden had been Jonson's schoolmaster at Westminster School and became his friend and mentor. The poem, the first one in the collection to celebrate an exemplar save for the one to King James (*E.* 4), opens with a very personal acknowledgment: "CAMDEN, most reverend head, to whom I owe / All that I am in arts, all that I know" (lines 1–2). It then moves outward from a private debt to a public one, acknowledging the country's obligation to Camden for his works *Britannia* (1586) and *Remaines of a Greater Worke Concerning Britaine* (1605). The center of the poem, based on two passages from Pliny's letters, celebrates the scholar as humanist hero:

> Then thee the age sees not that thing more grave,
>> More high, more holy, that shee more would crave.
> What name, what skill, what faith hast thou in things!
>> What sight in searching the most antique springs!
> What weight, and what authoritie in thy speech!
>> Man scarse can make that doubt, but thou canst teach.
>>> (lines 5–10)

These carefully balanced and dignified lines, the first half of each couplet centering on Camden, the second on the world around him, beautifully sum the antiquarian's commitment to discovering and disseminating knowledge and his discrimination in interpreting the artifacts of the past. The poem then contracts, turning inward to acknowledge Camden's own modesty and to conclude with Jonson's courteous self-effacement and personal devotion: "Many of thine this better could, then I, / But for their powers, accept my pietie" (lines 13–14). The word *pietie* in the final line recalls the opening couplet of the tribute to Francis Beaumont ("How I doe love thee BEAUMONT, and thy *Muse,* / That unto me dost such religion use" [*E.* 55, lines 1–2]), and it illustrates Jonson's keen attention to diction. Quite simply, "pietie" perfectly expresses the poet's devotion to the "reverend head" who is "more grave, / More high, more holy" than the age could desire and who has such faith in things. The poem, moving in a circular direction from the poet's own testimony and back again, is simultaneously a personal tribute to a much admired friend and a general celebration of the scholarly endeavor.[17]

"To William Roe" (E. 128) also illustrates well the complexity of Jonson's successful integration of public and private qualities. A poem of surpassing beauty, it pivots on the assumption that private virtues are prerequisite to public ones. A couplet-sonnet with a significant octet-sestet division, the initial eight lines bid the adventurous traveler farewell and culminate in a striking circle image, while the final six lines look forward to his safe return. A poem of leave-taking, it is firmly rooted in the particular circumstances of its occasion and it exploits the emotion potential to that occasion. The sweetness of its tone invests the whole with intensely personal feeling. Roe is a "joy" to name (line 1); Jonson wishes him "windes as soft as breath of kissing friends" (line 5); "blest" with his return (line 9), "We each to other may this voyce enspire" (line 11). The extraordinary courtesy and tenderness here convince readers of the poet's engagement and suggest his determined effort to restrain emotion even as he expresses it. A marvelous tension emerges from the poet's gentle well-wishing in the octet and his acknowledgment of danger in the sestet.

But the private emotions that Jonson feels are integrated into public concerns, and William Roe is understood finally to be not simply an individual friend of the poet but also a type of Aeneas whose anticipated trials will strengthen his essential integrity and provide a pattern for his friends (and others) to emulate. Moreover, because the opening of the poem echoes the *Odyssey*'s description of a voyage to "The cities of a world of nations, / With all their manners, mindes, and fashions,"[18] Roe is also a kind of Ulysses whose return will be a blessed homecoming. The classical allusions are purposeful. In the *Odyssey*, Ulysses is characterized chiefly in terms of his longing for home, his suffering, and his endurance. Thus, the opening lines that sing the adventure of Roe's travels also subtly acknowledge the hardships he must experience, although such trials are not made explicit until the sestet. Aeneas, in the *Aeneid*, literally passes "through fire, / Through seas, stormes, tempests" (lines 12–13). He was known in the Renaissance primarily for his piety and his faithfulness to the old traditions of Troy. Paradoxically, this piety and devotion to an old order qualify Aeneas to found a new and greater order, Rome.[19] Like Aeneas, Roe will be enriched and enlarged by his travels, but he will remain true to his "first thoughts" (line 10). It is significant that the subtle allusion to Ulysses in the octet is abandoned for an explicit evocation of Aeneas in the sestet. This movement parallels the progress in the poem from seeing Roe as an individual whose voyage ends in a simple homecoming to envisioning him explicitly as an epic type of the faithful traveler whose labors give birth to a new maturity.

Central to the poem is an implicit tension between internal and external worlds. Roe will digest and incorporate within himself the best of all he finds in the exotic places he visits. But he will come back essentially unchanged, enriched but not corrupted by the dangers he faces and the tests of fire and water he passes. The beautiful center of the poem, lines 4–8, introduces one of Jonson's favorite images—the circle—and it epitomizes the tension between the internal and the external. The circle is an emblem of perfection, a symbol of harmony and completeness. By hoping for Roe that his ends and beginnings "prove purely sweet, / And perfect in a circle alwayes meet" (lines 7–8), Jonson simply wishes the traveler well in a beautiful metaphor of perfect harmony borrowed from classical thought. Roe's circle is meet in the sense of being "true" or "perfect," and it is also meet in the witty sense that in completing a circle a line literally meets itself, in effect returning home to its beginnings. But what should not be overlooked is that the image also places Roe as the unchanging center of a circle that circumscribes hell and all the trials of Aeneas. Thus, the interior strength of Roe, his personal character, is measured by the external dangers to which he may be subjected. In another poem, Jonson writes, "He that is round within himselfe, and streight, / Need seeke no other strength, no other height" (E. 98, lines 3–4). Roe is thus celebrated as a public example of private integrity; his inner strength in the outer world earns him the epithet, "This man hath travail'd well" (line 14), in which the penultimate word punningly suggests both internal and external endurance. Concluding with a vision of homecoming, the poem completes its own circular pattern.

A number of the complimentary epigrams are addressed to accomplished women. These are important both because they are of very high quality and because they qualify Jonson's overstated reputation as a misogynist. In fact, Jonson is only rarely cynical in his attitude toward women, and the idealized portraits of noblewomen function as powerful antidotes to the unfavorable generalizations of a few satiric epigrams. The celebrations of women are among Jonson's liveliest and most satisfying poems, and they illustrate well some of his characteristic techniques, particularly the balance of idealism and experience to inform each other and his ability to freshen convention and invigorate tradition. In "To His Lady, Then Mrs. Cary" (E. 126), for instance, he self-consciously connects the contemporary and the classical. This playful and graceful integration of the idealized and the localized is not without irony:

> Retyr'd, with purpose your faire worth to praise,
>   'Mongst *Hampton* shades, and PHOEBUS grove of bayes,
> I pluck'd a branch; the jealous god did frowne,
>   And bad me lay th' unsurped laurell downe:
> Said I wrong'd him, and (which was more) his love.
>   I answer'd, DAPHNE now no paine can prove.
> PHOEBUS replyed. Bold head, it is not shee:
>   CARY my love is, DAPHNE but my tree.

Clearly, the poet's placing of Mrs. Cary within a mythic framework compliments her. Moreover, the intrusion of an actual place and a real person into the timelessness of mythology revitalizes the myth and testifies to the continuity of human experience. By integrating the idealized classical past and the realistic contemporary present, Jonson imparts surprise and resonance to a poem that might otherwise be tired and conventional (Spanos, 6–7). But this technique also creates a peculiar kind of irony that simultaneously undercuts the compliment and deepens it. The title, which pointedly emphasizes the past tense of the poet's attachment to Mrs. Cary, and the very violation of the Daphne-Apollo myth itself, ironically (and playfully) question the possibility of the ideal and call attention to the artificiality of its celebration. Thus, the poet's ingenious praise of Mrs. Cary is wittily undercut by the same technique used to compliment her. Paradoxically, however, the praise is also the greater for being more realistic and less idealized.

Three other poems addressed to women need to be singled out for their remarkable vitality: "On Lucy Countesse of Bedford" (*E.* 76), "To Susan Countesse of Montgomery" (*E.* 104), and "To Mary Lady Wroth" (*E.* 105). All three poems portray their subjects as ideals existing within a temporal world. Mary, Lady Wroth, restores in herself all the lost treasure of antiquity, measured in terms of classical exemplars from Ceres to Venus. She is "*Natures Index,* and restore, / I'your selfe, all treasure lost of th'age before" (lines 19–20). Playing tactfully with the biblical story of Susanna and the elders, Jonson asks in the poem on the countess of Montgomery, "Were they that nam'd you, prophets? Did they see, /

Even in the dew of grace, what you would bee?" (lines 1–2). The idealized portrait of Lucy, countess of Bedford, emerges from the poet's graceful participation in a knowing fiction. He enumerates the qualities he would have in the "creature I could most desire, / To honor, serve, and love; as *Poets* use" (lines 3–4). This paragon of his imagination should be fair, free, wise, "more good then great" (line 6), courteous, sweet, "Hating that solemne vice of greatnesse, pride" (line 10). But most of all, she should be independent and self-assured, combining in her traditionally "feminine" pursuits "masculine" qualities so as to become the embodiment of an androgynous ideal:

> Onely a learned, and a manly soule
>   I purpos'd her; that should, with even powers,
> The rock, the spindle, and the sheares controule
>   Of destinie, and spin her owne free houres.
>   (lines 13–16)

In these lines Jonson brilliantly domesticates the emblems of the Fates, attributing to his paragon believable control over her own free hours. The poem ends with the muse bidding "*Bedford* write, and that was shee" (line 18). This conclusion probably reflects Jonson's knowledge of the countess's distinctively "masculine" signature—the single word *Bedford* executed in bold, confident strokes and elaborately underlined. The poem is a shared fiction in which the imagined ideal is finally revealed as an actual person. It self-consciously, with knowing and playful insinuation, adopts artificial Petrarchan conventions to strain them, to shape them to its own purposes, gently mocking but never rejecting them. A kind of homage to Sidney's *Astrophil and Stella* I, wherein the muse finally bids the blocked speaker to look within his heart and write, Jonson's poem similarly feigns a poetical problem that is solved by the muse's intervention. Like Sidney's poem, Jonson's is also a poem about writing poetry.[20] What is most interesting about these idealized portraits of women is the way Jonson integrates in them fact and fiction, past and present. Although he addresses the ladies familiarly and even playfully, the women become embodiments of grace and virtue associated with the past. The poems celebrate enduring values in a living present.

Epigrams includes eight brief epitaphs that have often been praised. Among these are three poems that mourn the death of a close friend, the minor poet and soldier-adventurer Sir John Roe, who died in Jonson's arms (*E*. 27, 32, 33); an acrostic commemoration of Margaret Ratcliffe, maid of honor to Queen Elizabeth (*E*. 40); an imaginative tribute to a child actor (*E*. 120); a curious epitaph on the elusive Elizabeth L. H., whose last name Jonson lets "sleepe with death" (*E*. 124, line 10); and moving farewells to two of his own children (*E*. 22, 45). The best of these, the epitaphs for Salomon Pavy, the child actor, and for the poet's own children, are among the finest brief poems of the seventeenth century; and all eight are carefully executed. They contain pithy and memorable lines, as, for example, "Under-neath this stone doth lye / As much beautie, as could dye" (*E*. 124, lines 3–4), and they exhibit extraordinary metrical skill. As Jack D. Winner has observed, they "tend to contain emotion rather than to generate it and to pay tribute to the dead rather than to mourn them."[21] They also demonstrate well two aspects of Jonson's poetry that are often slighted: his capacity for deep feeling and his religious faith.

Only two poems in *Epigrams* are overtly religious, but they both establish attitudes mirrored in the epitaphs.[22] In "Of Life, and Death" (*E*. 80), Jonson contrasts earthly and heavenly life:

> This world deaths region is, the other lifes:
> And here, it should be one of our first strifes,
> So to front death, as men might judge us past it.
> For good men but see death, the wicked tast it.
>
> (lines 5–8)

The Christian stoicism and the faith in resurrection indicated here is restated in the aphoristic "Of Death" (*E*. 34):

> He that feares death, or mournes it, in the just,
> Shewes of the resurrection little trust.

These poems reflect a "rigorist" attitude toward mourning, reflecting the idea that rather than lamenting the death of a Christian one should rejoice at the soul's deliverance from this world and its translation to heaven.[23] The spiritual confidence of these abstract musings on death that prohibit mourning finds occasion for testing in the poems that confront the loss of loved ones. Jonson's resolution in the face of death is characteristic of his intellectual attitude in the epitaphs, but it is often countered by an emotional response that complicates the intellectual acceptance of death and gives to the best of the epitaphs great depth and power.

The three poems on Sir John Roe enact a process of coping with grief that involves tears yet culminates in a restatement of a rigorist position.[24] The first poem (*E.* 27) presents Jonson's tears and verse as "better ornaments" than the scutcheons that should deck the deceased's hearse yet insists that both mourned and mourners have attained a "happy state!" (lines 2, 8). Jonson here attempts to celebrate his friend's death, but the attempt is unsuccessful, for the tears are clearly tears of sadness, not of gladness. The second poem to Roe (*E.* 32) praises the soldier, who had fought abroad, for his heroism and fortitude and notes the irony that he should have died "at home in his repaire" (line 7). This poem again attempts to figure the death as a "blest fate" (line 8) but again is unsuccessful in this endeavor, because it more convincingly conveys the vulnerability and fragility of human life than the blessedness of death. In the final poem for his friend (*E.* 33), Jonson in effect acknowledges the failures of the previous two poems to achieve the stoic acceptance they attempt. Here he apologizes for his tears and places his friend's death in the larger context of humankind's common lot. From this perspective, he comes to terms with his own mortality:

> thou art but gone before,
> Whither the world must follow. And I, now,
> Breathe to expect my when, and make my how.
> Which if most gracious heaven grant like thine,
> Who wets my grave, can be no friend of mine.
> (lines 2–6)

If he meets death in the same manner that Roe did—"If any pious life ere lifted man / To heaven; his hath" (*E.* 27, lines 6–7)—then there will be no need to weep for him either. Jonson arrives at this rigorous position, and finally accepts the death of his friend, but only after having expressed a depth of grief that could not be suppressed by his rigorist intellectual beliefs.

The power of the poems occasioned by the deaths of his children stems directly from the conflict between Jonson's emotional response to personal loss and his intellectual, religious acceptance of death. "On My

First Daughter" (E. 22) mourns the death of a six-month-old infant. The first couplet, "Here lyes to each her parents ruth, / MARY, the daughter of their youth," is quietly but profoundly moving. The precision of the word *ruth* restrains the sentimentality inherent in the occasion, while the private loss the parents feel is evoked by the gentle nostalgia of the second line. By focusing on the parents' loss and by finding in the daughter's death evidence of their vulnerability—the passing of their daughter represents also the passing of their youth and reminds them of their own mortality—the opening couplet prepares for the religious consolation that forms the center of the poem. Significantly, the daughter's reception into a Christian afterlife comforts each of the parents in a particular way. By submitting himself to God's will, "all heavens gifts, being heavens due" (line 3), the father's grief is lessened. The baby's glory in joining the "virgin-traine" (line 9) of "heavens Queene, (whose name shee beares)" (line 7) assuages "her mothers teares" (line 8). This individualizing of the grief each parent feels and the comfort each finds helps personalize and make intimate what might easily be a conventional response to the death of an infant.

After finding religious consolation in the safety of the child's soul, however, Jonson turns to his daughter's small body. The "fleshly birth" (line 11), until it is reunited with her soul at the Resurrection, will remain in a grave, "Which," he pleads in the final line, "cover lightly, gentle earth" (line 12). This hope that the earth not weigh heavily upon a dead body is a persistent motif in classical epitaphs.[25] But Jonson is not simply accommodating a classical tradition within a Christian poem. His concern with his daughter's "fleshly birth" betrays his human grief even in the midst of sincerely felt religious consolation. The understated but strong tension between his acceptance of God's will and his feeling of personal loss is developed in the poem's oppositions of heaven and earth, soul and flesh. These oppositions finally yield to a larger opposition, unreconciled in the poem and indicated by implication rather than direct statement, between the poet's intellectual assurance of his daughter's ultimate resurrection and his irrational, emotional concern for her little body. Instead of moving from the physical to the transcendent, as is traditional in elegies, the poem ends where it began, with the grave in which the tiny body is interred. Precisely because it recognizes the conflicting emotions of a father who can accept orthodox doctrines intellectually but who nevertheless fails to feel emotionally the consolation such doctrines are supposed to confer, "On My First Daughter" is a deeply affecting and honest account of the grief occasioned by the loss of an infant.[26]

"On My First Sonne" (*E.* 45) also recognizes conflicting impulses in the response to loss. This poem, an elegy to which is appended an epitaph, attempts to provide a burial ritual and a gravestone inscription for a boy who probably had neither.[27] Jonson's son died of the plague in London while he was away in the country; the boy was probably unceremoniously buried in an unmarked grave. Hence, the poem may be motivated not only by Jonson's grief but also by his guilt at not having been present at his son's illness and death and perhaps, more generally, at having neglected his responsibilities as a parent. The poem's obsession with fatherhood and its conspicuous silence as to the boy's mother may both reflect Jonson's attempt to claim his son as his own.

Again, as in "On My First Daughter," the poem to the son is marked by tension between intellectual and emotional reactions. Jonson asks, "why / Will man lament the state he should envie?" (lines 5–6). His son has escaped through death all the miseries of life. The father knows that God is just, that his son was only lent to him, that the boy has been "Exacted by thy fate, on the just day" (line 4). But all this knowledge is at variance with his emotional response to the loss of his seven-year-old "lov'd boy" (line 2). "O, could I loose all father, now" (line 5), he exclaims, as his natural grief bursts the bonds of the intellectual restraint.

At the heart of the poem is the relationship of father and son and, more specifically, the reconciliation of a father to the loss of a son. This relationship is strikingly underlined by allusions, witty in their subtlety but austere and never indecorous. The first line, "Farewell, thou child of my right hand, and joy," alludes to the meaning of the boy's name, Benjamin, which means in Hebrew "son of the right hand." This meaning of the name is particularly touching because of the further allusion submerged in it to the account in Gen. 35:16–20 of the naming of Benjamin. The biblical child is given two contrasting names: his mother Rachel, dying in childbirth, calls him Ben-oni, child of sorrow; his father Jacob names him Benjamin. The contrast between child of sorrow and "child of my right hand, and joy" is important. In addition, the name Benjamin also carries such connotations as one on whom the father expects to count heavily for support and comfort. In this allusive and etymological context, Jonson's first line has enormous power and implication, and the borrowing and repaying metaphor of the third line is thereby given an Old Testament locus of legalistic justice. By emphasizing the happy relationship he had with his son, a child of joy, the father attempts to restrain his sorrow, to balance his present grief by memory of former happiness and by placing his son's death in a transcendental context of Christian history. What happens, however, is that while the Christian consolation yields intellectual satisfaction, the memory of the joy he took in his "lov'd boy" and the guilt he feels for his inordinate (and therefore sinful) hopes of support and comfort from his son intensify his feeling of loss.

In the tenth line, Jonson alludes to the Greek term for poet, *maker*, calling his son "his best piece of *poetrie*." This bilingual pun, prepared for by the phrase in the first line, "child of my right hand," which implies that the boy is the product of his pen (itself a pervasive pun in the Renaissance on penis), is an enormous tribute that equates procreation and poetic creation. It can be appreciated only in light of Jonson's profound respect for poetry and a knowledge of the immortality he hoped to achieve through it. If his son is his best piece of poetry, then the significance of the child's death is very great indeed. The gravestone inscription also reclaims Jonson's son as peculiarly his own, as though he created him without any help from the boy's mother. Moreover, by having the son speak the words, he receives from him "a verbal confirmation of his own love and his son's forgiveness."[28] The conflation of Jonson's initially discrete roles as poet and as father reverberates with implications for the whole poem. In retrospect, the wish to "loose all father, now" becomes even more haunting than it was originally. It expresses a wish to "lose" or escape the obligations and pain of fatherhood as well as a desire to let "loose" or unleash the powerful grief that the poem has hitherto restrained. The desire to "loose all father, now" is also sadly ironic, for the poem itself testifies to Jonson's continuing acceptance of his dual role as poet and father despite the pain such a role exacts of him.

The relationship of father and son is also pertinent to the ambiguous conclusion. The distinction Jonson makes in line 12 between "loves" and "like" is in part a distinction that stems from his obligations as a father and as a Christian.[29] As a father he is obligated to love his children and to be attentive to their welfare. As a Christian, he knows that his son's best interest is served by death. As a rigorist on the question of mourning, he knows that he should envy his son for having "so soone scap'd worlds, and fleshes rage, / And if no other miserie, yet age" (lines 6–7). But Jonson not only loves his son according to his obligations as a Christian father, he also genuinely likes the boy, and this latter affection makes the loss of his son difficult to bear even as he is able to place it within a Christian framework. Thus, the "sinne" of "too much hope of thee" in line 2 is also the liking too much in line 12. In the conclusion, the poet hopes henceforth to love only in a Christian context and never to reveal "of the resurrection little trust" (*E.* 34, line 2) by mourning the death of "the just" (*E.* 34, line 1). But the beauty of the poem, finally, is that Jonson never fully resolves this paradox of human love. The vow not to like those whom he loves is hardly a positive conclusion; it smacks of bitterness as well as sadness. At the end of the poem, the pain of loss exists alongside the Christian wisdom that is supposed to console, but that proves altogether inadequate. It is this complexity of feeling, as well as its masterful expression, that makes "On My First Sonne" one of Jonson's most moving poems.

The "Epitaph on S[alomon] P[avy] a Child of Q[ueen] El[izabeth's] Chappel" (*E.* 120) is a beautiful *tour de force.* The subject of the poem, a boy actor who performed in some of Jonson's own plays and who died at the age of 13, is celebrated as so consummate a player of old men that, ironically, the fates "thought him one, / He plai'd so truely" (lines 15 –16). The fates have since repented of their error and have sought to revive the boy, "But, being so much too good for earth, / Heaven vowes to keepe him" (lines 23 –24). The poem lacks the repressed emotion of the epitaphs for Jonson's own children, but its graceful tenderness reflects genuine feeling. The form of the work is very intricate, with its varying masculine and feminine endings and line lengths, but its artifice and theatricality are wholly in keeping with its subject. The hyperbole of the central conceit and the large personifications also call attention to the frankly artificial nature of the poem but without in any sense quali-fying its sincerity of tone. Indeed, one of the miracles of Jonson's art here is his ability to be at once playful and earnest, elaborate and restrained, witty and dignified, ironic and tender. This lovely tribute ranks among Jonson's wittiest and most imaginative achievements.

The epistolary "Inviting a Friend to Supper" (*E.* 101) is also among Jonson's finest works. Based on three of Martial's poems and infused with a spirit of classical urbanity, it is thoroughly Jonsonian.[30] It articu-lates a code of hospitality and grace that is central to Jonson's notion of civilized fellowship and enunciates a declaration of social principle in which courtesy, moderation, and freedom are the preeminent virtues. But its positive vision is seriously qualified in the poem by its acute awareness of the precariousness of its ideals in a harshly competitive and repressive society. The aesthetic and social values embodied in the poem are precisely those values the poet prizes in the commendatory epigrams when he hails his exemplary heroes and heroines as anachronistic emblems of earlier and better ages. But "Inviting a Friend to Supper" betrays the poet's consciousness of the dangers that threaten such values. Far more than a charming invitation to dinner, the poem both defines a social ideal and qualifies it with a dose of reality.

The poem breathes an air of self-confident control and shows Jonson's mastery of the pentameter couplet. The opening lines are marked by an air of courteous deference:

> To night, grave sir, both my poore house, and I
>> Doe equally desire your companie:
> Not that we thinke us worthy such a ghest,
>> But that your worth will dignifie our feast,
> With those that come; whose grace may make that seeme
>> Something, which, else, could hope for no esteeme.
>> (lines 1–6)

Despite the title, which might suggest intimacy, the invitation is addressed to a man of higher social status than the poet, probably a patron or prospective patron, and the poet acknowledges his social superiority. But as Michael Schoenfeldt points out, "The shrewd display of deference discharges the social burden that the situation imposes by redistributing the hierarchical privileges of guest and host."[31] "It is the faire acceptance, Sir, creates / The entertaynment perfect: not the cates," Jonson assures his guest, placing the onus on him for the success of the evening. Part of the good humor of this courtesy comes from the marvelous catalogue of "cates" that follows and from the capping line, "Ile tell you of more, and lye, so you will come" (line 17). The lavish fare that is promised is designed to be tempting and to demonstrate the host's taste and gracious consideration for his guest, but it is promised contingently, allowing for the probability that the host's generous intentions and vivid imagination may outstrip his financial resources. He may not be able to provide the kind of feast the guest deserves. A financially strapped poet may be better equipped at imagining a lavish feast than actually providing one.

But Jonson's menu features more than merely food, as he plans to incorporate the joys of literature into the rites of friendship. He and his guests will discuss Vergil, Tacitus, Livy, or "some better booke" (line 22). Following Martial's lead, the considerate host adds, "And Ile professe no verses to repeate" (line 24). He does, however, admit that his poetry may make an appearance nevertheless. It may be imprinted on the pastry he will serve (lines 25–26), alluding to the practice of using the pages of unsold books as wrappings in bakers' shops,[32] again subtly underlining his poverty and the neglect of poetry in his society. Indeed, the neglect of poetry in the society is directly responsible for his poverty and for his need of patronage. The feast will be accompanied by "that, which most doth take my *Muse,* and mee" (line 28): "a pure cup of rich *Canary*-wine, / Which is the *Mermaids,* now, but shall be mine" (lines 29–30). Evoking the inspiratory powers of wine and pointedly alluding to the immortalizing power of poetry, Jonson adds that had Horace or Anacreon tasted this wine, "Their lives, as doe their lines, till now had lasted" (line 32). As an antidote to the poet's self-consciousness about his social and financial inferiority to his guest, he implies the superiority of his own craft and hints at his ability to confer immortality on his patrons.

The whole poem and the social code it embodies are perceptibly deepened by the conclusion in which the poet declares "we will sup free, but moderately" (line 35). The last lines of the poem indicate more fully and more concretely the meanings of freedom and moderation Jonson intends:

> And we will have no *Pooly',* or *Parrot* by;
> Nor shall our cups make any guiltie men:
> But, at our parting, we will be, as when
> We innocently met. No simple word,
> That shall be utter'd at our mirthful boord,
> Shall make us sad next morning: or affright
> The libertie, that wee'll enjoy to night.
> (lines 36–42)

As so often in Jonson's poems, the concrete particulars of an immediate occasion unobtrusively come to symbolize large ethical issues that embrace far more than the particular or the immediate. The references to *Pooly* and *Parrot* are to government informers, the spies he attacks in *Epigram* 59. "Pooly" is probably Robert Poley who was present at the famous supper at which the young playwright and poet Christopher Marlowe was stabbed to death. The emphasis in the poem on trust, safety, innocence, moderation, mirth, and liberty reveals the ultimate seriousness beneath its veneer of lightness. The vision of the integrated life that Jonson evokes—one in which the sacred rites of friendship mirror the private and public virtues of courtesy, moderation, trust, and liberty, all infused with a passionate love of good verses—is countered by the realities of a repressive state in which poetry is unrespected and private intercourse dangerous. But the recognition of such realities makes the ideal all the more valuable. Hence, the dinner party that Jonson imagines is both an attempt to create a refuge and an attempt to preserve an ideal sorely threatened by the unsavory realities of life in seventeenth-century England. Courtesy and good fellowship can still flourish within a small circle of privacy and can help ameliorate the discontents of life in the larger world, but it can do so only on a very limited scale: The last word, "to night," not only calls attention to Jonson's characteristic circular strategy as it repeats the first word of the poem and invites a reconsideration of the beginning from the perspective of the ending but also emphasizes that the pleasures and safeties of the evening are for a brief time only.

As noted above, Jonson does not identify the guest in "Inviting a Friend to Supper." The only clues to his identity given in the poem are his superior social rank and his gravity. In light of Jonson's habit of meaningfully juxtaposing and pairing poems, however, the fact that the succeeding poem is an epigram addressed "To William Earle of Pembroke" (E. 102) may be significant. Pembroke, a nephew of Sir Philip Sidney and himself a poet, was Jonson's most reliable patron and a man deeply involved in governmental affairs. Jonson dedicated both *Epigrams* and *Catiline* to him and each year received from him the considerable sum of £20 to buy books. Moreover, Pembroke seems to have helped Jonson in his periods of disgrace after the performances of *Eastward Ho* and *Sejanus*. The Pembroke epigram and "Inviting a Friend to Supper" are linked by their common concern with the encroachment of virtue by vice and by their evocation of a repressive political climate. Just as private life in "Inviting a Friend to Supper" is threatened by government spies and the curtailment of liberty, so Pembroke is also depicted as a man under siege. His nobility "keeps one stature still, / And one true posture, though besieg'd with ill / Of what ambition, faction, pride can rase" (lines 14–16). These lines probably refer to the court party led by the earl of Northampton, who was an enemy of both Pembroke and Jonson. The epigram to Pembroke concludes in language reminiscent of "Inviting a Friend to Supper." They "that hope to see / The commonwealth still safe," Jonson tells his patron, "must study thee" (lines 19–20). Again, the emphasis is on vulnerability, though here the living presence of Pembroke provides a measure of guarded optimism, analogous perhaps to the cautious faith implicit in the proposed feast in "Inviting a Friend to Supper."

The variety and conscious artistry of *Epigrams* help explicate Jonson's claim for it as "the ripest of my studies." The volume concludes with the scatological mock-epic "On the Famous Voyage" (*E.* 133), a parodic poem whose indecorous subject is partially redeemed by infectious wit and comic delight.[33] Perhaps intended as a broad satire of Jacobean England, the poem has certain obvious affinities with the satiric epigrams, although not even by Jonson's broad conception of the genre could one classify "On the Famous Voyage" as an epigram. Jonson's volume, then, is more diverse than its name might suggest. Its 133 poems include celebrations of the poet's king and tender farewells to his children, the harsh attacks on foolish and vicious courtiers, and the commendations of contemporary heroes and heroines. But the unifying sensibility of Jonson emerges from this variety. His personality dominates all of these poems. Idealist and realist, moralist and parodist, in the *Epigrams* he is foremost a poet of his own times who brings to his responsibilities a sense of the past and a vision of the possible. He fulfills the obligations of the poet that he sketches in *Discoveries:* "Wee doe not require in him meere *Elocution;* or an excellent faculty in verse; but the exact knowledge of all vertues, and their Contraries; with ability to render the one lov'd, the other hated, by his proper embattaling them" (*Disc.,* lines 1038–41).

The Forest (1616)

The Forest first appeared in the 1616 folio *Works,* immediately following *Epigrams.* It consists of 15 poems in various forms and concerning diverse subjects. Although a small book, it includes lyrics, epistles, odes, and topographical poems and considers such subjects as love, hospitality, and religious devotion. In sum, it is very different from *Epigrams* in its size, the range of its content, and the variety of its verse forms, although the same moral and social preconceptions inform this collection as well.

The significance of Jonson's title and his high regard for this book can best be understood in light of the explanatory note "To the Reader" that he appended to the posthumous publication of *The Underwood* in the 1640–41 folio: "With the same leave, the Ancients call'd that kind of body *Sylva,* . . . in which there were workes of divers nature, and matter congested; as the multitude call Timber-trees, promiscuously growing, a *Wood,* or *Forrest:* so am I bold to entitle these lesser Poems, of later growth, by this of *Under-wood,* out of the Analogie they hold to the *Forrest,* in my former booke, and no otherwise." Thus, the title, on ancient authority, implies diversity of form and subject, and the sylvan analogy Jonson employs in naming his books indicates his higher regard for the poems of *The Forest* than for the later ones of *The Underwood.*[34] Actually, the two collections are of such different scope as to make such comparisons impossible. Still, it is true that the 15 poems of the earlier book are surprisingly various for their small number, and among them are some of Jonson's most famous and most admired poems. The collection is certainly not arranged sequentially, but it achieves coherence by virtue of its concern with recurrent themes, especially with defining the good life, and by virtue of the relatively large number of poems that address or celebrate various members of the illustrious Sidney family.

Seven of the 15 poems concern love, a subject in which Jonson is sometimes thought to lack interest. Admittedly, the poet himself helps to foster this impression. In *The Forest,* for instance, he entitles a poem "Why I Write Not of Love" (*F.* 1) and in another poem he expels Cupid, declaring, "His absence in my verse, is all I aske" (*F.* 10, line 21). And in several later poems, he presents himself as an unlikely lover: old, grayhaired, and with "so much wast, as she cannot imbrace / My mountaine belly, and my rockie face" (*U.* 9, lines 16–17). But the surprising diversity and large number of love poems in Jonson's canon, as well as the high quality of the best of them, suggest that in his erotic verse he is doing something more insistently engaging than merely demonstrating "that a poet should be able to write exhaustively about almost anything."[35] That Thomas Dekker, in *Satiro-mastix,* pictures Jonson laboring over a love lyric may indicate begrudging recognition of the poet's aspiration in this genre.[36] Noteworthy, too, is that Jonson read or quoted several of his own love poems on his famous visit to William Drummond of Hawthornden. Moreover, the very lyric that exiles Cupid serves as prelude to the "Epode" (*F.* 11), which sings of virtuous love. And the explanatory poem "Why I Write Not of Love" may itself be considered a love poem: It makes a subtle and touching statement about the human need for love. Further, in the poems that emphasize the speaker's unsuitability for love, Jonson cultivates a vital tradition of the *senex amans,* traceable at least to Horace, whose own complaint at having fallen in love with a beautiful boy at the unseemly age of 50 (*Odes,* 4.1) Jonson translates as *Underwood* 86. Finally, love is a dominant theme of the masques, those productions that "ought to be the mirrors

of mans life" (*L. T.*, lines 3–4). The love poetry, then, is not peripheral
to Jonson's total achievement but an integral part of it.

The love poems are, however, often quite unconventional. "Why I
Write Not of Love" (*F.* 1), for instance, imaginatively plays with the
reader's expectations in order to thwart them in an unpredictable manner. The poem pivots on the two different meanings of "Love"—as the
personification Cupid and as human emotion—and on a contrast of the
artificial and the real. It appears from its opening to be simply a witty
fable about Cupid but then deepens into a conclusion about human love
that starkly contrasts with the playfulness and artificiality of the beginning. The opening couplet, "Some act of *Love's* bound to reherse, / I
thought to binde him, in my verse," introduces the controlling imagery
of bondage, used in many senses throughout the poem. It also suggests
the idea, implied in the apologetic tone of the title as well, that poets are
bound to write of love and that by "binding" Cupid in their verse, the
poets reduce the power of love to the graceful mythology recounted in
the fable that follows. In the conclusion, however, Cupid flees the bonds
of art, but—in another and more important meaning—love does not:

> With which he fled me: and againe,
> Into my ri'mes could ne're be got
> By any arte. Then wonder not,
> That since, my numbers are so cold,
> When *Love* is fled, and I grow old.
> (lines 8–12)

The escape of Cupid is the poet's explanation of his refusal to write the artificial rehearsals of Love's acts, an example of which is the center of this very
poem (lines 3–7). But in the direct address to the reader of the last three
lines, the poet abandons the artificial and the mythological. He speaks as a
real person subject to age and death and in need of love. Paradoxically, his
explanation, "my numbers are so cold, / When *Love* is fled, and I grow old,"
actually binds the human emotion of love in art, and in an art more real
and more affecting than any fable of Cupid, Vulcan, and Venus could ever
be. "Why I Write Not of Love" is ultimately a love poem because it dramatizes in art an important distinction between conventional poetic treatments of love and the real human need for love in the face of time.[37]

The companion poems *Forest* 10 and 11 celebrate chaste neoplatonic
love. *Forest* 10 serves as prologue to *Forest* 11 and establishes the poet's
credibility. He abandons the conventional mythological subjects and

inspirations and declares, "I bring / My owne true fire" (lines 28–29). The end of *Forest* 10 introduces *Forest* 11: "Now my thought takes wing, / And now an *Epode* to deepe eares I sing" (lines 29–30). An epode is a classical form that alternates long and short lines and is usually serious in nature. Indeed, in an earlier version of this poem, Jonson specifically contrasts an epode with an elegy, the classical form most often used in love lyrics: "An elegie? no, muse; that asks a straine / to loose, and Cap'ring, for thy stricter veyne." The seriousness and strictness of *Forest* 11 is well conveyed by the dignified meter of the epode.

Commending the virtuous love of the Phoenix and the Dove (variously identified), *Forest* 11 disappoints in many ways. It is too long, too didactic, and too predictable. Nonetheless, it is important for the idealism of its attitude toward love and for its occasional moments of lyrical beauty. The opening of the poem establishes the moral tone of the whole: "Not to know vice at all, and keepe true state, / Is vertue, and not *Fate*" (lines 1–2). Jonson contrasts the passions of love that "still invade the minde, / And strike our reason blinde" (lines 29–30) with "true Love" (line 43) defined in neoplatonic terms. This reasonable love is celebrated in the poem's finest and best sustained passage:

> That is an essence, farre more gentle, fine,
> > Pure, perfect, nay divine;
> It is a golden chaine let downe from heaven,
> > Whose linkes are bright, and even,
> That falls like sleepe on lovers, and combines
> > The soft, and sweetest mindes
> In equall knots: This beares no brands, nor darts,
> > To murther different hearts,
> But, in a calme, and god-like unitie,
> > Preserves communitie.
> > > (lines 45–54)

In the last four of these lines, Jonson brilliantly juxtaposes neoplatonic and Petrarchan machinery in order to emphasize the peace and satisfaction of ideal love.[38] Jonson's neoplatonism is an important aspect of his love poetry, particularly that in *The Underwood*, where it is used more subtly and for greater effect than it is here.

Many of Jonson's love lyrics have a lightness of tone quite foreign to the seriousness of the "Epode." This playfulness dominates *Forest* 7,

"That Women Are But Mens Shaddowes." A lovely trifle, the poem dwells ingeniously on the paradoxical nature of courting rituals:

> Follow a shaddow, it still flies you;
> Seeme to flye it, it will pursue:
> So court a mistris, she denyes you;
> Let her alone, shee will court you.
>
> (lines 1–4)

The lyric is not weighty enough to be included among Jonson's best love poetry, but its sophisticated grace makes it far more than simply an exercise in a popular anti-Petrarchan mode. Surely Jonson's editors fail to apprehend the peculiar delicacy of tone here when they remark that the song reflects "faithfully enough the cynical view of women at large which no admiration for a few ever dislodged from his mind."[39] Jonsonian courtesy robs the poem of the cynicism potential to the tradition of paradoxical wit. This courtesy, in fact, helps distinguish Jonson's love poetry from much of that written by Donne and by the "Sons of Ben."

Jonson often individualizes his love poems by casting an aura of secrecy over the attachments they depict. The need for concealment in love is stressed by such different writers as Ovid and Baldassare Castiglione. The secrecy in Jonson's love poetry probably owes more to the latter, who, in *The Courtier,* emphasizes the importance of concealing virtuous love, than to the former, who, in *The Art of Love,* urges the practical necessity and amorous delights of concealing illicit relationships. At any rate, Jonson's fondness for identifying his subjects as existing in real time and locale outside of the poetic fiction makes the secretiveness of many of his love lyrics especially striking.

The lovers of *Forest* 6 exclude the envious world to create a private refuge of cleanly wantonness. Using a favorite Jonsonian technique of contrast, the speaker assures Celia that he is a "warie lover" (line 1) who "Can your favours keepe, and cover" (line 2) and not "the common courting jay" (line 3) who "All your bounties will betray" (line 4). This poem, partly an adaptation of Catullus 7, has been praised mainly for Jonson's superb anglicizing of the classical details.[40] But the theme of secrecy is thoroughly Jonsonian and Jonson's own. This motif helps convey a sense of the intimacy shared by the lovers, and it promotes a delicious feeling of mysterious sanctuary in the midst of an envious world.

Despite the emphasis on "stolne delights" (line 18), however, Jonson's poem avoids the libertinism of Catullus. A sweetness and a sincerity of tone in this and other Jonsonian persuasions to love differentiate them from the classical tradition of illicit pleasure. Nothing here, for instance, is equivalent to the furtiveness of Ovidian love. Jonson's individualized tone is achieved by the realistic details that place love's hyperbole in a recognizable setting, by the useful contrast of the "warie" speaker and the "common courting jay" eager to boast of amorous conquests, and by the essential innocence of the kisses.

The famous song "Come my Celia, let us prove" (F. 5) also employs the idea of secrecy, but the very lack of the speaker's innocence transforms what at first glance appears to be a persuasion to love into a cynical invitation to lust. The speaker's sinister *carpe diem* serves more to characterize him than to convince Celia. Heavily indebted to Catullus 5, Jonson's poem undercuts the Catullan spirit by gradually introducing moral values that become more and more explicit until the poem concludes with the cynical statement, "To be taken, to be seene, / These have crimes accounted beene" (lines 17–18). Even without knowledge of its original dramatic context in *Volpone,* readers cannot fail to grasp Jonson's satiric tone here.

One of Jonson's most nearly perfect lyrics depends for much of its tension on the premise of covert communication. "Drinke to me, onely, with thine eyes" (F. 9), based on several discrete passages from the letters of Philostratus, is finally much different from its classical sources, having a delicate tone completely foreign to them.[41] The inability of the speaker to communicate openly with Celia enables him to misinterpret her rejection of him. His need to believe that she returns his affection even in the face of contrary evidence reveals him as affectingly vulnerable and gives the poem considerable depth as well as grace. The lyric divides into two eight-line sections with corresponding and intricate rhyme schemes. The first section pleads for the lady to drink to the speaker or at least "leave a kisse but in the cup, / And Ile not looke for wine" (lines 3–4). The speaker's love is elevated by his compliment in lines 5–8:

> The thirst, that from the soule doth rise,
>   Doth aske a drinke divine:
> But might I of JOVE'S *Nectar* sup,
>   I would not change for thine.

Although the last two lines are sometimes interpreted to indicate that the speaker would prefer Jove's nectar to Celia's kisses, surely the more likely meaning is precisely opposite. The second section of the poem develops around the speaker's sending Celia a "rosie wreath" (line 9) that she returns. What gives the poem its touching quality is the rebuffed speaker's determined self-deception, his need to imagine that his lady returns his love as well as the rosy wreath. In the face of overwhelming evidence that Celia has no interest in him, the speaker persists in believing that they share a secret relationship. The perfect diction, delicate tone, and subtle betrayal of the speaker's vulnerability all make this one of Jonson's most beautiful poems.

Several of the poems in *The Forest* are verse epistles, a classical form especially congenial to Jonson because it calls for a familiar style and reveals the poet in his own person. As D. J. Palmer observes, "The epistolary form answered well to a new desire for a more informal use of language and a more empirical sense of reality. . . ."[42] Introduced into England in the late sixteenth century, the English adaptation was perfected by Donne and Jonson. The two most important classical masters of the form are Horace and Seneca, writers whose moral concerns and stoic philosophy are particularly attractive to Jonson. The most important aim of the classical form is to define the good life, an attempt congruent with Jonson's own notion of the function of poetry. The verse epistle is, thus, attractive to Jonson because it is a form at once public and private. It demands an intimate communication between poet and an addressed reader, yet it is an excellent medium for the expression of moral and social points of view. Rooted in the actual experience of the poet who speaks without an obvious mask, the verse letter applies the writer's observations to issues that transcend the personal.

The "*Epistle* To Elizabeth Countesse of Rutland" (*F.* 12) disappoints because it sacrifices intimacy in an attempt to accomplish disparate goals. Sent to the countess, a daughter of Sir Philip Sidney, as a New Year's Day gift in 1600, it makes much of the countess's relationship with her illustrious father and becomes itself a defense of poetry. Opening with a harsh attack on misplaced values in a gilded age, the poem deepens into a celebration of poetry's immortalizing power. The epistle's finest moment comes when Jonson contrasts poetry with wealth, beauty, and nobility:

> It is the *Muse,* alone, can raise to heaven,
>> And, at her strong armes end, hold up, and even,

> The soules, shee loves. Those other glorious notes,
>   Inscrib'd in touch or marble, or the cotes
> Painted, or carv'd upon our great-mens tombs,
>   Or in their windowes; doe but prove the wombs,
> That bred them, graves: when they were borne, they di'd,
>   That had no *Muse* to make their fame abide.
>
> (lines 41–48)

The confident dignity and subdued passion of these lines make them among the finest Jonson ever wrote. This faith in good verses is an important aspect of his personal philosophy, and it is not surprising to find it expressed in a verse epistle, which traditionally lends itself to discussions of literature. But in this poem it so overpowers the subject, who is defined only in terms of her devotion to a muse that may make her shine in conjunction with "that other starre" (line 65), Lucy, countess of Bedford, as to destroy any feeling of intimate communication between poet and subject. As presented in *The Forest,* the poem abruptly breaks off at line 93, with the notation "The rest is lost." Actually, the ending of the poem, which conveys the hope that the countess would soon bear a son, was suppressed because by the time of the publication of *The Forest* in 1616, the earl of Rutland was known to be impotent.

The "*Epistle.* To Katherine, Lady Aubigny" (*F.* 13) is altogether more successful; it is more familiar, and it more naturally integrates the poet's public and private concerns. Addressed to the wife of one of Jonson's closest friends, Esmé Stuart, Seigneur d'Aubigny, with whom Jonson lodged for five years, and to whom he addresses *Epigram* 127 and dedicates *Sejanus,* the epistle gains power by its intimacy of detail, sincerity of tone, and reliance on the poet's personal experience. In a characteristic Jonsonian manner, the poem opens by portraying a debased age in which virtuous individuals are a lonely few. The poet forcefully asserts his own integrity in the opening lines, an integrity maintained at high personal cost in a vicious world. Illustrating the Horatian observation that "The good hate vice because they love virtue" (*Epistles*1, line 52), he recounts his own suffering and stoic resolution, culminating in line 21 with the first mention of Lady Aubigny: "I, *Madame,* am become your praiser." The purpose of this self-congratulation is not mere indulgence. The personal experience of the poet establishes his credentials, and inasmuch as it is an exemplum of lonely virtue, it reflects the very qualities Lady Aubigny comes to embody in the course of the poem that mirrors the beauties of her mind.

Foremost of these qualities is her independence of thought and stoic indifference to fashion:

> wisely you decline your life,
>> Farre from the maze of custome, error, strife,
>> And keepe an even, and unalter'd gaite.
>>> (lines 59–61)

Like the poet, the lady finds comfort in her conscience, her isolated virtue, even amidst the "turning world" (line 64) and its vicissitudes. Beyond this, Lady Aubigny will triumph over the debased age, for she possesses virtue, which alone "can time, and chance defeat" (line 51). Jonson's praise for the beauty of the lady's mind is in contrast to the world's praise of superficial and cosmetic physical beauty, and it is reminiscent of the compliment extended to Lucy, countess of Bedford, in *Epigram* 76. Interestingly, Jonson also praises Lady Aubigny as an exemplary wife whose "chast love" (line 96) for her husband yields a "noble stemme" (line 97). The account of the love of Lord and Lady Aubigny, whose "soules conspire, as they were gone / Each into other, and had now made one" (lines 119–20), is gently intimate and helps make concrete what might otherwise seem a portrait of abstract virtue.

The epistle's final lines return to the controlling metaphor of the mirror and to the theme of Lady Aubigny's consistent independence of thought:

> and as long yeeres doe passe,
>> *Madame,* be bold to use this truest glasse:
>> Wherein, your forme, you still the same shall finde;
>> Because nor it can change, nor such a minde.
>>> (lines 121–24)

This is an especially effective conclusion, resolving a number of issues touched on earlier. It tactfully implies what is explicit in *Forest* 12, where the poet declares that—in contrast to poetry—beauty and wealth and blood are all subject to mutability and decay. At the end of this poem, Jonson looks ahead to the passing of time and recognizes that only in the frozen art of his "truest glasse" will Lady Aubigny's form remain untouched by time's passage. But whereas in *Forest* 12 poetry's immortalizing power is self-servingly, though movingly, asserted, here the promise of immortality stems from richer and more complex associations. It is the truth of the poem as a faithful mirror of Lady Aubigny's constant virtue that assures her immortality. Thus, the conclusion is not self-congratulatory; it is a graceful extension of the compliment that the poem as a whole represents. It explicates the earlier assurance that virtue "can time, and chance defeat" (line 51). By tactfully implying the physical changes inevitably to be wrought by time and finding a parallel between unchanging poetry and unchanging virtue, the conclusion is a moving declaration of faith in true poetry and true virtue at a time when both are imperiled.

"To Penshurst" (F. 2), which inaugurated a significant English tradition of poems in praise of country houses, may be Jonson's supreme success in creating verse that is simultaneously public and private.[43] Formally an ode and directed to the estate of Sir Robert Sidney, Lord Lisle, rather than to him personally, it is nevertheless very similar to the verse epistle because it addresses the country house as though it were a person. The poem's tone is one of dignified familiarity, thus creating an illusion of genuine communication between poet and patron, and Jonson bases his praise of the illustrious family on his own personal experience, casting himself as a recipient of Penshurst's hospitality. As J. C. A. Rathmell has demonstrated, the poem reveals the poet's knowledge of the estate's intimate domestic details and may be viewed as a discreet reminder to the financially troubled Lord Lisle of the true nature of his fortune.[44] But "To Penshurst" is clearly more than a poem of advice to an individual patron. It articulates an ideal of civilized life in a well-ordered society. It presents Penshurst as a paragon, a positive pattern to guide readers in search of the good life, and in doing so, it employs a negative formula of praise, contrasting the Sidney estate with others that fall short of that ideal. By these contrasts, it communicates an urgent awareness of the forces that threaten to undermine the values that Penshurst represents.

The opening of the poem establishes the bases of Penshurst's claim to praise. Unlike ostentatious new estates built to prideful and expensive "show" (line 1) and resented by their communities, Penshurst has grown from ancient traditions and is "reverenc'd" (line 6). Whereas the beauty of the other estates lies in gaudy decoration, the beauty of Penshurst is natural. Its "better markes" (line 7) are those of the four elements, and the estate comes to epitomize the harmonious coexistence of man and nature within God's great chain of being. In lines 45–47, another contrast between Penshurst and other country houses is implied. While the building of lavish estates often resulted from capitalistic exploitation and led to agrarian disruption, Penshurst's walls are "rear'd with no mans ruine, no mans grone, / There's none, that dwell about them, wish them downe" (lines 46–47). The enlightened, traditional social attitudes of the Sidneys earn them the respect and esteem of their tenants and neighbors. Moreover, the hospitality at Penshurst is in marked contrast to that of other great houses:

> And I not faine to sit (as some, this day,
>   At great mens tables) and yet dine away.
> Here no man tells my cups; nor, standing by,
>   A waiter, doth my gluttony envy.
>   (lines 65–68)

The complaint of a guest being served food inferior to that enjoyed by the host is a frequent one in classical literature, and Jonson undoubtedly intends his readers to recognize an allusion to Martial, *Epigrams* 3.9. But the contrast here between Penshurst and other great houses may be more localized and based on more than bookish knowledge, for Jonson apparently experienced in reality the same poor hospitality of which Martial complains. He told William Drummond that he protested to Robert Cecil, earl of Salisbury, owner of the lavish country estate Theobalds, "My Lord . . . yow promised I should dine with yow, bot I doe not. . . ." (*Conv.*, lines 318–19). A further contrast made in "To Penshurst" concerns the chastity of Lady Lisle, whose children her husband can be certain are his, "A fortune, in this age, but rarely knowne" (line 92). The domestic life at Penshurst thus incorporates a code of sexual morality that has become increasingly rare in the larger world. The poem concludes with a contrast paralleling that made in the opening lines:

> Now, PENSHURST, they that will proportion thee
>   With other edifices, when they see
> Those proud, ambitious heaps, and nothing else,
>   May say, their lords have built, but thy lord dwells.
>   (lines 99–102)

The precise diction here implies the true measure of Penshurst, not as a building but as a way of life transcending individual pride. The use of contrast is, of course, a characteristic technique of Jonson's praise throughout his works, but it functions particularly well in "To Pen-shurst" to establish a social context in which to view the ideal that the Sidney estate represents. This context gives the celebration an urgency it might otherwise lack.

Each of the two large divisions of the poem is organized to adhere to the hierarchical structure of the great chain of being and of the tradi-tional social order, itself a reflection of that chain. It is important to stress that these hierarchies are presented as nonoppressive and nurtur-ing. Just as the fish and the game and the fruit are described as eager to serve humanity, so each group of people is portrayed as looking with love and respect on those higher in the social order. As Don E. Wayne observes, "the 'chain of being' at Penshurst is also a chain of giving: the land gives of itself, animals give of themselves, peasants give of them-selves, ripe daughters give of themselves, ladies give of themselves to lords, lords give of themselves to kings."[45] Jonson's presentation of these hierarchies clearly mystifies actual social (and indeed natural) relation-ships, as it does labor itself, but he is, after all, devising an idealized rather than a realistic portrait. The first large section of the poem, lines 1–47, concentrates on the external features of the estate, emphasizing its natural harmony and bounty. The mythological figures introduced in lines 10–17 serve to connect the estate with classical ideals, particularly with Julius Caesar's estate at Tartessus, which was celebrated by Martial in *Epigrams* 9. 61, and to establish poetry as a natural part of the estate that contains "That taller tree" (line 13) planted in honor of the birth of Lord Lisle's deceased elder brother Sir Philip Sidney, in whom "all the *Muses* met" (line 14). Jonson's conception of Penshurst may be signifi-cantly influenced by the description of Kalander's house in Sir Philip's prose romance *The Arcadia,* so this courteous allusion to Penshurst's poetic son is especially appropriate.

Because poetry is a valued part of the estate's ancient traditions, it is not surprising to find the poet himself comfortably ensconced in the poem's second half, which depicts life indoors. The poet is assigned a middle position in the order that reflects the good life, as necessary to the social fabric as the peasants or the royalty who are also depicted. He is an honored guest, "all is there; / As if thou, then, wert mine, or I raign'd here" (lines 73–74), and the same hospitality extended to the poet is accorded King James and Prince Henry when they pay an unex-pected visit. As Michael Schoenfeldt remarks, "Lisle's hospitality, rather than forcing Jonson to taste his bitter subjugation, allows him to feel like a king" (73). It is noteworthy that the entertainment extended to the King and his son is "sodayne" but not "great" (line 82), fit but not lavish, perfectly in keeping with the ideal of moderation espoused in "Inviting a Friend to Supper" (*E.* 101). Lady Lisle's "high huswifery" (line 85) earns praise on that occasion, but her greater merit lies in being "noble, fruitfull, chaste withall" (line 90). Moreover, the Sidney children "are, and have beene taught religion" (line 93) and may "Reade, in their vertuous parents noble parts, / The mysteries of manners, armes, and arts" (lines 97–98). By introducing children into the poem, Jonson looks forward to the future, intimating the continuation of those values that the "ancient pile" (line 5) has inherited from the past. The "mysteries of manners, armes, and arts" are the lessons of an integrated life within a harmonious order in which man and nature, lord and tenant, poet and patron, husband and wife, parents and children all function to form an organic unit.

The verse epistle "To Sir Robert Wroth" (*F.* 3) is informed by the same vision expressed in "To Penshurst," but it is directed more narrowly toward praise of the country life. Moreover, its intention is not to articulate a social ideal but, more pointedly, to convince Wroth that his life in the country is happier than it would be in the city. It idealizes country life and satirizes city vice, but its portrayal lacks the stately dignity and broad scope of "To Penshurst." Influenced by a rich classical tradition of poems in celebration of rural retirement, a tradition that includes Horace's *Epode* 2 and Vergil's *Georgics,* it sings the "securer rest" (line 13) of the owner of the country estate Durrants and the husband of Sir Robert Sidney's daughter, Lady Mary. At Durrants, Wroth enjoys the pleasures of the Golden Age: rural sports, the variety of the seasons, mirth and cheer, poetry and dance, and the easy mingling of diverse social classes. The hospitality at Durrants is beautifully sketched in lines 53–60, the description of a winter festivity, which invokes the estate's connection with the Sidney family while simultaneously offering a vision of good fellowship that temporarily transcends class structure. Throughout the poem, Jonson contrasts the prideful acquisitiveness, competitiveness, and vice of the city and court with the natural bounty and innocence of the country. These contrasts have a far sharper satiric edge than those in "To Penshurst," as in lines 67–90. Within the poem, the vigor of such attacks gives force to Jonson's advice to Wroth to be content with his lot even if city life might superficially appear attractive and exciting.

The poem's argument for Wroth's acceptance of a country life is given religious justification in a conclusion indebted to Juvenal's tenth satire: God "alwayes gives what he knowes meet; / Which who can use is happy: Such be thou" (lines 98–99). The nature of this advice and the terms in which it is given prompt speculation that perhaps Wroth's retirement was not altogether voluntary. Jonson, although he apparently did not like him, actually knew Sir Robert fairly well, addressing his wife in *Epigrams* 103 and 105 and in *Underwood* 28 as well as dedicating *The Alchemist* to her. Yet he appears uncertain whether Wroth lives in the country by "choice, or fate" (line 2). Coupled with the poem's vociferous attack on city life, this studied uncertainty may suggest by reticence that Wroth's ambitions in the larger world have been frustrated. Jonson encourages him to adopt the Ciceronian viewpoint that it is blessed "for the soul, after having, as it were, finished its campaigns of lust and ambition, of strife and enmity and of all the passions, to return within itself, and, as the saying is, 'to live apart'!" (*De Senectute,* 14.49). Jonson fulfills his self-imposed obligation to advise his patrons discreetly but forthrightly. Whatever its immediate motivations, "To Sir Robert Wroth" is a fine tribute to the joys of life apart from the city's vice.

The celebration of country life in "To Penshurst," "To Sir Robert Wroth," and in other poems and masques makes clear the nature of Jonson's conservative ideal in a changing society. The contrast between town and country was particularly acute in the early seventeenth century, when the London metropolitan area was rapidly growing into a capitalist center dominated by "new men" whose fortunes were based on trade and finance rather than on the land. The decline of the old order and the rise of capitalism were accompanied by inevitable social strain and by the rise of religious Puritanism. Jonson directs much of his satire against the vices he particularly associated with the city: corruption and affectation, usury and financial exploitation, hypocrisy and intolerance. Conversely, he praises the countryside as the home of established order, proven tradition, and innocent pleasures. But it may be a mistake to read Jonson's criticism of urban life too literally as an attack on contemporary social conditions. The dispraise of cities and the celebration of rural retirement are persistent themes in classical literature, and the vices that the poet attacks are conventional targets. In any case, Jonson, among the most urban oriented of English poets, who lived almost his entire life in London, is also a poet with very deep affinities for the rural.

Like "To Sir Robert Wroth," another poem addressed to a member of the Sidney family also offers advice. The "Ode. To Sir William Sidney" (*F.* 14) celebrates its subject's twenty-first birthday in November 1611. A complexly organized, ceremonial poem usually designed for utterance on a public occasion, the ode is another form for which Jonson has a natural proclivity. The Sidney ode is written in the most complex stanzaic form of any of Jonson's poems. Despite the intricacy of rhyme and meter, however, the poem's diction is simple and its syntax natural. It frankly but gracefully advises the young man, the eldest son of Sir Robert Sidney, to "Strive all right wayes . . . / T'out-strip your peeres" (lines 25–26). Jonson pointedly stresses that the Sidney heir apparent cannot rely on the achievements of his famous forebears: "For they, that swell / With dust of ancestors, in graves but dwell" (lines 39–40). This advice may have been particularly welcomed by Sir William's parents, because the young man seems to have been a disappointment to his family. He sparked a scandal some years previous to the poem by seriously wounding his schoolmaster.[46] Throughout the ode, there is a fine tension between Jonson's desire to celebrate Sir William on his birthday and his need to admonish him to live up to his name and responsibilities. Jonson resolves this tension by creating a voice that is simultaneously—and naturally—celebratory and admonitory. The intricate song stanza contributes to the celebratory tone, thus helping make the admonition palatable. The advice itself stems naturally from the poem's ceremonial occasion: "This day sayes, then, the number of glad yeeres / Are justly summ'd, that make you man" (lines 21–22). The poem is a tactful but firm reminder of human and social responsibilities.

The Forest includes two remarkable poems that reveal Jonson in a melancholy mood and help to place in perspective the image of conviviality that he often cultivates. The first of these, "To the World" (*F.* 4), is subtitled *"A farewell for a Gentle-woman, vertuous and noble."* Having been abused and betrayed in her youth, this mature lady (who has not been identified) is repulsed by the decayed and corrupted world. She accepts unhappiness as her inevitable lot in a postlapsarian era:

> I doe know, that I was borne
> To age, misfortune, sicknesse, griefe:
> But I will beare these, with that scorne,
> As shall not need thy false reliefe.
> (lines 61–64)

She retreats from the contemptible world, finding peace in stoic resolution. She vows to "make my strengths, such as they are, / Here in my bosome, and at home" (lines 67–68). This ideal of the "gather'd selfe," as it is termed in *Epigram* 98, is frequently voiced in Jonson's work. It reflects his philosophical adherence to Christian stoicism and reveals another facet of the idealism that animates so much of his poetry. His contempt for the world and his attacks on the misplaced values of a debased age give urgency to the personal and public ideals he celebrates and add poignancy to the individual and social possibilities he envisions.

The speaker of "To Heaven" (*F.* 15) lacks the mature self-confidence of the gentlewoman in *Forest* 4. Among Jonson's most enigmatic poems, "To Heaven" is an intensely personal self-inquisition.[47] Its tension stems from the speaker's doubt of his own motives. More specifically, he is uncertain whether his discontent with the world, his longing for "ease" (line 4), his death wish, results from the dangerous despair of melancholy or from his soul's hunger to be with God. This is a crucial question, for the answer to it makes all the difference as to the speaker's salvation. Christian theologians almost unanimously condemn suicide, St. Augustine characterizing it as the one unforgivable sin, for the sinner has no opportunity to repent.[48] But not everyone who longs for death is guilty of suicidal impulses. Even St. Paul prayed for release from this life, as Jonson indicates in line 24, alluding to Rom. 7:24. The test for deciding whether a death wish is sinful or laudable is a test of the individual's motivation. John Donne, in his daring study of suicide, *Biathanatos,* explains the acceptable motive for wanting to die and cites John Calvin as his authority: "yet certainly S. *Paul* had some allowable reasons, *to desire to be dissolved, and be with Christ.* And Calvin by telling us upon what reason, and to what end he wished this, instructs us how we may wish the same. He sayes, Paul desired not death, for deaths sake, for that were against the sense of Nature, but he wished it to be with Christ."[49] "To Heaven" reveals Jonson in a troubled mood, "laden with my sinnes" (line 4), and longing for release from earthly life.

The most remarkable aspect of the poem is its speaker's acute self-consciousness. In *Epigram* 119, Jonson extols Sir Ralph Shelton, a wealthy Catholic, for knowing his own way, "Which is to live to conscience, not to show" (line 14). Here Jonson is not quite sure of his own conscience, and he wonders if he might not be living for show. The only certainty he knows is the spiritual crisis he feels. Long infatuated with worldly things, he unexpectedly feels God stoop to touch his heart (line 14). "Where have I beene this while exil'd from thee?" (line 13), he asks and implores God, "Dwell, dwell here still" (line 15). But his longing to be with God and to escape from the miseries of the world may itself be sinful, reflecting his melancholy weariness of life rather than his love of

God. Throughout the poem, he alternates between self-accusation and assertions of guiltlessness. He appeals to God as final arbiter, tellingly echoing Psalm 26, David's song of innocence:

> O, be thou witnesse, that the reynes dost know,
> And hearts of all, if I be sad for show,
> And judge me after: if I dare pretend
> To ought but grace, or ayme at other end.
>
> (lines 5–8)

The very intensity of the protest betrays self-doubt.

Jonson's self-doubt is also apparent in his moving assertion of self-knowledge. These lines, reminiscent of the gentlewoman's resignation from the world in *Forest* 4, acknowledge vulnerability:

> I know my state, both full of shame, and scorne,
> Conceiv'd in sinne, and unto labour borne,
> Standing with feare, and must with horror fall,
> And destin'd unto judgement, after all.
>
> (lines 17–20)

But whereas the lady's acceptance of the human condition in a corrupt world mirrors her secure self-reliance, this speaker's intellectual assessment of his state reflects a much more complex response. This difference is related to a fundamental difference between the two speakers: The gentlewoman's confident virtue insulates her from doubt, while the speaker in "To Heaven" undergoes a more immediate spiritual crisis in which he feels his guilt even as he protests his innocence. His genuine sense of sinfulness coexists with what he fears may be a prideful rejection of the world. The phrase "after all" in line 20, following as it does a list of tribulations to which we are heirs in this world, conveys a distinct hint of petulance: After all these earthly miseries, there is still the ordeal of judgment. The speaker adds, "I feele my griefes too, and there scarce is ground, / Upon my flesh to'inflict another wound" (lines 21–22). These telling lines, recalling Ovid's complaint that the gods are conspiring against him (*Epistulae Ex Ponto* 2.7. 41–42), sound a note of despair, make explicit the threat of self-destruction that haunts the poem, and indicate the depth of Jonson's spiritual crisis.

The conclusion resolves the issue of suicide. The speaker dares not

> complaine, or wish for death
> With holy PAUL, lest it be thought the breath
> Of discontent; or that these prayers bee
> For wearinesse of life, not love of thee.
>
> (lines 23–26)

This conclusion is unconvincing in the terms in which it is presented. The whole poem has been a complaint. The concern "lest it be thought" (line 24) parallels other statements in which Jonson fears his religious motivations might be misunderstood. But the earlier statements might be interpreted as reasonable fear that other people might think him a hypocrite (cf. Matt. 6:16–18), while the conclusion indicates apprehension that God might somehow err in judgment. This suggestion is ludicrous, even blasphemous, and incongruent with the earlier assertions of trust in God if the poem is taken to be a prayer. Actually, however, despite its title and its direct address to God, the poem is not so much a prayer as a self-inquisition into the speaker's longing for death. This self-examination is what in the seventeenth century might be described as meditation: "a diligent and forcible application of the understanding, to seeke, and knowe, and as it were to tast some divine matter; from whence doth arise in our affectionate powers good motions, inclinations, and purposes which stirre us up to the love and exercise of vertue, and the hatred and avoiding of sinne."[50] By meditating on his longings for death, the speaker attempts to avoid the sin to which the longings might lead. "To Heaven" is a fascinating exploration of religious consciousness and the one poem in which Jonson approaches the spiritual passion and introspection of Donne.

The Forest is a small but rewarding selection that reveals Jonson in a variety of moods and forms. In the brief span of this gathering, he is love poet, devotional poet, and public poet. He displays intensely private emotion as well as genuine engagement with social issues. He is both "morose Ben Jonson" and the convivial singer of hospitality. *The Forest* gives a good indication of Jonson's versatility and of his mastery of diverse forms from the love lyric and the familiar epistle to the formal ode. It is Jonson's most carefully pruned collection. His criteria for inclusion may have been many, but among them was the simple one of poetic excellence.

The Underwood (1640 – 41)

The Underwood was first published in the posthumous folio Works of 1640 – 41, seen through the press by Jonson's friend Sir Kenelm Digby, who gained access to the manuscripts upon the poet's death in 1637. Jonson apparently planned to publish the collection in 1631, when he wrote the brief, apologetic preface referring to its contents as "these lesser Poems, of later growth." It is impossible to determine exactly how much effort Jonson himself spent in the arrangement of the poems within the collection. There is, in fact, no obvious thematic organization, but there may be a rough chronological order: Most of the first 42 poems were probably written before Jonson's famous visit to Scotland in 1619, whereas the latter 46 were probably composed after the visit. According to Annabel Patterson, the effect of the collection as a whole "is a retrospective of his career, a retelling of his relations with the state, the stage, friends, patrons, politicians,"[51] but such a description, expansive as it is, overemphasizes the political and fails to do justice to the variety of theme and subject explored in The Underwood.

Dating from as early as 1600 and including some poems that were deliberately excluded from The Forest, the individual pieces of The Underwood vary widely in quality. But the collection itself is not much inferior to the Epigrams or The Forest. It contains far more successes than failures. Indeed, the later poems eloquently give evidence to Jonson's continuing power as a nondramatic poet throughout his life. Among the poems of The Underwood are some of Jonson's finest and most ambitious efforts. In this final gathering he continues to fulfill the social functions he accepted as his responsibility, but more frequently than in the earlier books he focuses upon himself as an idiosyncratic and vulnerable individual. Thus the book as a whole seems somewhat more personal than the two earlier ones.

The Underwood opens with a nonidiosyncratic though nevertheless personal work, the "Poems of Devotion" (U. 1), fittingly divided into three parts to form a contemplative trio of religious lyrics. Each of the three pieces is self-contained and may rightly be regarded as a separate poem, yet the series as a whole is greater than the sum of its parts. Each lyric progresses from a conviction of personal unworthiness to a meditation on God's love and culminates in an assurance of salvation, mirroring in effect the movement of the whole toward a celebration of Christ's nativity, the event that makes us all "heires of glory!" (1.3.21). In addition, each succeeding lyric builds upon the preceding one. The first piece ends with a vision of mystical union, thus imparting great confidence to the second, an assurance that expands into restrained but joyous celebration in the third. The series is personal but not eccentric. Throughout one is aware of an individual speaker's relationship with God; the thoughtful articulation of faith has very much a personal tone. But the details of sin, contrition, and manifestations of mercy are generalized. God's love is embraced as an offer of salvation to all, and not just to the speaker. The Christmas hymn ends with the universal question "Can man forget this Storie?" (1.3.24). There are moments of anguish and rapture, but in general the emotion is understated. This understatement may betray the influence of the medieval religious lyric, an influence that may also explain the intricate metrical patterns of the poems alongside the apparent simplicity of their religious feeling.[52]

The first of the lyrics, "The Sinners Sacrifice" (*U.*1.1), is subtitled "*To the Holy Trinitie.*" It is structured according to the meditative pattern of St. Bernard of Clairvaux (Cubeta, 103–5). The initial step in meditation is what Bernard describes as the *humilitas,* a process of purgation and self-knowledge. In this section, Jonson depicts himself as "harrow'd, torne, and bruis'd / By sinne, and Sathan; and my flesh misus'd" (lines 5–6). Presenting to "All-gracious God" (line 9) his broken heart, he begs forgiveness. In the second section, the *compassio,* Jonson moves from a narrow self-absorption to a comprehension of the plight of all human beings. Lovingly addressing each part of the Trinity, he makes a universal plea for "The gladdest light, darke man can thinke upon" (line 35). The final division of the lyric, the *contemplatio,* is an exalted adoration of God's tripartite mystery and an intensely felt vision of ultimate acceptance:

> My Maker, Saviour, and my Sanctifier:
> To heare, to mediate, sweeten my desire,
> With grace, with love, with cherishing intire.
>   (lines 41–43)

The lyric moves from personal anguish to an apprehension of the speaker as a member of the human community and, finally, to a mystical vision of unity with the three-personed God.

Jonson's treatment of the Trinity in this first lyric is an orthodox reflection of Anglican attitudes. The first of the articles of religion in the Anglican Church (as reestablished by the Convocation of 1563) is "Of Faith in the Holy Trinity." It declares that "in unity of this Godhead there be three Persons, of one substance, power, and eternity; the Father, the Son, and the Holy Ghost," a position restated by Jonson in his tenth stanza. Similarly, the poem is informed by the second article, "Of the Word or Son of God, which was made very Man." This article stresses Christ's duality: he "took Man's nature . . . so that two whole and perfect Natures, that is to say, the Godhead and Manhood, were joined together in one Person, never to be divided, whereof is one Christ, very God, and very Man; who truly suffered, was crucified, dead, and buried, to reconcile his Father to us, and to be a sacrifice, not only for original guilt, but also for actual sins of men." Jonson's second stanza reflects this theology, occasionally echoing the wording of the article itself. Jonson contemplates the Holy Ghost as "*Eternall Spirit,* God from both proceeding, / Father and Sonne" (lines 25–26), thus recalling the fifth article, which states, "The Holy Ghost, proceeding from the Father and the Son, is of one substance, majesty, and glory, with the Father and the Son, very and eternal God." Rooted as it is in the Anglican articles of religion, the poem testifies to the poet's reconciliation with the Established Church, a reconciliation that, he told Drummond, he celebrated by drinking up the whole cup of communion wine (*Conv.,* lines 314–16). Jonson's editors are correct when they remark of "The Sinners Sacrifice" that "he produces the current theology in the current phrases" (H. & S., 2:392), but they are wrong to see this as pedanticism or lack of personal commitment. The poems of devotion deliberately submerge individual eccentricity into a larger, more universal vision of the human community united by God's love. The echoes of communal religious belief are thus appropriate and meaningful.

The second lyric, although it admits the speaker's sinful nature and asks God to "Use still thy rod" (line 4), lacks the sense of spiritual doubt that pervades "To Heaven" (*F.* 15). Any potential anguish has been dissipated by the first lyric in the series and by the theological bias of the whole. In "A Hymne to God the Father" (*U.* 1. 2), Jonson accepts his sinfulness as original sin, "the fault and corruption of the Nature of every man, that naturally is engendered of the offspring of Adam; whereby man is very far gone from original righteousness, and is of his own nature inclined to evil, so that the flesh lusteth always contrary to the Spirit," as it is described in the articles of religion. He gladly embraces God's sacrifice of his Son "To free a slave" (line 20).

In the final piece, "A Hymne On the Nativitie of my Saviour" (*U.* 1. 3), Jonson focuses on that sacrifice, the issue of God's love.[53] He echoes the "gladdest light" of the first lyric in the opening couplet of the third: "I sing the birth, was borne to night, / The Author both of Life, and light." In lines packed with theological significance but presented with studied disingenuousness, the poet celebrates Christ's nativity, the birth of "the Babe, all innocence; / A Martyr borne in our defence" (lines 22–23). Jonson concentrates on Christ as *Theantropos*, the Word of God become human:

> Both wills were in one stature;
> And as that wisedome had decreed,
> The Word was now made Flesh indeed,
> And tooke on him our Nature.
>   (lines 15–18)

By emphasizing Christ's duality, the final lyric partakes of that unity of humankind with God that concluded "The Sinners Sacrifice." The simple statement and conversational ring of these lyrics, achieved within varied and intricate patterns, are reminiscent of the poetry of George Herbert. As with Herbert, Jonson's apparent simplicity, a simplicity born of tone and diction rather than of any poverty of ideas, gives his religious expression a feeling of humility in the presence of sacred mystery. In his works Jonson only occasionally appears truly humble; thus, the humility of these religious lyrics is all the more affecting.

A surprisingly large number of poems in *The Underwood* concern love. Although Jonson is seldom recognized as an important love poet, he merits such consideration, as the poems of *The Forest* suggest and those of *The Underwood* verify. He is often labeled cynical in his attitudes toward love and women, but apart from a few exercises in a tradition of wit in which he is both uncomfortable and ill equipped, this charge cannot be supported by the poetry itself. Even in poems in which he adopts the popular anti-Petrarchan stance, he characteristically tempers the cynicism common to such works. For instance, in the two *Underwood* poems in which he assumes a female persona to defend the promiscuity of women (*U.* 5 and 6), the poet prevents them from being read as serious indictments. Self-reflexive humor and a lightness of tone—a true Anacreontic gaiety—rescue them from that undercurrent of gravity that disturbs the superficial playfulness of Donne's poems on the same subject. Ringing changes on a familiar theme, the woman speaker of *Underwood* 6 defends inconstancy with great verve and wit. In closing, the poem neatly reverses itself to declare, "were the worthiest woman curst / To love one man, hee'd leave her first" (lines 23–24).

Rather than being cynical, Jonson is most often idealistic in his approach to love. His most important statement of ideal love is *Underwood* 88, his beautiful translation of a supposed fragment of Petronius Arbiter:

> Doing, a filthy pleasure is, and short;
> And done, we straight repent us of the sport:
> Let us not then rush blindly on unto it,
> Like lustfull beasts, that onely know to doe it:
> For lust will languish, and that heat decay.
> But thus, thus, keeping endlesse Holy-day,
> Let us together closely lie, and kisse,
> There is no labour, nor no shame in this;
> This hath pleas'd, doth please, and long will please; never
> Can this decay, but is beginning ever.[54]

The contrast between bestial lust and human love is a crucial one for Jonson. He opposes the guilt of the former to the innocence of the latter, the brief impermanence of lust to the enduring pleasure of love. Like Shakespeare's Sonnet 129, "Th' expense of spirit in a waste of shame," and Donne's "Farewell to Love," *Underwood* 88 realistically acknowledges conflicting impulses in the instinct to love. It avoids overt moralizing to concentrate on the fullness of emotional satisfaction. It thereby convinces by means of psychological insight rather than through conventional interdiction. For Jonson, the keeping of endless holiday is the liberating ideal of a love that continually renews itself. This ideal is never far from the poet's apprehension of love, even when he depicts relationships that question the possibility of the ideal.

Of immense significance to an understanding of Jonson's attitude toward love is the submerged neoplatonism of *Underwood* 88, a philosophy of love that subtly informs much of Jonson's serious amorous verse. Perhaps the most revealing gloss of *Underwood* 88 is the impassioned oration of Bembo in the fourth book of Castiglione's *Book of the Courtier,* a work that exerted great influence on Jonson. Bembo condemns physical love in terms similar to those of Jonson's translation, observing that sensual lovers, "as soone as they be come to the coveted ende . . . feele a fulnesse and lothsomnesse."[55] He also remarks that "Too unluckie were the nature of man, if oure soule (in the which this so fervent covetinge [of beauty] may lightlie arise) should be driven to nourish it with that onelye, which is commune to her with beastes, and could not tourn it to the other noble parte, which is propre to her" (352). Although beauty completely severed from the physical body that originally inspires it may be the most perfect, Bembo does allow Platonic lovers "lawfullye and without blame [to] come to kissinge," which is "a knitting together both of body and soule":

> the reasonable lover woteth well, that although the mouthe be a percell of the bodye, yet is it an issue for the wordes, that be the enterpreters of the soule: and therfore hath a delite to joigne hys mouth with the womans beloved with a kysse: not to stirre him to anye unhonest desire, but because he feeleth that, that bonde is the openynge of an entry to the soules. . . . Whereupon a kisse may be said to be rather a cooplinge together of the soule, then of the bodye, bicause it hath such force in her, that it draweth her unto it, and (as it were) separateth her from the bodye. For this do all chaste lovers covett a kisse, as a cooplinge of soules together. And therfore Plato the divine lover saith, that in kissing, his soule came as far as his lippes to depart out of the body. (355 –56)

Thus physical love can serve as a means to higher union. The ending of *Underwood* 88, which emphasizes the circular perfection of "endlesse Holy-day" and its "beginning ever," echoes the neoplatonic commonplace that "love is a circle, which turnes from good to good by an everlasting revolution,"[56] an idea further illuminated by Bembo's explanation that "beawtie commeth of God, and is like a circle, the goodnesse wherof is the Centre" (348).

Jonson often submerges the philosophical underpinning of his poetry. As a consequence, the idealistic cast to the love poetry has been mostly overlooked. Yet the importance of neoplatonism to Jonson's love poetry can hardly be overestimated. It may be that full appreciation of even a nonplatonic poem hinges on familiarity with neoplatonic documents. For instance, in "The Houre-glasse" (*U.* 8), Jonson questions his readers about the dust "running in the Glasse" (line 2):

> Could you beleeve, that this,
>   The body ever was
>   Of one that lov'd?
> And in his Mrs. flame, playing like a flye,
>   Turn'd to cinders by her eye?

> Yes; and in death, as life, unblest,
>> To have't exprest,
> Even ashes of lovers find no rest.
>   (lines 4–11)

Usually traced to Girolamo Amaltei's *Horologium Pulverum* (1603), this wry poem may be informed at least partially by the characterization in *The Courtier* of foolish women who attempt "to gete them a great number of lovers, and (if it were possible) they would have them al to burne and make asshes, and after death to retourn to lief, to die again" (285). Neoplatonism, then, is an essential ingredient in Jonson's poetry, adding depth and meaning to the realistic depictions of sexual attachments. Characteristically, Jonson's neoplatonism is a moderate philosophy that permits sensuality but not excess; he adopts a sensible, middle position that avoids both the unrequited worship of the Petrarchan lover and the otherworldly spiritual ecstasy of extreme neoplatonists like Marsilio Ficino but preserves the idealism of both. As Hugh Richmond observes of other poets who employ neoplatonic ideas, Jonson uses "the theories not for their own sakes but to illuminate essential features of the dramatic situations . . . in his lyrics."[57]

Apart from a few lyrics in a pastoral vein that celebrate idealized love in a mood of timeless holiday, most of Jonson's love poems are highly concretized inventions, set in real worlds of particularized locales and involving individualized characters. The realism of such poems is calculated to be measured against the ideals of the transcendent love described in *Underwood* 88 and implied within the particular poems themselves. The concreteness of experience tempers the philosophical and religious preconceptions of neoplatonism and concentrates them into private worlds of individual sensation, thereby rescuing the poetry from any tendencies toward the remote or the overtly didactic. On the other hand, the awareness of the transcendent deepens the experience of the actual, and the contrast of the real and the ideal sometimes leads to complex questioning of the experienced world and creates poetry of unusual power and implication.

"An Elegie" (*U.* 22), one of Jonson's finest poems, gains great emotional power when experience intrudes upon idealism. Singing a lady's perfect combination of beauty and virtue, the speaker reflects conventional neoplatonic attitudes. His hymn culminates in the lady's apotheosis into Love himself in lines 25–28. This graceful, conventionally exaggerated praise is suddenly deepened. In a startling merger of the realistic

with the ideal, the speaker asks for "One sparke of your Diviner heat /
To light upon a Love of mine" (lines 31–32):

> Which if it kindle not, but scant
> Appeare, and that to shortest view,
> Yet give me leave to 'adore in you
> What I, in her, am griev'd to want.
>   (lines 33–36)

This turn is no less disquieting for the casualness of its accomplishment.
The conclusion throws the whole poem into new perspective.[58] The
intrusion of the real on an idealized landscape forces a contrast between
the experienced real and the celebrated ideal. The contrast may expose
the artificiality of the ideal. But by revealing the speaker's private
attachment to a love at odds with the ideal he praises, the contrast also
adds deep and surprising poignancy to his public adoration of the lady's
neoplatonic virtue. The poem may be seen as a nostalgic tribute to idealized values almost extinct in the real world of the speaker's experience.

"My Picture left in *Scotland*" (*U.* 9) also demonstrates the failure of
neoplatonic ideals in an imperfect world. Brilliantly manipulating traditions such as Cupid's blindness and the *senex amans* convention, Jonson
achieves great pathos by portraying a vulnerable persona in realistic and
self-mocking detail. The poem is at once genuinely humorous and
deeply moving. It has an exactness of detail and title that convinces us
of the speaker's sincerity and of his pain, making the poem seem far
more personal than conventional. It is a poem in which experience challenges idealistic hopes. The defeat of those hopes is at the core of its pre-
carious balance of wit and pathos. The speaker's attempts to woo
through poetry have failed, not for any fault of his verse but because the
poetry cannot obscure his unattractive physical appearance. Indeed, the
realistically depicted lover—like Jonson, 47 years old, gray haired,
mountain bellied, and rocky faced—appears particularly incongruous in
an idealized landscape of the "shadow of *Apollo's* tree" (line 10). As noted
earlier, the *senex amans* convention is one Jonson knew firsthand from
Horace, and the question of whether an older man could be a lover is a
familiar one in both classical and Renaissance discussions of love. But if
Ovid thought that " 'Tis unseemly for the old man to soldier, unseemly
for the old man to love,"[59] the immediate impetus for Bembo's neoplatonic theorizing in *The Courtier* is to defend the proposition that "olde

menne maye love . . . more happilye then yonge" (342). Significantly,
Bembo urges lovers to "laye aside . . . the blinde judgemente of the
sense" and love with the eyes and ears, those "ministers of reason" (353).
But the speaker of Jonson's poem learns from his experience that the
ministers of reason are impaired: "I now thinke, Love is rather deafe,
then blind" (line 1). Even as Jonson exploits the inherent humor of the
speaker's self-mockery, a sense of failed idealism contributes to the
pathos of the poem.

"My Picture left in *Scotland*" in effect questions the power of poetry.
But with characteristic Jonsonian irony, the very questioning is tempered by the high quality of the poetry itself. If the speaker is an incongruous lover, he nevertheless is moving in his candor and convincing in
his command of language. The metrical *tour de force* of the first stanza
confirms his baroque virtuosity, while the self-deprecation of the second
persuades of the honesty of his "conscious feares" (line 11). The authenticity of feeling in "My Picture left in *Scotland*" is especially noteworthy
because the poem is frankly artificial, particularly in the first stanza
where the speaker duplicates the love poetry he describes. This authenticity results from the poem's solid rooting in experience and from Jonson's too-little-appreciated ability to convey fine shades of feeling. The
wit balances, then finally intensifies, the pathos. The speaker's self-
knowledge qualifies the brittle artificiality of the first stanza, and his
honesty precludes the maudlin self-pity potential in a poem of complaint.

As is apparent in "My Picture left in *Scotland*" and "An Elegie" (*U.*
22), Jonson makes his treatment of love concrete by imagining realistic
personae and by presenting carefully delineated dramatic situations.
Patrick Cruttwell comments of Shakespeare and Donne as love poets
that, "these two had a great deal in common, and what they had in
common was that the basic stance of both was a *dramatic* stance."[60] The
same could be said of Jonson. The drama of his poetry is expressed in a
number of ways: through the personal tone, through the adaptation of
conventional poses and exhausted conceits for new and unexpected
effects, and through the distinctive aura of secrecy—noticed earlier in
the love lyrics of *The Forest*—that gives a surprising number of poems
the illusion of private engagement.[61] Jonson's quiet but vivid articulation of dramatic context is at the center of his illumination of human
experience.

Essential to the drama of one of Jonson's most nearly perfect lyrics is
the secrecy motif. Beautiful and deceptively simple, the song "Oh doe

not wanton with those eyes" (*U.* 4) conceals fullness of emotion beneath a veneer of elegant polish. The suggestiveness and grace of this song earn it a place among the most intriguing and delightful of seventeenth-century minor lyrics. Reminiscent of a host of Petrarchan and neoplatonic lyrics that sing the importance of eyes in love, the poem recalls Spenser's *Amoretti* 7 in some specific details, but the compelling drama and powerful immediacy of Jonson's song make it unique.

The qualities central to "Oh doe not wanton with those eyes" stem from a dramatic situation in which secrecy is required. The speaker is hopelessly in love with the lady, so much so that he finds himself almost unbearably uncomfortable in her presence. However she conducts herself, she torments him. This discomfort arises from the fact that the two are unable to communicate openly. The sensitive, silent communication between the two may suggest an enviable intimacy, but such communication is rife with terror, particularly so if, as in the dramatic situation of *Forest* 9, the lady is uncooperative, perhaps even unaware of her effect on the speaker. If she "wantons" with her eyes, the speaker sickens because of the impossibility of fulfillment; if she casts them down, he fears they may be consumed by guilt. The lady's anger can kill him, and even her kindness can excite unrealistic hopes that may (with a sexual quibble) "spill" him. If the lady weeps, the lover will be slain with sorrow; if she becomes distracted with fear, which his own eyes "enough betray" (line 12), then their love may be exposed with presumably disastrous consequences. The suggestiveness of the poem, its consummate and economical exploitation of an implied dramatic situation, is remarkable. With shrewd psychological insight, Jonson reinvigorates a tired conceit to explore the painful isolation that a necessity for concealment exacts of the lovesick persona.

The peculiar circumstances that require secrecy in Jonson's sequence of love elegies, *Underwood* 38, 40, and 41, are not made explicit, but it may be that the lady is not only married but also of a much higher social rank than her "servant" who vows never to reveal her "blazon" (*U.* 40, line 13).[62] The sequence rivals "A Celebration of Charis" (*U.* 2) as Jonson's most ambitious exploration of love, and it is distinguished by a highly particularized dramatic situation. The first poem in the series is too long and repetitious, but it establishes the dramatic context, characterizes the narrator, and pleases with a fine urgency. The speaker has offended his mistress, perhaps by revealing her identity in a moment of drunkenness, and he addresses her in a mood of excited contrition. Throughout the poem, Jonson returns to the imagery of light and darkness that dominates the opening lines and continues the characterization of the speaker as resourceful and contrite. The narrator's nimbleness of thought prevents him from ever appearing exactly abject, but his adoration of the lady and his frank admission of error make him seem distinctly human. "Thinke it was frailtie, Mistris, thinke me man" (line 31), he pleads. The flaws of the narrator humanize the dramatic situation. His confession of weakness balances the exaggerated and unrealistic praise of the mistress. This balance particularizes the relationship of the two, making it seem distinctive and unconventional.

The narrator describes the lady in spiritual terms, often using analogies that equate her with divinity. For example, he tells her, "I am regenerate now, become the child / Of your compassion" (lines 39–40). Similarly, he asks her to "imitate that sweet Serenitie" (line 77) of God and to "view the mildnesse of your Makers state, / As I the penitents here emulate" (lines 85–86). But such witty idealism is tempered by the easy integration of realistic detail within the analogies, as in lines 87–98. The realism of such details serves further to particularize the dramatic context. It also places the celebrated love within a recognizable social setting, and it incorporates within that public milieu a space for the personal and the private.

Underwood 38 ends by establishing the dramatic context of leave-taking, the event with which the other poems in the series are more narrowly concerned:

> O, that you could but by dissection see
>   How much you are the better part of me;
> How all my Fibres by your Spirit doe move,
>   And that there is no life in me, but love.
> You would be then most confident, that tho
>   Publike affaires command me now to goe
> Out of your eyes, and be awhile away;
>   Absence, or Distance, shall not breed decay.
>   (lines 109–16)

There is exquisite feeling in this beautiful passage. These lines are a culmination of all that has preceded, and the narrator draws confidence from the success of his earlier arguments. He thus speaks with greater assurance and with a sincerity that has already been tested. The conventional tropes are freshened by the graceful but strong lines and by the very particularized dramatic situation in which they are placed. The dramatic context of situation, character, and event established here are assumed in the two other poems that follow in the sequence.

This dramatic situation compels the speaker in *Underwood* 40 to address a number of specific issues. Foremost, he assures his mistress that he will keep "The Jewell of your name, as close as sleepe / Can lock the Sense up" (lines 42–43). Separated from the lady, the lover may assuage his sorrow in drink, but—in lines 9–14, a fine passage that deepens the poet's cultivated image of sociability and beautifully attests to the essential privacy of individual emotion even on public occasions— he promises that he will not expose their secret. Moreover, in order to conceal the identity of his real love, he will even mislead others into thinking he loves elsewhere.

What makes this poem so interesting is that in it Jonson manages to do a number of things at once. The valediction explains how the lover copes with absence, characterizes the speaker as a highly individual lover who can be distinguished from various kinds of lovers, and reassures the mistress of the lover's trustworthiness. Poems about such subjects are at least potentially quite emotional, but Jonson restrains emotion here, allowing the various feelings evoked by the subjects to balance each other in a mood of assured tranquility, a mood more like the ending of *Underwood* 38 than its abrupt and agitated beginning. This restraint, coupled with an aura of secrecy, creates controlled tension. The secrecy motif contributes to the dramatic tension by prompting speculation on the reasons for secrecy, both helping make concrete an individualized relationship and providing an excuse for withholding specific details by which the characters within the poem could be identified in the world outside it.

The final lyric in the three-poem series of love elegies, *Underwood* 41 focuses more narrowly on the issue of leave-taking. In this poem, the tone modulates into a deeper strain, reflecting both the success of the other two poems in recovering the lady's trust and the imminence of the actual separation. The most concentrated and most moving of the three poems, it develops wholly conventional conceits into a fresh and unified statement of the pain of parting. The first third of the poem self-consciously skirts hyperbole to describe the effects of the mistress's absence:

It is as if a night should shade noone-day,
Or that the Sun was here, but forc't away;

> And we were left under that Hemisphere,
> > Where we must feele it Darke for halfe a yeare.
> > > (lines 5–8)

These lines may deliberately echo Sir Philip Sidney's *Astrophil and Stella* 89; certainly they develop the conceit that concludes *Underwood* 38, a passage that itself probably intends a slighting reference to Sidney's Stella in the phrase "common Stars":

> > Others by common Stars their courses run,
> > > When I see you, then I doe see my Sun,
> > Till then 'tis all but darknesse, that I have;
> > > Rather then want your light, I wish a grave.
> > > > (lines 119–22)

Along with this conventional trope, *Underwood* 41 also plays upon the familiar exchange of lovers' hearts, an idea intimated near the end of *Underwood* 38 when the narrator tells the lady, "Your forme shines here, here fixed in my heart" (line 117). *Underwood* 41 interestingly yokes together the two conceits:

> > Alas I ha' lost my heat, my blood, my prime,
> > > Winter is come a Quarter e're his Time,
> > My health will leave me; and when you depart,
> > > How shall I doe, sweet Mistris, for my heart?
> > > > (lines 11–14)

He refuses her offer to restore his heart, for such an offer is "worth a feare, / As if it were not worthy to be there" (lines 15–16). The conclusion is moving in its tender resignation to the necessary separation of the lovers, again echoing the close of *Underwood* 38:

> > Come what can become
> > Of me, I'le softly tread unto my Tombe;
> > Or like a Ghost walke silent amongst men,
> > > Till I may see both it [i.e., his heart] and you agen.
> > > > (lines 19–22)

The poem is a good example of Jonson's ability to infuse freshness and new grace into old conceits.

Underwood 41 succeeds in combining in a natural way several distinct love conventions that support rather than fracture the movement of the whole. The echoes that link *Underwood* 41 to *Underwood* 38 are important, for although *Underwood* 41 can stand alone without reference to *Underwood* 38 and 40, it gains greatly by being viewed as the culmination of a sequence. The other poems establish a dramatic situation that illuminates the nature of the relationship assumed here. And central to that relationship is a necessity for secrecy. This secrecy serves to isolate the lovers and to increase the poignancy of the speaker's duress. In addition, the motif helps illustrate how the dramatic situations reveal a great deal, but suggest more than they specify. Moreover, the sensitive reticence of the persona is an essential part of his individualized character and helps to create the distinctive tone of this series.

Jonson's most delightful love poem is the witty *tour de force* "A Celebration of Charis in ten Lyrick Peeces" (*U.* 2). Although the fourth lyric, "*Her Triumph,*" is frequently anthologized and is widely admired as one of Jonson's most beautiful songs, the sequence as a whole also merits careful attention.[63] It is sometimes misconstrued as a satirical attack on Charis and on the Jacobean court society that she is said to represent. But the tone of the celebration is too playful, and its execution too graceful, to be truly satiric. There are, of course, satiric and, especially, parodic moments within the sequence, which consists of mixed genres and styles, but "A Celebration of Charis" is written primarily in a comic mode. Foremost, it is an amused and bemused narrative of an unlikely love affair between an aging lover and a fashionable lady of great beauty. In many ways, the poem is reminiscent of "My Picture left in *Scotland*" (*U.* 9). Both present Jonson as a realistically depicted lover in competition with conventionally idealized younger suitors, both contrast idealistic and realistic attitudes toward love, and both question the power of poetry in love.

More specifically, "A Celebration of Charis" tests the premise that

> it is not always face,
> Clothes, or Fortune gives the grace;
> Or the feature, or the youth:
> But the Language, and the Truth,

> With the Ardor, and the Passion,
> Gives the Lover weight, and fashion.
>   (2.1.7–12)

Much of the humor in the sequence results from Jonson's self-conscious depiction of himself as an old and possibly ridiculous lover, completely barren of the conventional attributes of the successful wooer. "Let it not your wonder move, / Lesse your laughter; that I love" (2.1.1–2), he pleads. In the second lyric, he describes his appearance after having been struck by his lady's "Lightning" (2.2. 23):

> I stood a stone,
> Mock'd of all: and call'd of one
> (Which with griefe and wrath I heard)
> *Cupids* Statue with a Beard,
> Or else one that plaid his Ape,
> In a *Hercules*-his shape.
>   (2.2.27–32)

But if Jonson lacks the face, clothes, fortune, feature, and youth of the conventional lover, he is a poet, and—to reverse line 5 of the first lyric—poets, though human, are divine. The language and the truth, the ardor and the passion of a poet are tools he commands in this war of love. Indeed, in the individual lyrics of the sequence, he demonstrates a marvelous ability to ape various styles of love poetry.

The purpose of these imitations is not so much to satirize conventional love poetry as to illustrate the aging poet's baroque artistry, his ability to have fun with issues that are quite serious to him. The variety of form and style in these lyrics—which include the gorgeously elegant "*Her Triumph*" (2.4); the Donne-like, dramatically abrupt persuasion to love beginning "For *Loves*-sake, kisse me once againe" (2.7.1); and the Petrarchan parody of Cupid's voice in "*His discourse with* Cupid" (2.5)—demonstrates the poet-lover's facility and the range of his weapons in the contest for Charis. In the third lyric, he narrates his hopeless predicament as a victim of Cupid's arrow, but points to his poetry as a means of revenge:

> all my wreake
> Is, that I have leave to speake,

> And in either Prose, or Song,
> To revenge me with my Tongue.
>
>   (2.3.21–24)

This revenge with his tongue consists of his virtuoso poetic performances such as "*Her Triumph*." Appropriately, and wittily, these performances are rewarded by Charis's kisses, a *quid pro quo* explicitly enunciated in lyric 6, where he asks "if such a verse as this, / May not claime another kisse" (2.6.35–36). For all his indulgence in lover's complaints, Jonson actually is confident enough in the power of his poetry to tease his lady about it. For example, he slyly intimates that she is but one of his muses (2.5.7–9); he places his praise of her in a long tradition of love poetry in celebration of Venus, a traditional ploy that the lady might not find altogether pleasing because it qualifies her uniqueness and since one of Vulcan's wives was named Charis; and he playfully takes credit ("What my Muse and I have done" [2.6.5]) for Charis's triumph at the Whitehall wedding described in lyric 6, thus claiming another kiss by desert.

Whether the poet is finally successful in winning his lady is a matter of debate and hinges on interpretation of lyric 9, where Charis describes an ideal lover. Her description apparently contradicts the major premise of the sequence as a whole, for she seems to prize precisely those attributes of face, clothes, fortune, feature, and youth that Jonson hopes do not invariably ensure success in love. But Charis's description is so idealized as to stretch credibility and thus invites suspicion that the final quatrain of her "*Dictamen*" may in fact amount to a subtle declaration of love for Jonson with whom she intends to continue a secret relationship:

> Such a man, with every part,
> I could give my very heart;
> But of one, if short he came,
> I can rest me where I am.
>
>   (2.9.53–56)

In effect, she declares herself content with her poet-lover unless she should find the idealized young man she has described, an event so unlikely as to be scarcely possible. The lady thus indicates her willingness to accept the realistically flawed poet in the absence of an impossibly idealized suitor.

The phrase "if short he came" is almost certainly intended innocently by Charis, but it is given bawdy implications in the final lyric, spoken by a coarse lady who has overheard Charis's pronouncement. Insofar as the phrase can be construed to indicate Charis's need for a flesh-and-blood lover rather than an idealized imaginary one, Jonson intends it to be suggestive and witty. But unlike the lady of the final lyric, Charis herself is not vulgar. In lyric 5, she is identified with Venus in every respect except one: "All is *Venus:* save unchaste" (2.5.42), an epithet further clarified by the graceful tribute that closes the lyric, when Jonson tells Cupid:

> this Beauty yet doth hide
> Something more than thou hast spi'd.
> Outward Grace weake love beguiles:
> Shee is *Venus,* when she smiles,
> But shee's *Juno,* when she walkes,
> And *Minerva,* when she talkes.
> (2.5.49–54)

The qualities of Juno's dignity and Minerva's wisdom, which Charis possesses in addition to Venus's beauty, are utterly lacking in the lady of the final lyric, whose concerns are frankly and exclusively sexual. "What you please, you parts may call, / 'Tis one good part I'ld lie withall" (2.10.7–8), she declares. Her coarseness serves to characterize her own values rather than to implicate Charis in the courtly corruption. Indeed, the contrast between the two ladies may explain why Charis is determined to keep secret her alliance with a poet-lover who may appear ridiculous to those who value only titles, clothes, youth, beauty, and sexual endowment.

"A Celebration of Charis" is especially interesting for the easy integration of realism and idealism in its depiction of the lovers' attachment. Although Jonson affectionately parodies the extreme forms of Petrarchan worship and is clearly interested in a sensual relationship with Charis, the poem is nevertheless infused with idealistic but commonsensical neoplatonic feeling. Part of the difficulty in interpreting the poem arises from the fact that so much of it is parodic, as Jonson demonstrates his ability to celebrate his love in various styles. But the gentle parody of Petrarchan conventions does not amount to a rejection of idealism in love. The sensual motives of the aging lover are not inconsistent with the moderate neoplatonism of Jonson's philosophy of love. The essential innocence of the relationship between Charis and the poet can best be measured in comparison with the blatant and exploitative sexuality of the final lyric. Even lyric 7, which parodies the sexual urgency of Donne's anti-Petrarchanism, is—it must be recalled—an invitation to a kiss. The lover's plea, "What w'are but once to doe, we should doe long" (2.7.12), distinguishes his desire from the purely sexual impulse, the fulfillment of which results in guilt and revulsion if it is unaccompanied by love, as explained in the apt opening lines of *Underwood* 88. Though it is neither the unrequited worship of the Petrarchan lover nor the antisexual otherworldliness of the neoplatonic theorist, Jonson's love of Charis is idealistic.

Jonson's idealism is also revealed in several poems that focus on friendship. These poems make clear that the poet valued friendship highly and that he recognized the difficulties in achieving intimate relationships with others. He characteristically contrasts false or casual friendship—the "issue of the Taverne, or the Spit" (*U.* 45, line 8)—with a more sublime notion, sometimes using his own failures in friendship as a means of defining the ideal he seeks. Conceding that his idiosyncratic bluntness "is a Drug austere / In friendship" (*U.* 37, lines 17–18), he strives for freedom, honesty, and self-knowledge, elevating friendship into a union of hearts and souls. If Jonson's exaltation of friendship sometimes echoes classical models, it nearly always is rooted in concretely personal situations.[64]

The poet's awareness of his own failure to live up to the ideal of a friend colors several of the poems, investing them with a sincerity that makes them convincing and quietly moving. "An Epistle to Master *Arthur Squib*" (*U.* 45), for instance, opens with a statement of disarming honesty: "What I am not, and what I faine would be, / Whilst I informe my selfe, I would teach thee" (lines 1–2). The speaker discovers that, true to classical friendship theory, real friendship is based on virtue alone and that he must be "Friend to himselfe, that would be friend to thee" (line 22). The implied defensiveness of this poem is even more noticeable in the eminently tactful "An Epistle to a friend" (*U.* 37), where Jonson argues for the "comelie libertie" (line 20) of intimacy, the right of friends honestly to "mixe spirits" (line 12). This "comelie libertie" is equivalent to the "Freedome, and Truth" that "Epigram. To a Friend, and Sonne" (*U.* 69, line 5) insists friends owe one another. As a friend, Jonson prized integrity and independence. In "An Epistle answering to one that asked to be Sealed of the Tribe of *Ben*" (*U.* 47), the speaker, who dwells "as in my Center, as I can" (line 60), discovers self-knowledge and trust as essential ingredients in true friendship: "First give me faith, who know / My selfe a little. I will take you so" (lines 75–76). Although most of the poem is a satirical attack on the false friend, probably the poet's collaborator and antagonist Inigo Jones, it also gives ethical and, with the witty biblical allusion of the title (Rev. 7:1–8), even religious significance to the circle of friends and "sons" Jonson gathered about him for evenings of wine and wit at the Mermaid and the Apollo Taverns.

In "An Epistle to Master *John Selden*" (*U.* 14), Jonson pays a warm tribute to an accomplished friend and also celebrates the learned Selden's friendship with his chamberfellow Edward Hayward. The center of the poem is a beautiful passage that echoes several earlier poems, most notably "To William Camden" (*E.* 14) and "To William Roe" (*E.* 128). The poet portrays Selden, an eminent historian and legal scholar, as the consummate humanist. Lines 29–38 brilliantly convey the excitement of scholarship. Jonson sees Selden as a vicarious type of the epic hero. Secure in his own gathered self, the scholar adventurer explores the world about him and observes the past and present, informing his knowledge with commitment and trust, with "faith in things" (line 36).

After rehearsing Selden's wide learning and good instruction, the tribute culminates in the praise of Hayward, to whom Selden had dedicated his work *Titles of Honor* (1614). Hayward will not only love and cherish Selden, but—as a scholar himself—he can also appreciate the pains of scholarship. From his work in the "Mines of knowledge" (line 76), Hayward has brought "Humanitie enough to be a friend, / And strength to be a Champion" (lines 77–78). Jonson depicts the friendship of Hayward and Selden as a natural fruit of their humanistic learning. Their friendship in turn provides concrete evidence that Selden, like Hayward, has translated his knowledge and "faith in things" into humanity and strength.

Jonson's greatest poem on the theme of friendship is his dazzling "To the immortall memorie, and friendship of that noble paire, Sir *Lucius Cary,* and Sir *H. Morison*" (*U.* 70). Among the earliest Pindaric odes in English, the poem is immensely complex.[65] Occasioned by the early death in 1629 of Sir Henry Morison, whose "life was of Humanitie the Spheare" (line 52), it balances classical and Christian responses to life and death in a carefully modulated and superbly orchestrated elegy. Moving from classical stoicism in its opening stanzas to a Christian consolation, the poem envisions a "bright eternall Day" (line 81) in which the poet himself will finally rest with Morison and his friend Cary. Jonson apparently was much more closely associated with Sir Lucius Cary than with the deceased, and the poem uses the friendship of Morison and Cary as a means of making intimate and poignant its consideration of issues raised by the premature death of a promising young man. Jonson intrudes himself into the poem to make clear his personal involvement in the mourning of a young man whom he may not have known very well. The poem is an elegy for Morison, a consolatory tribute to Cary, a celebration of friendship, and a deeply felt response to premature death. If a poem as complex as this can be said to have a single theme, it is that the quality of a person's life is more significant than its length.

The poem begins by meditating on two negative exempla, the "Brave Infant of *Saguntum*" (line 1), whose return to his womb teaches a lesson about life's miseries, and the "Stirrer," a man who "out-liv'd his Peeres / And told forth fourscore years" (lines 25–26), yet did nothing but die late. In contrast, Morison died young yet lived fully, neither retreating from life nor merely vexing his time to no good end. Interestingly, the quality of Morison's life is judged by aesthetic standards, criteria that might well be applied to a poem or a musical composition:

> Life doth her great actions spell,
> By what was done and wrought
> In season, and so brought
> To light: her measures are, how well
> Each syllab'e answer'd, and was form'd, how faire;
> These make the lines of life, and that's her ayre.
> (lines 59–64)

Although Morison's life was brief, it was as graceful as a lyric:

> All Offices were done
> By him, so ample, full, and round,
> In weight, in measure, number, sound.
> (lines 48–50)

The loveliest stanza in the poem, lines 65–74, makes the theme explicit ("In small proportions, we just beautie see: / And in short measures, life may perfect bee" [lines 73–74]), and it illustrates the qualities of grace, ease, and proportion that Morison's own life is said to have embodied. The lyrical perfection of Morison's brief life prepares us for the graceful deference of the conclusion where Jonson ascribes the immortality of the Cary-Morison friendship not to his poem but to their deeds and their love, presenting the surviving friend with wine and laurel and assuring him that "thy *Morison's* not dead":

> Hee leap'd the present age,
> Possest with holy rage,
> To see that bright eternall Day:
> Of which we *Priests,* and *Poets* say,
> Such truths, as we expect for happy men,
> And there he lives with memorie.
>
> (lines 78–84)

The end of the poem focuses on the friendship itself. The exaltation of the Cary-Morison friendship draws on tropes derived from classical theory and familiar in the large body of seventeenth-century friendship literature. It also reflects the very qualities Jonson stresses in his other poems on friendship. Neither formed by chance or "leased out to'advance / The profits for a time" (lines 100–101), nor the issue of the tavern or the spit, the friendship of Cary and Morison stems from "simple love of greatnesse, and of good" (line 105). Characterized by honesty and self-knowledge, Cary and Morison's ideal friendship makes them examples to future generations. The elegiac consolation, in which the friends are translated into the Dioscuri, with Morison shining in heaven and Cary on earth, yields to their celebration as "one Starre: / Of hearts the union" (lines 98–99). The Cary-Morison ode may rightly be regarded as the triumphant culmination of Jonson's treatment of friendship.

The Underwood contains a number of tributes to worthy persons whom Jonson casts as virtuous exemplars for their own and future ages. Many of these seem formulary, and the ambitious enshrinement of Lady Venetia Digby as "Eupheme" (*U.* 84) is incomplete and uneven. Others, the best example of which may be the epistle to Sir Edward Sackville (*U.* 13), confront the question of the proper relationship of poet and patron. Some of the tributes are distinguished by the intimacy of Jonson's address and the subtlety of his didacticism. For instance, a gentleness and a specificity of detail give "An Epitaph on Master *Vincent Corbet*" (*U.* 12) surprising and understated power. The tributes to gifted women such as Lady Mary Wroth (*U.* 28) and the countess of Rutland (*U.* 50), are similarly marked by tactful familiarity and detailed knowledge and frequently enlivened by wit. Wit, indeed, is the most striking feature of the "Epistle. To my Lady *Covell*" (*U.* 56) and "An Elegie On the Lady *Jane Pawlet*" (*U.* 83). But whereas the self-deprecatory play of the poem to Lady Covell yields unsurprisingly to a graceful compliment, the wit of the elegy is far more complex.

The elegy for Jane Pawlet is a virtuoso piece, brilliantly inventive, daring in its conceits, and self-assured in stretching the boundaries of decorum. The speaker's self-dramatization gives the work a theatrical quality reminiscent of poems by Donne. Its frequent changes of tone are similar to those in the Cary-Morison ode, although here the changes are abrupt and call attention to themselves, dramatically juxtaposing one mood with another. The elegy is almost as long as the ode, but it has more energy and less delicacy, and consequently the experience of reading it is more compressed and more immediately pronounced. The poem begins with a private drama in which the poet himself is a participant but concludes with a triumphant celebration of faith accessible to all Christians.

The initial encounter of the speaker and the "gentle Ghost, besprent with *April* deaw" (line 1) self-consciously emphasizes the grotesqueness of the graveyard setting. "Stiffe! starke! my joynts 'gainst one another knock!" (line 9), the agitated narrator exclaims. The poem then modulates into an apparently conventional recitation of Lady Jane's genealogy and her individual virtues. But even these familiar topics of praise are heightened by the histrionic response of the poet. "Had I a thousand Mouthes, as many Tongues, / And voyce to raise them from my brazen Lungs" (lines 23–24), he could not adequately sound the lady's virtue. The drama of Jane Pawlet's deathbed is exaggerated in a famous passage that approaches the comic, lines 49–56. She meets death with such confidence and faith that she "taught the Standers-by, / With admiration, and applause to die!" (lines 61–62). In heaven, Lady Jane "through circumfused light . . . lookes / On Natures secrets" (lines 69–70) and "Beholds her Maker! and, in him, doth see / What the beginnings of all beauties be" (lines 73–74). The poem then addresses the lady's parents, enjoining them to be sad only "If you not understand, what Child you had" (line 78), using enjambment for surprise. The conclusion affirms Christian faith, echoing but not testing the conventional sentiments of "On My First Sonne" (*E.* 45), and culminates in a sober and victorious coda:

When we were all borne, we began to die;
And, but for that Contention, and brave strife
The Christian hath to'enjoy the future life,
Hee were the wretched'st of the race of men:
But as he soares at that, he bruiseth then
The Serpents head: Gets above Death, and Sinne,
And, sure of Heaven, rides triumphing in.
(lines 94–100)

The elegy for Lady Jane Pawlet is a *tour de force* in which Jonson skirts an excess of metaphysical wit to embrace a common religious consolation. Pleasing with its energy and its frenetic combination of the conventional and the startling, the poem demonstrates Jonson's ability in a mode of poetry he used only infrequently.

As the Cary-Morison ode and the Jane Pawlet elegy brilliantly demonstrate, Jonson's poetic powers did not wane in his later years. But many of Jonson's late poems concern specific personal problems, some of them occasioned by age and illness. His house burned in 1623, and in the fire he lost his library and several manuscripts. During the reign of Charles I, his prestige at court declined; with the ascendancy of Inigo Jones, he was employed less frequently in writing masques and other courtly entertainments, and consequently he was often in financial straits. A stroke paralyzed him in 1628 and confined him to bed for a long period. In 1629, his return to the popular stage met with disaster. Jonson experienced enough misfortune in his last years to have become an enfeebled and embittered old man. That he did not may be testimony to his own "faith in things," that favorite tribute of his to friends he admired.

Few of the late poems are self-pitying, and many are imbued with a comic spirit surprising in light of the circumstances of their composition. "An Execration upon *Vulcan*" (*U.* 43), prompted by the fire of 1623, while it contains much satire in passing, is remarkably good humored in its burlesque attack on the god of fire who is such a fool he "would his owne harvest spoile, or burne!" (line 150). Even in "An Ode. To himselfe" (*U.* 23), Jonson avoids the bitterness and self-pity of his immediate reaction to the failure of *The New Inn*. In *Underwood* 23, he castigates himself for "ease and sloth" (line 2) and resolves to "sing high and aloofe, / Safe from the wolves black jaw, and the dull Asses hoofe" (lines 35–36). His contempt for his age and for "that strumpet the Stage" (line 34) remains, but it is subordinated to his positive and healthy regard for his own poetic power, a gift for which he assumes full responsibility. In the "Epistle To Mr. *Arthur Squib*" (*U.* 54), he jokingly uses his own large girth as an opportune pretext to borrow money from his friend.

As a partial solution to his monetary problems, Jonson petitioned in 1630 "th'best of Monarchs, Masters, Men, King *Charles*" (*U.* 76, title) for an increase in the "free Poetique Pension" (line 10) that King James had granted him in 1616. The request was honored, but the payment was sometimes late. In an epigram to a clerk in the Exchequer (*U.* 57) and in "An Epigram, To the House-hold" (*U.* 68), the poet complains, "If the'Chequer be emptie, so will be his Head" (*U.* 57, line 28). The best of these begging verses is "To the Right Honourable, the Lord high Treasurer of *England*. An Epistle Mendicant" (*U.* 71), where the poet, using siege imagery, admits that

> *Disease,* the Enemie, and his Ingineeres,
> *Want,* with the rest of his conceal'd compeeres,
> Have cast a trench about mee, now, five yeares.
>
> (lines 4–6)

As a consequence, "The *Muse* not peepes out, one of hundred dayes" (line 9). The poet asks for "some saving-*Honour* of the *Crowne*" (line 13) to relieve his "*Bed-rid* Wit" (line 15). But for all the pathos inherent in the situation of a proud man wracked by illness and poverty, there is nothing maudlin in the poem. It maintains dignity in part by the martial imagery and the comparison of the poet with a distressed city but more because of its note of honest and unsentimentalized need.

In his later years, Jonson regularly fulfilled the obligations of poet laureate, producing poems on the loss of the royal couple's first child (*U.* 63), the birth of the future Charles II (*U.* 65), and royal anniversaries (*U.* 67, 72). These poems are filled with the royalist fervor that mark the praise of King James in the *Epigrams*. Occasionally, Jonson also reveals an awareness of the growing political problems facing his monarch. In "An Epigram. To K. *Charles* for a *100.* pounds he sent me in my sicknesse" (*U.* 62), the poet alludes to the old belief that the king's touch could cure scrofula (popularly known as the King's Evil). The ceremony itself asserts that the king's authority derives from God and not from the will of his unruly subjects.[66] Jonson uses the king's personal kindness to him as the occasion for a political statement, one especially appropriate in 1629 when the king dissolved his increasingly rebellious parliament: "What can the *Poet* wish his *King* may doe, / But, that he cure the

Peoples Evill too?" (lines 13–14). The growing discontent that would later fester into civil war is also at the core of "An Epigram. To our great and good K. *Charles* On his Anniversary Day" (*U.* 64). Beginning "How happy were the Subject, if he knew, / Most pious King, but his owne good in you!" (lines 1–2), Jonson attacks his countrymen—particularly the Puritans among them—for failing to appreciate their sovereign. "How is she barren growne of love! or broke! / That nothing can her gratitude provoke!" (lines 15–16), the poet asks of his unhappy country; he attributes the discontent to "Surfet bred of ease, / The truly Epidemicall disease!" (lines 17–18). The poem celebrates the beleaguered king by portraying him as a prophet without honor in his own country. Jonson was a keen observer of his age. His poems reflect his awareness of unhappiness in the land, and he correctly perceives in this discontent danger to his monarch.

A large and uneven collection that the poet himself did not live to see through the press, *The Underwood* is nevertheless a work of Jonson's mature genius; its poems exhibit the poet in a variety of moods and predicaments and, like the earlier collections, attest to the large range of his interests. The book in general reveals Jonson's personality more intimately and with greater warmth than do the previous gatherings. It contains poems that are both playful and serious, often simultaneously witty and moving. It features a number of fine love lyrics and an almost equally distinguished group of poems focusing on friendship. In addition, a number of poems unhesitatingly treat personal events and problems in the aging poet's life. Throughout the work, Jonson appears more idiosyncratic and more vulnerable than in the earlier collections, and more frequently than before he casts himself as a character in the poems, writing about his personal life in a way that is affecting but not sentimental. He remains an idealist and a moralist in these poems and more of a public than a private poet. But his idealism often functions to unveil realistic human imperfections that are not despised, and his didacticism translates into a large and humane vision of individual and social possibilities. For all its unevenness and occasional failures, *The Underwood* is a fitting capstone to the career of a man who dedicated his life to the arduous and sometimes unrewarding art of poetry.

Ungathered Verse

Jonson's ungathered verse is a motley group of poems that he did not see fit to publish in his three collections. Most of these poems were written as prefatory or complimentary verses for works by friends or acquaintances or as contributions to miscellaneous anthologies, and some are poems that Jonson deliberately chose to suppress, as, for example, the wedding poem for the ill-fated Robert Carr, earl of Somerset (U. V. 18). The uncollected poetry includes an intricate religious poem, "*The Ghyrlond* [Garland] of the blessed Virgin *Marie*" (U. V. 41), assorted epitaphs and literary compliments, attacks on Inigo Jones (U. V. 34, 35, 36), and several royalist encomia.

The most famous and the finest of the ungathered verse is a literary compliment addressed to William Shakespeare. "To the memory of my beloved, The Author *Mr. William Shakespeare:* And what he hath left us" (U. V. 26) was first published in the 1623 folio of Shakespeare's *Works,* collected by John Heminges and Henry Condell, actors in Shakespeare's company and friends of Jonson. Jonson's own folio of 1616 provided an important precedent for the publication of plays in folio and Jonson undoubtedly encouraged the publication of Shakespeare's work, perhaps even to the point of collaborating on the prefatory letter, "To the Great Variety of Readers," signed by Heminges and Condell.[67] Although the poem betrays aspects of what Roger B. Rollin diagnoses as the "anxiety of identification" attendant on Jonson's feelings of "sibling rivalry" toward his "dark brother," it nevertheless constitutes a generous tribute from one great poet to an even greater one.[68]

It is true that Jonson disapproved of what he considered Shakespeare's occasional lapses of decorum and of verisimilitude and that he thought Shakespeare should have revised more often than he was rumored to do: "*I remember,* the Players have often mentioned it as an honour to *Shakespeare,* that in his writing, (whatsoever he penn'd) hee never blotted out line. My answer hath beene, Would he had blotted a thousand" (*Disc.,* lines 647–50). Drummond reports, perhaps not entirely accurately, that his visitor declared, "Shaksperr wanted Arte" (*Conv.,* line 50), a blunt statement explicitly contradicted in the poem that gives nature and art equal credit in fashioning the poet. Jonson took great pains to clarify his position regarding Shakespeare, and in doing so he praised both the man and his genius: "I lov'd the man, and doe honour his memory (on this side Idolatry). . . . He was (indeed) honest, and of an open, and free nature: had an excellent *Phantsie;* brave notions, and gentle expressions. . . . hee redeemed his vices, with his vertues. There was ever more in him to be praysed, then to be pardoned" (*Disc.,* lines 654–68). In the poem to his fellow poet, Jonson honors the dead man's memory; to do so, he tends to make Shakespeare over in his own image, refiguring him as the *poeta* or maker that Jonson describes in *Discoveries,* attributing his great peer's success to exercise, imitation, revision, and art, as well as to nature. He insists that "a good *Poet's* made, as well as borne" (line 64), and credits Shakespeare with those very qualities of labor and art that he seemed to deny him in *Conversations.*

The poem opens with a long introduction in which Jonson details in what traditional ways he will not praise Shakespeare. He will not be motivated by ignorance, blind affection, or crafty malice. Having established his judiciousness, independence, and sincerity—that is, the fact that he is fully capable of the task of praising his great rival—he strikes a triumphant note: "Soule of the Age! / The applause! delight! the wonder of our Stage!" (lines 17–18). This expansive new beginning releases the energy restrained in the cautionary introduction and intimates the two interconnected concerns developed more fully in the tribute that follows. Shakespeare is celebrated as a national hero and as an embodiment of *Zeitgeist.* But as the poem proceeds, he comes to be seen as one whose art conquers any limitations of time and space. To render Shakespeare justly, he cannot be compared with his English contemporaries John Lyly, Thomas Kyd, and Christopher Marlowe, but with Jonson's hallowed humanist heroes, the classical masters of tragedy and comedy "that insolent *Greece,* or haughtie *Rome* / Sent forth, or since did from their ashes come" (lines 39–40). Shakespeare is a national hero, but he merits international acclaim: "Triumph, my *Britaine,* thou hast one to show, / To whom all Scenes of *Europe* homage owe" (lines 41–42). In this context of nationalistic celebration, Jonson's glance at his subject's "small *Latine,* and lesse *Greeke*" (line 31)—often regarded as a snide comment on Shakespeare's relative lack of classical learning—may be seen as a compliment "in that Shakespeare's achievement expressed in the native idiom and forms of the English vernacular exceeds the classical models."[69] And if he is the "Soule of the Age!" (line 17), he is also "not of an age, but for all time!" (line 43).

The two external factors that bear upon the poem—Shakespeare's death in 1616 and the publication of the folio in 1623—are naturally integrated. The poem is an elegy, but it is also a commendatory verse for a book. The central theme of the poem is Shakespeare's immortality, but that state results more insistently from "what he hath left us" than from the conventional consolation in which the dead poet is stellified. Thus, Shakespeare is "a Moniment without a tombe / And art alive still, while thy Booke doth live, / And we have wits to read, and praise to give" (lines 22–24). His mind and manners shine "In his well torned, and true-filed lines" (line 68). Even when the "Sweet Swan of *Avon*" (line 71) is transfigured into the constellation Cygnus, the stellar poet influences the "drooping Stage" (line 78) through his "Volumes light" (line 80). As the poem easily integrates the two parts of its double function, it also exploits the tension inherent in them. Shakespeare is dead; his art lives. Although the man can no more return than can *"Eliza,* and our *James"* (line 74), who so enjoyed his work, the "Starre of *Poets"* (line 77) triumphs over his own death through the continuing vitality of his book.

Jonson's tribute to Shakespeare is a dignified but seriously witty celebration of a great artist. Like "On My First Sonne" (*E.* 45), the poem is filled with semantic play that never violates decorum. The puns on Shakespeare (lines 37, 69), on Kyd and Lyly (lines 29–30), on issue and race (line 66), and on influence (line 78) give the poem a liveliness that contributes to the triumphant tone of the whole. Elegiac verse demands extravagant praise, but even within the conventions of compliment, Jonson's tribute is extraordinarily generous. Yet for all its generosity and conventional exaggeration, it is also a just, critical estimate that simultaneously recognizes in Shakespeare both his natural genius and his art. If Jonson remakes Shakespeare in his own image, he does not disfigure him in the process. Indeed, Jonson's acuity in recognizing his late rival's unique status among his contemporaries does both him and Shakespeare credit. The poem convinces and touches because of the sincerity and aptness of its sentiments. The great lines and epithets of the poem have by constant repetition become clichés, but as Ian Donaldson observes, they were brave words in 1623: "no one until then had so positively asserted the perennial and enduring nature of Shakespeare's genius, hailing him so boldly as a writer *for all time."*[70] The sentiments have been repeated precisely because in them Jonson conveys an appreciation of Shakespeare's genius that has struck succeeding generations of readers as entirely appropriate.

Although they do not approximate the Shakespeare elegy in ambition or achievement, the two most recent additions to Jonson's canon are also elegies for theatrical personages. One, an elegy for one of Jonson's early collaborators, Thomas Nashe, dates from the turn of the seventeenth century. In it, Jonson addresses those who are left behind after Nashe's death, instructing them to

> View here a trophee of that tyrant deathe
> And let the object strike your melting eyes

> blind as the night, when you but reade, Here lies
> Conquerd by destiny & turnd to earthe
> The man whose want hathe causd a generall dearthe
> Of witt; throughout this land: none left behind
> to equall him in his ingenious kynd.[71]

Like the Shakespeare elegy, it is a generous tribute, yet appropriately
measured. Nashe is credited with preeminence in a particular form of
ingenuity. The epigram on the actor Richard Burbage, who died in
1619, is reminiscent of the epitaph for Salamon Pavy (*E.* 120) in its wit
but lacks the tenderness of the earlier poem:

> Tell me who can when a player dies
> In which of his shapes againe hee shall rise?
> What need hee stand att the judgment throne
> Who hath a heaven and a hell of his owne?
> Then feare not Burbage heavens angry rodd,
> When thy fellows are angells and old Hemmings is God.[72]

As Brandon Centerwall remarks, the epigram is "neatly and delicately
balanced between eulogy and satire" (29). While the poem's theological
conceit is facetious, its theatricality is fitting for a famous actor. Like
John Heminges, who is referred to in the final line, Burbage was a
member of Shakespeare's company, the King's Men. He played the leading roles in many of Shakespeare's plays and probably appeared as
Sejanus, Mosca, Face, and Cicero in productions of Jonson's works. The
poem acknowledges Burbage's noted versatility and wittily celebrates
the protean quality and good fellowship of the acting profession.

Conclusion

Ben Jonson is one of the greatest poets of the earlier seventeenth century. In his various art, he mingles public and private concerns, Christian and classical points of view, idealistic and realistic attitudes, celebratory and satirical modes. He captures the fullness of Jacobean society,
depicting it as it actually was, alternately sordid and magnificent,
debased and robust, corrupt and just, but always measuring it against
an exalted vision of human possibilities. On everything he wrote, he

stamped the impress of his own vivid personality. His notion of the good life is a personal as well as a social ideal, and within his poetic commonwealth he insists upon room for the private emotions. Expressed in a style of passionate plainness admitting of wide tonal range, his individual sensibility is many faceted. Jonson may be the greatest occasional poet in English literature, but the occasions that prompted his poetry were not only public ones but also personal occasions of love, friendship, and grief.

As a serious writer single-mindedly dedicated to his talent, Jonson thought himself neglected in his own time: "*Poetry,* in this latter Age, hath prov'd but a meane *Mistresse,* to such as have wholly addicted themselves to her. . . ." (*Disc.,* lines 622–24). He offered his work to posterity, confident of its verdict: "An other Age, or juster men, will acknowledge the vertues of his studies: his wisdome, in dividing: his subtilty, in arguing: with what strength hee doth inspire his Readers; with what sweetnesse hee strokes them: in inveighing, what sharpnesse; in Jest, what urbanity hee uses. How he doth raigne in mens affections; how invade, and breake in upon them; and makes their minds like the thing he writes. Then in his Elocution to behold, what word is proper: which hath ornament: which height: what is beautifully translated: where figures are fit: which gentle, which strong to shew the composition *Manly.* And how hee hath avoyded faint, obscure, obscene, sordid, humble, improper, or effeminate *Phrase.* . . ." (*Disc.,* lines 786–99). The very qualities Jonson enunciates here are those that distinguish his own carefully wrought poetry. They can be seen most clearly in the brilliant and affecting epigrams, the dignified yet familiar odes and epistles, the graceful and elegant songs, the touching and dramatic explorations of the need to love. These varied poems honestly earn Ben Jonson the immortality he honestly sought.

Chapter Six

The Prose

Apart from dedications and miscellaneous writings, only two of Jonson's prose works survive. As he laments in "An Execration upon Vulcan" (*U.* 43), the fire that destroyed his library in late 1623 burned, among other of his compositions still in manuscript, "a Grammar . . . / To teach some that, their Nurses could not doe, / The puritie of Language" (lines 91–93); a narrative of "my journey into *Scotland* . . . / With all th'adventures" (lines 94–95); his translation of John Barclay's Latin romance *Argenis* (1621), "Three bookes not afraid / To speake the fate of the *Sicilian* Maid / To our owne Ladyes" (lines 95–97); his history "Of our fift[h] *Henry,* eight of his nine yeare" reign (line 98); and "twice-twelve-yeares stored up humanitie, / With humble Gleanings in Divinitie, / After the Fathers, and those wiser Guides / Whom Faction had not drawne to studie sides" (lines 101–04), probably compilations along the lines of the surviving *Discoveries.* Modern readers lament with Jonson the loss of his travel book, his history of Henry V's reign, the "humanitie" that he "stored up" in the notebooks of his early and middle years, and his "Gleanings" in nonfactious divinity. All would certainly enrich our picture of Jonson and his age. Fortunately, after the fire he did rewrite his *English Grammar,* at least in part, and the *Timber: or, Discoveries* published in the 1640–41 folio may be partially a memorial reconstruction of his earlier notebooks as well as a continuation of them. The former is important in that it is the first grammar of English written by a professional writer, and it shows both Jonson's keen interest in the history of his native tongue and his care for precision in its use. The latter is a treasure trove of humanistic thought, observations on people and manners, and literary criticism.

The English Grammar (1640–1641)

The English Grammar as published posthumously in the second volume of the 1640–41 folio is Jonson's second version of the work, and it seems somewhat sketchy. A separate half title in the folio gives this information: "Made by Ben. Iohnson. For the benefit of all Strangers, out of his observation of the English Language now spoken, and in use."

As the complete title suggests and the preface makes clear, this *Grammar* is ostensibly designed as an aid to foreigners "who are to live in communion, and commerce with us" (lines 1–2), though it is difficult to see how they would particularly profit from it. Jonson's *Grammar* consists of two books, the first on etymology, the second on syntax. Book 1 contains discussions of the individual letters of the alphabet, accompanied by copious Latin notes printed on the facing pages, and an explanation of the parts of speech. Book 2 sets out rules of syntax and illustrates each with quotations from English writers.

The English Grammar may have had its genesis in notes for lectures that Jonson, as deputy professor of rhetoric, delivered at Gresham College in the early 1620s.[1] In writing it, he employed several sources. Foremost among these are Petrus Ramus's *Grammatica* (1572), which he used extensively for organization as well as approach. Other continental sources, used more sparingly, include Ramus's *Scholae in Liberales Artes* (1578) and J. C. Scaliger's *De Causis Linguae Latinae* (1540). Jonson's two primary sources by English writers are Thomas Smith's *De recta et emenda Linguae Anglicae scriptione,* which sought to reform English spelling, and Richard Mulcaster's *The First Part of the Elementarie which entreateth chefelie of the right writing of our English tung.*[2] As in his other works, however, Jonson absorbs his sources, tests them with his own observations, and makes of them a statement that is his own.

One of Jonson's chief intellectual impulses in writing the *Grammar* is patriotic. He desires to raise the status of the vernacular, considered by many academicians to be inferior to the learned classical languages, to a position at least equal with them. In his preface, Jonson proudly announces, "Wee free our Language from the opinion of Rudenesse, and Barbarisme, wherewith it is mistaken to be diseas'd; We shew the Copie of it, and Matchablenesse, with other tongues" (lines 5–8). To do this, he does not seek so much to impose the rules of Latin or Greek on English as to discover the unique character of his native language as it has already developed and to subject its conventions to "Experience, Observation, Sense, Induction," which are "the fower Tryers of Arts" (lines 12–13). Although Jonson's *Grammar* is heavily indebted to the works of others, he has—following the example of his schoolmaster and mentor William Camden—tested empirically most of its pronouncements, for "It is ridiculous to teach any thing for undoubted Truth, that Sense, and Experience can confute" (lines 13–14). Arching over all that he writes of the English language is Jonson's sense of English history, as evinced by his frequent references to "our Fore-fathers" and "the *English-Saxons.*"

Jonson's *Grammar* is notable for several reasons, chief among them his continuation of Thomas Smith's quarrel with the oddities of English spelling, his groundbreaking attention to phonetics and use of illustrative quotations in the discussion of syntax, and his promulgation of a multipurpose punctuation system. In the case of spelling, Jonson is as condemnatory as Smith of superfluous letters, but he is pragmatic enough to know that he cannot alone reform English custom. For example, while condemning *c* as "a letter, which our Fore-fathers might very well have spar'd in our tongue" (because it duplicates the sounds of both *k* and *s*), Jonson nevertheless concedes, "since it hath obtained place, both in our Writing, and Language, we are not now to quarrell *Orthographie, or Custome*" (1.4.5–8). Even though he cannot alter conventions, Jonson still rails—with considerable wit—at what he considers to be absurdities. "Q," he writes in an anthropomorphic vein, echoing Smith, "Is a Letter we might very well spare in our *Alphabet,* if we would but use the serviceable *k* as he should be, and restore him to the right of reputation he had with our Fore-fathers. For, the *English-Saxons* knew not this halting *Q,* with her waiting-woman *u,* after her" (1.4.127–32). After discussing whether *h* is a letter or "an *Aspirate* meerely," he concludes: "But, be it a Letter, or Spirit, we have great use of it in our tongue, both before, and after *Vowells.* And though I dare not say, she is, (as I have heard one call her) the *Queene mother of Consonants:* yet she is the life, and quickening of them" (1.4.197, 200–204).

The innovativeness of the first book of Jonson's *Grammar* lies in its concern with phonetics. Although Ramus and others had systematized the phonetics of Latin and Greek, Jonson is the first to attempt such a task with English. This feature informs his discussion of most of the letters of the alphabet, but is best seen in chapter 3, "Of the Vowels." There he differentiates the multiple sounds of each and notes the use of the terminal *e* to alter the sound of the vowel preceding it (as in *mad* and *made*). By the standards of modern linguistics, Jonson's discussions of the sounds of letters and the way they are produced may seem crude, but they testify to his concern with the language as spoken, and they are of considerable value to anyone interested in the pronunciation of early modern English.

Jonson's handbook is most revolutionary in its second book, devoted to syntax. There he introduces the use of quotations to illustrate the rules of syntax, and he advocates a system of punctuation that had recently been developed by continental humanists. As a part of his strategy of testing the rules of grammar by "Observation," Jonson offers as examples 118 quotations from 12 different authors, illustrating every concept from the *"Apostrophus"* (chapter 1) through *"the* Syntaxe *of a* Verb *with a* Noune" (chapter 5) to *"the Distinction* [i.e., Punctuation] *of Sentences"* (chapter 9). The quoted authors range from the pioneers of English vernacular poetry in the fourteenth and fifteenth centuries (Chaucer, Gower, and Lydgate) to notable prose writers of the sixteenth (Ascham, Cheke, Foxe, Jewel, and More). And Jonson uses as well quotations and paraphrases of the Bible in its Authorized Version.[3] Indeed, although Jonson occasionally seems to force Latin grammar on the English language (as in his discussions of the conjugations of verbs, chapters 17–20), most often one gets the impression that the rules of syntax that he promulgates are arrived at, or at least tested, empirically, growing out of his observations of how English writers have actually used the language. N. E. Osselton calls Jonson's treatment of syntax "unique" and remarks, "one has to go into the eighteenth century before finding anyone systematically giving quotations to illustrate grammatical patterns."[4]

At first, Jonson's heavy reliance on Chaucer (27 quotations), Gower (28), and Lydgate (13) may seem surprising. He did, after all, write elsewhere that *"Spencer,* in affecting the Ancients, writ no Language" (*Disc.,* lines 1806–07); and he advised that youthful students not be allowed to read *"Gower,* or *Chaucer* at first, lest falling too much in love with Antiquity, and not apprehending the weight, they grow rough and barren in language onely" (*Disc.,* lines 1799–1802). But Jonson no doubt also thought of these earlier poets as the "antique springs" (*E.* 14, line 8) of the English language, and he uses them to add authority to his discussions of it, much as Camden had used Britain's ancient past to explain and glorify its present.

The final chapter of the second book is devoted to punctuation, and in it Jonson introduces into English grammar the concept of multipurpose punctuation devised by the continental humanists, notably Ramus. He alludes to two of those purposes in the first paragraph. After remarking, "All the parts of *Syntaxe* have already been declared," he continues:

> There resteth one generall Affection of the whole, dispersed thorow every member thereof, as the bloud is thorow the body; and consisteth in the breathing, when we pronounce any *Sentence;* For, whereas our breath is by nature so short, that we cannot continue without a stay to speake long together; it was thought necessarie, as well for the speakers ease, as for

the plainer deliverance of the things spoken, to invent this meanes,
whereby men pausing a pretty while, the whole speech might never the
worse be understood. (2.9.1–11)

In this brief passage, Jonson combines two approaches to punctuation,
the rhetorical (with its emphasis on speaking), which had been in use in
England for some time, and the hermeneutic (with its emphasis on
understanding), which had been newly developed by continental
humanists. In the paragraph that follows, he adds the third approach,
the logical or what is now referred to as grammatical, assigning marks
on the basis of the *"perfect,* or *imperfect"* nature of clauses (2.9.12–13). As
a consequence of seeing the purposes of punctuation as tripartite, Jonson, following the continental humanists, advocates heavy marking, and
he introduces into the discussion of English punctuation new marks
devised by those humanists, notably the semicolon and parentheses.[5]
What is perhaps more striking, however, is that Jonson conceives of
punctuation not simply as a system of imposed marks but as the "bloud"
that, by analogy, courses through writing, causing it to live and breathe.

Although Jonson's *English Grammar* may not satisfy modern grammatical theorists such as Emma Vorlat, who finds it to be "incomplete,
sketchy and carelessly composed" and complains that it "contains inconsistencies and omits essential data,"[6] it is nevertheless worthwhile.
Despite the fact that much of it is derivative and that it is incomplete
and somewhat eccentric, Jonson's *Grammar* is valuable for its celebration
of the vernacular, its pioneering study of English phonetics, its introduction of illustrative quotations in the discussion of syntax, and its empirical approach. Moreover, the fact that its author wrote some of the clear-
est and most resonant English poetry and prose in the early modern
period lends authority to its dicta.

Timber: or, Discoveries (1640–1641)

Discoveries was first published posthumously in the second folio of Jonson's *Works.* On its separate half title, dated 1641, it is given a lengthy
descriptive title: *Timber: or, Discoveries; Made upon Men and Matter: As
They have flow'd out of his daily Readings; or had their refluxe to his peculiar
Notion of the Times.* At the head of the first page of text stands an additional title: *Explorata: or, Discoveries.* Its individual sections probably
written, or rewritten, for the most part during the last decade of Jonson's life, *Discoveries* is his longest extant prose work. A rich repository of

his reflections on human nature, it is a compilation indispensable to understanding Jonson's critical, ethical, and political stances.

As the full title suggests, there are different kinds of discourse in *Discoveries*. Parts of the book record what "flow'd out of [Jonson's] daily Readings" and consist mostly of free translations and paraphrases of both classical and humanist writers on a variety of subjects.[7] Other parts are reflections of his own "peculiar Notion of the Times," his "Explorata" of individuals and society that are informed by a flowing back ("refluxe") of what Jonson had digested from the works of others but in the process had transformed by selection, arrangement, and new applications—as well as by striking additions of his own observations—into essentially original comments on Jacobean and Caroline England. Still other parts, not specifically signaled in the complete title, seem to be embryonic textbooks or treatises along with notes for future compositions. As a consequence of the varied contents of *Discoveries,* it is difficult to assign a generic label to the whole compilation. Some critics have referred to it as a commonplace book, but as Timothy Murray points out, "*Discoveries* differs in style and form from other extant English commonplace books of its period. It is not arranged according to readily identifiable commonplaces whose order is determined by alphabetization or theme. Nor does the text bear an index. . . . And most significant, the authors and sources of the extracts . . . are not clearly identified."[8] But neither is it, as Richard Newton has claimed, simply an "expository prose work";[9] for that designation suggests a kind of order and overarching design that *Discoveries* lacks. A more accurate generic category is a reader's and writer's notebook, because that term can encompass all of the multiform parts of the whole. Moreover, such a designation suggests as well that the book was not intended for publication in its present randomly organized, unfinished state. As a reader, Jonson recorded in *Discoveries* what most impressed and convinced him in the works of others; as a writer, he recorded drafts of essays and treatises, as well as suggestions for future compositions. *Discoveries* is a miscellaneous collection of works either in epitome, in embryo, or in progress, not a finished, polished work ready for publication. Its tentativeness and its function as a reader's and writer's notebook are suggested by the names applied to the work. As Richard Peterson points out, " 'Timber' suggests good building materials" and *Discoveries* "the idea that such material has been brought back."[10] Hence, the work may be thought of as a repository of raw materials that Jonson might use to fashion more polished work of his own at some future time.

Earlier in this century, most critics of *Discoveries* complained of its lack of originality. Reflecting the Romantics' equation of "original" with "new," even Percy Simpson, who was to become a major editor of Jonson, doubted in 1907 if *Discoveries* contained "a single original remark";[11] and in 1952 was still of that opinion: "The discoveries were made by other men. [Jonson] fuses, rearranges, and adapts his borrowed matter; the weakness of the collection is that he seems to have thought out little or nothing for himself."[12] But it is precisely in fusing, rearranging, and adapting—as well as selecting—earlier materials that writers and readers of the early modern period, sensitive to the widespread practice of *imitatio,* located originality. By those standards, *Discoveries* is an original work. Jonson gleans from his reading and his memory statements of what he himself has tested and found, through his own experience, to be true, and he augments or illustrates them with passages in his own voice, thereby producing something uniquely his, something new. Recognizing Jonson's procedure, more recent critics have been kinder to the book, assessing it on its own terms as a supremely useful compilation of Jonson's own convictions, regardless of whether they are stated in his words or in the words of others. George Parfitt, for example, views *Discoveries* as "Jonson's reflections on how life should be lived, how it is lived, and on the nature and function of art." He finds the virtues of "Jonson's good man" as reflected in *Discoveries* to be "self-awareness, reason, truth, wisdom, fortitude, honesty, and dignity."[13]

As might be expected in a writer's notebook, more than one half of *Discoveries* is devoted to literary concerns. Several passages are ostensibly directed toward teaching others to read well, speak well, and write well; while the final section—the longest sustained passage in the book, unfortunately left unfinished—is dedicated to setting out Jonson's own *ars poetica.* As he does in the parts of *Discoveries* that treat of other matters, Jonson relies heavily on the words and ideas of other writers in these passages on literature. But through selection, arrangement, and augmentation he constructs an aesthetic that, although it might not be as comprehensive or as subtle as some might wish, largely reflects his own literary values.[14] The major points in these passages that concern literature—particularly the characteristic Jonsonian stress on imitation and revision—have already been discussed in chapter 1 of this present book under the heading "The Artistic Stance" and need no further comment here.

The passages of *Discoveries* that read most like commonplace book entries are the brief miscellaneous bits of moral wisdom that are scattered, singly and in groups, throughout the book. Many—though not all—are translated or paraphrased from classical or humanist works, and all have their topics designated in the margins by the Latin categories one expects in a commonplace book: *Fama, Opinio, Hypocritia,* and the like. Typical of them is the brief passage labeled *Calumniae fructos*: "I am beholden to *Calumny,* that shee hath so endeavor'd, and taken paines to bely mee. It shall make mee set a surer Guard on my selfe, and keepe a better watch upon my *Actions*" (lines 206–09). In a similarly personal vein, the paragraph designated *Fortuna* begins: "Ill *Fortune* never crush't that man, whom good *Fortune* deceived not. I therefore have counselled my friends, never to trust to her fairer side, though she seem'd to make peace with them: But to place all things she gave them so, as she might aske them againe without their trouble" (lines 1–5). The first of these passages is apparently original with Jonson, the second a translation of a classical source, Seneca's *Consolatio ad Helviam*; yet the latter as well as the former resonates with Jonson's own voice. As might be expected from the late period in which most of *Discoveries* was written, many of these *sententiae* are tinged with bitterness or disillusionment, yet informing all is at least an attempt at stoic acceptance.

Jonson's overtly political statements are scattered throughout *Discoveries* (lines 65–115, 242–50, 972–1019, 1116–1297, and 1306–22), and they are informed and buttressed by his reading not only such ancients as Seneca, Suetonius, and Plutarch but also the works of several political theorists of the early modern period, notable among them Farnese, Lipsius, Machiavelli, Patricius, and Vives.[15] Jonson's attitude toward government, and particularly toward the monarchs under whom he lived and wrote, were complex and, of necessity, flexible. If his tragedies are any indication of his political beliefs, what Jonson saw as an ideal form of government was something akin to the ancient Roman republic. But he envisioned no possibility of such a government in England during his own lifetime, and he supported the monarchs under whom he lived and worked as the only feasible alternatives to chaos. It is not surprising, then, given the divisive times during which he wrote *Discoveries* that he should affirm his allegiance to monarchy. It is also not surprising, given his vatic calling as poet, that he should insist on ethical behavior and moral probity in a monarch.

Jonson's devotion to monarchy is nowhere more strongly stated than in the following passage, which is apparently original with him: "*After God,* nothing is to be lov'd of man like the Prince: He violates nature, that doth it not with his whole heart. For when hee hath put on the care of the publike good, and common safety; I am a wretch, and put of[f] man, if I doe not reverence, and honor him: in whose charge all things *divine* and *humane* are plac'd" (lines 986–91). Conversely, in an earlier passage, also original with him, he is scornful of the multitude: "*The vulgar* are commonly ill-natured; and alwayes grudging against their *Governours:* which makes, that a Prince has more busines, and trouble with them, then ever *Hercules* had with the Bull, or any other beast: by how much they have more heads, then will be rein'd with one bridle. There was not that variety of beasts in the Arke; as is of beastly natures in the multitude; especially when they come to that iniquity, to censure their *Soveraign's* actions" (lines 971–79). Worth noting in the last clause of the first quoted passage is the yoking of church and state under the king's rule. Jonson's condemnation of the vulgar (consistent with his treatment of mobs in his tragedies) probably reflects his suspicion of the religious individualism of extreme Protestantism. Jonson feared religious dissension as politically divisive. Precisely because Jonson sees the multitude as factious in both church and state affairs, he supports the idea of a strong monarch as a unifying force.

Yet Jonson is not an absolutist in any simple sense. His royalism is not an unthinking adherence to the first two Stuart monarchs and their insistence on the divine right of kings. He fully realizes that throughout history there have been bad kings as well as good ones, and he is as much a foe of the tyranny of an individual as he is of mob rule. "A *good King,*" he writes, "is a publike Servant" (lines 1232–33). To that end, Jonson outlines and defends, on historical and moral grounds, the attributes of a good king. He insists that a monarch should always follow the dictates of religion: "*The strength* of Empire is in Religion. . . . Nothing more commends the *Soveraigne* to the Subject, then it. For hee that is religious, must be mercifull and just necessarily. And they are two strong ties upon mankind" (lines 1197–1202). Indeed, Jonson confronts directly and scornfully refutes the cruelty allowed to princes in Machiavelli's version of *Realpolitik*: "*A Prince* should exercise his cruelty, not by himselfe, but by his Ministers: so hee may save himselfe, and his dignity with his people, by sacrificing those, when he list, saith the great *Doctor* of *State, Macchiavell.* But I say, he puts off man, and goes into a beast, that is cruell. No vertue is a *Princes* owne; or becomes him more, then his *Clemency:* And no glory is greater, then to be able to save with his power" (lines 1158–65). In refutation of Machiavelli's dictum that it is better for a prince to be feared than loved, Jonson, translating from Seneca's *De Clementia,* asserts that: "the mercifull *Prince* is safe in love, not in feare. Hee needs no Emissaries, Spies, Intelligencers, to intrap true Subjects. Hee feares no Libels, no Treasons. . . . He is guarded with his owne benefits" (1191–96).

In addition to exercising clemency, a good king should exhibit prudence. Englishing a passage from Farnese's *Diphthera Jovis,* Jonson writes: "the *Princes* Prudence is his chiefe Art, and safety. In his Counsels, and deliberations, hee forsees the future times. In the equity of his judgement, hee hath remembrance of the past; and knowledge of what is to bee done, or avoyded for the present" (lines 1010–15). To that end, a good prince should be well read. Paraphrasing Lipsius's *Politica* but reflecting his own exaltation of learning, Jonson asserts: "*A Prince* without Letters, is a Pilot without eyes. All his Government is groping. In *Soveraignity* it is a most happy thing, not to be compelled; but so it is the most miserable not to be counsell'd. And how can he be counsell'd that cannot see to read the best Counsellors (which are books.) for they neither flatter us, nor hide from us" (lines 1234–39). Finally, a good king should show a constant concern for the governed and take care not to abuse them. Quoting Lipsius, Jonson writes: "a *Prince* is the Pastor of the people. Hee ought to sheere, no[t] to flea his sheepe; to take their fleeces, not their fels" (lines 1254–56).

Among the most interesting extended reflections on people and manners in *Discoveries* are its handful of self-contained familiar essays.[16] Ralph Walker has pointed out four rather lengthy ones, assigning these titles to them: "Of Envy" (lines 258–312), "Of Talking Overmuch" (lines 330–404), "Of Worthless Aims" (lines 1323–1467), and "Of Flatterers" (lines 1586–1635).[17] But since early essayists frequently wrote compositions of only a page in length, it is justifiable to add to Walker's list four briefer passages, to which one might give the following titles: "Of Courtesies to Others" (lines 446–71), "Of Memory" (lines 479–507), "Of the Danger in Excusing Vices" (lines 543–69), and "Of Ignorance and Knowledge" (lines 801–20).

Ironically, Jonson's only comment on the essay as a genre in *Discoveries* is disparaging.[18] Writing of the different kinds of wits, he describes essayists as false wits who

> turne over all bookes, and are equally searching in all papers, that write out of what they presently find or meet, without choice; by which meanes it happens, that what they have discredited, and impugned in one worke, they have before, or after, extolled the same in another. Such are all the *Essayists,* even their Master *Mountaigne.* These, in all they

write, confesse still what bookes they have read last; and therein their
owne folly, so much, that they bring it to the *Stake* raw, and undigested:
not that the place did need it neither; but that they thought themselves
furnished, and would vent it. (lines 719–29)

It is true that the early modern essayists reflected their current reading
in their own essays. But what Jonson is criticizing in this passage is not
the borrowing of other men's ideas—he, least of all his contemporaries,
could afford to cast a stone on that subject—but the inconsistencies of
attitude occurring in some collections labeled essays. In the best of those
early essayists, however, as in Jonson's own essays, an underlying philosophy—Christian stoicism—lends unity to their ostensibly random
ideas.

Indeed, an apparent randomness is one of the features of the early
essay, a genre developed by humanists to explore facets of human
nature. It invites a free range in the choice and ordering of specific
points, and it moves from subject to subject in what appears to be a free
association of ideas. Other features of the form are a tentative approach,
distinguishing it from the inclusive and definitive posture of the treatise,
and a conversational style. Elsewhere in *Discoveries* Jonson himself
defines that style. Paraphrasing a passage from the continental humanist
Vives, he rejects both the extended loftiness of Cicero and the periodic
terseness of Seneca in favor of a position somewhere in between, favor-
ing a language that "is plaine, and pleasing: even without stopping,
round without swelling; all well-torn'd, compos'd, elegant, and accurate" (lines 2045–47). In a more famous passage, he declares, "Pure and
neat Language I love, yet plaine and customary" (lines 1870–71).
Finally, the early essay invites the thoughts of others, either in quotation
or paraphrase. And like Jonson, the best essayists of the period avoid
bringing their borrowings "to the *Stake* raw." They digest them into a
personal statement, autobiographical in illustration and application.[19]

A good example of the essays in *Discoveries* is Jonson's exploration of
the worthless aims that control men's lives (lines 1323–1467). This
selection begins with a brief but forceful statement of theme: "*A good
man* will avoide the spot of any sinne." Then, using the *Apology* of the
second-century Latin writer of romances Apuleius, Jonson contrasts the
evil man with the innocent one. After affirming that "*An Innocent* man
needs no *Eloquence*: his *Innocence* is in stead of it," he launches into what
Maurice Castelain has deemed "the longest and most important" original addition made to the translations and paraphrases that make up

most of *Discoveries*.[20] Discussing those who maliciously accuse innocent men of faults, Jonson leaves his model to write from personal experience:

> I have beene accus'd to the Lords, to the *King;* and by great ones: but it hap'ned my accusers had not thought of the Accusation with themselves; and so were driven, for want of crimes, to use invention, which was found slander. . . . Nor were they content, to faine things against mee, but to urge things, fain'd by the Ignorant, against my profession. . . . They objected, making of verses to me, when I could object to most of them, their not being able to reade them, but as worthy of scorne. Nay, they would offer to urge mine owne Writings against me; but by pieces, (which was an excellent way of malice) as if any mans Context, might not seeme dangerous, and offensive, if that which was knit to what went before, were defrauded of his beginning; or that things, by themselves utter'd, might not seeme subject to Calumnie, which read entire, would appear most free.

This first-person passage expressing Jonson's anger at his detractors and his scorn for the fools who cannot read him properly or—if they do—quote him out of context, Castelain sees only as "a spirited defense of his own conduct and a contemptuous onslaught on his enemies . . . forced in between two extracts from the *Apology* of Apuleius" (Castelain, xvi). But Jonson's outcry here is more than just another manifestation of his querulousness. It is an example of his characteristic use of autobiographical incident to transform his raw materials into a statement very much his own, a technique that is a hallmark of the essay genre.

After lashing out at his detractors, Jonson returns to his model for a passage on poverty. Although it is for the most part a paraphrase of Apuleius's *Apology,* a personal intensity animates Jonson's rendition of it: "At last they upbraided my poverty; I confesse, shee is my Domestick; sober of diet, simple of habit; frugall, painefull; a good Counsellor for me; that keepes me from Cruelty, Pride, or other more delicate impertinences, which are the Nurse-children of Riches." In the late 1620s, when this essay was written, Jonson was living in poverty, not merely reading of it, and it is his own experience—not Apuleius's—that imparts force to this passage.

Turning to a consideration of the wrong uses of wealth, Jonson borrows materials from a letter by Seneca the philosopher (*ad Lucilium,* 110) that points up our enslavement to our "gullet, and groyne," interrupting his source this time to illustrate from personal observation the

folly of serving *"Fame,* and Ambition." Referring to the costly but
ephemeral celebrations attendant on the 1606 state visit of Christian IV
of Denmark, brother of James I's consort Anne, among which was a
performance of Jonson's own *Entertainment of the Two Kings at Theobalds,*
he writes: "Have not I seen the pompe of a whole Kingdome, and what
a forraigne King could bring hither also to make himselfe gaz'd, and
wonder'd at, laid forth as it were to the shew, and vanish all away in a
day? And shall that which could not fill the expectation of few houres,
entertaine, and take up our whole lives? when even it appear'd as superfluous to the Possessors, as to me that was a Spectator."[21] Besides being
an excellent example of an essayist's reliance on personal experience, this
passage is a remarkable testament to Jonson's honesty with himself,
because it criticizes an extravagance of the court—expensive entertainments and masques—that at various times during his life afforded him a
large part of his income. After this illustration drawn from his personal
observation, Jonson ends his essay on worthless aims with an abstract of
another of Seneca's letters (115), a passage condemning fancy dress and
other deceptive facades and urging in their stead the stoic ideal of virtue
kept plain and private.

The personal essays in *Discoveries* are an impressive achievement in a
relatively new form. Although Swinburne may exaggerate in judging
"Jonson's notes or observations on men and morals, on principles and on
facts . . . superior to Bacon's [*Essays*] in truth of insight, in breadth of
view, in vigour of reflection and in concision of eloquence," he is right to
contrast the "dry curt style of the statesman, docked and trimmed into
sentences that are regularly snapped off or snipped down at the close of
each deliverance" with the "fresh and vigorous spontaneity" of the
"poet's" essays in *Discoveries.*[22] In his prose, Jonson exhibits the clarity,
unobtrusive control, and suggestiveness that is the hallmark of his
poetry.

As received, *Discoveries* is a problematic work. Its lack of logical organization, the fragmentary nature of many of its parts, and its heavy
reliance on the words and ideas of others are stumbling blocks that must
be overcome if one is to judge it fairly. Seeing it as a reader's and writer's
notebook not intended for publication can help alleviate the first two
difficulties. The third disappears when one considers it in the context of
the early modern concept of originality. Indeed, *Discoveries* as a whole
may be best seen as essayistic, a series of explorations of various subjects,
none of which aim at completeness, that mixes materials from the
author's reading with his own thoughts and observations. What give the

book its character and interest are what give the personal essay those same qualities: its voice and the mental processes that it chronicles. In the case of *Discoveries,* the voice and those processes are those of a dedicated humanist who was fascinated with the world around him, who revered the ancients but constantly tested received wisdom by personal observation and experience, who developed strong opinions and the ability to state them effectively, who respected art as a mirror of life, and who was moral without being priggish and bookish without being pedantic.

Chapter Seven

Jonson's Reputation

When Ben Jonson died in 1637, he was recognized as the greatest man of letters his age had produced. His death was marked by an outpouring of elegies and commemorative tributes that mourned him, in English, Latin, and Greek, as "the most Excellent of English *Poets*," the "Mirror of our *Age!*" and the lawgiver to the stage.[1] Even in a period of extravagant commemorative verse, this praise from fellow poets is extraordinary. More significantly, it is a measure of the position Jonson enjoyed late in his life as "rare Ben Jonson," a unique literary personality who had influenced a host of lyric and dramatic disciples. Indeed, apart from his own work, Jonson's greatest legacy is the pervasive influence he exerted on his contemporaries and "Sons."[2] The "Tribe of Ben" included poets as individual and accomplished as Robert Herrick, Thomas Carew, Sir John Suckling, and Richard Lovelace as well as such fine lesser voices as Thomas Randolph, Richard Corbett, James Shirley, and William Habington. But Jonson's influence reached further than those who, like Herrick, recall with such vividness "those *Lyrick* Feasts" at London taverns "Where we such clusters had, / As made us nobly wild, not mad."[3] Almost no poet of the earlier seventeenth century escaped the impact of Jonson's humanist vision. It affected the whole age, even exerting influence on John Donne and touching the still greater genius of John Milton.

From Dryden to Eliot

Jonson's best early critic is John Dryden, whose generous estimate concludes with what had already become almost obligatory, a comparison of Jonson and Shakespeare: "If I would compare him with Shakespeare, I must acknowledge him the more correct poet, but Shakespeare the greater wit. Shakespeare was the Homer, or father of our dramatic poets; Jonson was the Virgil, the pattern of elaborate writing; I admire him, but I love Shakespeare."[4] Although Jonson might well have appreciated being likened to Vergil, the ideal poet of *Poetaster,* Dryden's comparison established the terms by which Jonson's reputation precipitously declined in the eighteenth century, a decline that has been reversed only recently. The most popular comedies continued to be produced throughout much of the eighteenth century, but Jonson—both the man and the artist—was sacrificed upon the altar of Shakespearean bardolatry. The bardolators attacked Jonson as a means of praising Shakespeare. As Jonas Barish has observed, they came "to see in Shakespeare a Christ figure, and in Jonson both the Judas and the mob demanding blood."[5]

The polemicist William Gifford, who in 1816 issued the first scholarly edition of Jonson's works, largely silenced the attacks on the poet's character.[6] But with the rise of Romanticism, the decline of Jonson's artistic reputation accelerated in the nineteenth century. The plays were produced less often than in the previous century, and the poetry utterly failed to satisfy the Romantic appreciation of the exquisite sensibility belonging to a more aureate tradition. To nineteenth-century readers, Jonson seemed to lack those qualities they valued most highly: a soaring imagination, a delicate tone, a unique soul. His realism was seen as a failure of inspiration and an inability to convey psychological subtleties. Although praised as a dramatist and poet of learning and self-conscious classicism, he was dismissed as a plodding pedant, devoid of the "natural" gift of lyric so abundant in Shakespeare; and even his learning sometimes became evidence of his lack of originality.

The nineteenth century did, however, produce some defenses of the poet other than those of Gifford and his scholar friend Octavius Gilchrist. Critics as diverse as Coleridge and J. A. Symonds offered incidental appreciations.[7] Colonel Francis Cunningham revised and reissued Gifford's edition in 1875,[8] and in 1889, Algernon Charles Swinburne published *A Study of Ben Jonson*. Although an eccentric critic limited by his own impressionistic ardor, itself the product of late Victorian sentimentality, Swinburne deeply appreciated Jonson. Much of his book recapitulates standard critical prejudices, as does his opening sentence, which draws the inevitable contrast between Shakespeare and Jonson in terms of a distinction between "gods of harmony and creation" and "giants of energy and invention": "the supremacy of Shakespeare among the gods of English verse is not more unquestionable than the supremacy of Jonson among its giants" (Swinburne, 3). But if Swinburne felt that Jonson was deficient in imagination and passion, he fully credited his "weight of matter, the solidity of meaning, the significance and purpose of the thing suggested or presented." And he affirmed that the author of *Discoveries* "was in every way worthy to have been the friend of Bacon and of Shakespeare" (Swinburne, 6, 181). Despite Swinburne's efforts, however, Jonson in the nineteenth century became a figure to be consigned to literary history, a footnote rather than a living author to be reinterpreted by each new generation. Thus T. S. Eliot began his 1919 essay on Jonson by remarking that his reputation "has been of the most deadly kind that can be compelled upon the memory of a great poet. To be universally accepted; to be damned by the praise that quenches all desire to read the book; to be afflicted by the imputation of the virtues which excite the least pleasure; and to be read only by historians and antiquaries—this is the most perfect conspiracy of approval."[9]

The Current View

In the twentieth century, Jonson's reputation has undergone a remarkable recovery, due largely to a number of academic critics who have appreciated the artist on his own terms.[10] The modernist reaction against the late Romantic sensibility and Eliot's critical belief that poetry should transform individual feeling into generalized truth set the stage for a sympathetic revaluation of Jonson's achievement as playwright and poet. Eliot called for "intelligent saturation in Jonson's work as a whole" as the necessary prerequisite for a new appreciation of him (Eliot, 148). This task was made immeasurably easier by the massive scholarly edition of C. H. Herford and Percy and Evelyn Simpson, issued in 11 volumes between 1925 and 1952. Twentieth-century studies of Jonson have revealed the accuracy of the plays' depiction of the men and women of seventeenth-century England, their mastery of form and seriousness of purpose. The masques have come to be seen as more than ephemeral spectacles and to be appreciated for their combination of the topical and the transcendent. More recently, the nondramatic poetry, which had been eclipsed by Donne's, has been recognized as remarkable in its "range and strength and art," its dignity and scope.[11]

If Jonson has now been restored to his place as a major figure in English literature, that is not to say that there is a consensus as to the exact nature of his achievement. There is, in fact, disagreement among Jonson's leading critics as to almost every facet of his work and life, ranging from expected differences of opinion as to the interpretation of specific works to polarized conceptions of his personality. Still, what has been most illuminating about the recent revaluation of Jonson is how his works are susceptible to fruitful analysis through many different approaches. Critics applying the perspectives and presuppositions of new historicism and cultural materialism have illuminatingly demonstrated how Jonson's plays, masques, and poems confront the political and social issues of his day and have more precisely located him within the competitive world of the Stuart courts, while commentators employing more traditional methodologies have offered a deeper understanding of his literary techniques and dramaturgy as well as of his ideas and influences. Identifying him as the first major literary figure to assimilate thoroughly the impact of printing, scholars have recognized his contribution to the creation of the conditions under which literary study and systematic criticism could flourish, even as they have also explored with ever more precision the nature of his antitheatricalism and the dynamics of his relationship with his various audiences. The vitality of the recent criticism and scholarship devoted to Jonson witnesses to the continuing interest of his work and to the centrality of Jonson's achievement for a grasp of seventeenth-century English culture. Most interestingly, Jonson remains an unsettling figure, mired in the morass of his own time and his own labored attempt to achieve transcendence. As Richard Helgerson has observed, "Instead of a flight, his work is an agon, an unresolved struggle of the self against the very conditions of its expression. But that struggle gives Jonson's plays, poems, and masques much of their troubling power—and it has made Jonson himself one of the enduring presences in our literature. In the labor of self-presentation, rather than in a transcendently achieved laureate self, *The Works of Ben Jonson* find their true, though unacknowledged self" (Helgerson, 184).

Jonson is among the greatest writers in English literature. Of the poets and playwrights of his own time, he yields place only to Shakespeare, Donne, and Milton. A professional man of letters, whose livelihood derived directly or indirectly from his pen, he always looked beyond his own age, self-consciously writing for posterity. He took seriously the moral obligations of art, yet he is earnest without being sober, moral without being grim. A literary critic and theorist, he imposed discipline on his work but did not sacrifice either spontaneity or vigor. More vividly than anyone else, he sketched the manners of his age, yet he probed beneath the superficial and the transient to reveal universal longings and common failings. A satirist who excoriated vice and folly, he is also supremely a poet of human possibilities. He never lost his "faith in things" (*U.* 14, line 36), and his humanist vision expressed "the life of man in fit measure, numbers, and harmony" (*Disc.,* lines 2349–50). The variety and quality of his achievement merit the respect of all who love literature. More pointedly, the greatness of his art entitles Jonson to the "legitimate fame" (*E.* 17, line 3) he sought from intelligent readers.

Notes and References

Chapter One

1. For detailed accounts of the times during which Jonson lived, see the relevant volumes of *The Oxford History of England:* J. B. Black, *The Reign of Elizabeth, 1558–1603,* 2d ed. (Oxford: Clarendon Press, 1959; hereafter cited in text as Black), and Godfrey Davies, *The Early Stuarts, 1603–1660,* 2d ed. (Oxford: Clarendon Press, 1959); Christopher Hill, *Intellectual Origins of the English Revolution Revisited* (Oxford: Clarendon Press, 1997); C. A. Patrides and Raymond B. Waddington, eds., *The Age of Milton* (Ithaca, N.Y.: Cornell University Press, 1980); Blair Worden, ed., *Stuart England* (Oxford: Phaidon, 1986); and Graham Parry, *The Seventeenth Century: The Intellectual and Cultural Context of English Literature, 1603–1700* (London: Longman, 1989). On Jonson's detailed knowledge of the social, political, economic, and religious currents of his day, see L. C. Knights, *Drama and Society in the Age of Jonson* (London, 1937; reprint, New York: Norton, 1968; hereafter cited in text as Knights).

2. Of the rich scholarship on the theaters, the acting companies, and the audiences of Jonson's day, see, for example, Alfred Harbage, *Shakespeare's Audience* (New York: Columbia University Press, 1941); M. C. Bradbrook, *The Rise of the Common Player: A Study of Actor and Society in Shakespeare's England* (London: Chatto & Windus, 1962); and G. E. Bentley, *The Jacobean and Caroline Stage,* 7 vols. (Oxford: Clarendon Press, 1941–68; hereafter cited in text as Bentley 1941–68); Michael Hattaway, *Elizabethan Popular Theatre: Plays in Performance* (London: Routledge and Kegan Paul, 1982); David Bradley, *From Text to Performance in Elizabethan Theatre: Preparing the Play for the Stage* (Cambridge: Cambridge University Press, 1992); and Paul Whitfield White, *Theatre and Reformation: Protestantism, Patronage, and Playing in Tudor England* (Cambridge: Cambridge University Press, 1993).

3. Letter of the Papal Secretary of State Cardinal Como to the papal nuncio in Madrid, written in December of 1580; quoted in Black, 178.

4. William Camden, *The Historie of the Most Renowned and Victorious Princesse Elizabeth, Late Queen of England,* trans. Robert Norton of *Annales rerum Anglicarum...regnante Elizabetha* (London, 1630), bk. 2, 68–69.

5. Volume 1 of H. & S. has a detailed life of Jonson and also includes *Conversations with Drummond,* John Aubrey's notes on Jonson, and legal and official documents relating to the poet. Volume 11 contains supplemental notes to Jonson's life and a reprint of Thomas Fuller's charming but brief and unreliable biography (1662). Marchette Chute's *Ben Jonson of Westminster* (New York: Dutton, 1953) is a very readable lengthy account. The earlier biographers have

243

recently been supplemented by four excellent biographical studies: E. Pearlman, "Ben Jonson: An Anatomy," *English Literary Renaissance* 9 (1979): 364–93; Rosalind Miles, *Ben Jonson: His Life and Work* (London: Routledge, 1986; hereafter cited in text as Miles 1986); David Riggs, *Ben Jonson: A Life* (Cambridge, Mass.: Harvard University Press, 1989; hereafter cited in text as Riggs); and W. David Kay, *Ben Jonson: A Literary Life* (London: Macmillan, 1995; hereafter cited in text as Kay 1995).

 6. J. B. Leishman, ed., *The Three Parnassus Plays, 1598–1601* (London, 1949), 1.2.293, 296–99; reprinted in H. & S., 11:364. Frank L. Huntley has argued strongly for Joseph Hall's authorship of the second part of *The Returne;* see his *Bishop Joseph Hall, 1574–1656: A Biographical and Critical Study* (Cambridge: D. S. Brewer, 1979; hereafter cited in text as Huntley), 29–45.

 7. Alexander Gill the Younger, "Uppon Ben Jonsons Magnettick Ladye," Bodleian MS. Ashmole 38, p. 15, lines 52–56; printed in H. & S., 11:346–48.

 8. Jonson may have had other children; see Mark Eccles, "Jonson's Marriage," *Review of English Studies* 12 (1936): 257–72; and the cautionary discussion of Eccles' findings and conclusions in H. & S., 11:574–77.

 9. "Ben Jonson," in Bentley 1941–68, 4:618, 625.

 10. G. E. Bentley, *The Profession of Dramatist in Shakespeare's Time, 1590–1642* (Princeton, N.J.: Princeton University Press, 1971; hereafter cited in text as Bentley 1971), 227–34.

 11. Jonas A. Barish, "Jonson and the Loathed Stage," in *A Celebration of Ben Jonson,* ed. William Blissett, Julian Patrick, and R. W. Van Fossen (Toronto: University of Toronto Press, 1973), 38.

 12. Anonymous; first printed in *Wits Recreations* (London, 1640) as epigram 269 but circulated in manuscript much earlier.

 13. W. David Kay, "The Shaping of Ben Jonson's Literary Career: A Reexamination of Facts and Problems," *Modern Philology* 67 (1970): 236 (hereafter cited in text as Kay 1970). On the importance of the 1616 folio, see also the seminal essay by Richard C. Newton, "Jonson and the (Re)-Invention of the Book," in *Classic and Cavalier: Essays on Jonson and the Sons of Ben,* ed. Claude J. Summers and Ted-Larry Pebworth (Pittsburgh: University of Pittsburgh Press, 1982; hereafter cited in text as Summers and Pebworth 1982), 31–55; the essays in *Ben Jonson's 1616 Folio,* ed. Jennifer Brady and W. H. Herendeen (Newark: University of Delaware Press; London: Associated University Presses, 1991; hereafter cited in text as Brady and Herendeen); and Douglas Brooks, " 'If He Be at His Book, Disturb Him Not': The Two Jonson Folios of 1616," *Ben Jonson Journal* 4 (1997): 81–101. More generally, on Jonson's attitudes toward authorship, see also Bruce Thomas Boehrer, "The Poet of Labor: Authorship and Property in the Work of Ben Jonson," *Philological Quarterly* 72 (1993): 289–312 (hereafter cited in text as Boehrer 1993).

 14. For discussions of Drummond's assessment of Jonson's personality and of *Conversations* in general, see, for example, Ralph S. Walker, "Literary

Criticism in Jonson's Conversations with Drummond," *English* 8 (1951): 222–27; George Parfitt, *Ben Jonson: Public Poet, Private Man* (London: Dent, 1976), 17–24; and Jennifer Brady, "Jonson's Elegies of the Plague Years," *Dalhousie Review* 65 (1985): 208–30 (hereafter cited in text as Brady).

15.   Inigo Jones, "To his false friend mr: Ben Jonson," British Library MS. Harleian 6057, fol. 30r., line 42; printed in H. & S., 11:385–86.

16.   Robert Herrick, "His Prayer to Ben Jonson," *The Complete Poetry of Robert Herrick,* ed. J. Max Patrick (New York: New York University Press, 1963; hereafter cited in text as Herrick), 282.

17.   Sir Edward Walker, Garter, August 17, 1637; quoted in H. & S., 1:115. There is some confusion as to the exact date of Jonson's death, some accounts having it occur on August 16 and others on August 6. See Wayne H. Phelps, "The Date of Ben Jonson's Death," *Notes & Queries,* n.s., 27 (1980): 146–49.

18.   These are the labels of the two parts of the collection of satiric poems that apparently touched off the vogue for satire in the late 1590s, Joseph Hall's *Virgidemiarum* (1597–98); see Huntley, 10–26. Cf. Jonson's acknowledgment of his own reputation for satirical bite: "And, howsoever I cannot escape, from some, the imputation of sharpnesse, but that they will say, I have taken a pride, or lust, to be bitter, and not my youngest infant but hath come into the world with all his teeth. . . ." (*Vol.,* Dedication, lines 47–50).

19.   For a discussion of Jonson's critical principles, see the introduction to James D. Redwine Jr., ed., *Ben Jonson's Literary Criticism* (Lincoln: University of Nebraska Press, 1970); and Richard Dutton, *Ben Jonson: Authority: Criticism* (London: Macmillan, 1996). These volumes select and categorize various critical comments and passages from throughout Jonson's canon. On Jonson's status as a "laureate poet" and on the literary system of his day, see Richard Helgerson, *Self-Crowned Laureates: Spenser, Jonson, Milton, and the Literary System* (Berkeley: University of California Press, 1983; hereafter cited in text as Helgerson).

20.   Douglas Bush, *English Literature in the Earlier Seventeenth Century, 1600–1660,* 2d ed., rev. (Oxford: Clarendon Press, 1962; hereafter cited in text as Bush), 111.

Chapter Two

1.   For detailed information on the social background of Jonson's comedies and on Jonsonian realism, see Knights; and Jonathan Haynes, *The Social Relations of Jonson's Theater* (Cambridge: Cambridge University Press, 1992; hereafter cited in text as Haynes).

2.   For some of the remarks by Jonson's contemporaries, see D. Heyward Brock's introduction to the Scolar facsimile of *The Workes of Benjamin Jonson, 1616* (London: Scolar, 1976), iii.

3.   On this point, see Gabriele Bernhard Jackson, *Vision and Judgment in Ben Jonson's Drama,* Yale Studies in English, vol. 166 (New Haven, Conn.: Yale University Press, 1968; hereafter cited in text as Jackson), 57–69.

4.   On Jonson's characterization, see Lawrence Danson, "Jonsonian Comedy and the Discovery of the Social Self," *PMLA* 99 (1984): 179–93.

5.   For interesting discussions of Jonson's language, see Edward B. Partridge, *The Broken Compass: A Study of the Major Comedies of Ben Jonson* (London: Chatto and Windus; Cambridge, Mass.: Harvard University Press, 1958; hereafter cited in text as Partridge 1958); Jonas A. Barish, *Ben Jonson and the Language of Prose Comedy* (Cambridge, Mass.: Harvard University Press, 1960; reprint, New York: Norton, 1970; hereafter cited in text as Barish); and Peter Womack, *Ben Jonson* (Oxford: Blackwell, 1986; hereafter cited in text as Womack).

6.   See John Jacob Enck, *"The Case Is Altered:* Initial Comedy of Humours," *Studies in Philology* 50 (1953): 195–214, reworked and condensed in Enck, *Jonson and the Comic Truth* (Madison: University of Wisconsin Press, 1957), 21–33; and Robert L. Mack, "Ben Jonson's Own 'Comedy of Errors': 'That Witty Play,' *The Case Is Altered," Ben Jonson Journal* 4 (1997): 47–63. *The Case Is Altered* is usually assigned to 1598, but Kay (1970) suggests 1597 as the more likely date (226–27).

7.   See Joseph A. Bryant Jr., "Jonson's Revision of *Every Man in His Humour," Studies in Philology* 59 (1962): 641–50; A. Richard Dutton, "The Significance of Jonson's Revision of 'Every Man in His Humour,' " *Modern Language Review* 69 (1974): 241–49; Ralph Alan Cohen, "The Importance of Setting in the Revision of *Every Man in His Humour," English Literary Renaissance* 8 (1978): 183–96; and James A. Riddell, "Jonson and Stansby and the Revisions of *Every Man in His Humour," Medieval & Renaissance Drama in England* 9 (1997): 81–91.

8.   On *Every Man in His Humour* as a satiric comedy that parodies popular theatrical fare (such as cuckolding farces, prodigal son fables, and romantic tragedies) and flouts audience expectations, see Robert N. Watson, *Ben Jonson's Parodic Strategy: Literary Imperialism in the Comedies* (Cambridge, Mass.: Harvard University Press, 1987; hereafter cited in text as Watson), 19–46.

9.   See chapter 2 of Judd Arnold, *A Grace Peculiar: Ben Jonson's Cavalier Heroes,* The Pennsylvania State University Studies, no. 35 (University Park: Pennsylvania State University, 1972; hereafter cited in text as Arnold 1972), especially 16–17.

10.   Edward B. Partridge, "Ben Jonson: The Makings of the Dramatist (1596–1602)," in *Elizabethan Theatre,* Stratford-upon-Avon Studies, no. 9 (New York: St. Martin's Press, 1966), 228; see also Lawrence L. Levin, "Clement Justice in *Every Man in His Humor," Studies in English Literature* 12 (1972): 291–307.

11.   For provocative discussions of the comical satires, see Alvin Kernan, *The Cankered Muse: Satire of the English Renaissance* (New Haven, Conn.: Yale

University Press, 1959), 156–64; C. G. Thayer, *Ben Jonson: Studies in the Plays* (Norman: University of Oklahoma Press, 1963; hereafter cited in text as Thayer), 25–49; Robert E. Knoll, *Ben Jonson's Plays: An Introduction* (Lincoln: University of Nebraska Press, 1964; hereafter cited in text as Knoll), 45–65; R. B. Parker, "The Problem of Tone in Jonson's 'Comicall Satyrs,'" *Humanities Association Bulletin* 28 (1977): 43–64; L. A. Beaurline, *Jonson and Elizabethan Comedy: Essays in Dramatic Rhetoric* (San Marino, Calif.: Huntington Library, 1978; hereafter cited in text as Beaurline 1978), 110–55; Richard Dutton, *Ben Jonson: To the First Folio* (Cambridge: Cambridge University Press, 1983; hereafter cited in text as Dutton 1983), 34–53; and Lawrence Danson, "Jonsonian Comedy and the Discovery of the Social Self," *PMLA* 99 (1984): 179–93. On the importance of the comical satires to Jonson's literary career and on their critical and popular reception by his contemporaries, see Kay 1970, 229–37. On the relationship of the comical satires to contemporary verse satire, see Frank Kerins, "The Crafty Enchaunter: *Ironic Satires* and Jonson's *Every Man Out of His Humour,*" *Renaissance Drama,* n.s., 14 (1983): 125–50.

12. Anne Barton, *Ben Jonson, Dramatist* (Cambridge: Cambridge University Press, 1984; hereafter cited in text as Barton), 65. On the play's experiments with theatricality, see also Helen M. Ostovich, " 'So Sudden and Strange a Cure': A Rudimentary Masque in *Every Man Out of His Humour,*" *English Literary Renaissance* 22 (1992): 315–32. On the play as "a parody of literature and the ease with which literary forms are imitated," see Terrance Dunford, "Consumption of the World: Reading, Eating, and Imitation in *Every Man Out of His Humor,*" *English Literary Renaissance* 14 (1984): 131–47; and Watson, 47–79.

13. See E. M. Thron, "Jonson's *Cynthia's Revels:* Multiplicity and Unity," *Studies in English Literature* 11 (1971): 235–47; and Joseph Loewenstein, *Responsive Readings: Versions of Echo in Pastoral, Epic, and the Jonsonian Masque* (New Haven, Conn.: Yale University Press, 1984; hereafter cited in text as Loewenstein), 57–92.

14. Bednarz argues that *Histriomastix* was written as a critique of *Every Man out of His Humour* and that Jonson's disparagement of *Histriomastix* in *Every Man out* was subsequently added to the acting script of the comical satire as a rejoinder to Marston's attack. See "*Histriomastix* and the War of the Theaters," *Medieval & Renaissance Drama in England* 6 (1993): 103–28.

15. See Ernest William Talbert, "The Purpose and Technique of Jonson's *Poetaster,*" *Studies in Philology* 42 (1945): 225–52; and Eugene M. Waith, "The Poet's Morals in Jonson's *Poetaster,*" *Modern Language Quarterly* 12 (1952): 13–19. The fullest discussion of the play and its contexts is Tom Cain's excellent introduction to his edition of *Poetaster* (Manchester: Manchester University Press, 1995; hereafter cited in text as Cain), 1–60.

16. See Robert B. Pierce, "Ben Jonson's Horace and Horace's Ben Jonson," *Studies in Philology* 78 (1981): 20–31; James D. Mulvihill, "Jonson's *Poetaster* and the Ovidian Debate," *Studies in English Literature* 22 (1982): 239–55; Helgerson, 110–16; and Cain, 10–14, 19–23.

248 NOTES AND REFERENCES

17. D. A. Scheve, "Jonson's *Volpone* and Traditional Fox Lore," *Review of English Studies*, n.s., 1 (1950): 242–44; amplified by Charles A. Hallett, "The Satanic Nature of Volpone," *Philological Quarterly* 49 (1970): 41–55. See also R. B. Parker, "*Volpone* and *Reynard the Fox*," *Renaissance Drama*, n.s., 7 (1976): 3–42.

18. Although some of its readings are unconvincing, see S. L. Goldberg, "Folly into Crime: The Catastrophe of *Volpone*," *Modern Language Quarterly* 20 (1959): 233–42. See also Harold Skulsky, "Cannibals vs. Demons in *Volpone*," *Studies in English Literature* 29 (1989): 291–308.

19. See C. J. Gianakaris, "Identifying Ethical Values in *Volpone*," *Huntington Library Quarterly* 32 (1963): 45–57. Cf. A. K. Nardo, "The Transmigration of Folly: Volpone's Innocent Grotesques," *English Studies* 58 (1977): 105–9, which argues that Nano, Androgyno, and Castrone are the only characters in the play who neither gull others nor are themselves victimized.

20. For discussions of the relationship between the plots, see Jonas A. Barish, "The Double Plot in *Volpone*," *Modern Philology* 51 (1953): 83–92; Judd Arnold, "The Double Plot in *Volpone*: A Note on Jonsonian Structure," *Seventeenth-Century News* 23, no. 4 (1965): 47–48, 50–52; Dorothy E. Litt, "Unity of Theme in *Volpone*," *Bulletin of the New York Public Library* 73 (1969): 218–26; and Alexander Leggatt, "*Volpone*: The Double Plot Revisited," in *New Perspectives on Ben Jonson*, ed. James Hirsh (Madison, N.J.: Fairleigh Dickinson University Press; London: Associated University Presses, 1997; hereafter cited in text as Hirsh), 89–105.

21. See Charles A. Hallett, "Jonson's Celia: A Reinterpretation of *Volpone*," *Studies in Philology* 68 (1961): 50–69; Ian Donaldson, "Volpone: Quick and Dead," *Essays in Criticism* 21 (1971): 123–24; and the answer to Donaldson by G. A. E. Parfitt, "Volpone," *Essays in Criticism* 21 (1971): 411–12. On the literary and cultural contexts of Jonson's representation of Celia "as Heaven within an urban bestiary, canonized as ideal wife, recanonized as whore, countercanonized as saint," see Martin Andrew, " 'Cut So Like [Her] Character': Preconstructing Celia in *Volpone*," *Medieval & Renaissance Drama in England* 8 (1996): 94–118.

22. See Arnold 1972, 45. But for a contrary view, see John Creaser, "A Vindication of Sir Politic Would-be," *English Studies* 57 (1976): 503–14.

23. On the antagonism between Mosca and Volpone, see Alexander Leggatt, "The Suicide of Volpone," *University of Toronto Quarterly* 39 (1969): 19–32; and Stephen J. Greenblatt, "The False Ending in *Volpone*," *Journal of English and Germanic Philology* 75 (1976): 90–104. On the homoeroticism in their relationship, see Howard Marchitell, "Desire and Domination in *Volpone*," *Studies in English Literature* 31 (1991): 287–308; Richmond Barbour, " 'When I Acted Young Antinous': Boy Actors and the Erotics of Jonsonian Theater," *PMLA* 110 (1995): 1006–22 (hereafter cited in text as Barbour); and Mario DiGangi, "Asses and Wits: The Homoerotics of Mastery in Satiric Comedy," *English Literary Renaissance* 25 (1995): 179–208.

24. See James D. Redwine Jr., "Volpone's 'Sport' and the Structure of Jonson's *Volpone*," *Studies in English Literature* 34 (1994): 301–21.

25. On the significance of the Venetian setting, see David C. McPherson, *Shakespeare, Jonson, and the Myth of Venice* (Newark: University of Delaware Press, 1990); and Leo Salingar, "The Idea of Venice in Shakespeare and Jonson," in *Shakespeare's Italy: Functions of Italian Locations in Renaissance Drama*, ed. Michele Marrapodi et al. (Manchester: Manchester University Press, 1993), 171–84. On the limits of materialism, see Harriet Hawkins, "Folly, Incurable Disease, and *Volpone*," *Studies in English Literature* 8 (1968): 335–48.

26. See Ronald Broude, "Volpone and the Triumph of Truth: Some Antecedents and Analogues of the Main Plot in *Volpone*," *Studies in Philology* 77 (1980): 227–46.

27. On this point, see James Hirsh, "Cynicism and the Futility of Art in *Volpone*," in Hirsh, 106–27.

28. John Dryden, "An Essay of Dramatic Poesy," in *Essays of John Dryden*, ed. W. P. Ker, 2 vols. (Oxford, 1900; reprint, New York: Russell and Russell, 1961; hereafter cited in text as Dryden), 1:83. But see also Freda L. Townsend, *Apologie for Bartholomew Fayre: The Art of Jonson's Comedies* (New York: Modern Language Association, 1947), 91–97; Ray L. Heffner Jr., "Unifying Symbols in the Comedy of Ben Jonson," in *English Stage Comedy*, ed. W. K. Wimsatt Jr. (New York: Columbia University Press, 1955), 74–97; Mark A. Anderson, "The Successful Unity of *Epicoene*: A Defense of Ben Jonson," *Studies in English Literature* 10 (1970): 349–66; and Beaurline 1978, 200–13.

29. On this point, see Jonas Barish, "Ovid, Juvenal, and *The Silent Woman*," *PMLA* 71 (1956): 213–24; and John Ferns, "Ovid, Juvenal, and 'The Silent Woman': A Reconsideration," *Modern Language Review* 65 (1970): 248–53.

30. Several critics discuss Jonson's setting and his relationship to his audience in *Epicoene*. See, for example, Michael Shapiro, "Audience vs. Dramatist in Jonson's *Epicoene* and Other Plays of the Children's Troupes," *English Literary Renaissance* 3 (1973): 400–17; and P. K. Ayers, "Dreams of the City: The Urban and the Urbane in Jonson's *Epicoene*," *Philological Quarterly* 66 (1987): 73–86.

31. The best discussion of the gallants is in Arnold 1972, 47–54. But see also J. A. Bryant Jr., *The Compassionate Satirist: Ben Jonson and His Imperfect World* (Athens: University of Georgia Press, 1973), 92–111. In "Silence, Wit, and Wisdom in *The Silent Woman*," *Studies in English Literature* 29 (1989): 309–35, Philip Mirabelli argues for the primacy of Truewit among the gallants. He finds Truewit the most impressive of Jonson's comic creations.

32. Diana Benet, " 'The Master-Wit is the Master-Fool': Jonson, *Epicoene*, and the Moralists," *Renaissance Drama*, n.s., 16 (1985): 121–29. Other recent studies that find the gallants less than admirable include Russ McDonald, "Jonsonian Comedy and the Value of *Sejanus*," *Studies in English Literature*

21 (1981): 287–305; Barton, 120–35; and Bruce Thomas Boehrer, *"Epicoene, Charivari, Skimmington," English Studies* 75 (1994): 17–33.

33. Steve Brown, in "The Boyhood of Shakespeare's Heroines: Notes on Gender Ambiguity in the Sixteenth Century," *Studies in English Literature* 30 (1990): 243–63 (hereafter cited in text as Brown), notes that the reference to Clerimont's "engle" is unusual in the period for being noncensorious; he concludes that Jonson's attitude toward same-sex sexual relationships in *Epicoene* is indulgent and genial.

34. See, for example, Edmund Wilson, "Morose Ben Jonson," in *The Triple Thinkers,* rev. ed. (New York: Oxford University Press, 1948), 213–14. Morose's humor must be placed in the context of Renaissance attitudes toward silence and noise. See Huston D. Hallahan, "Silence, Eloquence, and Chatter in Jonson's *Epicoene," Huntington Library Quarterly* 40 (1977): 117–27; and Michael Flachmann, *"Epicoene:* A Comic Hell for a Comic Sinner," *Medieval & Renaissance Drama in England* 1 (1984): 131–42.

35. See Alexander Leggatt, "Morose and His Tormentors," *University of Toronto Quarterly* 45 (1976): 221–35.

36. First discussed extensively in Partridge 1958,161–77.

37. See, for example, Phyllis Rackin, "Androgyny, Mimesis, and the Marriage of the Boy Heroine on the English Renaissance Stage," *PMLA* 102 (1987): 29–41; Mary Beth Rose, *The Expense of Spirit: Love and Sexuality in English Renaissance Drama* (Ithaca, N.Y.: Cornell University Press, 1988), 50–64; and Lorraine Helms, "Roaring Girls and Silent Women: The Politics of Androgyny on the Jacobean Stage," *Themes in Drama* 11 (1989): 59–73. For more positive views of Jonson's treatment of gender issues, see Barbara C. Millard, " 'An Acceptable Violence': Sexual Context in Jonson's *Epicoene," Medieval & Renaissance Drama in England* 1 (1984): 143–58.

38. For example, Knoll, 110.

39. See Barbara J. Baines and Mary C. Williams, "The Contemporary and Classical Antifeminist Tradition in Jonson's *Epicoene,"* in *Renaissance Papers, 1977,* ed. Dennis G. Donovan and A. Leigh DeNeef (Durham, N.C.: Southeastern Renaissance Conference, 1977), 43–58.

40. Barbour, 1006. See also Mario DiGangi, "Asses and Wits: The Homoerotics of Mastery in Satiric Comedy," *English Literary Renaissance* 25 (1995): 179–208; and Brown, 254–63.

41. For a provocative discussion of the ideological significance of the setting in a time of plague, see Cheryl Lynn Ross, "The Plague of *The Alchemist," Renaissance Quarterly* 41 (1988): 439–58.

42. See Alvin B. Kernan, "Alchemy and Acting: The Major Plays of Ben Jonson," *Studies in the Literary Imagination* 6, no. 1 (1973): 4–8.

43. On the tendency to ignore the play's good humor, see Richard Levin's excellent corrective, " 'No Laughing Matter': Some New Readings of *The Alchemist," Studies in the Literary Imagination,* 6, no. 1 (1973): 85–99. See

also Donald Gertmenian, "Comic Experience in *Volpone* and *The Alchemist*," *Studies in English Literature* 17 (1977): 247–58.

44. On the competition between Subtle and Face, see Joyce Van Dyke, "The Game of Wits in *The Alchemist*," *Studies in English Literature* 19 (1979): 253–69; and George E. Rowe, *Distinguishing Jonson: Imitation, Rivalry, and the Direction of a Dramatic Career* (Lincoln: University of Nebraska Press, 1988), 33–36.

45. See Edgar Hill Duncan, "Jonson's *Alchemist* and the Literature of Alchemy," *PMLA* 61 (1946): 699–710; the valuable appendix 1, "Jonson's Use of Alchemy and a Glossary of Alchemical Terms," in Alvin B. Kernan, ed., *Ben Jonson: The Alchemist*, The Yale Ben Jonson, no. 7 (New Haven, Conn.: Yale University Press, 1974), 227–39; and Michael Flachmann, "Ben Jonson and the Alchemy of Satire," *Studies in English Literature* 17 (1977): 259–80.

46. See Johnstone Parr, "Non-Alchemical Pseudo-Sciences in *The Alchemist*," *Philological Quarterly* 24 (1945): 85–89.

47. Gerard H. Cox, "Apocalyptic Projection and the Comic Plot of *The Alchemist*," *English Literary Renaissance* 13 (1983): 70–87 (hereafter cited in text as Cox). On the play's apocalypticism and millenarianism, see also the excellent essay by Robert M. Schuler, "Jonson's Alchemists, Epicures, and Puritans," *Medieval & Renaissance Drama in England* 2 (1985): 171–208 (hereafter cited in text as Schuler).

48. Wayne A. Rebhorn, "Jonson's 'Jovy Boy': Lovewit and the Dupes in *The Alchemist*," *Journal of English and Germanic Philology* 79 (1980): 355–75, especially 365–66 (hereafter cited in text as Rebhorn).

49. On this point, see Schuler, who documents the parallels between Puritanism and alchemy "as manifestations of the same moral and psychological weakness" and explains the rationale of Jonson's choice of the radical Anabaptists as the target of his satire.

50. On Jonson's depiction of Surly, see David F. Finnigan, "The Role of Surly in *The Alchemist*," *Papers on Language and Literature* 16 (1980): 100–104.

51. Jackson, 68. The most persuasive discussion of Lovewit as a dupe is that of Rebhorn, especially 368–75. William W. E. Slights, in *Ben Jonson and the Art of Secrecy*, (Toronto: University of Toronto Press, 1994; hereafter cited in text as Slights), sees Lovewit as similar to both the gulls and the rogues and concludes: "The difference between his trickery and Subtle's is that he uses established laws and social pressures of the community to do the work of Subtle's perverse, jargon-rich imagination. Lovewit is the cheater of everyday" (128).

52. On this point see William Blissett, "The Venter Tripartite in *The Alchemist*," *Studies in English Literature* 8 (1968): 333–34, and Judd Arnold, "Lovewit's Triumph and Jonsonian Morality: A Reading of 'The Alchemist,' " *Criticism* 11 (1969): 151–66, some of which is incorporated into Arnold 1972, 56–61. Nancy S. Leonard, "Shakespeare and Jonson Again: The Comic Forms," *Renaissance Drama*, n.s., 10 (1979): 45–69, regards Lovewit as the

most successful of the rogues. Cox sees Lovewit as triumphing by "enjoying himself here and now rather than striving to become some visionary version of himself" (86).

53.   Schuler, 202. Slights makes a similar point when he writes that "Jonson extends his study of the conspiratorial habit of mind to include the respectable and legitimate within the terms of the criminalized other. Lovewit, that is, gives us more of the same, establishing a fresh conspiracy with Face-Jeremy to replace the *'indenture tripartite'* " (126).

54.   Samuel Taylor Coleridge, "Table Talk," *The Complete Works*, ed. James Shedd, 7 vols. (New York: Harper, 1871; hereafter cited in text as Coleridge), 6:426. The other two are Sophocles' *Oedipus Tyrannos* and Henry Fielding's *Tom Jones*.

55.   On the depiction of women in the play, see Renu Juneja, "Eve's Flesh and Blood in Jonson's *Bartholomew Fair*," *Comparative Drama* 12 (1978–79): 340–55 (hereafter cited in text as Juneja); Kristen McDermott, "Femininity in *Bartholomew Fair*" (hereafter cited in text as McDermott), in *Renaissance Papers, 1993,* ed. Barbara J. Baines and George Walton Williams (Durham, N.C.: Southeastern Renaissance Conference, 1993), 91–115; Lorie Schroeder Haslem, " 'Troubled with the Mother': Longings, Purgings, and the Maternal Body in *Bartholomew Fair* and *The Duchess of Malfi*," *Modern Philology* 92 (1995): 438–59 (hereafter cited in text as Haslem); and Shannon Miller, "Consuming Mothers/Consuming Merchants: The Carnivalesque Economy of Jacobean City Comedy," *Modern Language Studies* 26 (1996): 74–97 (hereafter cited in text as Miller 1996).

56.   On the play's patterns of separation and reunion, see Richard Levin, "The Structure of *Bartholomew Fair*," *PMLA* 80 (1965): 172–79; and Leo Salingar, "Crowd and Public in *Bartholomew Fair*," *Renaissance Drama*, n.s., 10 (1979): 141–59.

57.   Beaurline 1978, 252. John Gordon Sweeney III, *Jonson and the Psychology of Public Theater* (Princeton, N.J.: Princeton University Press, 1985; hereafter cited in text as Sweeney), 164–70, contrasts *Bartholomew Fair* and *A Midsummer Night's Dream*.

58.   See chapter 3, " 'Days of Privilege': *Bartholomew Fair*," in Ian Donaldson, *The World Upside-Down: Comedy from Jonson to Fielding* (Oxford: Clarendon Press, 1970; hereafter cited as Donaldson 1970), 46–77.

59.   Haynes, 130. Haynes's chapter on *Bartholomew Fair* historicizes the meaning of festivity in the play and points out the complexity of Jonson's attitude toward the fair. See also Miller 1996, 86–97.

60.   On Smithfield's association with religious persecution and its consequence for the play, see Clifford Davidson, "Judgment, Iconoclasm, and Anti-Theatricalism in Jonson's *Bartholomew Fair*," *Papers on Language and Literature* 25 (1989): 349–63. See also G. M. Pinciss, "*Bartholomew Fair* and Jonsonian Tolerance," *Studies in English Literature* 35 (1995): 345–59 (hereafter cited in text as Pinciss). Pinciss reads the play as a plea for religious toleration. On the his-

torical background, see also Frances Teague, *The Curious History of Bartholomew Fair* (Lewisburg, Pa.: Bucknell University Press, 1985).

61. On the motif of enormity, see Mary W. Bledsoe, "The Function of Linguistic Enormity in Ben Jonson's *Bartholomew Fair,*" *Language and Style* 17 (1984): 149–60. Bledsoe demonstrates that the disordered syntax and inappropriate imagery of the dialogue is a key to understanding the characters and to establishing the theme and tone of the play.

62. Brian Gibbons, *Jacobean City Comedy: A Study of Satiric Plays by Jonson, Marston, and Middleton* (Cambridge, Mass.: Harvard University Press, 1968; hereafter cited in text as Gibbons), 186.

63. On this point, see McDermott, 95–98. In contrast, Haslem believes that Win is not pregnant at all but is merely feigning pregnancy to trick her mother into accompanying her to the fair to satisfy her longing to eat pig (444–47).

64. Pinciss sees Cokes as representative of English Catholics who might break free of Rome and Wasp as representative of the Roman Catholic hierarchy.

65. On Jonson's treatment of Puritanism in the play, in connection not only with Busy but also Justice Overdo, see Jeanette Ferreira-Ross, "Religion and the Law in Jonson's *Bartholomew Fair,*" *Renaissance and Reformation/Renaissance et Réforme*, n.s., 18 (1994): 45–66.

66. For good discussions of Grace Wellborn and her dilemma as a ward of marriageable age, see Juneja, 343–50; and McDermott, 108–11.

67. Debora K. Shuger, "Hypocrites and Puppets in *Bartholomew Fair,*" *Modern Philology* 82 (1984): 72.

68. This quotation had also been used by King James, so Jonson's use of it may be intended as a compliment to the king. See Gillian Manning, "An Echo of King James in Jonson's *Bartholomew Fair,*" *Notes and Queries,* n.s., 36 (1989): 342–44.

69. On the play's political context, see Leah S. Marcus, *The Politics of Mirth: Jonson, Herrick, Milton, Marvell, and the Defense of Old Holiday Pastimes* (Chicago: University of Chicago Press, 1986; hereafter cited in text as Marcus), 38–63; and by the same author, "Of Mire and Authorship," in *The Theatrical City: Culture, Theatre and Politics in London, 1576–1649,* ed. David L. Smith, Richard Strier, and David Bevington (Cambridge: Cambridge University Press, 1995), 170–81.

70. Donaldson 1970, 71. See also W. David Kay, "*Bartholomew Fair:* Ben Jonson in Praise of Folly," *English Literary Renaissance* 6 (1976): 299–316.

71. For detailed information concerning Jacobean monopolies and projectors and Jonson's accuracy in depicting them, see Knights, especially 71–88, 210–18. On the topical issues addressed in the play, see also the excellent discussions in Marcus, 85–105; and Robert C. Evans, "Contemporary Contexts of Jonson's *The Devil Is an Ass,*" *Comparative Drama* 26 (1992): 140–76.

72. Barton, 235. For extended, generally sympathetic treatments of the play, see in addition to Barton (219–36), Thayer, 156–77; Larry S. Champion,

Ben Jonson's "Dotages": A Reconsideration of the Late Plays (Lexington: University of Kentucky Press, 1967; hereafter cited in text as Champion), 22–44; Gibbons, 192–99; Watson, 172–209; and Rosalind Miles, *Ben Jonson: His Craft and Art* (London: Routledge, 1990; hereafter cited in text as Miles 1990), 198–209.

73. Jonson apparently angered someone influential at court with his satiric attack on this particular scheme. In fact, the earl of Argyle and Sir Robert Carr (a kinsman of the king's one-time favorite, the earl of Somerset) had "been granted patents to drain the fens of Norfolk and Lincolnshire and share the profits with the Crown" (Kay 1995, 151–52). Jonson complained to Drummond that he was "accused" by parties unnamed and that King James "desyred him to conceal" his discourse "of the Duke of Drown land" (*Conv.*, lines 409–15).

74. For an excellent discussion of this aspect of the play, see Devra Rowland Kifer, "*The Staple of News:* Jonson's Festive Comedy," *Studies in English Literature* 12 (1972): 329–44. Also provocative are the analyses in Richard Levin, "The Staple of News, The Society of Jeerers, and Canters' College," *Philological Quarterly* 44 (1965): 445–53; Champion, 45–75; Barton, 237–43; Katherine Eisaman Maus, *Ben Jonson and the Roman Frame of Mind* (Princeton, N.J.: Princeton University Press, 1984; hereafter cited in text as Maus), 160–64; Douglas M. Lanier, "The Prison-House of the Canon: Allegorical Form and Posterity in Ben Jonson's *The Staple of Newes*," *Medieval & Renaissance Drama in England* 2 (1985): 253–67 (hereafter cited in text as Lanier); Miles 1990, 232–39; Kay 1995, 165–68; and Karen Newman, "Engendering the News," in *The Elizabethan Theatre 14,* ed. A. L. Magnusson and C. E. McGee (Toronto: Macmillan of Canada, 1996), 49–69.

75. Knights, 223. But as Lanier points out, Pennyboy Canter "does not understand the problem of moral action in the world in all its complexity; he fails to see that good men may be used." As a consequence, he must be taught "the potentially reforming power of guile in a world of disguises" (262). Ironically, it is not a gallant who teaches him this, as in earlier Jonsonian comedies, but the foolish Pennyboy Junior.

76. This idea was first developed in Harriet Hawkins, "The Idea of a Theater in Jonson's *The New Inn*," *Renaissance Drama* 9 (1966): 205–26 (hereafter cited in text as Hawkins).

77. Cf. a similar situation in *U.* 42, lines 37–42.

78. In addition to Hawkins, see, for example, Partridge 1958, 189–205; Thayer, 198–232; Champion, 76–103; Douglas Duncan, "A Guide to *The New Inn*," *Essays in Criticism* 20 (1970): 311–26; Beaurline 1978, 256–75; Barton, 258–84; Patrick Cheney, "Jonson's *The New Inn* and Plato's Myth of the Hermaphrodite," *Renaissance Drama* 14 (1983): 173–94; Jon S. Lawry, "A Prospect of Jonson's *The New Inn*," *Studies in English Literature* 23 (1983): 311–27; Watson, 210–25; Miles 1990, 239–46; Julie Sanders, " 'The Day's Sports Devised in the Inn': Jonson's *The New Inn* and Theatrical Politics,"

Modern Language Review 91 (1996): 545–60; and Helen Ostovich, "Mistress and Maid: Women's Friendship in *The New Inn*," *Ben Jonson Journal* 4 (1997): 1–26. But see also Richard Levin's protest, "The New *New Inn* and the Proliferation of Good Bad Drama," *Essays in Criticism* 22 (1972): 41–47, answered by R. A. Foakes, "Mr. Levin and 'Good Bad Drama,' " *Essays in Criticism* 22 (1972): 372–79.

79. The most sympathetic discussions of the play are in Champion, 104–30; and Miles 1990, 246–52. See also the analyses in Partridge 1958, 205–12; Thayer, 232–46; and Barton, 285–99; and these more specialized studies: Ronald K. McFarland, "Jonson's Magnetic Lady and the Reception of Gilbert's *De Magnete*," *Studies in English Literature* 11 (1971): 283–93; George E. Rowe Jr., "Ben Jonson's Quarrel with Audience and Its Renaissance Context," *Studies in Philology* 81 (1984): 438–60; Martin Butler, "Ecclesiastical Censorship of Early Stuart Drama: The Case of Jonson's *The Magnetic Lady*," *Modern Philology* 89 (1992): 469–81; and Helen Ostovich, "The Appropriation of Pleasure in *The Magnetic Lady*," *Studies in English Literature* 34 (1994): 425–42.

80. Barton, 321–37; the quotation is from 321. See H. & S., 1:275–301, 3:3, and 9:267–75; W. W. Greg, "Some Notes on Ben Jonson's Works," *Review of English Studies* 2 (1926): 129–45; and Beaurline 1978, 274–86, especially 275. See also Frances Teague, "The Date of Ben Jonson's *A Tale of a Tub*," in *Renaissance Papers, 1979*, ed. A. Leigh DeNeef and M. Thomas Hester (Durham, N.C.: Southeastern Renaissance Conference, 1980), 49–57; and Kay 1995, 178–80. In addition to the appreciative studies of the play by Barton and Beaurline (1978) just cited, see John Lemly, " 'Make Odde Discoveries!': Disguises, Masques, and Jonsonian Romance," in *Comedy from Shakespeare to Sheridan: Change and Continuity in the English and European Dramatic Tradition*, ed. A. R. Braunmuller and J. C. Bulman (Newark: University of Delaware Press, 1986), 141–43; and Riggs, 334–37. Cf. Miles (1990), who finds the play a "total failure . . . on every level" (256).

81. On these points and their political implications, see Marcus, especially 132–35. See also Martin Butler, "Stuart Politics in Jonson's *Tale of a Tub*," *Modern Language Review* 85 (1990): 12–28; and by the same author, "Late Jonson," in *The Politics of Tragicomedy: Shakespeare and After*, ed. Gordon McMullan and Jonathan Hope (London and New York: Routledge, 1992), 179–84.

Chapter Three

1. Jonson may have written several tragedies early in his career. Francis Meres, in his *Palladis Tamia* (entered in the Stationers' Register on September 7, 1598), includes Jonson among the best contemporary tragic playwrights, and Jonson collaborated with other authors on several tragedies. On this point, and for interesting speculation as to why Jonson may have suppressed his early tragedies, see Kay 1970, 225–26.

2. On this point, see Robert Ornstein, *The Moral Vision of Jacobean Tragedy* (Madison: University of Wisconsin Press, 1965; hereafter cited in text as Ornstein), 85–86. See also David Farley-Hills, "Jonson and the Neo-Classical Rules in *Sejanus* and *Volpone*," *Review of English Studies*, n.s., 46 (1995): 153–73.

3. Philip J. Ayres, "The Nature of Jonson's Roman History," *English Literary Renaissance* 16 (1986): 168. See also Joseph A. Bryant Jr., "The Significance of Ben Jonson's First Requirement for Tragedy: 'Truth of Argument,' " *Studies in Philology* 49 (1952): 195–213; A. Richard Dutton, "The Sources, Text, and Readers of *Sejanus:* Jonson's 'integrity in the Story,' " *Studies in Philology* 75 (1978): 181–98 (hereafter cited in text as Dutton 1978); and Bruce Boehrer, "The War on History in Jonson's *Sejanus*," *Studia Neophilologica* 66 (1994): 209–21.

4. For an interesting account of the topical applications of history and drama, see the first chapter of B. N. DeLuna, *Jonson's Romish Plot: A Study of* Catiline *and Its Historical Context* (Oxford: Clarendon Press, 1967; hereafter cited in text as DeLuna), 1–30; and J. M. H. Salmon, "Seneca and Tacitus in Jacobean England" (hereafter cited in text as Salmon), in *The Mental World of the Jacobean Court,* ed. Linda Levy Peck (New York: Cambridge University Press, 1991), 169–88.

5. On Jonson's language in the tragedies, see Geoffrey Hill, *The Lords of Limit: Essays on Literature and Ideas* (London: Deutsch, 1984), 38–54.

6. See R. P. Corballis, "The 'Second Pen' in the Stage Version of *Sejanus*," *Modern Philology* 76 (1979): 273–77. Barton, 93–94, speculates that the "second pen" might have been Shakespeare.

7. Wilson F. Engel III, "The Iron World of *Sejanus*: History in the Crucible of Art," *Renaissance Drama*, n.s., 11 (1980): 95–114.

8. Annabel Patterson, *Censorship and Interpretation: The Conditions of Writing and Reading in Early Modern England* (Madison: University of Wisconsin Press, 1984), 44.

9. On this point and on the political meaning of the play generally, see Matthew H. Wikander, " 'Queasy to be Touched': The World of Ben Jonson's *Sejanus*," *Journal of English and Germanic Philology* 78 (1980): 345–57; Annabel Patterson, " 'Roman-Cast Similitude': Ben Jonson and the English Use of Roman History," in *Rome in the Renaissance: The City and the Myth,* ed. P. A. Ramsey (Binghamton, N.Y.: Medieval and Renaissance Texts and Studies, 1982; hereafter cited in text as Ramsey), 381–94; Anthony Miller, "The Roman State in *Julius Caesar* and *Sejanus*" (hereafter cited in text as Miller 1983), in *Jonson and Shakespeare,* ed. Ian Donaldson (London: Macmillan, 1983), 179–201; Philip J. Ayres, "Jonson, Northampton, and the 'Treason' in *Sejanus*," *Modern Philology* 80 (1983): 356–63; Albert H. Tricomi, *Anticourt Drama in England, 1603–1642* (Charlottesville: University Press of Virginia, 1989), 72–79; Salmon, especially 177–80; and Kay 1995, 68–74.

10. William Blissett, "Roman Ben Jonson," in Brady and Herendeen, 97.

11. For a discussion of the structural formula—the story of two intriguers who conspire and compete—and themes common to *Sejanus* and the comedies, see Russ McDonald, "Jonsonian Comedy and *Sejanus*," *Studies in English Literature* 19 (1981): 288–305.

12. Marvin L. Vawter, "The Seeds of Virtue: Political Imperatives in Jonson's *Sejanus*," *Studies in the Literary Imagination* 6, no. 1 (1973): 41–60. See also George A. E. Parfitt, "Virtue and Pessimism in Three Plays by Ben Jonson," *Studies in the Literary Imagination* 6, no. 1 (1973): 23–40; Frederick Kiefer, "Pretense in Ben Jonson's *Sejanus*," *Essays in Literature* 4 (1977): 19–26; and Dutton 1978.

13. Sweeney, 47–69; Riggs, 101–2. On the play's concern with familial relationships, see also Stuart Kurland, " 'No Innocence is Safe, When Power Contests': The Factional Worlds of Caesar and Sejanus," *Comparative Drama* 22 (1988): 56–57.

14. Gail Kern Paster, *The Idea of the City in the Age of Shakespeare* (Athens: University of Georgia Press, 1985), 115.

15. Bruce Smith, "Rape, Rap, Rupture: R-rated Futures on the Global Market," *Textual Practice* 9 (1995): 439. On dismemberment in the play, see also Christopher Ricks, "*Sejanus* and Dismemberment," *Modern Language Notes* 76 (1961): 301–8; Jonathan Goldberg, *James I and the Politics of Literature: Jonson, Shakespeare, Donne, and Their Contemporaries* (Baltimore: Johns Hopkins University Press, 1983; hereafter cited in text as Goldberg), 184–85; and Slights, 32–56.

16. J. W. Lever, *The Tragedy of State* (London: Methuen, 1971), 66.

17. Gerald Bentley, *Shakespeare and Jonson: Their Reputations in the Seventeenth Century Compared* (Chicago: University of Chicago Press, 1945), 1:109–12.

18. DeLuna, argues that "*Catiline* . . . was both intended and in some circles understood as a classical parallelograph on the Gunpowder Plot of 1605" (360). See also the discussion in Kay 1995, 121–25.

19. On the playwright's handling of his sources, see Bruce Boehrer, "Jonson's *Catiline* and Anti-Sallustian Trends in Renaissance Humanist Historiography," *Studies in Philology* 94 (1997): 85–102 (hereafter cited in text as Boehrer 1997).

20. A. R. Dutton, " 'What Ministers Men Must, For Practice, Use': Ben Jonson's Cicero," *English Studies* 59 (1978): 327.

21. For an analysis of Cicero's speech and its function in the play, see Womack, 87–96.

22. On Jonson's interpretation of history in *Catiline,* see Joseph A. Bryant Jr., "*Catiline* and the Nature of Jonson's Tragic Fable," *PMLA* 69 (1954), 265–77; and Boehrer 1997. It is worth noting that in 1609, Jonson contributed two prefatory poems (*E.* 110 and 111) to Clement Edmondes's *Observations upon Caesar's Commentaries.* In *E.* 110, he expresses his view of Caesar as an enemy of Rome, who robbed the city of its liberty. On these poems, see

Robert C. Evans, *Habits of Mind: Evidence and Effects of Ben Jonson's Reading* (Lewisburg, Pa.: Bucknell University Press, 1995), 218–44.

  23. Cf. Ornstein, 102–3.

  24. J. S. Lawry, "*Catiline* and 'the Sight of Rome in Us,'" in Ramsey, 399.

  25. Howard B. Norland, "The Design of Ben Jonson's *Catiline*," *Sixteenth Century Journal* 9, no. 4 (1978): 69.

  26. On the family imagery in *Catiline*, see Barton, 163–64. On another pattern of imagery in the play, related to serpents, see Clifford J. Ronan, "Snakes in *Catiline*," *Medieval & Renaissance Drama in England* 3 (1986): 149–63.

Chapter Four

  1. See Suzanne Gossett, "Recent Studies in the English Masque," *English Literary Renaissance* 26 (1996): 586–614, for bibliographical essays on the masque in general (586–605) and Jonson's masques in particular (605–14). On the development of the masque and its conventions, see, for example, Enid Welsford, *The Court Masque: A Study in the Relationship between Poetry & the Revels* (Cambridge, 1927; reprint New York: Russell and Russell, 1962); Allardyce Nicoll, *Stuart Masques and the Renaissance Stage* (London: Harrap, 1937); and Stephen Orgel, *The Illusion of Power: Political Theater in the English Renaissance* (Berkeley: University of California Press, 1975; hereafter cited in text as Orgel 1975). The two fullest and most influential studies of Jonson's masques are Stephen Orgel, *The Jonsonian Masque* (Cambridge, Mass.: Harvard University Press, 1965; hereafter cited in text as Orgel 1965); and John C. Meagher, *Method and Meaning in Jonson's Masques* (Notre Dame, Ind.: University of Notre Dame Press, 1966; hereafter cited in text as Meagher). Other useful studies include Ernest W. Talbert, "The Interpretation of Jonson's Courtly Spectacles," *PMLA* 61 (1946): 454–73; Dolora Cunningham, "The Jonsonian Masque as a Literary Form," *ELH* 22 (1955): 108–24; W. Todd Furniss, "Ben Jonson's Masques," in *Three Studies in the Renaissance: Sidney, Jonson, Milton* (New Haven, Conn.: Yale University Press, 1958; hereafter cited in text as Furniss), 89–179; Stephen Orgel, "To Make Boards to Speak: Inigo Jones's Stage and the Jonsonian Masque," *Renaissance Drama*, n.s., 1 (1968): 121–52, revised and expanded as the introduction to his edition, *Ben Jonson: The Complete Masques* (New Haven, Conn.: Yale University Press, 1969), 1–44; M. C. Bradbrook, "Social Change and the Evolution of Ben Jonson's Court Masques," *Studies in the Literary Imagination* 6, no. 1 (1973): 101–38; Mary Chan, *Music in the Theatre of Ben Jonson* (Oxford: Clarendon Press, 1980; hereafter cited in text as Chan), 138–304; Dutton 1983; Goldberg, 55–112; Loewenstein, 93–132, and "Printing and 'The Multitudinous Presse': The Contentious Texts of Jonson's Masques," in Brady and Herendeen, 168–91; Nathaniel Strout, "Jonson's Jacobean Masques and the Moral Imagination," *Studies in English Literature* 27 (1987): 233–47; Robert C. Evans, *Ben Jonson and the Poetics of Patronage* (Lewisburg, Pa.: Bucknell

University Press, 1989; hereafter cited in text as Evans), 222–45; and Miles 1990, 85–103.

2. On Jonson's collaboration with Jones, and their quarrel, see D. J. Gordon, "Poet and Architect: The Intellectual Setting of the Quarrel between Ben Jonson and Inigo Jones," *Journal of the Warburg and Courtauld Institutes* 8 (1945): 107–45; and Stephen Orgel and Roy Strong, *Inigo Jones: The Theater of the Stuart Court,* 2 vols. (Berkeley: University of California Press, 1973; hereafter cited in text as Orgel and Strong).

3. Sir Francis Bacon, "Of Praise," in *The Essayes* (London, 1625; reprint Menston, England: Scolar, 1971), 305–6.

4. See also *Disc.,* lines 1404–12, where Jonson criticizes the ephemeral entertainments prepared at great cost for the state visit of Christian IV of Denmark in 1606.

5. Barish, 244. See also Robert Behunin, "Classical Wonder in Jonson's Masques," *Ben Jonson Journal* 3 (1996): 39–57.

6. Leah Sinanoglou Marcus has excellent studies of the topical nature of Jonson's masques in " 'Present Occasions' and the Shaping of Ben Jonson's Masques," *ELH* 45 (1978): 201–25; "Masquing Occasions and Masque Structure," *Research Opportunities in Renaissance Drama* 24 (1981): 7–16; and Marcus, chapters 2–4. Both Riggs and Kay 1995 contextualize the masques and comment on their political contents.

7. A telling example of Jonson's daring in this regard is *The Gypsies Metamorphosed* (1621), where the poet may have intended to warn the king of the prodigality of his favorite, the earl (later duke) of Buckingham, who commissioned the masque. See the fascinating book by Dale B. J. Randall, *Jonson's Gypsies Unmasked: Background and Theme of* The Gypsies Metamorphos'd (Durham, N.C.: Duke University Press, 1975).

8. See, for example, D. J. Gordon, "The Imagery of Ben Jonson's 'The Masque of Blacknesse' and 'The Masque of Beautie,' " *Journal of the Warburg and Courtauld Institutes* 6 (1943): 122–41 (hereafter cited in text as Gordon); Allan H. Gilbert, *The Symbolic Persons in the Masques of Ben Jonson* (Durham, N.C., 1948; reprint New York: AMS Press, 1969); and Furniss. Meagher's *Method and Meaning* is perhaps the best study of Jonson's assimilation of a wide variety of philosophical influences. Much of the symbolism in Jonson's masques is derived from popular mythographical handbooks, such as Cesare Ripa's *Iconologia,* Natilis Comes's *Mythologia,* and Vicenzo Cartari's *Imagini.*

9. For Queen Anne's influence on Jonson's masques, including her political agenda, see Barbara Kiefer Lewalski, *Writing Women in Jacobean England* (Cambridge, Mass.: Harvard University Press, 1993; hereafter cited in text as Lewalski), 1–43. See also Suzanne Gossett, " 'Man-maid, begone!': Women in Masques," *English Literary Renaissance* 18 (1988): 96–113 (hereafter cited in text as Gossett); and Marion Wynne-Davies, "The Queen's Masque: Renaissance Women and the Seventeenth-Century Court Masque" (hereafter cited in text as Wynne-Davies), in *Gloriana's Face: Women, Public and Private, in the Eng-*

lish Renaissance, ed. S. P. Cerasano and Marion Wynne-Davies (New York: Harvester, 1992), 79–104.

10. Yumna Siddiqi, "Dark Incontinents: The Discourses of Race and Gender in Three Renaissance Masques," *Renaissance Drama* 23 (1992): 139, 146. See also Gordon; Loewenstein, 93–103; Joyce Green MacDonald, " 'The Force of Imagination': The Subject of Blackness in Shakespeare, Jonson, and Ravenscroft," in *Renaissance Papers, 1991,* ed. George Walton Williams and Barbara J. Baines (Durham, N.C.: Southeastern Renaissance Conference, 1992), 53–74; and Hardin Aasand, " 'To Blanch an Ethiop, and Revive a Corse': Queen Anne and *The Masque of Blackness,*" *Studies in English Literature* 32 (1992): 271–85.

11. Cf. *E.* 5, "On the Union," but see *E.* 14, "To William Camden," in which Jonson credits Camden with restoring the ancient name Britain to the island (line 5).

12. By the time that Jonson published *Hymenaei* in the 1616 folio, Frances Howard had been disgraced. In a scandalous proceeding, she had obtained an annulment of her marriage to Essex; married Robert Carr, earl of Somerset; and been accused of murdering her new husband's ex-secretary, Sir Thomas Overbury. As a consequence, Jonson suppressed all mention of the specific occasion of this masque celebrating her first marriage. See David Lindley, "Embarrassing Ben: The Masques for Frances Howard," *English Literary Renaissance* 16 (1986): 343–59. See also, by the same author, *The Trials of Frances Howard: Fact and Fiction at the Court of King James* (London: Routledge, 1993).

13. Luckily, many of Jones's designs survive and are often reproduced. In their lavishly illustrated and beautifully printed *Inigo Jones,* Orgel and Strong reproduce many of Jones's sketches for masques. Orgel's distillation of that work, *The Illusion of Power,* includes photographs of three of Jones's designs for *The Masque of Queens:* the costume of one of the masquers, the headdress worn by Queen Anne, and a sketch of the House of Fame.

14. On this point, see Meagher, 155–56.

15. See, for example, Gossett, 99–101; Margaret Maurer, "Reading Ben Jonson's *Queens,*" in *Seeking the Woman in Late Medieval and Renaissance Writings,* ed. Sheila Fisher and Janet E. Halley (Knoxville: University of Tennessee Press, 1989), 233–63; John F. Moffitt, "Il Filarete and Inigo Jones: The House of Fame in Ben Jonson's 'The Masque of Queens,' " *Arte Lombardo* 90 (1989): 61–66; Stephen Orgel, "Jonson and the Amazons," in *Soliciting Interpretation: Literary Theory and Seventeenth-Century English Poetry,* ed. Elizabeth D. Harvey and Katharine Eisaman Maus (Chicago: University of Chicago Press, 1990), 119–39; Wynne-Davies, 82–86; Lewalski, 36–39; Eugene R. Cunnar, "(En)Gendering Architectural Poetics in Jonson's *Masque of Queens,*" *LIT: Literature Interpretation Theory* 4 (1993): 145–60 (hereafter cited in text as Cunnar); and Lawrence Normand, "Witches, King James, and *The Masque of Queens*" (hereafter cited in text as Normand), in *Representing Women in Renaissance*

England, ed. Claude J. Summers and Ted-Larry Pebworth (Columbia: University of Missouri Press, 1997), 107–20.

16. Cunnar, 150. Moffitt's proposal is announced in "Il Filarete and Inigo Jones."

17. See Goldberg, 142.

18. See the introduction to Orgel 1965, 9–25. But as pointed out in Bruce Louis Jay, "The Role of Verse and the Dynamics of Form in Jonson's Masques," *Études Anglaises* 29 (1976): 129–43 (hereafter cited in text as Jay), "Jonson's resistance to the encroaching glitter of Jones' spectacles was compromised by the royal taste and his own slim pocketbook" (141).

19. For an excellent discussion of *Oberon,* see Jay, 136–38.

20. See Willa McClung Evans, *Ben Jonson and Elizabethan Music* (Lancaster, Pa., 1929; reprint New York: Da Capo Press, 1965), 78–121; and Chan, 232–304.

21. Orgel 1965, 162. See also Richard S. Peterson, "The Iconography of Jonson's *Pleasure Reconciled to Virtue,*" *Journal of Medieval and Renaissance Studies* 5 (1975): 123–53; and John Mulryan, "Mythic Interpretations of Ideas in Jonson's *Pleasure Reconciled to Virtue,*" *Ben Jonson Journal* 1 (1994): 63–76.

22. Peter Walls, "Jonson's Borrowing," *Theatre Notebook* 28 (1974): 80–71, notes similarities in the antimasques of *Pleasure Renconciled to Virtue* and Robert White's *Cupid's Banishment,* which had been staged the previous May with Queen Anne in the audience. Robert C. Evans, " 'Other Men's Provision': Ben Jonson's Parody of Robert White in *Pleasure Reconciled to Virtue,*" *Comparative Drama* 24 (1990): 55–77, offers detailed parallels from the two masques and proposes that Jonson was trying to outdo White, whom he saw as a possible rival for royal patronage. The fact that many members of the audience of *Pleasure Reconciled to Virtue* had seen White's masque on nearly the identical subject a few months earlier may account for its less-than-enthusiastic reception.

23. Leah Sinanoglou Marcus, "The Occasion of Ben Jonson's *Pleasure Reconciled to Virtue,*" *Studies in English Literature* 19 (1979): 279.

24. For an excellent discussion of the relationship between *Pleasure Reconciled to Virtue* and *A Maske,* see Orgel, *The Jonsonian Masque,* 151–53.

Chapter Five

1. Useful comparisons of Donne and Jonson include J. B. Leishman, *The Monarch of Wit* (London, 1951; reprint New York: Harper and Row, 1966), 11–29; Wesley Trimpi, *Ben Jonson's Poems: A Study of the Plain Style* (Palo Alto, Calif.: Stanford University Press, 1962; hereafter cited in text as Trimpi), 1–40; and Joseph H. Summers, *The Heirs of Donne and Jonson* (New York and London: Oxford University Press, 1970; hereafter cited in text as Summers), 13–40.

2. C. A. Patrides, "A Poet Nearly Anonymous" (hereafter cited in text as Patrides), in Summers and Pebworth 1982, 3–16; on *imitatio,* see Richard S.

Peterson, *Imitation and Praise in the Poems of Ben Jonson* (New Haven, Conn.: Yale University Press, 1981; hereafter cited in text as Peterson 1981). On Jonson's classicism, see also, for example, George A. E. Parfitt, "Compromise Classicism: Language and Rhythm in Ben Jonson's Poetry," *Studies in English Literature* 11 (1971): 109–23; Earl Miner, *The Cavalier Mode from Jonson to Cotton* (Princeton, N.J.: Princeton University Press, 1971; hereafter cited in text as Miner): 84–99; and Don E. Wayne, "Mediation and Contestation: English Classicism from Sidney to Jonson," *Criticism* 25 (1983): 211–37.

3. On this point, see Geoffrey Walton, "The Tone of Ben Jonson's Poetry," in *Metaphysical to Augustan* (London: Bowes and Bowes, 1955), 23–44; Hugh Maclean, "Ben Jonson's Poems: Notes on the Ordered Society," in *Essays in English Literature from the Renaissance to the Victorian Age, Presented to A. S. P. Woodhouse,* ed. Millar MacLure and F. Watt (Toronto: University of Toronto Press, 1964), 43–68; L. C. Knights, "Ben Jonson: Public Attitudes and Social Poetry," in *A Celebration of Ben Jonson,* ed. William Blissett, Julian Patrick, and R. W. Van Fossen (Toronto: University of Toronto Press, 1973), 167–87; and Anthony Mortimer, "The Feigned Commonwealth in the Poetry of Ben Jonson," *Studies in English Literature* 13 (1973): 69–79.

4. Sara van den Berg, *The Action of Ben Jonson's Poetry* (Newark: University of Delaware Press, 1987; hereafter cited in text as van den Berg), 13. See also Stanley Fish, "Authors-Readers: Jonson's Community of the Same," *Representations* 7 (1984): 26–57.

5. For discussions of Jonson's style, see Trimpi, 96–237; G. A. E. Parfitt, "The Poetry of Ben Jonson," *Essays in Criticism* 18 (1968): 18–31; William V. Spanos, "The Real Toad in the Jonsonian Garden: Resonance in the Nondramatic Poetry," *Journal of English and Germanic Philology* 68 (1969): 1–23; Arthur F. Marotti, "All About Jonson's Poetry," *ELH* 39 (1971): 208–37; and Richard C. Newton, " 'Ben. / Jonson': The Poet in the Poems," in *Two Renaissance Mythmakers: Christopher Marlowe and Ben Jonson,* ed. Alvin Kernan (Baltimore: Johns Hopkins University Press, 1977; hereafter cited in text as Kernan), 165–95.

6. On Jonson's versification, see especially Richard Flantz, "The Authoritie of Truth: Jonson's Mastery of Measure and the Founding of the Modern Plain-Style Lyric," in Summers and Pebworth 1982, 59–75; and Susanne Woods, "The Context of Jonson's Formalism," in Summers and Pebworth 1982, 77–89. On Jonson's attitude toward language, see Martin Elsky, "Words, Things, and Names: Jonson's Poetry and Philosophical Grammar," in Summers and Pebworth 1982, 91–104.

7. See Ilona Bell, "Circular Strategies and Structures in Jonson and Herbert," in Summers and Pebworth 1982, 157–70; and Richard B. Wollman, " 'Speak that I may see thee': Aurality in Ben Jonson's Print Poetry," *Ben Jonson Journal* 3 (1996): 21–37. On Jonson's punctuation and contrastive techniques, see also Michael McCanles, *Jonsonian Discriminations: The Humanist Poet and the Praise of True Nobility* (Toronto: University of Toronto Press, 1992), 3–45.

8. T. K. Whipple, *Martial and the English Epigram from Sir Thomas Wyatt to Ben Jonson,* University of California Publications in Modern Philology, vol. 10 (Berkeley: University of California Press, 1925), 387ff.

9. On *Epigrams* as a coherent collection, see Rufus D. Putney, " 'This So Subtile Sport': Some Aspects of Jonson's Epigrams," *University of Colorado Studies,* Series in Language and Literature, 10 (1966): 37–56; David Wykes, "Ben Jonson's 'Chast Booke': The *Epigrammes,*" *Renaissance and Modern Studies* 13 (1969): 76–87; Edward Partridge, "Jonson's *Epigrammes:* The Named and the Nameless," *Studies in the Literary Imagination* 6, no. 1 (1973): 153–98 (hereafter cited in text as Partridge 1973); Bruce R. Smith, "Ben Jonson's *Epigrammes:* Portrait-Gallery, Theater, Commonwealth," *Studies in English Literature* 14 (1974): 91–109; R. V. Young Jr., "Style and Structure in Jonson's Epigrams," *Criticism* 17 (1975): 201–22 (hereafter cited in text as Young); Judith Kegan Gardiner, *Craftsmanship in Context: The Development of Ben Jonson's Poetry* (The Hague: Mouton, 1975), 12–53; James A. Riddell, "The Arrangement of Ben Jonson's *Epigrammes,*" *Studies in English Literature* 27 (1987): 53–70; and Robert Wiltenburg, *Ben Jonson and Self-Love: The Subtlest Maze of All* (Columbia, Mo.: University of Missouri Press, 1990; hereafter cited in text as Wiltenburg), 45–90.

10. See Jack D. Winner, "Ben Jonson's *Epigrammes* and the Conventions of Verse Satire," *Studies in English Literature* 23 (1983): 61–76. On Jonson's necessary discretion, see Evans, 82.

11. See Young, 214–15.

12. Robert Burton, *The Anatomy of Melancholy,* ed. Floyd Dell and Paul Jordan Smith (New York: Tudor, 1955), 504.

13. See the discussion of this poem in Young, 207–8.

14. For a discussion of this poem and of Jonson's attitude toward King James, see Jennifer Brady, "Jonson's 'To King James': Plain Speaking in the *Epigrammes* and the *Conversations,*" *Studies in Philology* 82 (1985): 380–98. See also Jean Le Drew Metcalfe, "Subjecting the King: Ben Jonson's Praise of James I," *English Studies in Canada* 17 (1991): 135–49. On Jonson's absolutism, see Goldberg, 219–30.

15. Partridge 1973, 198. See also Achsah Guibbory, "The Poet as Myth Maker: Ben Jonson's Poetry of Praise," *Clio* 5 (1976): 315–29; Don E. Wayne, "Poetry and Power in Ben Jonson's *Epigrammes:* The Naming of 'Facts' or the Figuring of Social Relations," *Renaissance and Modern Studies* 23 (1979): 70–103; and Jonathan Z. Kamholtz, "Ben Jonson's *Epigrammes* and Poetic Occasions," *Studies in English Literature* 23 (1983): 77–94.

16. On Jonson's complicated relations with Cecil, who may be the person Jonson admits to having praised undeservingly in "To My Muse" (*E.* 65), see Robert Wiltenburg, " 'What need hast thou of me? or of my *Muse?*': Jonson and Cecil, Politician and Poet," in *"The Muses Commonweale": Poetry and Politics in the Seventeenth Century,* ed. Claude J. Summers and Ted-Larry Pebworth (Colum-

bia: University of Missouri Press, 1988; hereafter cited in text as Summers and Pebworth 1988), 34–47; and Evans, 95–107.

17.   On the significance of Camden for Jonson, see W. H. Herendeen, "Like a Circle Bounded in Itself: Jonson, Camden, and the Strategies of Praise," *Journal of Medieval and Renaissance Studies* 11 (1981): 137–67.

18.   Homer, *The Odyssey,* bk. 1, line 506, in *Chapman's Homer,* ed. Allardyce Nicoll, 2 vols. (New York: Pantheon, 1956), 2:12. Peterson, in *Imitation and Praise in Ben Jonson's Poems,* points out that behind the poem also lie works by Catullus, Horace, and their imitator, Statius, "so that there is good reason to believe that Jonson saw his poem as descended from these, a new and worthy link in a chain of imitation" (35).

19.   On this point, see Young, 212. For a discussion of the circle image which figures so prominently in the poem, see Thomas M. Greene, "Ben Jonson and the Centered Self," *Studies in English Literature* 10 (1970): 325–48.

20.   For a reading of the poem in the context of the patronage system, see Mary Thomas Crane, " 'His Owne Style': Voice and Writing in Jonson's Poems," *Criticism* 32 (1990): 31–50.

21.   Jack D. Winner, "The Public and Private Dimensions of Jonson's Epitaphs," in Summers and Pebworth 1982, 111.

22.   On the presence of Jonson's religious beliefs in his poetry, see James P. Crowley, "The 'Honest Style' of Ben Jonson's *Epigrams* and *The Forest,*" *Renaissance and Reformation / Renaissance et Réforme* 20 (1996): 33–56; see also George A. E. Parfitt, "Ethics and Christianity in Ben Jonson," in Hirsh, 77–88.

23.   On rigorism and its presence in Jonson's poetry, see G. W. Pigman III, "Suppressed Grief in Jonson's Funeral Poetry," *English Literary Renaissance* 13 (1983): 203–20.

24.   On Jonson's friendship with Sir John Roe and his mourning for him, see Brady, 216–30.

25.   See Richmond Lattimore, *Themes in Greek and Latin Epitaphs* (Urbana: University of Illinois Press, 1962), 65–74.

26.   See Ann Lauinger, " 'It Makes the Father, Lesse, to Rue': Resistance to Consolation in Jonson's 'On My First Daughter,' " *Studies in Philology* 86 (1989): 219–33. Lauinger attributes the poet's resistance to consolation to "his understanding of fatherhood as it contrasts with motherhood and conflicts with God" (233).

27.   On the poem as an elegy describing or evoking a burial ceremony and concluding with an epitaph and on the poem as Jonson's attempt to pay back his son for his neglect, see Joshua Scodel, "Genre and Occasion in Jonson's 'On My First Sonne,' " *Studies in Philology* 86 (1989): 235–59. On Jonson's guilt and grief for his son, see also Brady, 213–16.

28.   Ilona Bell, "The Most Retired and Inmost Part of Jonson's 'On My First Sonne,' " *College Language Association Journal* 29 (1985): 179. See also H. W. Matalene, "Patriarchal Fatherhood in Ben Jonson's Epigram 45," in *Traditions and Innovations: Essays on British Literature of the Middle Ages and the*

Renaissance, ed. David G. Allen and Robert A. White (Newark: University of Delaware Press, 1990), 102–112.

29.   The Christian context of the poem is discussed by the following: L. A. Beaurline, "The Selective Principle in Jonson's Shorter Poems," *Criticism* 8 (1966): 64–74, revised and reprinted in *Ben Jonson and the Cavalier Poets,* ed. Hugh Maclean (New York: Norton, 1974), 516–25 (hereafter cited in text as Beaurline 1974); Francis Fike, "Ben Jonson's 'On My First Sonne,' " *Gordon Review* 11 (1969): 205–20; W. David Kay, "The Christian Wisdom of Ben Jonson's 'On My First Sonne,' " *Studies in English Literature* 11 (1971): 125–36; J. Z. Kronenfeld, "The Father Found: Consolation Achieved through Love in Ben Jonson's 'On My First Sonne,' " *Studies in Philology* 75 (1978): 64–83; and Lauren Silberman, "To Write Sorrow in Jonson's 'On My First Sonne,' " *John Donne Journal* 9 (1990): 149–55. But cf. Peter Hyland, "The Failure of Stoicism: A Reading of Ben Jonson's 'On My First Sonne,' " *Concerning Poetry* 17 (1984): 35–42.

30.   On Jonson's imitation of Martial in this poem, see Thomas M. Greene, *The Light in Troy: Imitation and Discovery in Renaissance Poetry* (New Haven, Conn.: Yale University Press, 1982), 278–82. In *The Action of Ben Jonson's Poetry,* van den Berg also associates the poem with three colloquies of Erasmus (52–61).

31.   Michael Schoenfeldt, " 'The Mysteries of Manners, Armes, and Arts': 'Inviting a Friend to Supper' and 'To Penshurst' " (hereafter cited in text as Schoenfeldt), in Summers and Pebworth 1988, 65. Evans, 205–10, also situates the poem within a social context. See also Joseph Loewenstein, "The Jonsonian Corpulence, or The Poet as Mouthpiece," *ELH* 53 (1986): 491–518; and Bruce Thomas Boehrer, "Renaissance Overeating: The Sad Case of Ben Jonson," *PMLA* 105 (1990): 1071–82.

32.   See Roger Cognard, "Jonson's 'Inviting a Friend to Supper,' " *Explicator* 37, no. 3 (1979): 4.

33.   For discussions of "On the Famous Voyage," see J. G. Nichols, *The Poetry of Ben Jonson* (New York: Barnes and Noble, 1969; hereafter cited in text as Nichols), 105–11; Peter E. Medine, "Object and Intent in Jonson's 'Famous Voyage,' " *Studies in English Literature* 15 (1975): 97–110; van den Berg, 103–8; and Bruce Thomas Boehrer, "The Ordure of Things: Ben Jonson, Sir John Harington, and the Culture of Excrement in Early Modern England," in Hirsh, 174–96.

34.   On Jonson's title and the arrangement of the book, see Jonathan Kamholtz, "Ben Jonson's Green World: Structure and Imaginative Unity in *The Forrest,*" *Studies in Philology* 78 (1981): 170–93; David Hill Radcliffe, "Sylvan States: Social and Literary Formations in Sylvae by Jonson and Cowley," *ELH* 55 (1988): 797–809; and Catherine Bates, "Much Ado about Nothing: The Contents of Jonson's *Forrest,*" *Essays in Criticism* 42 (1992): 24–35. See also George Parfitt, "The 'Strangeness' of Ben Jonson's *The Forest,*" *Leeds Studies in English* 18 (1987): 45–54; van den Berg, 109–42; and Wiltenburg, 91–123.

35. Summers, 27. See also Lawrence Venuti, "Why Jonson Wrote Not of Love," *Journal of Medieval and Renaissance Studies* 12 (1982): 195–220.

36. See H. & S., 11:366–67.

37. See Anne Ferry, *All in War with Time: Love Poetry of Shakespeare, Donne, Jonson, Marvell* (Cambridge, Mass.: Harvard University Press, 1975; hereafter cited in text as Ferry), 163–68.

38. On the relationship of neoplatonism and Petrarchanism, see Trimpi, 280–81, n. 18.

39. H. & S., 2:389.

40. For example, see Nichols, 23–29; and Summers, 28. On the Catullan influence on Jonson, see Patrides in Summers and Pebworth 1982, 3–16; Stella P. Revard, "Classicism and Neo-Classicism in Jonson's *Epigrammes* and *The Forrest*," in Brady and Herendeen, 138–67; and Bruce Boehrer, "Ben Jonson and the *Traditio Basiorum*: Catullan Imitation in *The Forrest* 5 and 6," *Papers on Language and Literature* 32 (1996): 63–84.

41. See Beaurline 1974, 523–24.

42. D. J. Palmer, "The Verse Epistle" in *Metaphysical Poetry,* ed. Malcolm Bradbury and David Palmer (London, 1970; reprint Bloomington: Indiana University Press, 1971; hereafter cited in text as Bradbury and Palmer), 73.

43. Studies of the country house poem include G. R. Hibbard, "The Country House Poem of the Seventeenth Century," *Journal of the Warburg and Courtauld Institutes* 19 (1956): 159–74; Charles Molesworth, "Property and Virtue: The Genre of the Country-House Poem in the Seventeenth Century," *Genre* 1 (1968): 141–57; William A. McClung, *The Country House in English Renaissance Poetry* (Berkeley: University of California Press, 1977); Heather Dubrow, "The Country-House Poem: A Study in Generic Development," *Genre* 12 (1979): 153–79; and Don E. Wayne, *Penshurst: The Semiotics of Place and the Poetics of History* (Madison: University of Wisconsin Press, 1984; hereafter cited in text as Wayne).

44. J. C. A. Rathmell, "Jonson, Lord Lisle, and Penshurst," *English Literary Renaissance* 1 (1971): 250–60. See also Gayle E. Wilson, "Jonson's Use of the Bible and the Great Chain of Being in 'To Penshurst,' " *Studies in English Literature* 8 (1968): 77–89; Paul Cubeta, "A Jonsonian Ideal: 'To Penshurst,' " *Philosophical Quarterly* 42 (1963): 14–24; Jeffrey Hart, "Ben Jonson's Good Society: On the Growth of a Place and a Poem," *Modern Age* 7 (1963): 61–68; Alistair Fowler, "The Locality of Jonson's *To Penshurst*," in *Conceitful Thought: The Interpretation of English Renaissance Poems* (Edinburgh: Edinburgh University Press, 1975), 114–34; and Hugh Jenkins, "The Alchemy of Penshurst," *Clio* 25 (1985): 165–80.

45. Wayne, 75. The classic statement of the mystification of social relations in "To Penshurst" is Raymond Williams, *The Country and the City* (Oxford: Oxford University Press, 1973), 28–34. For important qualifications of Williams's argument and further consideration of the ideology of the poem, see also Wayne; Schoenfeldt, 69–79; Richard Harp, "Jonson's 'To Penshurst': The

Country House as Church," *John Donne Journal* 7 (1988): 73–89; and Thomas D. Marshall, "Addressing the House: Jonson's Ideology at Penshurst," *Texas Studies in Literature and Language* 35 (1993): 57–77.

46. See Lisle Cecil John, "Ben Jonson's 'To Sir William Sydney, on his Birthday,' " *Modern Language Review* 52 (1957): 168–76; and Anthony Miller, " 'These Forc'd Ioyes': Imitation, Celebration, and Exhortation in Ben Jonson's Ode to Sir William Sidney," *Studies in Philology* 86 (1989): 42–68.

47. See William Kerrigan, "Ben Jonson Full of Shame and Scorn," *Studies in the Literary Imagination* 6, no. 1 (1973): 199–217 (hereafter cited in text as Kerrigan).

48. Augustine, *De Civitate Dei,* 1.16–27. Cited in Kerrigan, 202, 209.

49. John Donne, *Biathanatos,* ed. J. William Hebel (New York: Facsimile Text Society, 1930), 121. Cited in Kerrigan, 210.

50. From a treatise on "The Practical Methode of Meditation," prefaced to Richard Gibbons's translation of *An Abridgment of Meditations . . . by the R. Father Vincentius Bruno . . .* (1614), quoted in Louis L. Martz, *The Poetry of Meditation* (New Haven, Conn.: Yale University Press, 1954), 14. See also Paul M. Cubeta, "Ben Jonson's Religious Lyrics," *Journal of English and Germanic Philology* 62 (1963): 95–110 (hereafter cited in text as Cubeta).

51. Annabel Patterson, "Lyric and Society in Jonson's *Under-wood,*" in *Lyric Poetry: Beyond New Criticism,* ed. Chaviva Hosek and Patricia Parker (Ithaca, N.Y.: Cornell University Press, 1985), 153. In a companion essay, Patterson further suggests that *The Underwood* is carefully organized by Jonson to form "an elliptical history of the Jacobean and Caroline era." See "Jonson, Marvell, and Miscellaneity?" in *Poems in Their Place: The Intertextuality and Order of Poetic Collections,* ed. Neil Fraistat (Chapel Hill: University of North Carolina Press, 1986), 95–118. But telling against Patterson's argument is the fact that the collection as published in 1640–1641 contains three poems that are definitely not by Jonson. Had Jonson organized the collection as elaborately and complexly as Patterson contends, surely he would have excised the poems by Donne, Wotton, and Godolphin. A writer as scrupulous about authorship as Jonson would hardly have included works by others in his collection. Notwithstanding the excessiveness of Patterson's claims for the authorial organization and arrangement of *The Underwood,* her essays contain valuable insights into the political content of some of the poems in the collection. For a more convincing account of the organization of *The Underwood,* see van den Berg, 170–81.

52. On this point, see Cubeta, 97–98. For an intricate analysis of Jonson's structuring the poem through numerological principles, see Sibyl Lutz Severance, " 'To Shine in Union': Measure, Number, and Harmony in Ben Jonson's '*Poems* of Devotion,' " *Studies in Philology* 80 (1983): 183–99.

53. See A. B. Chambers, "Christmas: The Liturgy of the Church and English Verse of the Renaissance," *Literary Monographs,* vol. 6, ed. Eric Rothstein and Joseph Anthony Wittreich (Madison: University of Wisconsin Press, 1975), especially 140–42.

54.   As Herford and Simpson explain, "The original is not by Petronius, but it was printed in Linocerius' edition, Paris, 1585." See H. & S., 11:109; and Petronius, trans. Michael Heseltine, Loeb Classical Library (London: Dent, 1913), 340, 358–61. That Jonson chose to translate this supposed fragment, so different from the licentiousness of most of Petronius's authentic work, is telling. For an appreciation of Jonson as translator, see Nichols, 135–37.

55.   Baldassare Castiglione, *The Book of the Courtier,* trans. Sir Thomas Hoby, (London, 1900; reprint New York: Penguin, 1967), 344. Subsequent quotations from *The Courtier* are from this edition and are cited by page number in the text.

56.   Nicholas Caussin, *The Holy Court: Fourth Tome* (1638), sig. A4v. Quoted in Meagher, 126.

57.   Hugh Richmond, *The School of Love: The Evolution of the Stuart Love Lyric* (Princeton, N.J.: Princeton University Press, 1964), 207.

58.   See Ferry, 168–71.

59.   Ovid, *Amores* 1.9.3–4. Quoted from *Heroides and Amores,* trans. Grant Showerman, Loeb Classical Library (Cambridge, Mass.: Harvard University Press, 1914), 35. In addition to those works of Horace, Ovid, and Castiglione discussed in the text, the *senex amans* debate includes, among other documents, *Anacreontea,* Odes 7 and 51; Plato, *The Symposium;* Cicero, *De Senectute;* Tibullus, 1.8; Seneca, *Epistles* 12 and 68; and Ficino, *Commentary on Plato's* Symposium. Richard S. Peterson, "Virtue Reconciled to Pleasure: Jonson's 'A Celebration of Charis,'" *Studies in the Literary Imagination* 6, no. 1 (1973): 219–68 (hereafter cited in text as Peterson 1973), suggests the importance of Ronsard's *Sonnets pour Helene* and of emblematic literature; see 221, nn. 3, 4, and 5. Trimpi identifies the aging persona of "My Picture Left in *Scotland*" with Socrates as presented in *The Symposium* and interpreted by Ficino; see 228.

60.   Patrick Cruttwell, "The Love Poetry of John Donne: Pedantique Weedes or Fresh Invention?" in Bradbury and Palmer, 16.

61.   Peterson (1973) discusses the motif of secrecy, 259–68. Ovid stresses the need for secrecy in *Ars Amatoria,* 2.601–40; Castiglione, throughout *The Courtier,* but especially 284–87. Peterson also suggests Montaigne's essay "Upon some verses of Virgill," Sidney's Songs 8 and 9 from *Astrophil and Stella,* and Chapman's *Ovids Banquet of Sense* as possible influences on Jonson's use of this motif.

62.   Because *Underwood* 39 was printed with Donne's *Poems* in 1633, the authenticity of Jonson's authorship of it and of *Underwood* 38, 40, and 41 has sometimes been in doubt. Evelyn Simpson, "Jonson and Donne," *Review of English Studies* 15 (1939): 274–82, argues convincingly for the ascription of *Underwood* 38, 40, and 41 to Jonson; this attribution is now generally accepted. *Underwood* 39 does not form part of the sequence under discussion. It is accepted as Donne's by most of his modern editors; see the text and commentary in *The Elegies,* vol. 2 of *The Variorum Edition of the Poetry of John Donne,* gen. ed. Gary A. Stringer (Bloomington, Ind.: Indiana University Press, 2000).

63. See Paul Cubeta, " 'A Celebration of Charis': An Evaluation of Jonsonian Poetic Strategy," *ELH* 25 (1958): 163–80; Trimpi, 209–27; G. J. Weinberger, "Jonson's Mock-encomiastic 'Celebration of Charis,' " *Genre* 4 (1971): 305–28; Peterson 1973; Sara Van Den Berg, "The Play of Wit and Love: Demetrius' *On Style* and Jonson's 'A Celebration of Charis,' " *ELH* 41 (1974): 26–36; R. V. LeClercq, "The Reciprocal Harmony of Jonson's 'A Celebration of Charis,' " *Texas Studies in Language and Literature* 16 (1975): 627–50; Raymond B. Waddington, " 'A Celebration of Charis': Socratic Lover and Silenic Speaker," in Summers and Pebworth 1982, 121–38; and Nathaniel Strout, "Reading 'A Celebration of Charis' and the Nature of Jonson's Art," *Texas Studies in Language and Literature* 26 (1984): 128–43.

64. On Jonson's friendship topos and the influence of Cicero, see Richard Finkelstein, "Ben Jonson's Ciceronian Rhetoric of Friendship," *Journal of Medieval and Renaissance Studies* 16 (1986): 103–24 (hereafter cited in text as Finkelstein). See also William Cain, "Self and Others in Two Poems by Ben Jonson," *Studies in Philology* 80 (1983): esp. 163–76.

65. See Ian Donaldson, "Jonson's Ode to Sir Lucius Cary and Sir H. Morison," *Studies in the Literary Imagination* 6, no. 1 (1973): 139–52; Mary I. Oates, "Jonson's 'Ode Pindarick' and the Doctrine of Imitation," *Papers on Language and Literature* 11 (1975): 126–48; Susanne Woods, "Ben Jonson's Cary-Morison Ode: Some Observations on Structure and Form," *Studies in English Literature* 18 (1978): 57–74; Peterson 1981, 195–232; Stella P. Revard, "Pindar and Jonson's Cary-Morison Ode," in Summers and Pebworth 1982, 17–29; Finkelstein, 120–23; and W. Scott Blanchard, "*Ut Encyclopedia Poesis*: Ben Jonson's Cary-Morison Ode and the 'Spheare' of 'Humanitie,' " *Studies in Philology* 87 (1990): 194–220.

66. A useful history of this belief is Raymond Crawford, *The King's Evil* (Oxford: Clarendon Press, 1911). Cf. Robert Herrick's "TO THE KING, To Cure the Evill"; and see Claude J. Summers, "Herrick's Political Poetry: The Strategies of His Art," in *"Trust to Good Verses": Herrick Tercentenary Essays,* ed. Roger B. Rollin and J. Max Patrick (Pittsburgh: University of Pittsburgh Press, 1978), 171–83.

67. See E. A. J. Honigmann, *The Stability of Shakespeare's Text* (Lincoln: University of Nebraska Press, 1965), 34. But note that the preface repeats the claim, first reported by Jonson in *Discoveries,* that Shakespeare almost never revised, betraying a lack of concern with his texts that Jonson deplored.

68. Roger B. Rollin, "The Anxiety of Identification: Jonson and the Rival Poets," in Summers and Pebworth 1982, 139–54. See also T. J. B. Spencer, "Ben Jonson on his beloved The Author Mr. William Shakespeare," in *The Elizabethan Theatre 4,* ed. G. R. Hibbard (Hamden, Conn.: Archon, 1974), 22–40; Peterson 1981, 158–94; van den Berg, 146–54; and Barbara L. DeStefano, "Ben Jonson's Eulogy on Shakespeare: Native Maker and the Triumph of English," *Studies in Philology* 90 (1993): 231–45 (hereafter cited in text as DeStefano).

69. DeStefano, 242. As Peterson (1981) notes, the phrase is presented "as a paradox rather than a slight" (179).

70. Donaldson, " 'Not of an Age': Jonson, Shakespeare, and the Verdicts of Posterity" (hereafter cited as Donaldson 1997), in Hirsh, 197. Donaldson notes that in the late twentieth century, Shakespeare, like all other writers, is no longer regarded as a timeless and transhistorical genius "but as a textual phenomenon that is constantly reconstructed, constantly reinvented, constantly reinterpreted by every age according to its needs, priorities, and preconceptions."

71. Quoted from Katherine Duncan-Jones, " 'They say a made a good end': Ben Jonson's Epitaph on Thomas Nashe," *Ben Jonson Journal* 3 (1996): 1–19.

72. Quoted from Brandon S. Centerwall, " 'Tell Me Who Can When a Player Dies': Ben Jonson's Epigram on Richard Burbage and How It Was Lost to the Canon," *Ben Jonson Journal* 4 (1997): 27–34 (hereafter cited in text as Centerwall).

Chapter Six

1. First suggested by C. J. Sisson, "Ben Jonson of Gresham College," *Times Literary Supplement,* Sept. 21, 1951, p. 604, and endorsed by George Burke Johnston, "Ben Jonson of Gresham College," *Times Literary Supplement,* Dec. 28, 1951, p. 837. Miles (1986, 222–24), terms the Gresham professorship a "suggestion that fits in well with the framework of other events and developments for [Jonson] at that time" and discusses the *Grammar* in that context, as does Kay 1995, 161.

2. On Jonson's sources, see the commentary on *The English Grammar* in H. & S., 11:165–210; and Otto Funke, "Ben Jonsons *English Grammar,*" *Anglia* 64 (1940): 117–34.

3. H. & S., 11:201, lists most of the sources of the quotations from English writers but is silent on the Biblical quotations and paraphrases.

4. N. E. Osselton, "Ben Jonson's Status as a Grammarian," *Dutch Quarterly Review of Anglo-American Letters* 12 (1982): 207.

5. The definitive study of this subject is Sara van den Berg, "Marking his Place: Ben Jonson's Punctuation," *Early Modern Literary Studies* 1, no. 3 (December 1995), 2.1–25 (URL: http://purl.oclc.org/emls/01–3bergjons.html).

6. Emma Vorlat, *The Development of English Grammatical Theory 1586–1737* (Louvain: University Press, 1976), 18.

7. For the more than thirty classical and humanist writers that Jonson quotes, paraphrases, or translates in *Discoveries,* see H. & S., 11:210–94, and the following: Paul J. McGinnis, "Ben Jonson's 'Discoveries,' " *Notes & Queries* 202, no. 4 (April 1957): 162–63; W. A. Murray, "Ben Jonson and Dr. Mayerne," *Times Literary Supplement,* Sept. 2, 1960, p. 561; J. K. Houck, "An Unidentified Borrowing in Jonson's 'Discoveries,' " *Notes & Queries* 213, no.

10 (October 1968): 267–68; Hugh Maclean, "Ben Jonson's *Timber,* 1046–1115, and Falstaff," *Papers on Language and Literature* 10 (1974): 202–6; Margaret Clayton, "Ben Jonson, 'In Travaile with Expression of Another': His Use of John of Salisbury's *Policraticus* in *Timber,*" *Review of English Studies* 30 (1979): 397–408; and W. David Kay, "Jonson, Erasmus, and Religious Controversy: *Discoveries,* Lines 1046–1062," *English Language Notes* 17 (1979): 108–12.

    8. Timothy Murray, *Theatrical Legitimation: Allegories of Genius in Seventeenth-Century England and France* (New York and Oxford: Oxford University Press, 1987), 48.

    9. Richard C. Newton, " 'Ben./Jonson': The Poet in the Poems," in Kernan, 182.

    10. Peterson 1981, 10. On the lack of a logical organization in *Discoveries,* see H. & S., 8:558–59. In an attempt to impose order on the book, Ralph S. Walker, ed., *Ben Jonson's Timber or Discoveries* (Syracuse: Syracuse University Press, 1953; hereafter cited in text as Walker), rearranges Jonson's text under seven categories, frequently fusing disparate parts into unified essays and treatises. James A. Riddell and Stanley Stewart, *Jonson's Spenser: Evidence and Historical Criticism* (Pittsburgh: Duquesne University Press, 1995), see the book as a "written equivalent" to memory that "entails the probability that some readers—for whose use it was not intended—may find its arrangement haphazard, just as matter retained word-for-word in the memory is 'haphazard' " (91). Neil P. Probst, "A Topical Index to Jonson's *Discoveries,*" *Ben Jonson Journal* 3 (1996): 116–26, provides a useful guide through the book's randomly arranged contents.

    11. Percy Simpson, " 'Tanquam Explorator': Jonson's Method in the 'Discoveries,' " *Modern Language Review* 2 (1907): 202.

    12. H. & S., 11:213. The commentary is largely Simpson's.

    13. George Parfitt, *Ben Jonson: Public Poet and Private Man* (London: Dent, 1976), 24, 28. Although he does not explore the practice in *Discoveries,* Peterson, in *Imitation and Praise* (1981), offers the best discussion of Jonson's use of *imitatio,* which he describes as "the creative use of the thoughts and words of the ancients in the spirit of emulous rivalry" (xiii). See also Jennifer Brady, "Progenitors and other Sons in Ben Jonson's *Discoveries,*" in *New Perspectives on Ben Jonson,* ed. Hirsh, who sees *Discoveries* as a critical handbook concerned with "how best to equip his readers with a constructive model of responsive and responsible humanism" that judges received wisdom by experience (20).

    14. For adverse assessments of Jonson's literary criticism in *Discoveries,* see, for example, Paul R. Sellin, *Daniel Heinsius and Stuart England* (Leiden: University Press, 1968), who concludes of the passages in which Jonson discusses poetry that "the material assembled in the *Discoveries* cannot be regarded as focused into an integrated doctrine of poetry which Jonson 'made his own' out of the snippets gathered from his reading. . . . The *Discoveries* does not present a system of ideas on poetry, and the treatise seems to be little more than a mere

collection of ideas, a commonplace-book" (162); and Boehrer (1993, 289–312), who finds Jonson's discussions of such terms as art and nature to be contradictory.

15.   On the political passages in *Discoveries,* see especially chapter 7, *"The Discoveries:* Jonson's Moral Rejection of Machiavelli," in Daniel C. Boughner, *The Devil's Disciple: Ben Jonson's Debt to Machiavelli* (New York: Philosophical Library, 1968), 138–51; and chapter 4, "Lipsius, Jonson, James, and Charles," in Robert C. Evans, *Jonson, Lipsius and the Politics of Renaissance Stoicism* (Wakefield, N.H.: Longwood Academic, 1992), 111–30.

16.   For a lengthier study of this subject, see Ted-Larry Pebworth, "Jonson's *Timber* and the Essay Tradition," in *Essays in Honor of Esmond Linworth Marilla,* ed. Thomas A. Kirby and W. John Olive (Baton Rouge: Louisiana State University Press, 1970), 115–26. See also Pebworth, "Not Being, but Passing: Defining the Early English Essay," *Studies in the Literary Imagination* 10, no.2 (Fall 1977): 17–27.

17.   Walker, 20–21, 25–34. In addition, on pp. 21–25 and 34–35, Walker constructs two additional essays from scattered passages: "Of the Diversity of Wits" (lines 669–800, 846–61, 948–58) and "Of Picture and Poetry" (lines 1509–40, 1549–85).

18.   Cf. *Epicoene* 2.3.48–50, where the foolish Daw dismisses Seneca and Plutarch, whom Clerimont deems "grave authors," as "Grave asses! meere *Essaists!* a few loose sentences, and that's all."

19.   On the digestion of sources into a new concoction, see Bruce Thomas Boehrer, *The Fury of Men's Gullets: Ben Jonson and the Digestive Canal* (Philadelphia: University of Pennsylvania Press, 1997), especially 118–24.

20.   Maurice Castelain, ed., *Discoveries: A Critical Edition* (Paris: Hachette, 1907; hereafter cited in text as Castelain), xvi.

21.   H. & S., 11:255. Walker (32, n. 29) sees this passage as referring to the wedding of Princess Elizabeth to the Elector Palatine in February 1613, but Jonson could not have witnessed the celebrations of that event as he was in France at the time, tutoring Wat Ralegh (Riggs, 190–91).

22.   Algernon Charles Swinburne, *A Study of Ben Jonson* (1889), ed. Howard B. Norland (Lincoln: University of Nebraska Press, 1969; hereafter cited in text as Swinburne), 129–30.

Chapter Seven

1.   Many of these elegies were printed in *Jonsonus Virbius,* a collection compiled by Bishop Brian Duppa (London, 1638), reproduced in H. & S., 11:428–81. The quotations in the text are from William Habington, p. 446, and Edmund Waller, p. 447. James Clayton begins his tribute by asking, "Who first reform'd our *Stage* with justest *Lawes,* / And was the first best *Judge* in his owne *Cause"* (450).

2. Excellent studies of Jonson's influence on his contemporaries include Bush, 107–25; Summers; and Miner.

3. Robert Herrick, "An Ode for Him," in Herrick, 380.

4. Dryden, "An Essay of Dramatic Poesy," in Dryden, 1:82–83.

5. Jonas A. Barish, introduction to *Ben Jonson: A Collection of Critical Essays* (Englewood Cliffs, N.J.: Prentice-Hall, 1963), 4. Barish's concise historical survey of Jonson's reputation is very valuable. See also David H. Craig, *Ben Jonson: The Critical Heritage, 1599–1798* (London: Routledge, 1990); and Donaldson 1997,197–214.

6. *The Works of Ben Jonson,* ed. William Gifford, 9 vols. (London, 1816).

7. Coleridge, "Notes on Ben Jonson," in Coleridge, 4:185–99; J. A. Symonds, *Ben Jonson,* English Worthies Series (London, 1886). On Jonson's fortunes in the nineteenth century, see the first chapter of Ejner Jensen, *Ben Jonson's Comedies on the Modern Stage* (Ann Arbor: UMI Research Press, 1985; hereafter cited in text as Jensen), 7–25.

8. *The Works of Ben Jonson,* ed. William Gifford, with introduction and appendixes by Lieutenant-Colonel Francis Cunningham, 9 vols. (London, 1875).

9. T. S. Eliot, "Ben Jonson" (hereafter cited in text as Eliot), in *Selected Essays* (London: Faber and Faber, 1951), 147.

10. The introduction to D. Heyward Brock and James M. Welsh, *Ben Jonson: A Quadricentennial Bibliography* (Metuchen, N.J.: Scarecrow, 1974), 11–32, surveys the trends in twentieth-century criticism. See also William L. Godshalk, "Ben Jonson," in *The New Intellectuals: A Survey and Bibliography of Recent Studies in English Renaissance Drama,* ed. Terence P. Logan and Denzell S. Smith (Lincoln: University of Nebraska Press, 1977), 3–116. For a survey of Jonson's comedies on the twentieth-century stage, see Jensen, 28–124.

11. The quoted phrase is from Summers, 18.

Selected Bibliography

Only book-length studies of Jonson are included here. Readers should also consult important works cited in the notes and references.

Primary Sources

1. Important Early Editions

The Workes of Benjamin Jonson. London: William Stansby, 1616; reprinted in facsimile, with an introduction by D. Heyward Brock, London: Scolar, 1976. Contains seven comedies, two tragedies, two collections of poems, and several masques and entertainments.

The Workes of Benjamin Jonson. 2 vols. London: R. Bishop et al., 1640–41. The first volume is a reprint of the 1616 *Workes;* the second volume is in two parts, the former prepared by Jonson and the latter assembled by Sir Kenelm Digby after Jonson's death.

2. Modern Critical Editions

Ben Jonson. Edited by C. H. Herford, Percy Simpson, and Evelyn Simpson. 11 vols. Oxford: Clarendon Press, 1925–52. Contains a life, critical and textual introductions to each work, textual notes, commentaries, and corollary materials.

The Complete Plays of Ben Jonson. Edited by George Wilkes. 4 vols. Oxford: Clarendon Press, 1981. Modernized texts based on the Herford and Simpson edition.

Individual plays, edited by noted scholars, with critical introductions, textual notes, and commentaries appear in such distinguished series as the Yale Ben Jonson, the New Mermaid Editions, and the Revels Plays. Modern critical editions of the poetry include *The Complete Poetry,* ed. William B. Hunter Jr. (New York: New York University Press, 1963); *Poems of Ben Jonson,* ed. Ian Donaldson (Oxford: Clarendon Press, 1975); and *Selected Poems of Ben Jonson,* ed. Ted-Larry Pebworth and Claude J. Summers (Binghamton, N.Y.: Medieval and Renaissance Texts and Studies, 1995).

Secondary Sources

1. Biography and Bibliography

Bates, Steven L., and Sidney D. Orr. *A Concordance to the Poems of Ben Jonson.* Athens: Ohio University Press, 1978. Concordance to the nondramatic poetry keyed to volume 8 of H. & S.

Brock, D. Heyward. *A Ben Jonson Companion.* Bloomington: Indiana University Press; Brighton, England: Harvester Press, 1983. Convenient reference work on Jonson's life, works, times, and critics.

Chute, Marchette. *Ben Jonson of Westminster.* New York: Dutton, 1953. Popular, well-written biography, but now dated; often questionable in its critical assessments.

Craig, D. H. *Ben Jonson: The Critical Heritage, 1599–1798.* London: Routledge, 1990. Documents criticism of Jonson through the eighteenth century.

Jenson, Ejner J. *Ben Jonson's Comedies on the Modern Stage.* Ann Arbor: UMI Research Press, 1985. Documents the stage history of Jonson's comedies from 1899 to 1972; also contains a chapter on Jonson in the nineteenth century.

Judkins, David C. *The Nondramatic Works of Ben Jonson: A Reference Guide.* Boston: G. K. Hall, 1982. Annotated bibliography spanning the years 1615–1978, arranged by year.

Kay, W. David. *Ben Jonson: A Literary Life.* London: Macmillan, 1995. Stimulating account of Jonson's literary career.

Lehrman, Walter D., Dolores J. Sarafinski, and Elizabeth Savage. *The Plays of Ben Jonson: A Reference Guide.* Boston: G. K. Hall, 1980. Annotated bibliography spanning the years 1911–1975. Includes reviews and dissertations.

Miles, Rosalind. *Ben Jonson: His Life and Work.* London: Routledge, 1986. Lively biography, accessible and trustworthy.

Riggs, David. *Ben Jonson: A Life.* Cambridge, Mass.: Harvard University Press, 1987. The standard scholarly biography. Its critical comments on the works are often acute.

2. Scholarly and Critical Books and Monographs

Arnold, Judd. *A Grace Peculiar: Ben Jonson's Cavalier Heroes.* The Pennsylvania State University Studies, no. 35. University Park: Pennsylvania State University, 1972. Emphasizes the importance of the witty gallants as keys to discerning the tone of many of the comedies. An important corrective.

Bamborough, J. B. *Ben Jonson.* British Writers and Their Work, no. 112. London and New York: Longmans, 1959; reprinted in the collected British

Writers and Their Work, no. 11. Lincoln: University of Nebraska Press, 1966. Brief general introduction to Jonson and his work.

————. *Ben Jonson.* Hutchinson University Library. London: Hutchinson, 1970. An expanded version of the earlier pamphlet. Generally insightful discussions of the plays; slights the nondramatic poetry.

Barish, Jonas A. *Ben Jonson and the Language of Prose Comedy.* Cambridge, Mass.: Harvard University Press, 1960; reprint New York: Norton, 1970. Thorough and illuminating study of the complex variety in Jonson's prose comedies; contains incidental important remarks on the verse plays as well.

Barton, Anne. *Ben Jonson, Dramatist.* Cambridge: Cambridge University Press, 1984. Invariably interesting and intelligent discussions of Jonson's plays. Significant.

Beaurline, L. A. *Jonson and Elizabeth Comedy: Essays in Dramatic Rhetoric.* San Marino, Calif.: Huntington Library, 1978. Emphasizes the diversity of Jonson's rhetoric and the complexity of audience response demanded by his comedies. Important.

Boehrer, Bruce Thomas. *The Fury of Men's Gullets: Ben Jonson and the Digestive Canal.* Philadelphia: University of Pennsylvania Press, 1997. Explores Jonson's fascination with alimentary matters. Often illuminating.

Bryant, J. A., Jr. *The Compassionate Satirist: Ben Jonson and His Imperfect World.* Athens: University of Georgia Press, 1973. Balanced discussion of the comedies; stresses Jonson's abiding faith in goodness.

Burt, Richard. *Licensed by Authority: Ben Jonson and the Discourses of Censorship.* Ithaca, N.Y.: Cornell University Press, 1993. Comprehensive study of the effect of censorship on Jonson's works.

Cave, Richard Allen. *Ben Jonson.* New York: St. Martin's, 1991. Survey of Jonson's achievement as a dramatist.

Champion, Larry S. *Ben Jonson's "Dotages": A Reconsideration of the Late Plays.* Lexington: University of Kentucky Press, 1967. Sustained attempt to rehabilitate the last four comedies. Provocative insights.

Chan, Mary. *Music in the Theatre of Ben Jonson.* Oxford: Clarendon Press, 1980. Studies the function of music in Jonson's plays and masques.

DeLuna, B. N. *Jonson's Romish Plot: A Study of* Catiline *and Its Historical Context.* Oxford: Clarendon Press, 1967. Argues that *Catiline* was intended as a "parallelograph" on the Gunpowder Plot. Interesting, but not altogether convincing in its details.

Dessen, Alan C. *Jonson's Moral Comedy.* Evanston, Ill.: Northwestern University Press, 1971. Discusses Jonson's debt to earlier dramatic modes and emphasizes the moral intention of the comedies.

Donaldson, Ian. *The World Upside-Down: Comedy from Jonson to Fielding.* Oxford: Clarendon Press, 1970. Discusses *Epicoene* and *Bartholomew Fair* in the context of social disorder; traces Jonson's influence on later comic writing.

Duncan, Douglas. *Ben Jonson and the Lucianic Tradition.* Cambridge: Cambridge University Press, 1979. Explores the influence of the Lucianic tradition—including works by Lucian, Erasmus, and More—on Jonson's plays.

Dutton, Richard. *Ben Jonson: To the First Folio.* Cambridge: Cambridge University Press, 1983. Discusses the dramatic and nondramatic works published in the 1616 Folio. Often incisive and insightful.

Enck, John J. *Jonson and the Comic Truth.* Madison: University of Wisconsin Press, 1957. A chronologically arranged discussion of Jonson's achievements in comedy. Emphasizes Jonson's awareness of the ultimate imperfectability of humanity and society. Provocative.

Evans, Robert C. *Ben Jonson and the Poetics of Patronage.* Lewisburg, Pa.: Bucknell University Press; London: Associated University Presses, 1989. Reads Jonson's poetry and some plays within the context of the period's elaborate patronage system. Important.

———. *Habits of Mind: Evidence and Effects of Ben Jonson's Reading.* Lewisburg, Pa.: Bucknell University Press; London: Associated University Presses, 1995. Reports on the markings in Jonson's copies of significant books, including works by Seneca, Apuleius, Chaucer, More, and Edmondes.

———. *Jonson and the Contexts of His Time.* Lewisburg, Pa.: Bucknell University Press; London: Associated University Presses, 1994. Explores the "micropolitics" of Jonson's enmeshment in the social relations of his day, including his friends and rivals.

———. *Jonson, Lipsius, and the Politics of Renaissance Stoicism.* Wakefield, N.H.: Longwood Academic, 1992. Studies Jonson's response to the political thought of Justus Lipsius; examines Jonson's markings in his copy of Lipsius's *Six Books of Politics or Civil Doctrine.*

Gardiner, Judith Kegan. *Craftsmanship in Context: The Development of Ben Jonson's Poetry.* The Hague: Mouton, 1975. Useful study of Jonson's poetic development, emphasizing the distinctive traits of each period of the poet's career.

Haynes, Jonathan. *The Social Relations of Jonson's Theater.* Cambridge: Cambridge University Press, 1992. Emphasizes Jonson as a realist and explores the social dynamics of selected plays from the perspective of the new social history.

Jackson, Gabriele Bernhard. *Vision and Judgment in Ben Jonson's Drama.* Yale Studies in English, vol. 166. New Haven, Conn.: Yale University Press, 1968. Emphasizes Jonson's view of humanity's lofty potentiality and his poetic function as judge of human realities. Tends to ignore Jonson's good-humored compromises.

Johnson, A. W. *Ben Jonson: Poetry and Architecture.* Oxford: Clarendon Press, 1994. Studies Jonson's aesthetic as reflected in the structure of his poems and masques.

Johnston, George Burke. *Ben Jonson: Poet*. Columbia University Studies in English and Comparative Literature, no. 162. New York: Columbia University Press, 1945. An important attempt to revive interest in the nondramatic poetry; dated and impressionistic, but still valuable.

Knights, L. C. *Drama and Society in the Age of Jonson*. London: Chatto and Windus, 1937; reprint New York: Norton, 1968. An important, pioneering study of the social and economic structures of Jacobean England as they are embodied in the plays of Jonson, Dekker, Heywood, Middleton, and Massinger. Offers invaluable insights into the drama it discusses.

Knoll, Robert E. *Ben Jonson's Plays: An Introduction*. Lincoln: University of Nebraska Press, 1964. Chronologically arranged readings of the plays. Generally appreciative.

Leggatt, Alexander. *Ben Jonson: His Vision and His Art*. London: Methuen, 1981. Insightful assessment of Jonson's achievement in both dramatic and nondramatic works.

Loewenstein, Joseph. *Responsive Readings: Versions of Echo in Pastoral, Epic, and the Jonsonian Masque*. Yale Studies in English, vol. 192. New Haven, Conn.: Yale University Press, 1984. Cultural history of Echo, featuring *Cynthia's Revels* and the masques.

Maus, Katherine Eisaman. *Ben Jonson and the Roman Frame of Mind*. Princeton, N.J.: Princeton University Press, 1984. Studies the effects of the Roman moralists on the way Jonson construes ethical, social, and artistic issues.

McCanles, Michael. *The Humanist Poet and the Praise of True Nobility*. Toronto: University of Toronto Press, 1992. Densely written survey of the nondramatic poetry in light of the *vera nobilitas* tradition.

Meagher, John C. *Method and Meaning in Jonson's Masques*. Notre Dame, Ind.: University of Notre Dame Press, 1966. Especially valuable for its exposition of the philosophical and thematic contexts of the masques.

Miles, Rosalind. *Ben Jonson: His Craft and Art*. London: Routledge, 1990. Companion volume to the author's 1986 biography. Surveys the entire canon.

Miner, Earl. *The Cavalier Mode from Jonson to Cotton*. Princeton, N.J.: Princeton University Press, 1961. Jonson is the central figure in this important critical account of cavalier poetry. Contains sensitive readings of individual poems.

Nichols, J. G. *The Poetry of Ben Jonson*. New York: Barnes and Noble, 1969. Interesting and informative study of the nondramatic poetry, emphasizing Jonson's variety and careful craftsmanship.

Orgel, Stephen. *The Illusion of Power: Political Theater in the English Renaissance*. A Quantum Book. Berkeley: University of California Press, 1975. Jonson's masques discussed as the center of this study of theater at the Stuart court.

———.*The Jonsonian Masque*. Cambridge, Mass.: Harvard University Press, 1967. Thorough and perceptive study of Jonson's development as a writer of masques.

Parfitt, George. *Ben Jonson: Public Poet and Private Man.* London: Dent, 1976. Concentrates on the nondramatic poetry and attempts an integrated view of Jonson's life, social concerns, and artistry. Examines individual works in light of his total achievement.

Partridge, Edward B. *The Broken Compass: A Study of the Major Comedies of Ben Jonson.* London: Chatto and Windus; Cambridge, Mass.: Harvard University Press, 1958. A detailed study of imagery. An important, provocative study.

Peterson, Richard S. *Imitation and Praise in the Poems of Ben Jonson.* New Haven, Conn.: Yale University Press, 1981. Concentrates on Jonson's celebratory poems; views them from the perspective of imitation. Illuminating.

Riddell, James A., and Stanley Stewart. *Jonson's Spenser: Evidence and Historical Criticism.* Pittsburgh: Duquesne University Press, 1995. Explores the significance of Jonson's annotations in his copy of Spenser.

Rowe, George E. *Distinguishing Jonson: Imitation, Rivalry, and the Direction of a Dramatic Career.* Lincoln: University of Nebraska Press, 1988. Traces Jonson's attempt to create a literary identity. Concentrates on the plays.

Slights, William W. E. *Ben Jonson and the Art of Secrecy.* Toronto: University of Toronto Press, 1994. Emphasizes the importance of secrecy in Jonson's plays, especially *Sejanus, Volpone, Epicoene, The Alchemist, Catiline,* and *Bartholomew Fair.* Reliable and often acute.

Smith, Barbara. *The Women of Jonson's Poetry: Female Representation in the Non-Dramatic Verse.* Aldershot, England: Scolar Press, 1995. Examines Jonson's representation of women in the poetry.

Summers, Joseph H. *The Heirs of Donne and Jonson.* New York and London: Oxford University Press, 1970. Argues that Jonson and Donne jointly influenced nearly all of the poets of the seventeenth century. Important both for its criticism of Jonson's poetry and for its documentation of his influence.

Sweeney, John Gordon, III. *Jonson and the Psychology of Public Theater.* Princeton, N.J.: Princeton University Press, 1985. Studies Jonson's vexed relationship with the public theater and how it changed in the course of his career from the comical satires through *Bartholomew Fair.*

Swinburne, Algernon Charles. *A Study of Ben Jonson.* London: Chatto and Windus, 1889; annotated reprint, edited by Howard B. Norland, Lincoln: University of Nebraska Press, 1969. Highly impressionistic and dated, but offering many valuable insights.

Teague, Francis. *The Curious History of* Bartholomew Fair. Lewisburg, Pa.: Bucknell University Press; London: Associated University Presses, 1985. Explores the rise and fall of the play's reputation.

Thayer, C. G. *Ben Jonson: Studies in the Plays.* Norman: University of Oklahoma Press, 1963. Chronologically arranged, appreciative analyses of the plays.

Trimpi, Wesley. *Ben Jonson's Poems: A Study of the Plain Style.* Palo Alto: Stanford University Press, 1962. Excellent account of the nondramatic poetry and Jonson's characteristic style.

van den Berg, Sara. *The Action of Ben Jonson's Poetry.* Newark: University of Delaware Press; London: Associated University Press, 1987. Interprets the nondramatic poetry as a set of complex actions. Important.

Watson, Robert N. *Ben Jonson's Parodic Strategy: Literary Imperialism in the Comedies.* Cambridge, Mass.: Harvard University Press, 1987. Discusses Jonson's comedies as acts of literary imperialism that parody hackneyed plots and stage conventions of popular drama. Stimulating readings and intelligent observations.

Wayne, Don E. *Penshurst: The Semiotics of Place and the Poetics of History.* Madison: University of Wisconsin Press, 1984. Exploration of the ideological and cultural meanings and intersections of "To Penshurst" and the place it addresses.

Wiltenburg, Robert. *Ben Jonson and Self-Love: The Subtlest Maze of All.* Columbia: University of Missouri Press, 1990. Traces Jonson's treatment of the theme of self-love in selected plays, poems, and masques. Perceptive.

Womack, Peter. *Ben Jonson.* Oxford: Blackwell, 1986. A provocative study that concentrates on the plays and emphasizes the ideological implications of Jonson's work.

3. Collections of Essays

Barish, Jonas, ed. *Ben Jonson: A Collection of Critical Essays.* Twentieth-Century Views. Englewood Cliffs, N.J.: Prentice-Hall, 1963. Reprints essays by T. S. Eliot, L. C. Knights, Harry Levin, Edmund Wilson, C. H. Herford, Jonas Barish, Paul Goodman, Edward B. Partridge, Ray L. Heffner Jr., Joseph Allen Bryant Jr., and Dolora Cunningham. The introduction a useful historical survey of Jonson's reputation.

Blissett, William, Julian Patrick, and R. W. Van Fossen, eds. *A Celebration of Ben Jonson.* Toronto: University of Toronto Press, 1973. Contains previously unpublished essays by Clifford Leech, Jonas Barish, George Hibbard, D. F. McKenzie, Hugh Maclean, and L. C. Knights.

Brady, Jennifer, and W. H. Herendeen, eds. *Ben Jonson's 1616 Folio.* Newark: University of Delaware Press; London: Associated University Presses, 1991. Contains previously unpublished essays on the significance of the 1616 Folio and its contents by W. H. Herendeen, Kevin J. Donovan, Katharine Eisaman Maus, William Blissett, Sara van den Berg, Stella P. Revard, Joseph Loewenstein, and Jennifer Brady.

Bloom, Harold, ed. *Ben Jonson.* Modern Critical Views. New York: Chelsea House, 1987. Reprints essays and chapters by Jonas A. Barish, Edward B. Partridge, Geoffrey Hill, Stephen Orgel, William Blissett, Thomas M. Greene, William Kerrigan, A. Richard Dutton, Jonathan Haynes, Jonathan Dollimore, Joseph Loewenstein, Stanley Fish, John Hollander, and Marijke Rijsherman.

————, ed. *Ben Jonson's Volpone, or the Fox.* Modern Critical Interpretations. New York: Chelsea House, 1988. Reprints essays and chapters by Stephen Greenblatt, Leo Salingar, L. A. Beaurline, C. N. Manlove, Anne Barton, and William W. E. Slights.

Donaldson, Ian, ed. *Jonson and Shakespeare.* London: Macmillan, in association with Australian National University Press, 1983. Includes essays on Jonson by Alvin B. Kernan, D. H. Craig, F. H. Mares, Ann Blake, J. B. Bamborough, Peter Barnes, Francis Berry, and Peter Walls.

Donaldson, Ian. *Jonson's Magic Houses: Essays in Interpretation.* Oxford: Clarendon Press, 1997. Essays and lectures on Jonson by a leading Jonsonian.

Hirsh, James, ed. *New Perspectives on Ben Jonson.* Madison, N.J.: Fairleigh Dickinson University Press; London: Associated University Presses, 1997. Contains previously unpublished essays on both the dramatic and nondramatic works by James Hirsh, Jennifer Brady, Anne Lake Prescott, Robert C. Evans, George A. E. Parfitt, Alexander Leggatt, Kate D. Levin, Carol P. Marsh-Lockett, Frances Teague, Bruce Thomas Boehrer, and Ian Donaldson.

Kernan, Alvin, ed. *Two Renaissance Mythmakers: Christopher Marlowe and Ben Jonson.* Selected Papers from the English Institute, 1975–76, n.s., 1. Baltimore: Johns Hopkins University Press, 1977. Contains previously unpublished essays on Jonson by Gabriele Bernhard Jackson, Ian Donaldson, and Richard C. Newton.

Summers, Claude J., and Ted-Larry Pebworth, eds. *Classic and Cavalier: Essays on Jonson and the Sons of Ben.* Pittsburgh: University of Pittsburgh Press, 1982. Contains previously unpublished essays on Jonson's poetry by C. A. Patrides, Stella P. Revard, Richard C. Newton, Richard Flantz, Susanne Woods, Martin Elsky, Jack D. Winner, Raymond B. Waddington, Roger B. Rollin, Ilona Bell, and Robert B. Hinman.

Thomas, Mary Olive, ed. "Ben Jonson: Quadricentennial Essays." A special issue of *Studies in the Literary Imagination* 6, no. 1 (April 1973). Contains previously unpublished essays by Alvin B. Kernan, George A. E. Parfitt, Marvin L. Vawter, L. A. Beaurline, David McPherson, Richard Levin, M. C. Bradbrook, Ian Donaldson, Edward Partridge, William Kerrigan, and Richard S. Peterson.

Index

For abbreviations, see "A Note on the Texts," pp. xv–xvi.

The Authors

Claude J. Summers and Ted-Larry Pebworth are both William E. Stirton Professors in the Humanities and Professors of English at the University of Michigan–Dearborn. They have collaborated on a number of articles and are coeditors of *The Poems of Owen Felltham, Selected Poems of Ben Jonson,* and of collections of essays on a wide variety of seventeenth-century topics. They are the organizers of the University of Michigan–Dearborn Biennial Renaissance Conferences.

Claude Summers earned his Ph.D. at the University of Chicago. He has published widely on both seventeenth- and twentieth-century literature. He is author of numerous essays and of book-length studies of Christopher Marlowe, Christopher Isherwood, E. M. Forster, and twentieth-century English and American gay fiction. His recent transnational and transhistorical anthology entitled *The Gay and Lesbian Literary Heritage* received a Lambda Literary Award. He is a past president of the John Donne Society.

Ted-Larry Pebworth received his doctorate from Louisiana State University. Author of *Owen Felltham* (TEAS 189) and of numerous critical and textual studies of Renaissance literature, he is a senior textual editor and member of the advisory board of *The Variorum Edition of the Poetry of John Donne.* He has served as president of the John Donne Society.

The Editor

Arthur F. Kinney is the Thomas W. Copeland Professor of Literary History at the University of Massachusetts, Amherst, and the Director of the Center for Renaissance Studies there; he is also an adjunct professor of English at New York University. He has written several books in the field: *Humanist Poetics, Continental Humanist Poetics, John Skelton: Priest as Poet,* and the forthcoming *Lies Like the Truth: 'Macbeth' and the Cultural Moment* are among them. He is the Founding Editor of the journal *English Literary Renaissance* and Editor of the book series, "Massachusetts Studies in Early Modern Culture."